PUZZLING

LING

ASSEM

BLIES

FOREWORD

by **THOM MAYNE**

In the ever-evolving landscape of architecture, where the boundaries of form and function are constantly challenged, Dwayne Oyler and Jenny Wu stand as dynamic disruptors. Their work, as captured in *Puzzling Assemblies*, is a testament to the relentless pursuit of complexity and the power of the unconventional. As someone who has spent a lifetime challenging the status quo as it relates to exploring the intersections of art, architecture, and urbanism, I find their approach both invigorating and essential. Oyler Wu's methodology is not merely about constructing buildings; it is about assembling ideas. Their projects are not static entities but dynamic systems that engage with their environments and users in profound ways.

This book delves into their unique process, one that foregrounds the model as the central artifact. Their oeuvre embodies a philosophy that resonates deeply—by aspiring to provoke thought, challenge norms, and inspire dialogue.

In *Puzzling Assemblies*, Oyler and Wu invite us into a world where the act of assembly becomes an art form. Their work is characterized by an obsessive attention to detail, an embrace of emerging technologies, and a commitment to pushing the boundaries of what architecture can be. They explore the friction and harmony between parts, creating spaces that are as intellectually stimulating as they are visually captivating.

Their projects, much like the puzzles they construct, reveal a strategy of creative constraint and result in unexpected, even hidden relationships within architectural forms, encouraging a perceptual shift in how we understand space. This approach reminds us that architecture should be a compelling narrative, one that transcends conventional aesthetics to engage with the complexities of human experience.

As we stand on the precipice of a new architectural era, *Puzzling Assemblies* serves as a timely reminder of the power of innovation. Oyler Wu's work is a beacon for those who are interested in challenging the ordinary, who seek to redefine the possibilities of design. It is a call to action for architects to embrace the unknown, to revel in the challenges that lie ahead, and to create spaces that are as dynamic and diverse as the world we inhabit.

PREFACE

by DWAYNE OYLER
& JENNY WU

A constant force over the course of our twenty-year history as an office is the idea of "making" as a generator for architectural ideas. We believe that architecture reaches its full potential when it operates as an art form, affecting human experience, from large architectural strategies to intimate forms of engagement. Through obsessively mining small objects and experiments for big ideas, and vice versa, our methodology relies on a continuous exchange of ideas at various scales. It's this back and forth that we find particularly exciting, and our ambition for this book is to share some of the dialogues that have enlivened this spirited exchange.

This book traverses an important period of evolution for us. Our earliest work consisted largely of things that we built ourselves. Eager to test our ideas and impatient in our desire to see how they played out, we turned to our own love of building as the generator for experimentation, transforming small projects with modest budgets into testing grounds for design. This way of working originally grew out of necessity, where our insistence on detail-driven work allowed the design process to continually respond to feedback that came about in the fabrication process.

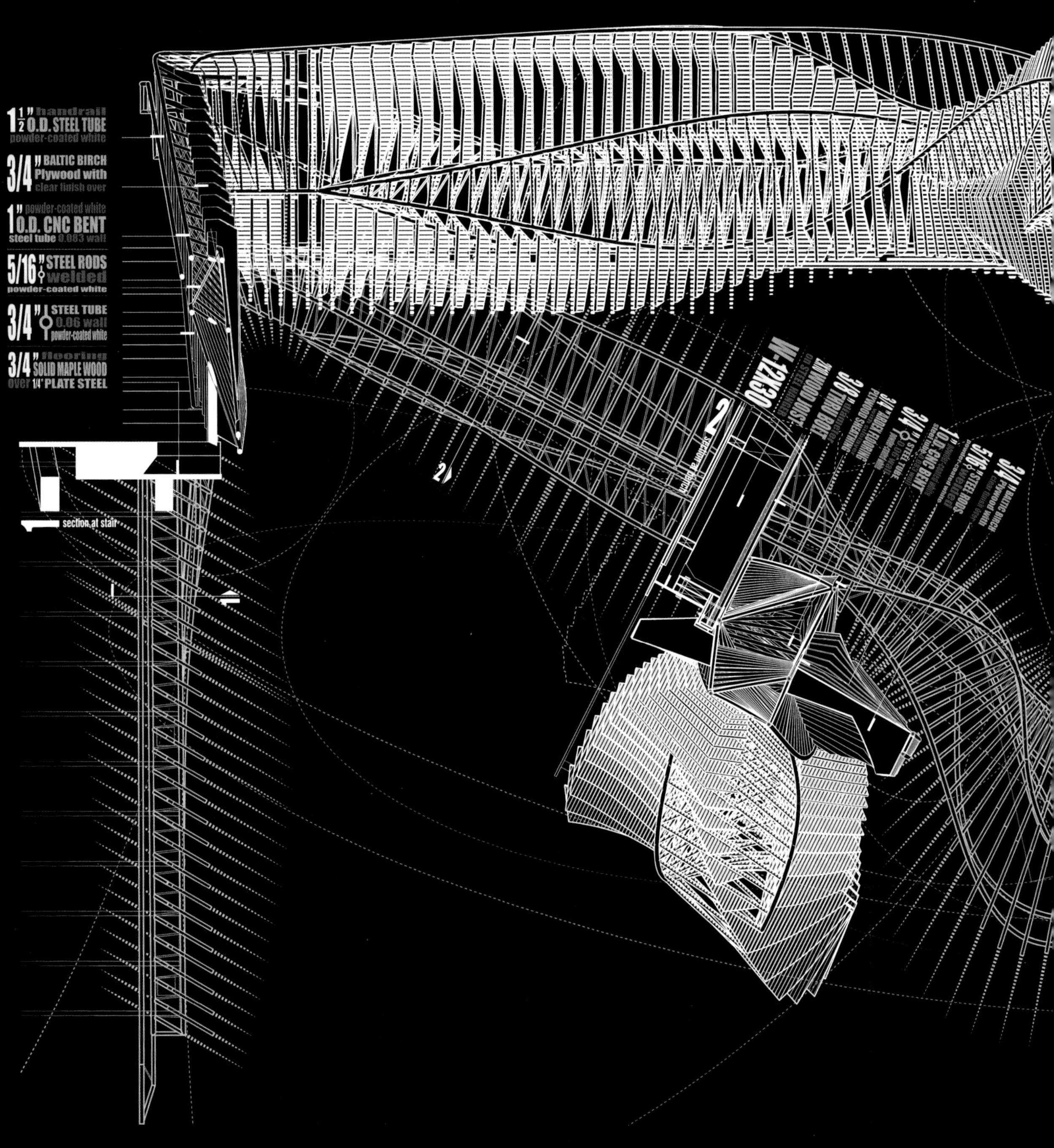

1 1/2" handrail O.D. STEEL TUBE powder-coated white
3/4" BALTIC BIRCH Plywood with clear finish over
1" powder-coated white O.D. CNC BENT steel tube 0.083 wall
5/16" STEEL RODS welded powder-coated white
3/4" STEEL TUBE 0.06 wall powder-coated white
3/4" flooring SOLID MAPLE WOOD over 1/4" PLATE STEEL
section at stair
1
2
W-12X30

This focus led us to discoveries in how materials connect, through a tectonic invention that was enriched by the difficult but profoundly rewarding task of realizing the work in various settings. In both the line-based and volumetric projects included in this book, we found common ground in methods of assembly, at various scales, as a primary creative and conceptual driver. Different contexts introduced new and often unexpected concepts for building that went beyond material or physical interpretation—and we continued to seek more engaging ways to express ideas about architecture's use and human interaction.

As we've developed more complex projects, we continue to rely on the dialogue between design and making, but we've come to realize that the kinds of hands-on approaches that were so essential to those early projects would need to evolve. We would need to find new ways of thinking that are comprehensive— evaluating the perceptual, organizational, and programmatic possibilities of development across scales. To do that, we redefined our experiments as collections of exploratory investigations where we could interrogate objects more intensely. As we continue to adapt to architectural challenges, we believe that this intense experimentation is a fundamental philosophy and will be key to our continued growth and evolution. We recognize that perhaps the greater value

IDEAS
SECTION 1

INVESTIGATIONS
SECTION 2

PROJECTS
SECTION 3

Fundamental to almost any architectural act is the assembly of parts. From stacking bricks to organizing program, few things consume as much intellectual capital as the consideration given to the way elements come together. Yet, ways of working on different forms of assembly are often compartmentalized into conventional territories of architectural investigation—program, massing, site, detailing, etc.—each with an established disciplinary methodology for how parts relate (and often without using the term "assembly"). By redefining these conventional territories, we are interested in the potential cross-fertilization of all architectural scales of design—from tectonic details to site context and every stage in between. Ultimately, we seek to reinvent forms of assembly—what we call "puzzle logics"—as being more than a connection of materials, but as the primary driver for a larger exploration of architecture.

IDEAS
SECTION 1

PUZZLE LOGICS

Occupying a unique territory that intersects cognitive engagement, organization, and design, puzzles—particularly physical puzzles—possess diverse characteristics that compel human interaction. Finding resolution is a process that requires discerning relationships between individual parts, as well as an adept manipulation to discover an inter-relatability beyond the mere adjacency of parts. Puzzled parts connect in ways that are interlocked, contained, linked, wrapped, snapped, rotated, zipped, fastened, clicked, screwed, and hinged, to name a few.

Although two-dimensional puzzles immediately come to mind, three-dimensional puzzles, with their interconnected structures and accompanying features, offer greater insight into the nuances of assemblies and operations than their two-dimensional cousins. They can impact and inform architectural ideas in more engaging ways, and are tied to the qualities of spatial experiences, organizational principles, and the character of parts. Moreover, they suggest a tightly wound and robust dialogue not found in typical assembled or arranged forms like piles, stacks, or grids. This makes three-dimensional puzzles especially thought-provoking and productive for shaping new areas of architectural thought, and we find a number of characteristics essential to our understanding:

(1) Puzzles are made of interlocking parts.

From relatively simple designs with only a few pieces, to a volumetric matrix of components, the diverse shape and design of each piece of a puzzle is carefully formed to create a fitted connection. These connections are not simple juxtapositions: three-dimensional fits involve wraps, locks, and nests of various kinds. The properties of each component are considered based on how it connects with others. And when components interlock, they reveal this relationship in unexpected ways; what may appear as individual traits in isolation may actually be fragments of a larger strategy.

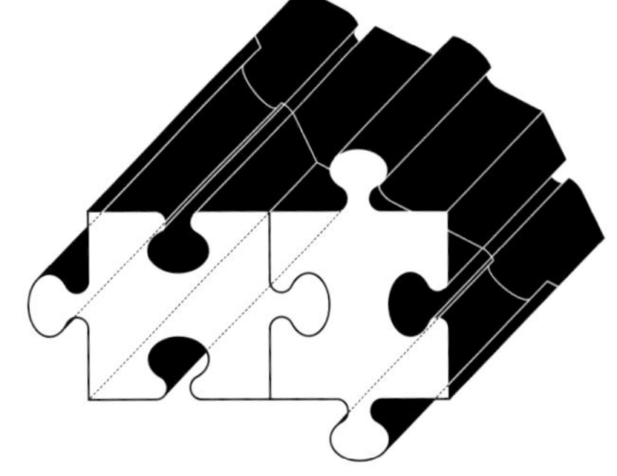

(2) Puzzles rely on careful examination and active engagement.

Puzzles require an investigation of the shape and structure of their parts through progressive trial and error. A puzzle can only be solved through one's innate ability to perceive and recognize solid and void relationships. Sometimes curious voids and seams meander through the puzzle, and traits cannot always be determined through visual cues alone. It is the process of assembling or disassembling that illuminates a sense of discovery and further understanding.

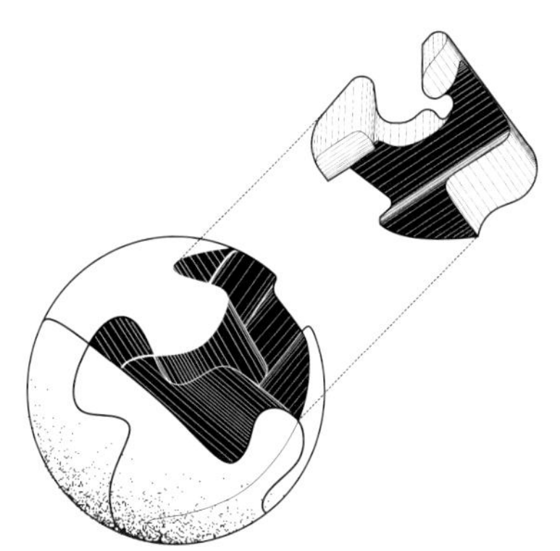

(3) Puzzles strive for a sense of completion.

Parts of a puzzle are intentionally designed to provide just enough information to require engagement between them, and yet remain elusive. Discoveries of their assembly are motivated by the continued reward of finding a fit, as the puzzler slowly builds parts into an overall shape. Each part has a unique interaction, and if parts are too similar or too different, this interaction is harder to discern. Additionally, completed puzzles tend to avoid overly sculptural or figural forms, instead resolving into simpler geometries of rectilinear or primitive shapes that serve as a recognizable guide for finding resolution. This simplicity of the final form allows the puzzler to focus on part-to-part compatibility, as seams, notches, edges, and gaps encourage a curiosity about the systemic nature of how these parts uniquely interact with each other.

(4) Puzzles are designed to conceal their process of assembly.

They evade immediate understanding, and consequently are slow to reveal their assembly logic. Although at first puzzles may appear to have a sensible arrangement, in most cases they do not resolve easily through repetition or a systematic approach to assembly. Instead, through intelligent differentiation, the unique signatures that are embedded in individual parts eventually disclose the correct assembly sequence in an ever-changing process of observation and experimentation.

(5) Puzzles are precise.

Each puzzle demands absolute precision, defining each part and method of assembly through an intentional logic. This precision confirms how parts fit together. However, each part only needs to be precise to the degree necessary to convey a clear sense of having found its proper location within the whole—a tight fit is not always a requirement. Creating figural spaces from gaps and openings between puzzle pieces can be an active agent of the puzzle's assembly logic. This occasional loose-fit strategy also opens up the possibility for more dissonant relationships to be conveyed between parts that would not exist otherwise.

(6) Puzzles are inherently complex.

Puzzles often use a proliferation of geometry in both their external and internal form. Each piece has a hyper-specific relationship to the other and contains the individual characteristics necessary to convey how they puzzle together. While containing the DNA of how they combine and connect, the proliferation of their geometries in non-operative form can also disguise detection of how they fit together.

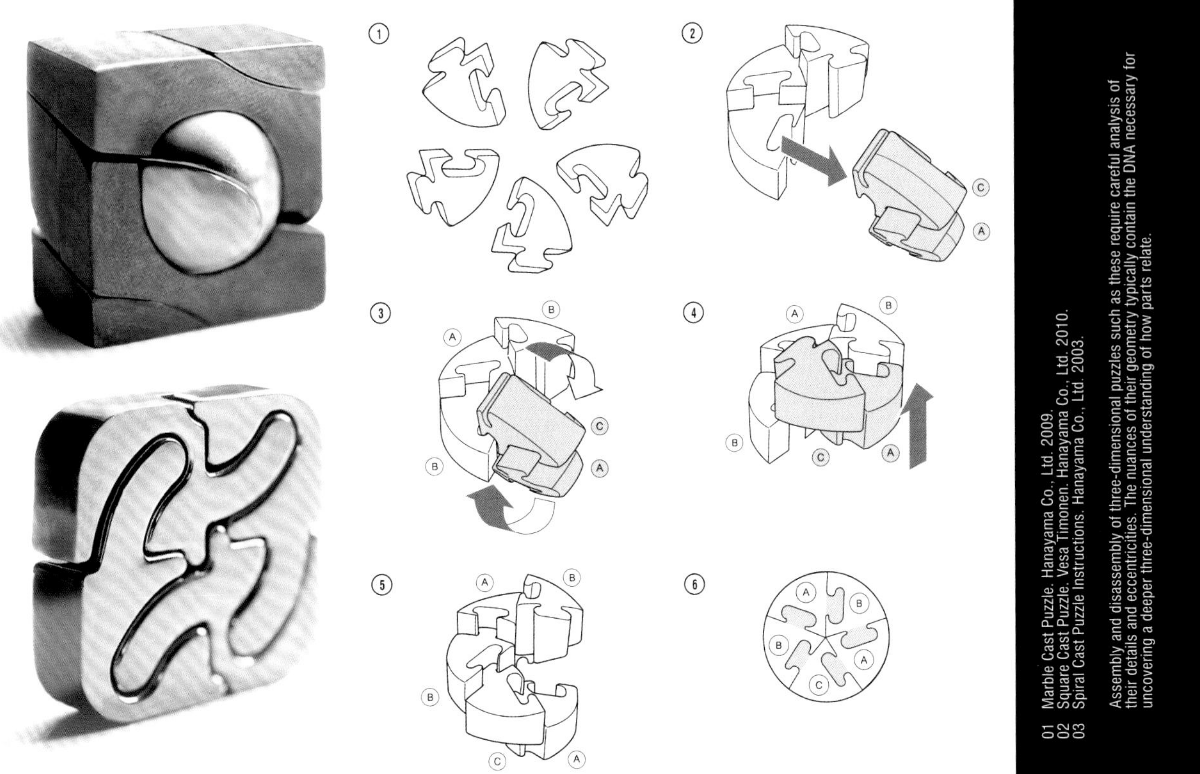

Puzzle Adjacent: From Machines to Sculpture

With these diverse characteristics, the typical three-dimensional puzzle provides a lexicon of useful methodologies for how things join together, yet our inquiry into puzzle logics is not limited to puzzles alone, and looks to two other, perhaps more familiar sources of assembly: machines and sculpture. Understanding methods of assembly, in all its manifestations, is critical to productively applying this exploration to architectural ideas. Located adjacent to what might typically be thought of as puzzles, both machines and sculpture embody characteristics we draw from. Their relationship to architectural ideas resonates in two distinctly different realms—the physical, evident in their operational features, and the conceptual, communicated as a set of associations or meanings produced by those physical characteristics.

Machines organize components to produce coordinated movements. They can be fascinatingly complex, using physical parts to create precise connections, with inventive forms of interlocking geometry and eccentric configurations. Their application to the world of architectural detailing and technical assembly is immeasurable, creating movements and interactions that are akin to how puzzles physically operate. But unlike a puzzle, machines also have a performance requirement. For example, a mechanism can help propel parts through space, or synchronize moving parts to align and attach together—they are principally assembled for this purpose, without regard to overall aesthetic expression. Puzzles, at least in conventional thinking, are not designed to perform a function other than to be assembled. Their ASSEMBLY is their function.

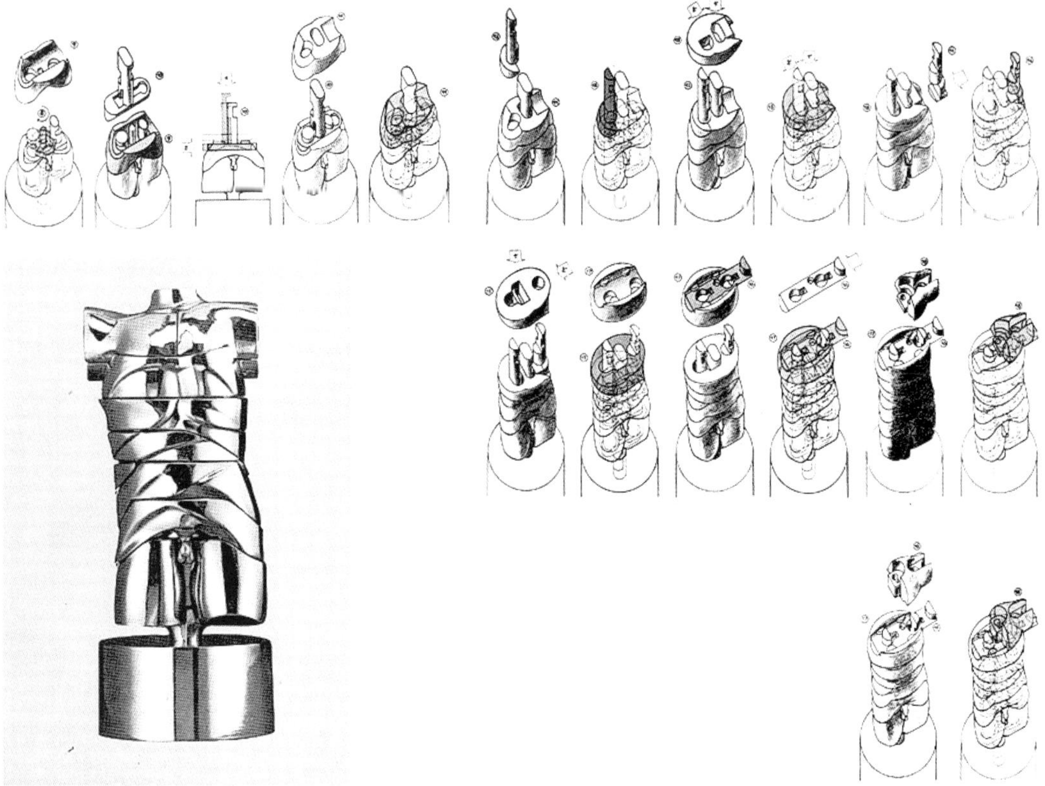

04 Mini David. Instructions for assembly. Miguel Berrocal. Antologica Berrocal (1955–984), Pages 169–170. 1969.
05 Le Bijou. Image of assembly and parts. Miguel Berrocal. Rome. 1960.
06 Poem Cube. Saloua Raouda Choucair. 1965.

Sculptures, however, rely upon three-dimensional shaping regardless of functionality, realistically or abstractly representing modeled forms in diverse ways. Unlike puzzles and machines, they express a presence that exists outside of the tactical methods of assembly, physically embodying conceptual thought. We refer especially to two sculptors whose tectonic invention and formal experimentation offer creative contributions to the idea of puzzle logics.

For over forty years, Spanish sculptor Miguel Ortiz Berrocal produced highly detailed modular sculptures in cast metal from a small foundry in Verona, Italy. Highlighting the complex connections of simple forms, his most compelling works used systems of assembly ranging from figural busts to abstract aggregations of rounded volumes. Producing modular sculptures in series, and often detailing their puzzle-like features, his works use tectonic forms as the key ingredient of their physical appearance. Developing his concepts in iteration, Berrocal manufactured objects of remarkable technical achievement, demonstrating an almost surgical precision and meticulous analysis of exact proportions. With an oeuvre of large and small sculptures, many possessing hidden inclusions within their interior volume, his work invites curiosity and interaction. Manifested through his intricate formal style, Berrocal's works are conceptually rich methods of assembly.

Tectonically similar to Berrocal, the works of Lebanese painter and sculptor Saloua Raouda Choucair present her formal investigations with a similar

disposition to the nature of compatible objects, but do this with a sensitivity that configures this relationship as being in poetic repose. Exploring the dialogue between "inversely mated" objects, her three-dimensional forms present compatibility through a sharing of space. Imagined as "duals," her sculptures create entanglements, from objects that are side by side, as well as interlock together to construct simple geometries. With careful attention to the intimate positioning of their fit, Choucair's works emphasize the dialogue between parts, introducing a shape language that creates a sense of their belonging to one another. Unlike conventional puzzles, they don't present an overt challenge to the viewer, however they are highly expressive of an idea embedded in how solid objects coherently interact. Imbuing these expressive characteristics isn't explicitly intended to compel physical interaction, but to produce a provocative reading of how parts are related, both physically and conceptually.

In the cases of Berrocal and Choucair, their skillful operations and techniques make their work tectonically compelling. Like machines, these objects provide physical and aesthetic characteristics that lend themselves to architectural thinking. But it's the interesting layers of meaning and interpretation that differentiate these sculptures from machines and make them particularly relevant to a more expansive form of architectural thinking. Architecture's most enduring qualities are produced through the slow revelation of multiple readings, and in turn how those readings create meaningful and layered experiences. An architectural approach to puzzling is closely

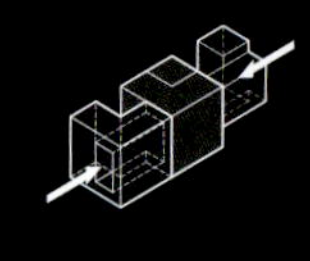

07 Joinery Assemblies, partition walls and panels. Suburban Intervention. Oyler Wu Collaborative. 2008.
08 Armchairs. Oyler Wu Collaborative. 2000.
09 Diagrams of common wood joints.

Some of our earliest projects involved the exploration of wood joinery and connection techniques as primary drivers for the design sensibility. As our work evolved into steel and aluminum, the specifics of the connection methods adapted; however, an interest in connectivity as a primary driver remains.

related to sculpture in this sense, but the conceptual and formal dialogue should go beyond its perception as art by building on precision, performance, and the full spectrum of ideas found in the territory between machines and sculpture.

All of these facets of puzzle logics—interlocking parts, active engagement, discovery and completion, concealment, precision, complexity, function, and meaning—enrich the concept of "assembly" in architecture. Through expanding and reinterpreting the definition of assembly in this way, we apply puzzled logics as the active driver in architectural design at every scale—from tectonic connection to site context.

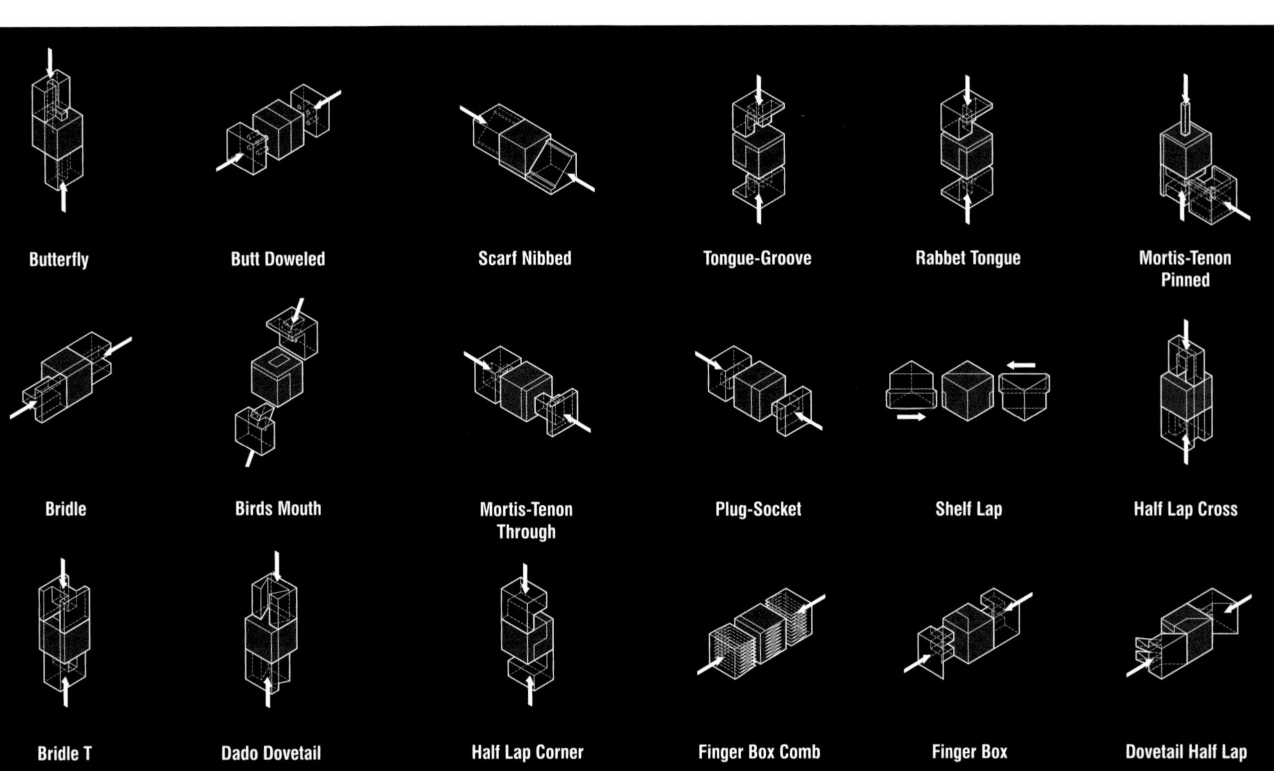

ASSEMBLY & TECTONICS

In architecture, an "assembly" usually refers to the connection of materials and parts in an overall building system. Whether referring to a window assembly, a door assembly, or any other combination of materials, they are typically thought of as systems with a shared purpose for building. Beyond their association with construction techniques, however, we propose a contemporary lexicon of assemblies with a more open-ended and expansive understanding.

Assemblies have multiple manifestations. In their physical application to architecture, there are several examples of assemblies that organize the methods for simple connections to great effect—for instance, forming an arch using shaped bricks: a basic and primitive strategy that permeated an entire era of Roman architectural expression. Practical and ubiquitous, the stacking and coursing of brickwork is a relatively simple and tectonically restrained assembly method.

Japanese joinery, on the other hand, treats this same part-to-part process differently, achieving a precision and craftsmanship that demonstrates a mastery of assembly and construction. Using profoundly resilient and beautifully crafted connections, this traditional wood construction configures joints with fittings carefully designed to interlock. Called "tsugite" and "shiguchi," as beam and column joinery, these systems combine the physical properties and bearing forces of compatible parts to create rigid intersections from solid materials.[1] These joints are shaped to wedge and groove, unifying parts together to harmoniously coexist, exposing the intricate

1   Matsui, Gengo; Sumiyoshi, Torashichi. *Wood Joints in Classical Japanese Architecture*. Tokyo, Japan: Kajima Institute Publishing Company, 1991.

and elegant techniques of their tectonic structures, making them a premier example of puzzled form in architecture. These joints provoke a sense of wonder about the relationship of each element, how they are made, and how they fit together to perform in structural and material equilibrium.

Focusing on newer materials and techniques, Carlo Scarpa's body of work portrays a strong sense of physical and material intimacy as well, exploring tectonics at various scales. Interestingly, his projects tend to avoid a larger formal reading—but in their organization and expression they promote a profound sense of human engagement. Through collections of uniquely detailed, tactile forms, Scarpa created intricate configurations in precious dialogue with one another. At first glance, his interventions seem fragmented and incomplete, but as they are encountered in physical space, the juxtaposition of these elements stitch together into a cohesive experience.

Scarpa's completed design for the Fondazione Querini Stampalia is just one great example of this approach. Organizing disparate elements, the doorways, halls, stairs, and passageways reinforce a series of spaces as being interlinked, where thresholds that form the path of this movement combine the ground floor and courtyard using subtle tectonic shifts and openings that connect new and old elements. Produced at a time when his contemporaries were quick to foreground how manufacturing processes might play a role in the production of new forms of architecture, Scarpa's method was artistic and nuanced. However, with a building industry that

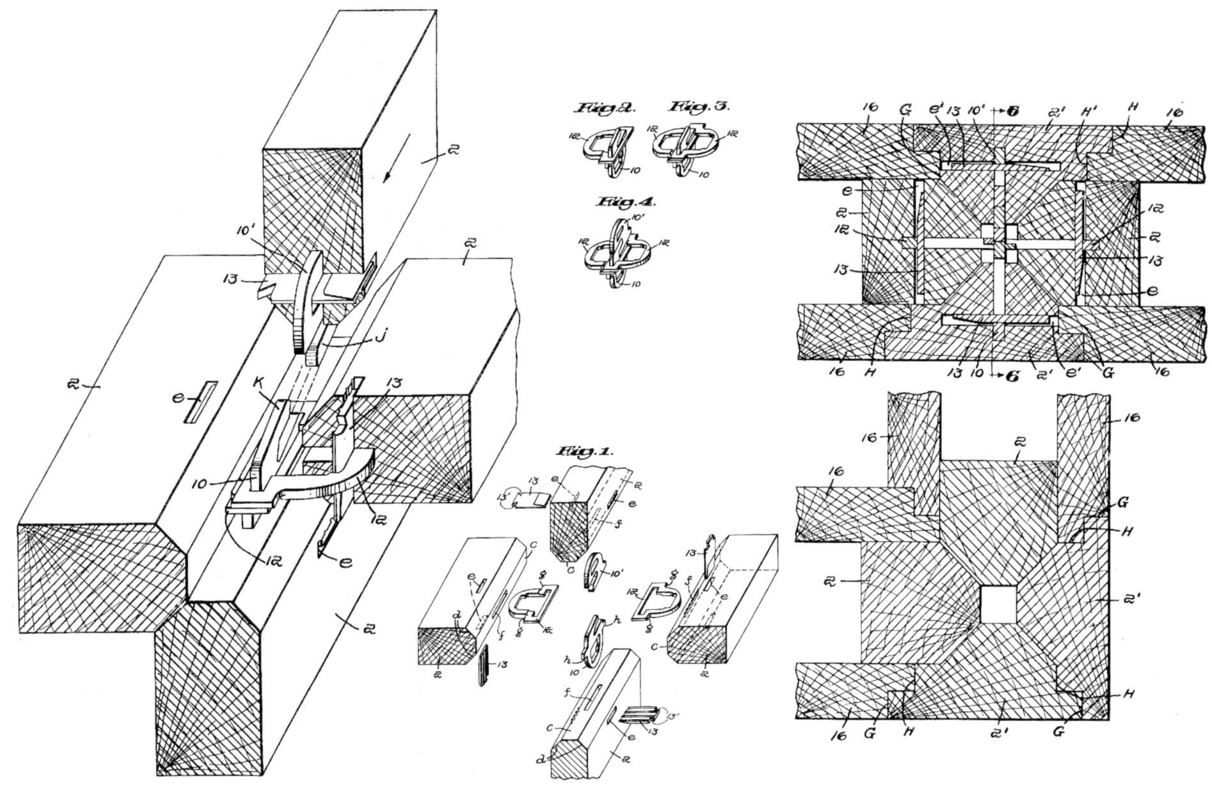

fully embraced modern methods of assembly and efficiency, these sophisticated methods—and their engaging qualities of intimacy—have faded from use. Today, these transformative techniques tend to be relegated to academic discussions and are somewhat incompatible with contemporary methods of construction in the profession. Yet assembly is an inescapable reality of building that presents opportunities we believe should be proactively re-engaged to consider multiple scales in parallel.

Interested in assembly techniques that fit emerging advancements of this era, Walter Gropius and Konrad Wachsmann designed the Packaged House to strategically consider scale, aligning manufacturing with an artful design intelligence. Identifying efficient methods of construction to create a repetitive and modular system for building, they leveraged technological advancements of prefabricated assemblies. Designed to create a more universal approach to how parts come together, the system offers a part-to-part armature for easy assembly on site. Simple in its overall building composition, the uniformity and precision of unitization make it adaptable to various configurations, linking partitions, floors, and ceilings with coordinated sets of universal "wedge connector" joints.[2] In its final assembly, the exterior appearance of the Packaged House is modest in architectural expression; its real innovation is the tectonic design and construction of its parts. Using prefabricated parts, the Packaged House concept considers building assemblies as a tactical intervention and presents an inventive catalog of connected components that are key to assembly.

---

2   Herbert, Gilbert. *Dream of the Factory-Made House: Walter Gropius and Konrad Wachsmann*. Cambridge, Massachusetts: MIT Press, 1984.

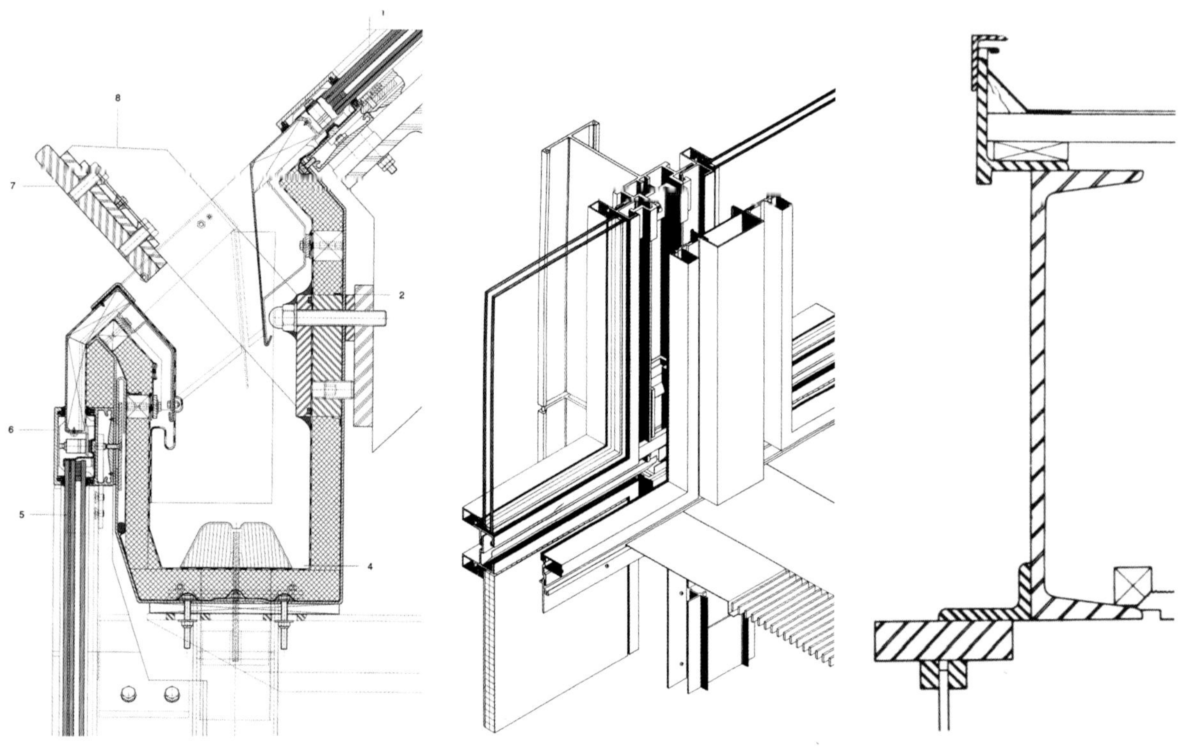

Gropius and Wachsmann's inventiveness in the Packaged House came about during a period of rapidly evolving material and construction advancements. Consider the evolution of a prominent architectural assembly over the course of the twentieth century: the facade window. At an accelerated pace of development over the last hundred years, window assemblies have radically evolved into a wide range of connections that snap, screw, rotate, and slide together with incredible precision. Comparing a section detail of Philip Johnson's Glass House in 1949 to Mies van der Rohe's "Mullion Assembly" for the IBM Building in 1968, the leaps in sophistication of tectonic construction systems generated in just twenty years are astounding. This evolution has continued through material advancements, and in response to a wider range of building forms that require details to unify conflicts and incongruities in architectural systems. The bespoke window assemblies for the Seattle Public Library by OMA and LMN Architects are a prime example. What might be considered a typical construction detail for most buildings—a gutter and snow fence—is, in this case, an elaborate display of technical savvy that is becoming more emblematic of rigorous detailing in digital environments today. Comparing these window details also highlights the increasing difficulty of designing what was once considered an "honest" tectonic or material approach.

In parallel to technical advancements in building assemblies, a number of artful approaches have also evolved the definitions of assemblies in ways that expose construction techniques as an embedded language of the design. Artists Erwin Hauer and Malcolm Leland re-evaluated the typical modular approach using fabrication

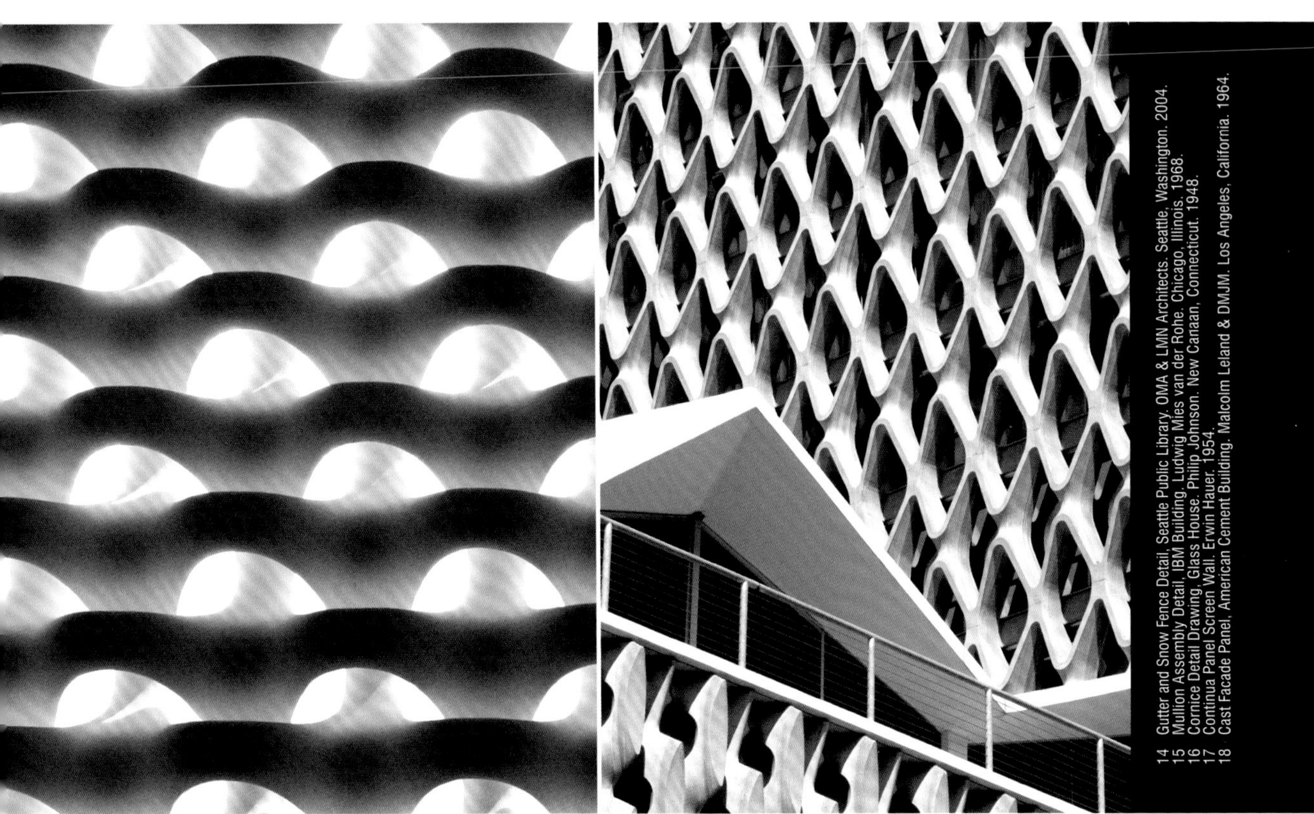

14 Gutter and Snow Fence Detail, Seattle Public Library. OMA & LMN Architects. Seattle, Washington. 2004.
15 Mullion Assembly Detail, IBM Building. Ludwig Mies van der Rohe. Chicago, Illinois. 1968.
16 Cornice Detail Drawing, Glass House. Philip Johnson. New Canaan, Connecticut. 1948.
17 Continua Panel Screen Wall. Erwin Hauer. 1954.
18 Cast Facade Panel, American Cement Building. Malcolm Leland & DMJM. Los Angeles, California. 1964.

techniques for pre-assembled parts with seamless geometries. This is most clear in their works on perforated wall systems—where their expertise elegantly showcases the performative potential of construction methods that aren't typical for standardized assembly. Hauer's inventively sculptural, modular paneling for architectural screens like Continua artfully enhances the functionality and aesthetic of the interior, while Leland's concrete construction becomes part of the larger architectural system bound to the performance of the facade. Enlisted in 1961 by architecture firm Daniel, Mann, Johnson and Mendenhall (DMJM), Leland's concrete facade for the American Cement Building in Los Angeles boasts repeatable modularity in its architectural expression. Embedding a dialogue of structure and form, the design uses 450 x-shaped precast concrete modules to create a sculptural latticework on the north and south facades, alleviating the need for columns on the building's interior.

Today, architects engage ideas that have evolved since Hauer and Leland, exploring this type of unitization in parametrically designed systems. Those same ideas now include dramatic variations between parts and must conform to formal differences only feasible through more advanced methods. Contemporary parallels to this type of specialty work are today embodied in the versatile fabrication techniques found in offices like A. Zahner and Company and Kreysler and Associates. Conventionally thought of as fabrication shops, both Zahner and Kreysler now create a necessary bridge between architectural design offices and one-of-a-kind construction—developing the details for sophisticated architectural components at scales both large and small.

There are also spectacular examples of architectural works that give form to complex ideas of assembly in multi-scalar ways. For Frei Otto, experimentation with maquettes was a fundamental part of his work. Observing natural structures in soap films, viscous fluids, and branching structures, his experiments focused on processes that reshaped materials and objects to balance structural efficiency with minimal surfaces.[3] With ingenious techniques for generating form, his observations became a systematic model for three-dimensional development, offering analytical tools for evaluating lightweight construction. Concentrating on lattice shell and tensile structures, his methods articulated a coherent relationship between his experiments with abstracted formal geometries and developing inventive technical details to construct them. His innovative experiments prolifically oscillated between these scales with ingenious results.

Where Otto's formal precision defines a more universal assembly of parts, Enric Miralles and Carme Pinós play out the relationship of architectural elements through human engagement. The Olympic Archery Range in Barcelona, for example, features inventive detailing that is curiously fragmented to be read at different scales. Creating a visually complex layering of roof slabs that lift above concrete walls, the systems of assembly express a physical connection between parts. Each element articulates a relationship to those around it, emphasizing a material dialogue that is essential to the way the work is experienced. The simplicity of these systems, left untreated in material appearance, emphasizes position and compatibility as necessary physical

components in the design. Not unlike Japanese joinery, this compatibility is simple and exposed, and presents a tectonic mastery that views assembly as both a means of construction and a larger conceptual idea.

The introduction of digital design software also brought new ways of thinking about the role of part-to-part relationships.[4] Along with technological advancements in material and fabrication techniques, the ability to create continuity between a building's overall expression and its details has become a more feasible endeavor. This has naturally led to the suggestion that details might simply be absorbed into the architecture, without an observable expression. While conceptually interesting, the human experience of architecture suffers when details are relegated to a subservient role. As the examples above demonstrate, we see the potential for assemblies to offer something curiously different, prolonging and articulating details in balance with an overall sense of discovery at many scales. We are interested in reclaiming assemblies as active players in design.

3   Bach, Klaus; Burkhardt, Berthold; Otto, Frei. *Forming Bubbles*. Stuttgart, Germany: Universität Stuttgart,
     Institut für leichte Flächentragwerke, 1988.

4   Ford, Edward R. *The Architectural Detail*. New York City, New York: Princeton Architectural Press, 2011.

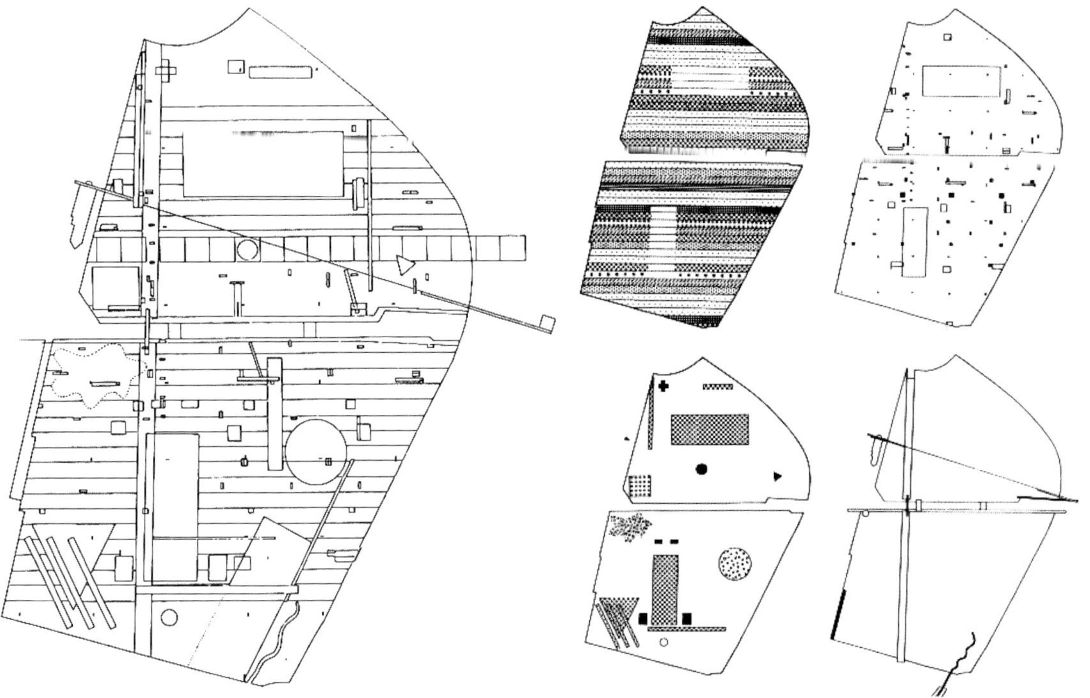

PROGRAM

Beyond material tectonics, we look to programming as another scale of experimentation with puzzled assemblies in architecture. When considered as volumetric objects, distinct pieces of program are capable of engaging one another and providing a built-in logic for their interlocking. Within most buildings, the criteria for spatial planning balances a blend of decisions between functionality and user experience. When thought of as a three-dimensional assembly, programming can use the inherent logic of puzzles to mediate complexity and sequence—as the order, positioning, and compatibility of spaces lend themselves to complex and unexpected juxtapositions. The formal tactics involved in the arrangement of puzzled parts have the potential to create coherence at both a global and local scale, as well as in the occupation of areas between programs.

At their best, puzzled programs aggregate internally to make generous room for the open and ambiguous readings of space. We are interested in this approach as a developing framework—one that treats spatial planning as being interwoven with form, yet operates to embolden architectural concepts that are often susceptible to constant change. This is best exemplified in the works of Rem Koolhaas and OMA in the early 1980s. With proposals that mixed unexpected adjacencies and overlaps, OMA's strategies for programming spaces brought an imaginative vitality essential to the experiences in their designs. In their proposal for the Parc de la Villette, Koolhaas argued for a larger organizational principle to proliferate the potential for unstructured interactions. Where elements of the park were left undefined, the programming offered

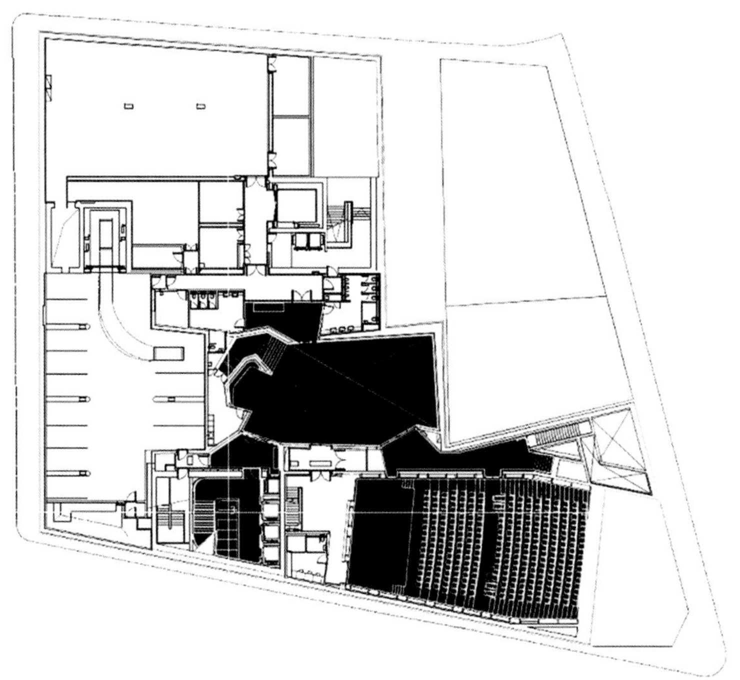

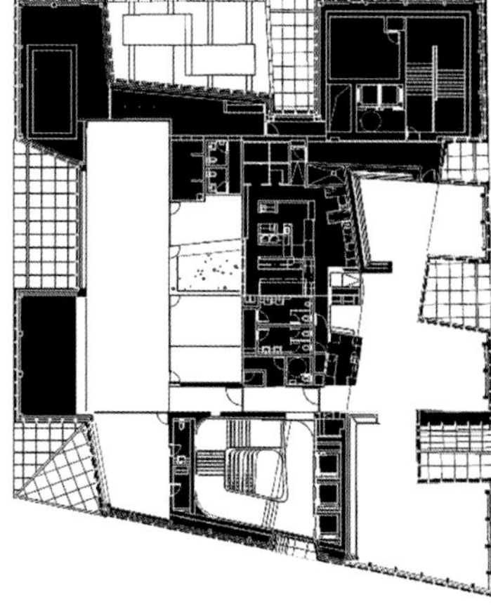

conceptual tactics for condensed programs, allowing the "invisible congestion" of how those spaces are used to play out as it fit the visitors. Strategically enlivening this concept with smaller "confetti"-like elements—like ticket stands and shops—the grounds were pollinated with these functional elements to entice and activate the life of the park.[5]

In another example, Herzog and de Meuron's Caixa Forum presents a conceptual approach that programs architectural spaces from the inside out. Surgically detaching the original brick facade of the Central Eléctrica del Mediodía, the design transforms the building's internal program through a kind of metamorphosis, redefining the open areas that exist on the site and within the building. Volumetrically, the building is elevated over the plaza like an overturned container for the large public spaces that are packed within it. Linked together in spatial sequence, the spaces squeeze through vertical openings to fill the public gallery levels within the hovering container above, while below, unrestrained by this container, the cultural programs more freely spill out into the plaza and to the auditorium and foyers underground.

James Stirling and James Gowan's innovative work for the Engineering Building at the University of Leicester exhibits a similar interplay of volumetric masses. Combining program and form with an industrial elegance, the design uses engineered solutions to arrange program volumes to fit together on the site. This shifting and shaping of volumes creates internal relationships that are expressed on the exterior, fitting the

5   Koolhaas, Rem; Mau, Bruce; O.M.A. *S,M,L,XL*. New York City, New York: The Monacelli Press, 1995.

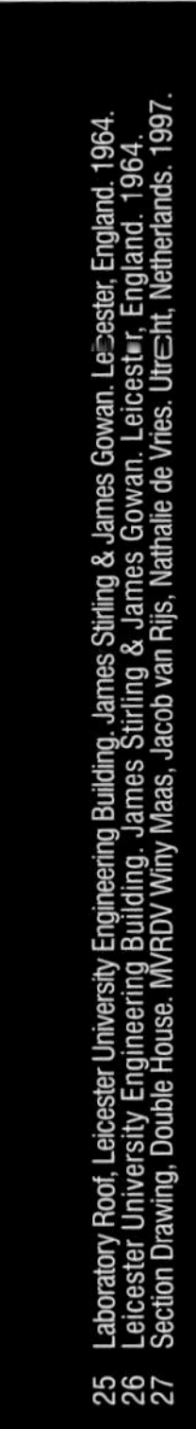

towers with lecture rooms and offices that change their shape. The towers reconfigure the functions of the school into vertical forms, extracting this program from the light-filled factory floor of laboratories at the ground level. Choreographing program and form, the overall massing can be read as building blocks that directly embody how the programs are organized and separated. Stirling and Gowan used this approach to conjoin the towers on the site with a straightforward shape language built to meet the demands of the program.

Rather than a volumetric reading of programs, a more literal example is the Double House by MVRDV. Constructed in Utrecht in 1997, its building components propose a meandering sequence of movements through a programmatic interlocking of "dwelling volumes."[6] Designed for two separate families sharing one building, the movements through the house are an inversely shared experience on either side of a central dividing wall. With one-room-deep living spaces on each side, the house balances the programs with pushes and pulls on each floor to find a compatible arrangement of internal spaces.

When building programs are viewed as volumetric parts of an assembly, their shape can engage three dimensionally, with both physical and spatial interactions that create opportunities for engaging architecture. They allow for much more than juxtaposition and adjacency—they reach across, overlap, interfere, and superimpose. They can volumetrically configure to cradle, blanket, surround, push through, and reach into

6   Ruby, Andreas; Ruby, Ilka; MVRDV. *MVRDV Buildings*. Rotterdam, Netherlands: nai010 Publishers, 2016.

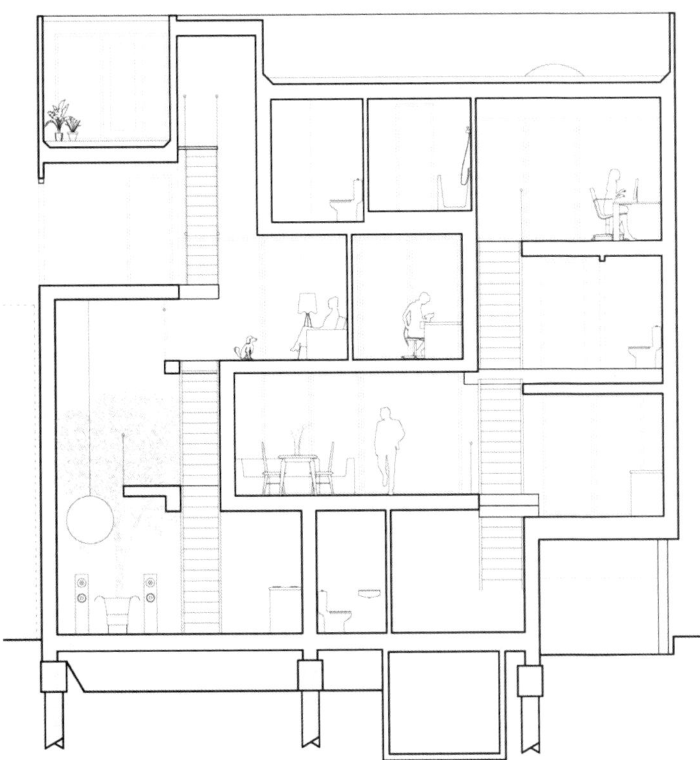

other areas with a conceptual flexibility that reinforces their continuity. Programs that belong to one area can unexpectedly emerge in another, giving a suggested or literal continuity to how spaces are used. As volumetric parts, they can be contained within one another and yet extend with a three-dimensional logic that resonates physically, spatially, and experientially.

SECTION

Section also serves as a critical territory for the exploration and examination of puzzled assemblies. Almost any three-dimensional puzzle has an internal logic, but some puzzles require careful examination beyond their external appearance to discover how parts engage and connect. In order to evaluate these connections more clearly and spatially, section drawings reveal the formal maneuvers that fit parts together in three dimensions. In their most basic sense, sections produce a planar "slice" through a building. And while they often include elevational information beyond this plane, sections are a snapshot of the conditions that exist at that particular slice. A critical analytical tool, the section clearly and explicitly reveals the dialogue between forms and spaces with precision—emphasizing their interaction. Sections are important to how architects develop ideas and understanding—uncovering otherwise imperceptible relationships by means of adjacencies and spatial connectivity.

The hidden internal logic in Jean Nouvel's 1986 proposal for the Tokyo Opera House is a prime example for sectional analysis. While the monolithic exterior conceals the forms within it, the section presents the tightly packed volumes behind its shell—the external mass shows only subtle inflections that correlate with those interior volumes. But in section, this nondescript envelope reveals spaces that counter its mysterious and dark appearance, with theater spaces suspended in a three-dimensional arrangement of golden volumes. Similar to hidden parts in a puzzle, the section reveals an understanding of otherwise hidden relationships that defy the building's external appearance.

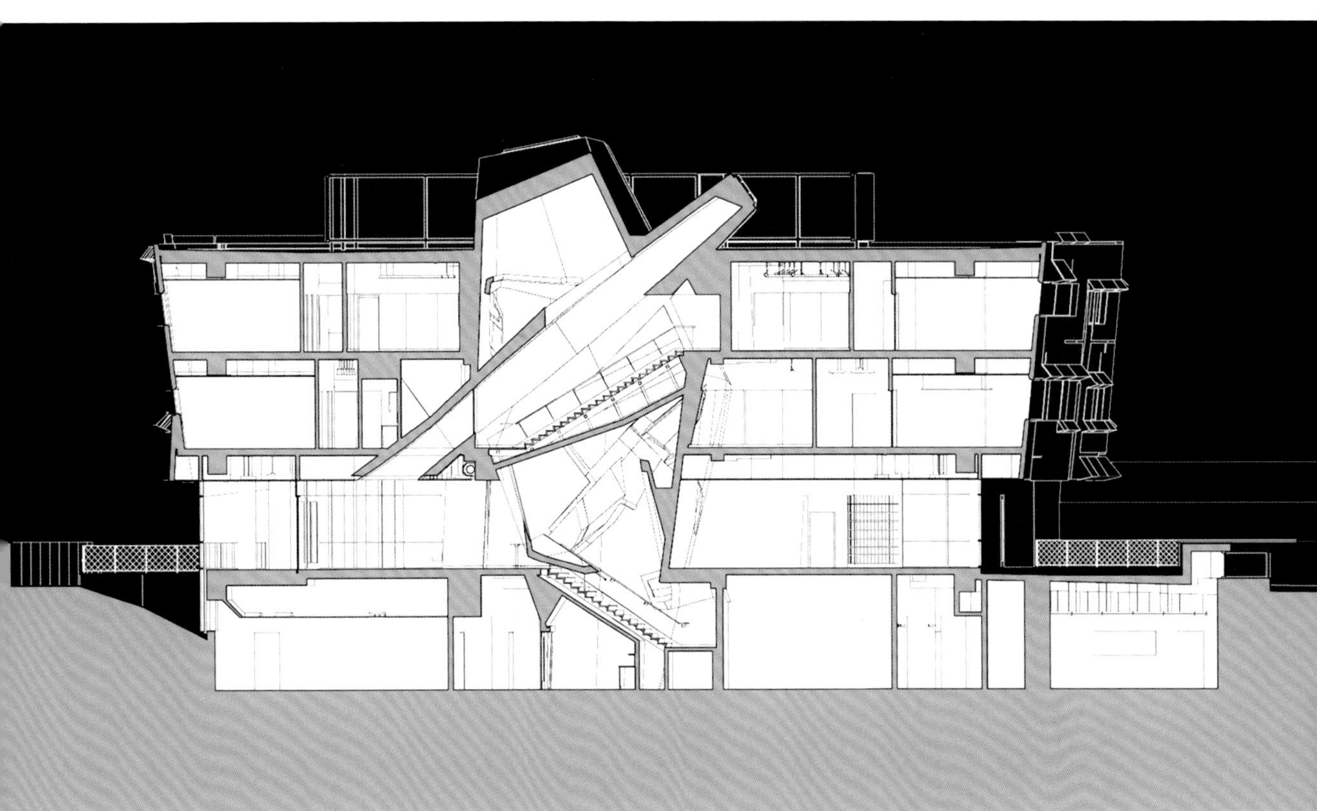

Not only do sections enable a more complete understanding of the configurations of objects in space, but at times, sections can reveal formal fragments that invite a more volumetric analysis. Section drawings for projects like the Cahill Center at Caltech and 41 Cooper Square at Cooper Union, both designed by Morphosis, express embedded volumes that jostle to find a formal fit on the interior, producing fractures and slots, tilted surfaces and slanted openings. The interactions of these volumes are truncated by the section, which cannot provide a full understanding of these forms, but does convey a spatial language and perceived interaction that is tectonically advanced, abstracting the interactions of solid objects in spatial arrangements. Actively engaging both volume and program, the section is representative of the inner workings of the building, and provides a tool for experimentation that is especially beneficial to the design process.

Sectional ideas are also an ideal tool for revealing internal voids within a building. In the case of puzzled assemblies, these voids have specific logics and spatial choreography that differentiate them from other approaches. They exist as networks of spaces between parts that are further heightened in the case of loose-fit parts. Loose-fit puzzle connections tend to reach out, wrap around, and interlock into adjacent parts. Voids can appear in ways that are outside of typical architectural approaches—for instance, instead of a central atrium, decentralized, voided spaces might produce interconnected networks. Unlike a typical translation of this void space into functional architectural elements, such as interconnected hallways or conventional circulation,

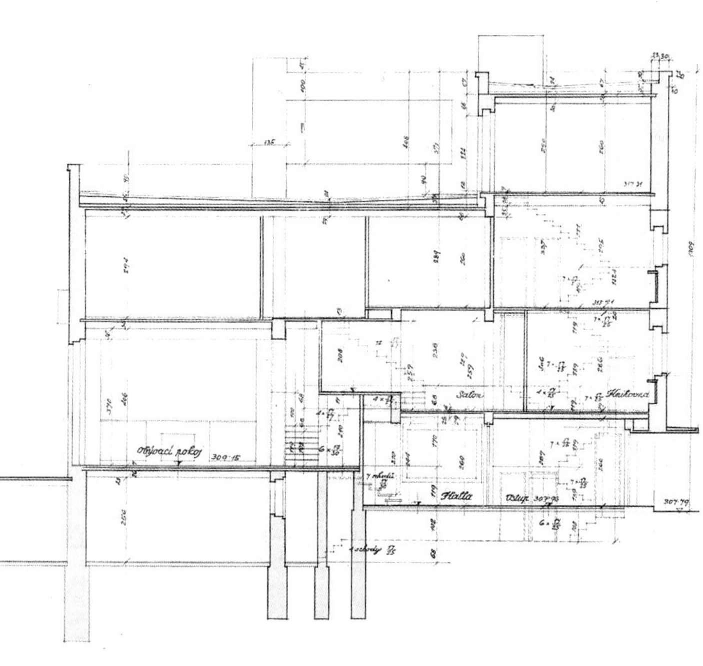

these voids are bound spatially by their coherence with geometries that are object-based. Giving definition to how this volumetric puzzle can be represented in section, we turn to two projects that consider voids differently—whether introducing their expressive qualities with clear definition, or as contiguous organizers of space.

Built in 1930 in Prague, Adolf Loos' Villa Müller presents loose-fit voids as a balance between the formal proportion and spatial arrangement of the internal elements. Freely flowing from one space to another without clear definitions, rooms spill into ancillary nooks and vestibule-like landings that step and meander room to room. This sectional sophistication breaks floors into various heights, adjusting to an imaginary axis that avoids a centrality, but instead intentionally weaves the spaces with a continuity that can be felt in the movement through the house.

Focusing on an abstract yet coherent figural space, Herzog and de Meuron's Elbphilharmonie Hamburg's most distinctive features are only revealed in section. From the exterior, the character of the building presents little semblance of its dynamically shaped concert hall. Voluptuous caverns scrape, sweep, and tunnel through the public spaces, and around the chandelier-like envelope of the grand hall, dramatically sculpting crevasses that erode the interior. With interiors that formally express an interplay of programs from within the building envelope, they are meant to be experienced through direct engagement.

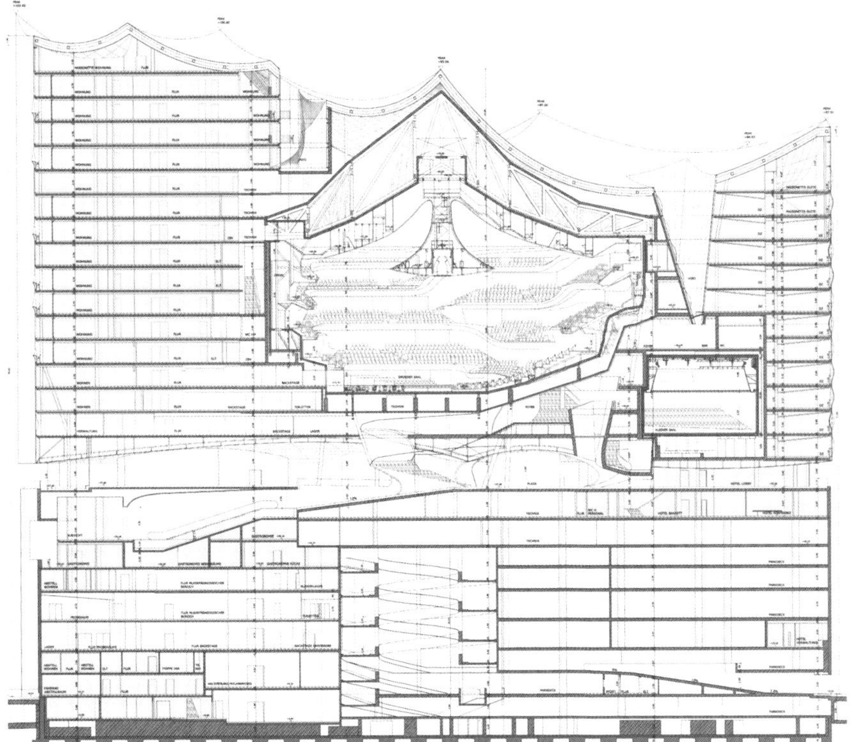

In our teaching at SCI-Arc and elsewhere, we focus on sectional strategies that work from object to building and back again. These strategies typically begin as abstract physical models in the early stages, with a focus on maintaining the three-dimensional interaction of parts, and are translated into building ideas as they develop. In a constant exchange, the buildings are assessed and analyzed through sectional models, preserving the dynamic interactions of volumetric spaces and ensuring a dialogue between parts. Throughout most of our object-based studies, we intentionally use primitive shapes like cubes and rectangles to serve as hosts for this exploration, establishing the visual bounds for manipulation constrained in volumetric geometries that are clearly identifiable. This sets the stage for the completed object to be conceived of like a physical section, both by isolating parts, as well as by combining them.

These sectional models give an internal vantage point that looks past the space in a drawn section, revealing the sectional features of loosely fitted objects, and the spaces between them. These openings play a significant role in creating coherence between objects, and emphasize opportunities between them that were not previously considered. This approach offers a more open-ended examination of parts that allows for their connective logic to take precedent in the process. It also ensures that parts developed in section are not simply a product of their exterior logic, but take into account the internal spatial and programmatic logics and their potential for affecting human experience.

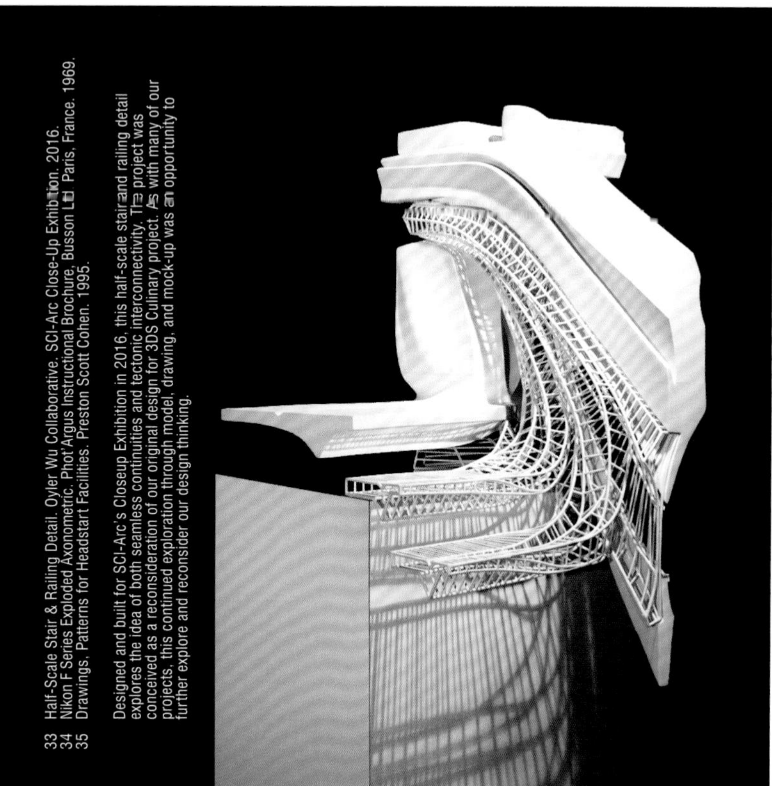

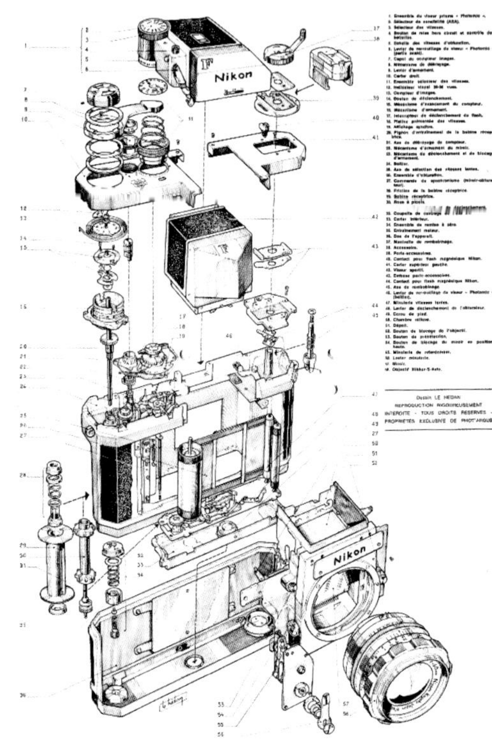

REPRESENTATION

For all that architectural sections offer, the complex and dynamic interactions of puzzled forms present both challenges and opportunities for representation that sections alone are unable to fully address. One challenge is accurately describing how elements are intertwined in x, y, and z directions. Embedded in the anatomy of a puzzle is a set of rules that govern the appearance of each piece and its interactions with others. Representing this three-dimensional logic in drawn form requires a process of abstraction.

One of the most successful representation methods for conveying these logics is the axonometric drawing. Acting like a set of "instructions" these drawings are oftentimes orthographic projections to convey space and distance, or exploded axonometric drawings, maintaining both the scale of their parts as well as their relationships to one another. Extraordinary examples of these types of drawings populate the user manuals and technical drawings of complex machines, like the cutaway drawings in *Popular Mechanics* magazine, or instructional pamphlets for scale models. As representations of functional machines, these drawings convey complex interactions between parts with a technically comprehensive understanding of how every element fits together.

Another challenge is capturing not just the physical relationships at play, but the dynamism of that interaction. Drawings of puzzles and machines describe the assembly of parts using arrows, notations, and other symbols to convey movement. These symbols and notations clarify processes, and like architectural construction

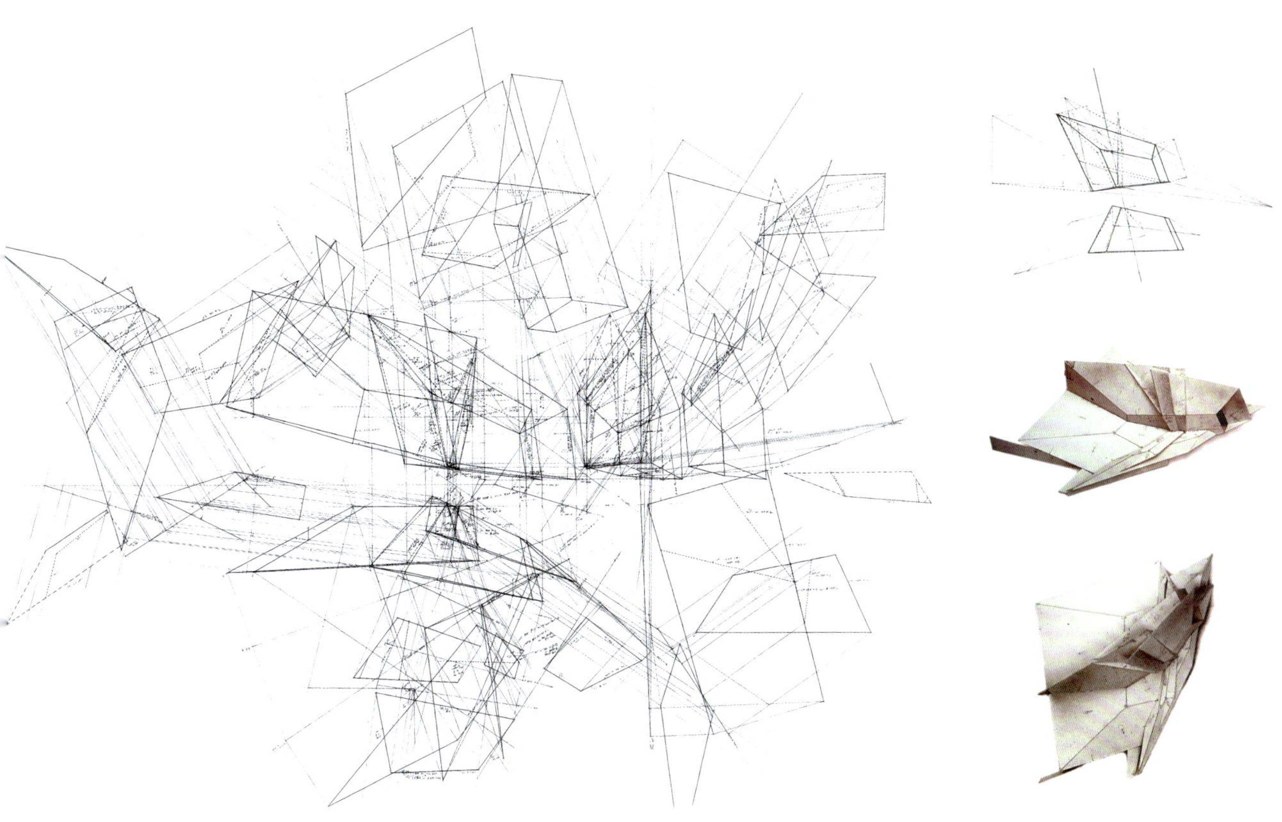

drawings, they are intended to convey only descriptive information, as opposed to artistic gestures or visual effects. Using these types of drawings, we heavily employ the disciplinary tools of line drawing and projection to convey all aspects of our work, without relying on perspective, rendering, or painterly gestures.

Our approach to drawing has been to represent how constructable objects and their assembly can be both analytical and expressive. Combining material notation, dimensions, and descriptive projection lines with the elements being described, the drawings are layered with information that logically gives graphic description to the ways elements connect in space. As a way of furthering that three-dimensional reading, we often produce "skewed" elevations or plans that are not in alignment with the primary axis, producing a curious (semi) three-dimensional effect. Unlike most axonometric or isometric drawings, ours illustrate only two out of the three (x, y, z) axes. Although these drawings fall squarely within an architectural history of two-dimensional projection drawings, they suggest a three-dimensional representation. We are interested in elevating what may be historically thought of as pure construction information to a higher status—one that is simultaneously expressive of its conceptual intent, yet remains true to the disciplinary nature of architectural drawing.

Representation, in its most productive architectural form, is more than a method of description—it is a tool for generating ideas. Its methods of abstraction take the work to another place so it might be examined through a different lens, with a different set of

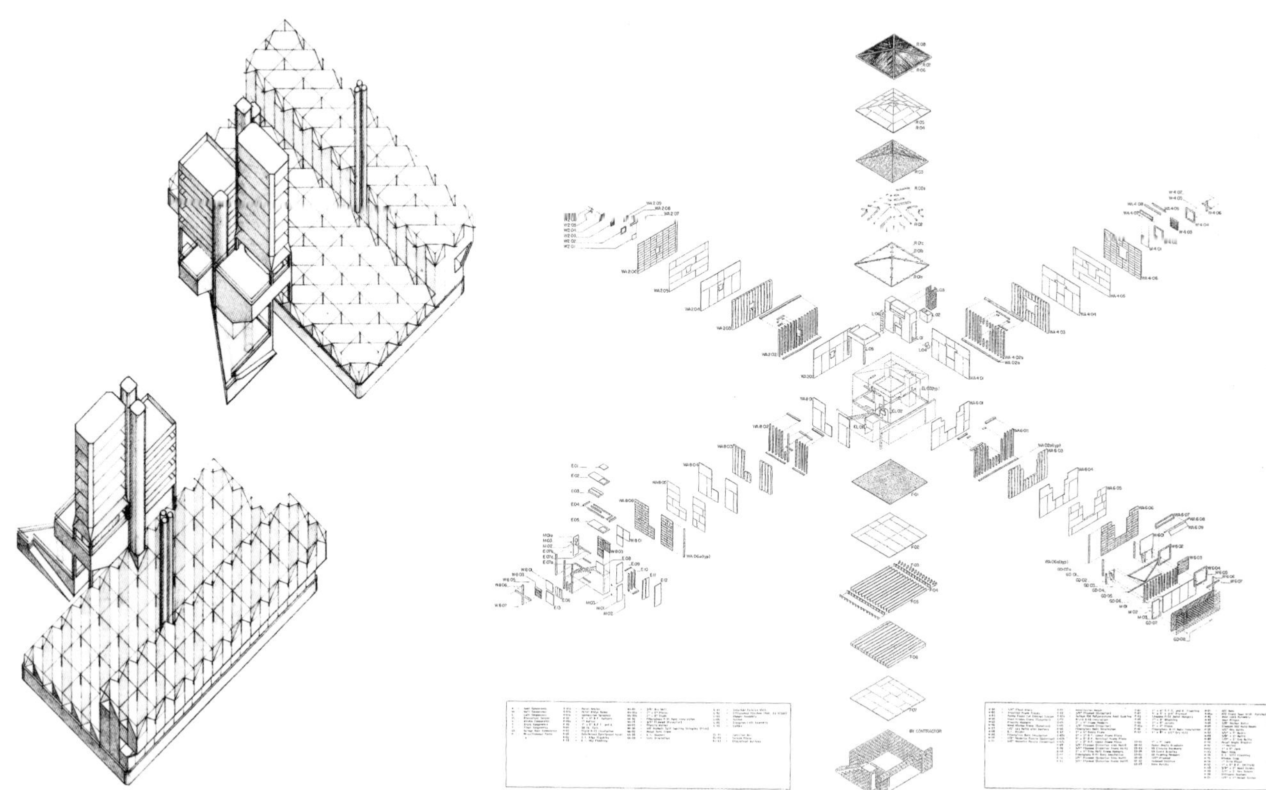

criteria to evaluate not only the drawing, but the architecture itself. These criteria may be as simple as the clarity of proportions seen in an elevation, or it may be as complex as the suggestion of spatial depth implicit in the space of a drawing projection. This idea is seen in the work of Preston Scott Cohen; his deep interest in descriptive geometry highlights a set of relationships, bringing to light what would otherwise go unrecognized. What makes these drawings especially powerful are the dynamic spatial implications seen in the space of projection. In this sense they are more than simple descriptors; they are design generators.

Drawings can also suggest the presence of the unseen, like a hidden line used to convey something behind or beyond, or they can reveal a set of internal workings, as seen in section drawings. Architects have grappled with these challenges in various ways—often with the intention of synthesizing the three-dimensional, perceptual, and generative approaches.

James Stirling's axonometric drawings, for example, encapsulate a formal logic that presents all components of the building as completely fixed. This technique is a hallmark of Stirling's, making each part legible through deliberate compositions of solid masses. In many ways, this drawing technique corresponds to the composition of his buildings, representing the primitive blocks that find balance in a strong volumetric dialogue. In axonometric drawing, space can be represented in a more malleable way, giving greater detail to how forms assemble. Drawings of

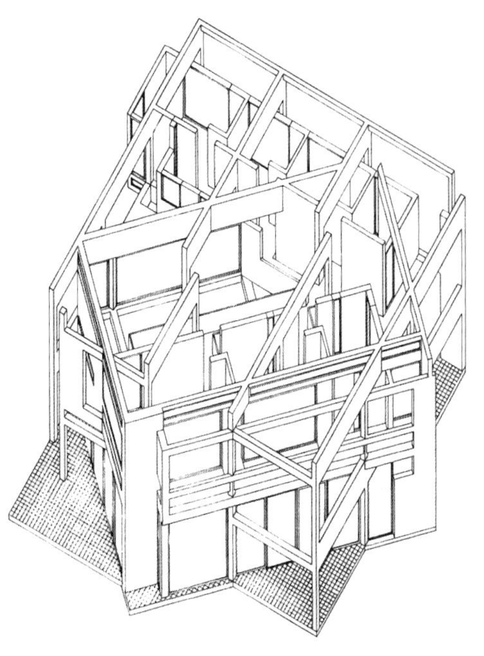

the 2-4-6-8 House by Morphosis in 1978 obsessively document this technique, systematically exposing the layered components of the house in multiple dimensions. They are distinct in showing the transformation of parts, elaborating on the anatomy of the house's construction by expanding its layers outward in x, y, and z directions. Axonometric projection not only offers an ideal analysis for examining the assembly of parts, but also in depicting design transformation and evolution.

Peter Eisenman's sequential drawings for House IV present a step-by-step procedure through which the design intention emerges. The collection of drawings coalesces in precise order to produce a crisp understanding of spatial operations, carefully examining intersecting geometries. This series presents the design of the house as being a result of these combined configurations in rectilinear space.

Similarly, Frank Gehry's proposal for the Mid-Atlantic Toyota Distributors in 1978 depicts this procedural examination as well, but his exploration portrays a much different attitude for how geometries interface, challenging their rectilinear boundaries to project how the interiors are shaped. For both Eisenman and Gehry, the assemblies of wall partitions, windows, door openings, structure, and spaces are represented with refined attention to their deliberate interactions. Informing operations of design in orthographic space, the uniquely tectonic language of these drawings allows for overlaps to occur, and provides moments where architectural elements intersect.

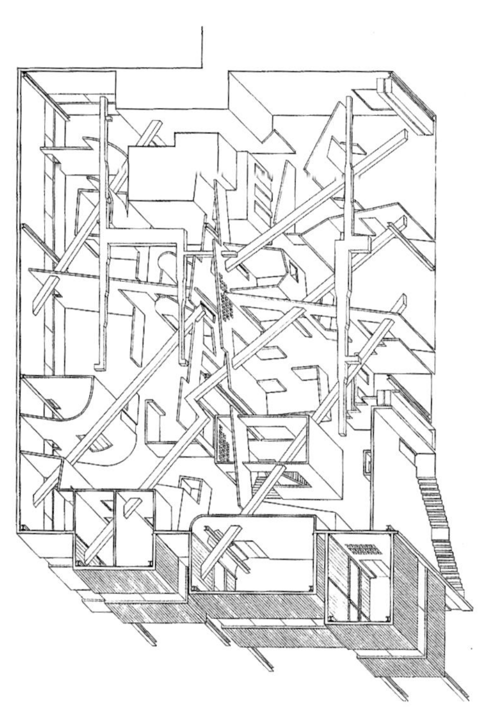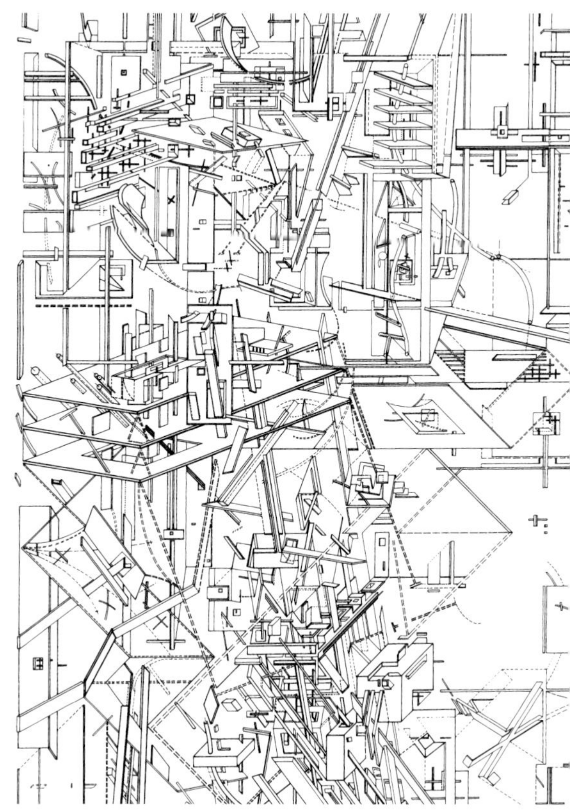

Removing the boundaries surrounding these interactions, Daniel Libeskind's Micromegas unravel these relationships in search of exploring the same superimposition, but in a scattered field. Parts are explored through local relationships, indeterminate in open space. Developing an expressive codex of superimposed artifacts, this representation, though suspiciously perspectival, carefully composes intersecting parts to reveal the part-to-part states of assembly.

Our own work has also used representation as both a descriptive tool and as a driver for the work. Pendulum Plane, one of our earliest projects from 2009, consists of a complex field of bent aluminum tubing that hovers over a gallery space. Made up of sixteen modules, each includes multiple moving elements and counterweights that rotate and fold in such a way that parts of the ceiling plane can drop down into the space to form exhibition hangers. Our drawings of the project make intense use of notational devices to describe the range of literal movements, but also use projection lines to describe the relationship between drawings on the page. In some cases, the drawn elements are rotated on the page (adjusting their skewed projection into an orthographic orientation), with a corresponding description of this rotation drawn as a projection line. The drawings, unlike the work itself, don't literally move—yet their suggested qualities may be equal to if not more powerful than the literal movement of the piece. This kind of visual description, along with the intense layering of linework that permeates the drawing, conveys more than a simple arrangement of elements, and is aimed at cultivating the perceptual and experiential qualities of the project itself.

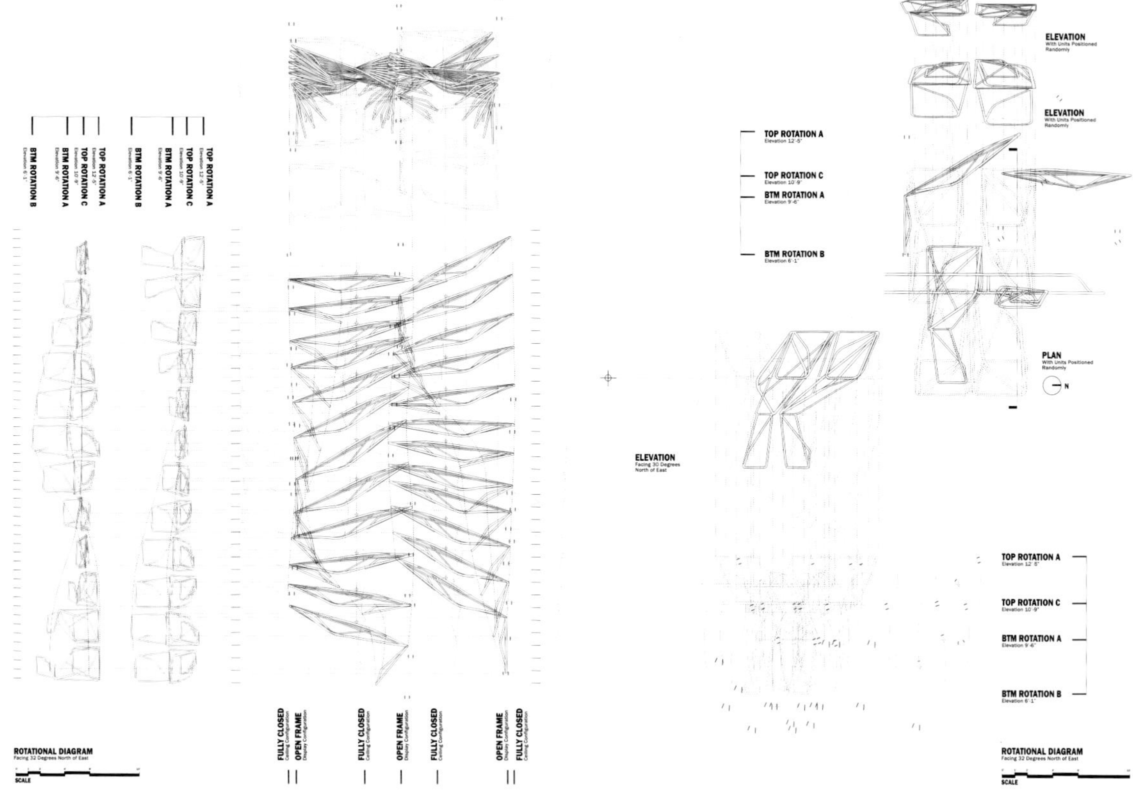

As our work has evolved, we've moved away from the kind of literal movement seen in Pendulum Plane, and increasingly toward more perceived forms of movement and connectivity. Projects like Live Wire, also from 2009, and Closeup from 2016, use fluid and repetitive geometries that capture the spirit of movement. Like Marcel Duchamp's *Nude Descending a Staircase*, there is a sense of movement through space, as if capturing multiple moments in a single frame, or in the case of architecture, in three-dimensional space. Our most recent work increasingly investigates implied or perceptual ideas of assembly and employs a more nuanced set of relationships between parts. We create an experience where the user may subtly perceive the shifting of a part by recognizing the remaining void, the implied continuity of an object as it passes through another, or the impressions left on a surface that suggest a relationship to an entity no longer sharing that space.

In many ways, representation has been an essential tool for defining the aspirations of all of our work at all phases. Our hope is to continue to build on these representational techniques, with the intention of driving the work in new and fruitful directions.

INTER-SCALAR: SITE/CITY/DETAIL

The experience of assembly in architecture translates to the full range of architectural conditions and design phases. We're especially interested in moving ideas through a project at various scales in a non-linear way, for example, starting with the small scale, jumping to issues of site, grappling with the scale of building assembly, and then back to detail. Sometimes with radically different and seemingly unrelated challenges to a design, these shifts in thinking stretch how techniques are applied, superimpose misfits, and introduce an environment where strategies can be freely transposed. We've found this way of working offers a different perspective at every scale, and often arrives at solutions that encompass the full breadth of an architectural problem. For every new scale an idea encounters, it must be interrogated for a range of possible applications. In some cases, there may be direct tectonic or formal applications, and in other cases, it may be purely conceptual. A hinge, for example, may find tectonic application in a set of moving partitions. A site strategy may make use of that same idea as a way of producing rotational movement of visitors around or through a site. The range of approaches between those literal and conceptual methodologies, as well as the degree to which they are interchangeable, lies at the heart of our investigations.

Detailing, site strategies, building, program—regardless of scale, each of these architectural territories share a set of perceptual issues that make them especially impactful to the human experience. Solving a problem, like a puzzle, engages our ability to find solutions through deduction and experimentation. Discovery also relies on the perception of new elements, or in the completion of specific tasks—and,

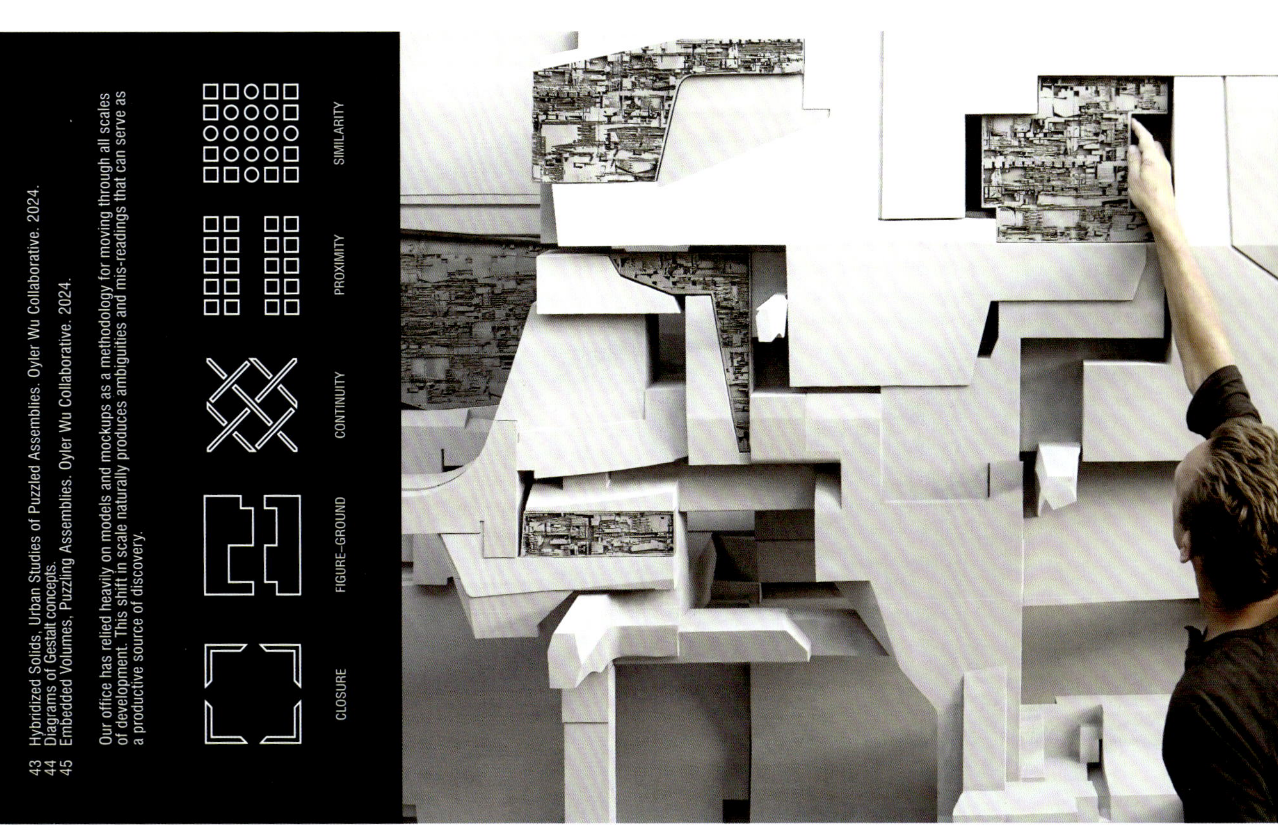

43 Hybridized Solids, Urban Studies of Puzzled Assemblies. Oyler Wu Collaborative. 2024.
44 Diagrams of Gestalt concepts.
45 Embedded Volumes, Puzzling Assemblies. Oyler Wu Collaborative. 2024.

Our office has relied heavily on models and mockups as a methodology for moving through all scales of development. This shift in scale naturally produces ambiguities and mis-readings that can serve as a productive source of discovery.

importantly, perception can jump across scales. Perception in design leans heavily on foundational principles best described in Gestalt theory.[7] The human mind finds order in our everyday experiences by grouping similar elements, recognizing patterns, and simplifying complex images. These principles create a framework for understanding not only how puzzles work, but for designing the human experience in architecture:

Similarity: Elements that are similar in shape, size, proportion, and appearance are perceived to be part of a whole even if they are not in proximity to each other.

Proximity: Elements that are positioned near each other tend to be perceived as a group, as their complexities and eccentricities are simplified into a collective entity.

Continuity: Parts that seemingly continue in the same direction are often considered to be related, where their orientation along a path is perceived to continue. Continuity becomes legible through visual alignments, symmetry, directionality, and orientation.

Figure–Ground: Foreground and background elements are instinctively isolated. Anything perceived as being in the foreground tends to be the more prominent focus of attention.

Closure: Even if parts are missing, the mind perceives a complete whole, connecting voided parts to see the overall form.

7   Ellis, Willis D. *A Source Book of Gestalt Psychology*. Milton Park, Abingdon, Oxfordshire: Routledge, 2013.

46   Vertical Volumes. Puzzling Assemblies. Oyler Wu Collaborative. 2024.
47   South and East Elevation. Storer House. Frank Lloyd Wright. Los Angeles, California. 1923.
48   Scissor Arches, Wells Cathedral. William Joy. Somerset, England, United Kingdom ca. 1183–1260.

Much of our urban work has been motivated by the idea that small-scale "bottom–up" interactions lie at the heart of a city's vitality. In response to this idea, our studies have explored ways of weaving these small-scale elements into tapestries of urban interactions, with puzzle logics serving as a key driver for ensuring robust interconnectivity and interaction.

Much of our work relies on our interest in these principles of perception, using implied relationships as an almost ephemeral factor that perceptually connects individual parts and can integrate architectural gestures at any scale. In the shift from object to architecture, perceptual readings provoke active exploration and vivid curiosity.

The most interesting methods of what we call an "inter-scalar" way of thinking leverage this type of abstraction and are perceptible in the diverse formations of a design, from the scale of the detail to the scale of urban networks. Striving for robust interactions and cohesive design strategies at multiple scales can be challenging to implement, especially in elements larger than a building. At the scale of the site, where a diversity of conditions influences early design decisions, and where interventions may resist design legibility in order to confront these conditions, we've found puzzling strategies to be especially helpful to guide the means and measure of their application. To clarify this, it is important to recognize how inter-scalar approaches can play out in design, and what this thinking offers when applied to architecture in different ways.

As an example, the inter-scalar approach of Gothic works is comprehensive, as pointed arches influence the formal and spatial shaping of almost every facet of the architecture. Gothic apertures create a raised posture through vaulted geometries, which its naves, galleries, and arcades all adopt in some variation of scale. From

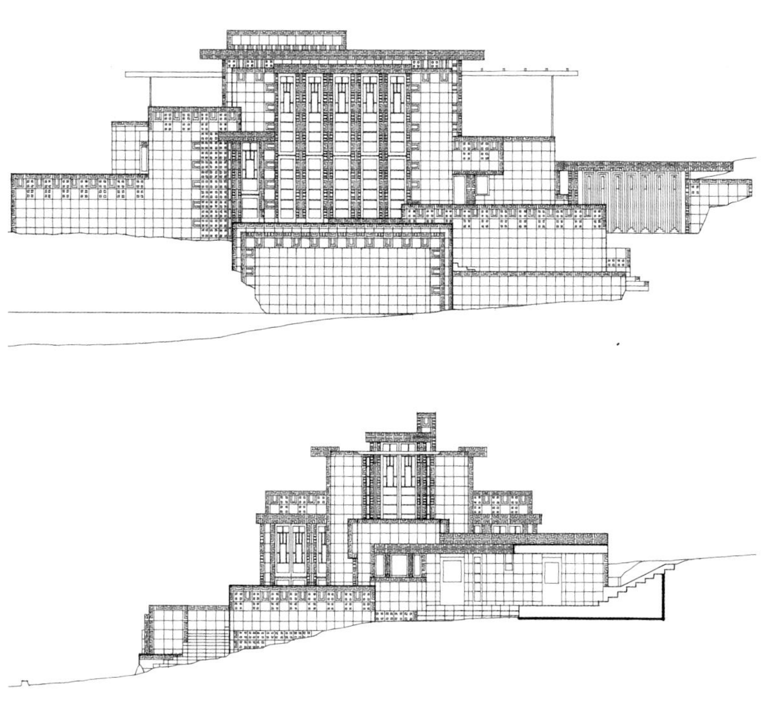

arched openings to the embedded features on the surface of the walls, the adorning of ornate railings, and the articulation of the window tracery, the rhythm of these geometries traverses various scales, elaborately unified through this shared motif.

Frank Lloyd Wright's modular designs for textile blocks explore his fascination with scale as well, but instead of holistically applying this approach to every formal aspect of the design, he focuses on the design of the modular block and the overall building massing. Developed for four different houses in the Los Angeles area between 1923 and 1925, these custom-fabricated masonry units were woven together with cast-in-place steel rods to create a block construction system that buttressed the external walls. Textured on both sides with patterns that mimicked the conceptual arrangement of the house's interior, this modular membrane prioritizes the assembly of units to create a unifying architectural element. In both the Gothic and Wright's modular block houses, features at one scale are transposed onto another in powerful ways. Taken to an extreme, however, this strategy does have the potential to become superficially stylized without formal or spatial logics. Puzzles are not simply shapes. Three-dimensional puzzles require physical manipulation, spatial reasoning, logic, and creativity to find a solution, and yet operate through parts that move like latch, lock, tab, or groove. They often involve disentangling, rearranging, and repeated testing to determine compatible forms, through explicit movements. Their varied operations can be applied to architectural ideas that use their implicit language to address a new or changing context.

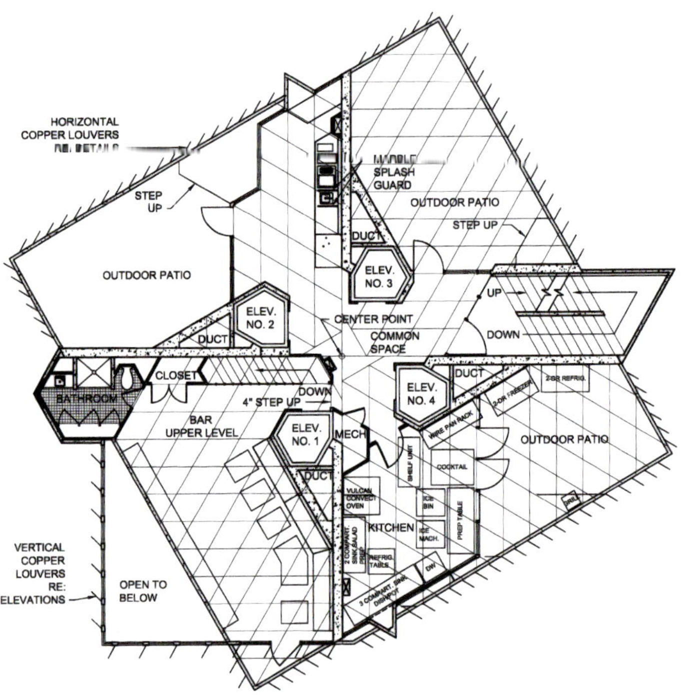

Another interesting example by Frank Lloyd Wright that takes this inter-scalar idea further is the 1952 Price Tower in Bartlesville, Oklahoma. The plan employs a pinwheel strategy used in a variety of decorative modernist motifs that proved to be especially fruitful as an inter-scalar design idea. In the case of the Price Tower, Wright rotates the building on the site while leaving the orthographic orientation of the primary interior walls in alignment with the site boundaries. The result is a dramatic spatial and organizational effect that produces a tension between the incongruent geometries. It also produces triangular geometries at all scales. What could easily have been viewed as an architectural problem became an opportunity for invention by Wright, playing out in everything from decorative motifs in copper panels, to unique stair landings and balconies, to a decentralized and spatially dynamic interior lobby located at the nexus of the pinwheel plan. This same powerful spatial effect is seen in numerous modernist plans—from Mies van der Rohe's 1923 Brick Country House to Paul Rudolph's Bass Residence. One key distinction between Wright's approach to the Price Tower and the Gothic is the difference between the operational idea of the pinwheel and the two-dimensional idea of the pointed arch. Extruded through space, they both have the potential to produce spatial outcomes. But the action inherent in the pinwheel relies less on repetitive motifs and symbolic associations, and more on the experiential qualities it has the potential to produce.

The translation of inter-scalar ideas has the same potential for affecting the placement of a building on a site. At its simplest, a site plan aims to create cohesion in either real

or implied interactions with the building's surroundings. And at its best, a site plan elaborates with a specificity that expresses how previously imperceptible elements are now understood. A building's relationship to the ground solidifies it as being a connected entity to its site—relating this with building components that in some way indicate its positioning. For example, a building can nestle into a site in the same way a puzzle piece finds a fit amongst its assembly. When architects speak of a building that is "of its site," most wouldn't generally use the terms puzzled or assembly, but this way of thinking is ideal for communicating how its features are conceptually bonded to the site. Viewing the two as being connected, or puzzled, the nuances of their assembly can offer ways to emphasize and activate this relationship between the two.

What we find particularly compelling is the tension produced between a building and its site. The specifics of each site require different approaches. Open sites, such as those found in rural, suburban, or parklike settings, allow for the manipulation of the site in ways that suggest a provocative fit within the surrounding landscape. These operations can be fitted to the ground, locked into it, leaving little doubt about its compatibility. In other contexts, physical features can be exaggerated through objects that scrape the site, or building elements that reshape it, revealing their interaction and imprint on one another. Like a "snow angel" creates loose impressions through the sweeping movements of the body that shaped it, a building can also nestle into the ground in a loose fit. Or site manipulations could suggest the idea that a building

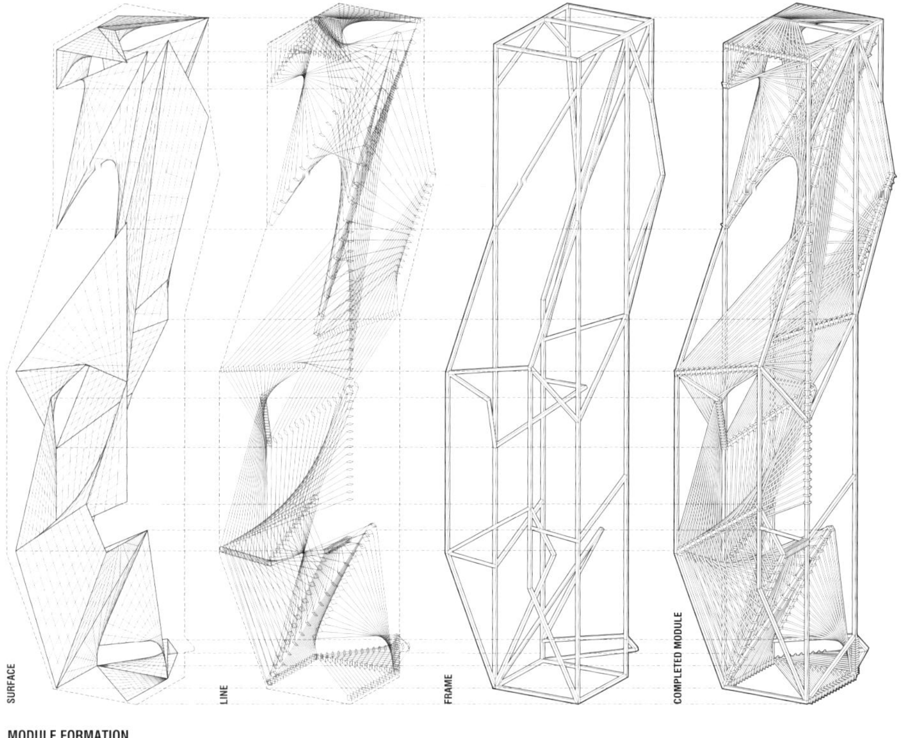

might have shifted, rotated, and slid across a site, leaving the tell-tale signs of its initial placement and repositioning. Formally fitted together in engaging ways, this ground manipulation can produce variation in section, diverse spaces between solid and void, and a sense that the building and site harmoniously coexist through their unique interaction.

From an urban design standpoint, consider the idea that the building itself can be thought of as the missing piece in a larger puzzle. An urban infill project may look to adjacent building features, existing alignments, and connective tissues that tightly embed the building into the site. Or in the case of new urban developments, they may deploy a more holistic strategy for interlocked and interwoven urban fabric that more comprehensively juxtaposes three-dimensional urban spaces with diverse building programs. When applied to urban networks, puzzling strategies resist the deficiencies of many large-scale urban gestures that often fail to consider a fine-grain tapestry of landscape, history, and culture within the public space—as streets, plazas, squares, and parks coalesce in context. Cities are enlivened networks that eccentrically organize buildings, landmarks, and focal points that are constantly in flux. When urban gestures ignore the specifics of an urban fabric, they tend to operate in ways that holistically unify the particularities of this framework into a "top–down" method, and in many ways seem antithetical to the part-to-part logic that puzzling presents. Our investigations navigate this logic, working from the "bottom–up," to explore puzzled form as an active player in configuring the urban context.

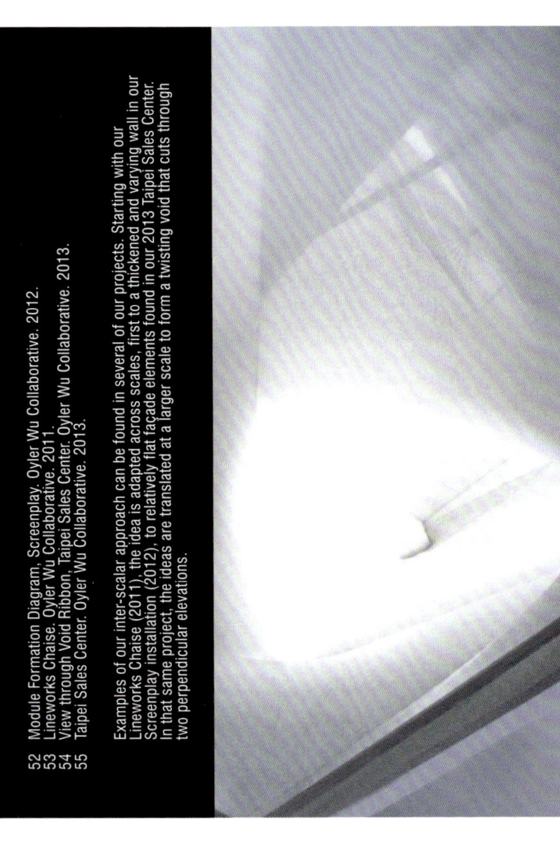

52 Module Formation Diagram, Screenplay. Oyler Wu Collaborative. 2012.
53 Lineworks Chaise. Oyler Wu Collaborative. 2011.
54 View through Void Ribbon, Taipei Sales Center. Oyler Wu Collaborative. 2013.
55 Taipei Sales Center. Oyler Wu Collaborative. 2013.

Examples of our inter-scalar approach can be found in several of our projects. Starting with our Lineworks Chaise (2011), the idea is adapted across scales, first to a thickened and varying wall in our Screenplay installation (2012), to relatively flat façade elements found in our 2013 Taipei Sales Center. In that same project, the ideas are translated at a larger scale to form a twisting void that cuts through two perpendicular elevations.

Materials, textures, and other tectonic features play an important role in the urban scale of assembly as well, and can bring a tactility that supports the logical reading of architectural space—one with distinct edges, surfaces, and textures. In dialogue with ground formations, and often drawing on principles of perception, these features can accentuate ideas that both sharpen and blur boundaries of site and building. Particular features of architectural space may leave an observable trace through this interplay. Like when a notched element is seemingly dislodged, or a gap between similarly shaped surfaces is revealed, these features offer glimpses that clarify their abstraction, bringing their formal maneuvers to the forefront. Apart from these aesthetic relationships, the interventions that embed site and building can be conceptually linked as well—punctuating program and experience in ways capable of expanding into a larger scale of design through abstraction, translating the physical nature of puzzles into something more ephemeral.

When considered at every scale, puzzles offer a theoretical model that is unlike any other, one that is full of characteristics that inform the exploration of complex construction. And although the strategies vary in application, the process of experimenting with assemblies in multiple phases and conditions generates new discoveries and operations. In punctuating assemblies, puzzles present a transformational language for architectural study, revealing a hidden physicality and operability that goes beyond a formal or figural approach. Through investigation and interrogation, puzzled assemblies activate the critical dialogue between design and making.

56 Church of St. John's in Vilnius. Johann Christoph Glaubitz. Vilnius, Lithuania. c.1426.

THE TECTONICS OF ANIMACY

by NADER TEHRANI

To ponder the extraordinary work of Oyler Wu is to confront the inevitable question of whether tectonics has anything to do with construction, even if that is its main preoccupation. It is a well-rehearsed argument that tectonics, if seen through the lens of its classical antecedents, is about the "effects" of construction. The entasis of the Doric order, an oft-cited example, illustrates how the weight of the entablature above is manifest through the bulge on the column below. That the temple is fabricated of stone is no obstacle: the laborious carving of masonry has never limited the voluptuousness of expression, as we have witnessed in the work of masons and sculptors alike.

Consider the Porch of the Maidens at the Erectheion, located meters away from the Parthenon atop the Acropolis: do we challenge the impact of gravity on the body of the maidens, the subtle dialogue between the articulation of flesh and draped fabric that adorns their figures? I suspect not, if only because the realism that is insinuated in the carving of the figures allows us to read the structure within, accepting gravity as a central ingredient of their representation. Animate as they seem to be in their capacity to bring to life the effects of gravity, the human figures—and the columns of the Parthenon nearby—both embody this desire for architecture to live, breathe, or somehow move.

To better situate the work of Oyler Wu, it is helpful to reflect on the idea of animacy as it is captured by other architectures—not so much to demonstrate a teleology, but rather to expand on the cultural context of their work when situated within an expanded history. For instance, it is hard to imagine why the Church of St. John's in Vilnius might need such a myriad of columns to reinforce its front facade. Spaced narrowly together, so redundant are its columns, that one can hardly perceive the wall of the facade itself. Compressed one against the next, the columns vie for attention, distorting the plane of the facade, as if the crowding of the columns forces some to recess as pilasters and others to step forth as full-fledged rotund columns. There emerges in this facade an animate logic that defies the mere necessity of structure, hence reinforcing the argument that tectonics is more about visual rather than technical performance.

Similarly, in Alvar Aalto's Hochhaus in Bremen, we discover a planimetric strategy that is somehow informed by two concurrent logics: the first, a rational appeal to orthogonal core infrastructural elements, and the second, an array of radial party walls that organize apartments with the curious capacity to maximize units as they conically expand toward the vista. This second logic balances "play" with real estate logic, the facade undulating in relationship to the views it is intended to capture. In tandem, this face also captures a semantic dimension beyond what buildings are conventionally called on to manifest; ambiguous as a signifier, the folded facade appears as an animate plane, a fabric in the breeze, a sinuous surface of sorts. Conceived less as a single object, the organizational system of the Hochhaus might better be interpreted through the idea of multiplicity: channeled through a set of parameters, the built version can be seen as only one of many solutions. The malleability of this animate system demonstrates the analytical potential of rule-based relationships.

The conceptual connection between analytical approaches and animate qualities is also captured by those architectures that embody the design process in their final instantiation, critically illustrated by Peter Eisenman's House IV. In some way, while the house satisfies programmatic, circulatory, and technical mandates, what defines the house are the rules that guide its design. These operations manifest as "traces" onto the final iteration of the house. That the analytical "process" has the capacity to coalesce into the building is a testament to the idea that the animate can also be captured as a frozen moment in time, drawing an entire method into the form of the artifact.[8]

Different as these examples might be, they capture a range of interpretations of animate tectonics that are also explored in the work of Oyler Wu. The connection between "animate form" and the digital turn is best articulated by Greg Lynn's book, the namesake of which illustrates how the instrumentality of emerging tools of drawing, modeling, and visualization produce new forms of architectural agency. Written in the late nineties, *Animate Form* brought together many of the ideas formed in the paperless studios at Columbia's GSAPP.[9] Positioned right between the analogue and digital generations—between their undergraduate and graduate years, Oyler and Wu would become the beneficiaries of the best of both cultures. Not only could they tap into the pedagogical foundations of tectonic culture, but also seamlessly navigate through digital protocols as they came together in graduate studies, eventually merging them strategically through their work. If most of the work of the nineties was centered on form making, generative strategies, and visualization, the question of the means and methods of fabrication was not part of the debate at Columbia.

Others at that time would take on the problem of digital fabrication head on, either fueled by well-endowed patronage—like Frank Gehry, or supported more modestly through academic endowments with installations, mock-ups, and detail studies. In the infancy of that moment, we would witness the transition from mass production to customization, accompanied by a rhetoric of rationality, ease, and infinite malleability. For those who built in that era, they would also come to confront the immediate challenges between the rhetoric and reality of the argument: there were, and remain today, significant difficulties to get the construction trades to buy into technologies, to train their staff in the necessary skills, and to invite the dexterity of complexity. For this reason, even for complex projects, practicing architects continue to develop systems of aggregation that rely on repetition with relative variation to bring projects within financial reach. Here, the appearance of animate surfaces may be tamed by scales of pixelation and subdivision, allowing for greater deployability.

8   Eisenman, Peter. *The Formal Basis of Modern Architecture*. Baden, Switzerland: Lars Müller Publishers, 2006.

9   Lynn, Greg. *Animate Form*. New York City, New York: Princeton Architectural Press, 1999.

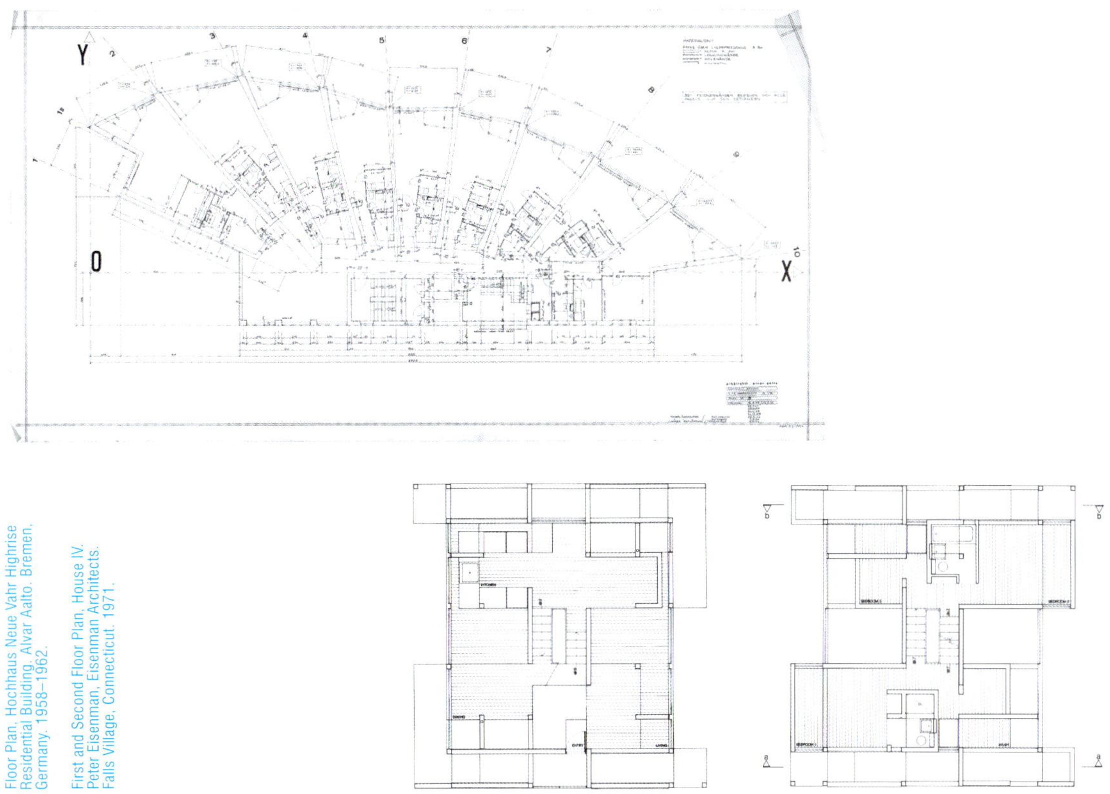

57 Floor Plan, Hochhaus Neue Vahr Highrise Residential Building, Alvar Aalto, Bremen, Germany, 1958–1962.

58 First and Second Floor Plan, House IV, Peter Eisenman, Eisenman Architects, Falls Village, Connecticut, 1971.

As they launched their practice, Oyler Wu would be positioned perfectly to oversee these evolutions. If both came to architecture with substantial ambitions, a couple of biographical twists may shed light on the apparent ease with which they have exercised their skills, from drawing to construction. With a background in arts and fabrication, Dwayne Oyler spent two arduous years in a foundry, casting iron, and effectively being educated in metal works. That is to say that while architecture would eventually emerge as a focused discipline, his lens into the métier would invariably be informed by a detailed understanding of welding, casting, and other related protocols. Through this construction tutelage, Oyler would mitigate the otherwise unchecked costs of subcontractor's bids, overcoming the deadly spiral of value engineering and compromises that befall other practices. Meanwhile, at the other end of the scalar spectrum, Jenny Wu was researching digital printing, seizing the moment as the economies of metal printing became affordable. With formidable geometric literacy, she would tinker with small experiments, delicate as they were, to form necklaces, rings, and jewelry that would become objects of desire at the very lectures, exhibitions, and events to which she would become a significant voice. This interest would eventually allow her to launch LACE, the company she continues to lead as part of a commitment to design within an expanded field. Between these two spheres of fabrication, Oyler Wu understand not only the "what" of design, but equally importantly the "how." The exuberance of their formal zeal is bracketed by a consistent co-presence of the figurative—the organic, the shapely, the sculpted, and the configurative—what becomes realized in the details of their aggregations and the metamorphic assemblies they undertake. If the architectural figure is somehow indifferent to questions of construction, Oyler Wu's bottom–up focus on detailed configurations of metal rods, wood studs, and mesh emphasizes material agency as a central part of their formal imagination.

59   Stormcloud, SCI-Arc Graduation Pavilion. Oyler Wu Collaborative. Los Angeles, California. 2013.

60   The Exchange. Oyler Wu Collaborative. Columbus, Indiana. 2017.

With a healthy portfolio of installations, pavilions, small projects, and a few upcoming larger projects, the couple's emerging challenge will be the predicament of scaling up. The sheer accomplishment of the installations cannot be casually overlooked: what remained for a prior generation an improbable fascination with drawings, models, and renderings is manifest through robust material reality in the work of Oyler Wu. Complex arrangements of lines, planes, and volumes—what others speculatively model with facility in Rhino, overlooking any regard to construction tolerances—Oyler Wu build with impeccable craft and confidence. I am reminded of Richard Serra's *Verb List* as I attempt to identify distinct configurational differences in each project: to bend, to fold, to droop, to twist, etc. While certainly not immune to compound curvature, their operations lead us through thoughtful material assemblies stemming from construction and labor protocols.

Pedagogical in their approach, Oyler Wu's projects are somehow didactic in their composition. Unmistakable as a defined geometric territory, The Exchange in Columbus, Indiana, identifies its site through the extraction of volumes from a perfect cubic mass. Composed as a combination of solids, planes, and lines, these elements are fabricated to reveal the anatomy of their thinking: stereotomic solids remain tectonically abstract— presumably in plaster, hovering gently over a reveal in relationship to the ground. Though observant of the limits of the cube on the outside, the inside of the volume is carved as if a monolithic mass, without recourse to panelization, seams, or details. Unconstrained by the geometry of the exterior, the internal figures appear free form, though precise in the way that they rehearse deformations and contortions through ruled surfaces—that is, developable surfaces modeled for fabrication purposes. Those very ruled surfaces become manifest through a skeleton of steel ribs, an apparition whose geometry extends the logic of solid masses; crisp in their delineation of geometric description, they recall the contours or isocurves of a computer model. Fashioned like an exploded axonometric, the installation reveals the anatomy of a project, not only describing the relationship between solids, voids, and screens, but also an architecture caught in the act of becoming; as the figures swirl, canopies transform into benches, walls become chaises longues, etc. The results, of course, transcend the limits of an analytical description; superimposed onto each other, nestled into the trees, framed as a protected environment, the entire space sponsors an experience that escapes verbal articulation—playing on light, shadow, nature, and spatial qualities that momentarily suspend the need for rational explanation.

Numerous in their qualities, other installations experiment with related issues, allowing ample slippage between material performance and geometric precision to make for uncanny discoveries. Played out in fabric, mesh, slats, tensile rods, and other media, the explorations are too many to enumerate in this text. However, a fragment of their body of work serves as an apparent outlier to these complex assemblies and tectonic explorations.

Two projects, the Suburban Intervention and the American Cement Building Loft, are characterized by their remarkable conventionalism in addressing wood construction, trabeated connections, and millwork assemblies as basis for architectural transformations. No less accomplished than any of the other projects, these two, in specific ways, both draw out a slightly different connotation of the term "tectonics" than what I have outlined above, and each develop a language of connections, details, and joinery that speaks to the core of the fabricational disciplines. These projects are composed of standard elements—studs, beams, plywood, etc.—and are not subjugated to larger figurative impulses. Rather, they patiently build up a restrained language whose invention reveals itself at the configurative scale of the detail: less form, more syntax. Though distinct from their other projects, these two still suggest an animate tectonic that layers the relationship between elements—such that the connections between columns and beams might slip past each other, rather than closing on a point. The formlessness of these two projects recalls the configurative biases of Greene and Greene's Gamble House or the interiors of Rudolf Schindler, not in the emulation of details, but in the dispersion of architectural attention: the detail is not reserved for a unique corner but is omnipresent as a distributed system throughout a field of relationships. The architectural effect is such that one inhabits the spatiality of the system, rather than seeing the detail as a precious object. These two projects potentially demonstrate a wider perspective of both their potential as designers and of things to come.

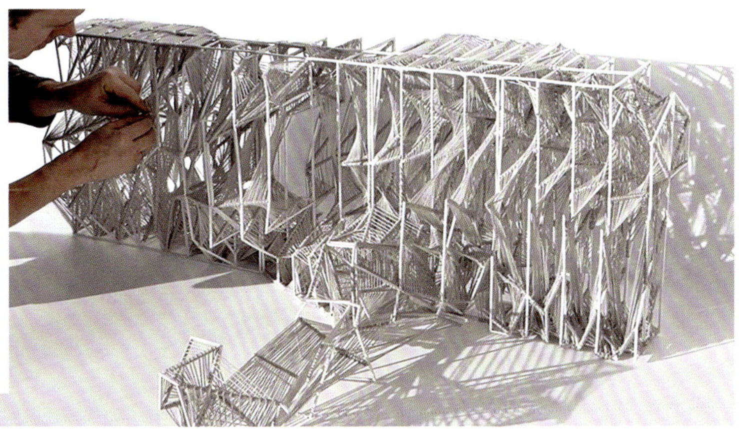

Whether as fabricators or architects, Oyler and Wu build: that is to say, they have built with their own hands, they have managed student teams in collaborative assemblies, and in turn, they have also coordinated broader construction teams towards complex scopes of work. Many of their generation have dreamed and drawn, but these two have delivered on certain architectural promises, what possibly allows us to discuss not just the extraordinary "what" and "how" of their architecture, but also the "why." If technology, patronage, finances, or means and methods were no obstacles, then presumably architects could build almost anything they desired, with only their critical judgment as obstacles or safeguards. It is possible that Oyler Wu have not yet crossed the threshold into what I will describe as a more complex territory of urban strategies, political entanglements, or collaborative community processes, all the things that stand to bring a different type of sobriety to exceptional talents. It is maybe in those moments where critical judgment allows us to see how the architects confront decorum and opportunity.

Premature as it may be as a declaration, this is the danger that awaits Oyler Wu as they gain new opportunities to design, build, and cement their authorship. The Monarch Tower in Taipei may give us a clue as to the predicaments that loom ahead, and how they might navigate them. A substantial residential tower in the skyline, just under twenty stories tall, the commission offered a challenge that few architects would refuse: an opportunity to exercise their intellectual speculations, to explore a shift in scale, and to experiment with a level of complexity to which they have not had prior access. At the same time, of all the building types, the residential tower is stubborn in both its technical mandates and financial economies; the desire of customization is almost always short-circuited by the requirements of stacked plumbing lines, repetitive formwork, and standardized units, among other development restrictions. In that light, the evident sophistication of architectural surplus in its outer skin—a combination of staggering balconies, metal scrims, and glass picture planes—deftly overcomes the barriers that are part and parcel of most developer projects. Unitized as they are, the modules of this second skin produce a recognizable figurative flourish in what is otherwise a simple extrusion of a tower.

The slippage between the regularity of floor plans—what the architects had no recourse to control—and the undulating skin—what they have mastered in the scale of installations, pavilions, and now this large building—produces what appears to be a unique identity for

all apartments: each with their particular set of relationships between amenities. And yet, behind this figurative impulse lies a yearning that I can only explain as a two-fold desire: at once, to form an iconicity for the tower that is conventionally reserved for cultural projects, but at the same time, to maintain an identifiable brand for their authorship, a language that sweeps across scales. To understand this better, it should be underscored that there is a genuine desire for developers to deliver products that are unique, with varied apartment layouts and amenities that offer bespoke choices; it is also true that there is a design tradition of developing modular variations for these building types such that there emerges a legible reciprocity between apartment unit and its identity as a type lodged within the larger figure of the building.

The ethic of reciprocity between the organization of a building as a configuration and its identity as a figure is, of course, entirely arbitrary. If anything, the rhetoric of functionalism and its desire to reveal an alleged "truth" in materiality has long been demythologized. If Le Corbusier's Five Points taught us anything about the free facade—and the curtain wall that was its technological prerequisite—it was that beyond the ribbon window, there was a range of phenomenal and representational opportunities the elevation could project.[10] Robert Venturi and Denise Scott Brown's "decorated shed" would eventually unburden the architect from the unnecessary guilt associated with the narration of a single truth.[11] Moreover, what both Le Corbusier and Venturi, Scott Brown would achieve together— unwittingly as it were—was to invoke new tectonic possibilities for the facade, untethered to the actual structural performance it might have been tied to in another era. In a period of parametric dexterity, interactive environments, and spectacular icons, there are fewer obstacles to restrain the architectural appetite, but in tandem, an even higher pressure to exercise critical discernment. This is what awaits the talents of Oyler Wu; indeed, the dexterity of their skills is captured aptly in the sinuous animacy of tectonic permutations. Still, as accomplished as they reveal themselves to be in a twenty-story tower, their capacity to continue to interpret the animate within an expanded field of varied guises will invariably allow them an even more critical posture towards the occasion of the ever-more-complex projects that appear to be forthcoming.

10   Le Corbusier. *Towards an Architecture* (French, 1923), translated by John Goodman. Los Angeles, California: Getty Research Institute, 2007.

11   Venturi, Robert; Scott Brown, Denise; Izenour, Steven. *Learning from Las Vegas*. Cambridge, Massachusetts: MIT Press, 1972.

THOUGHTS ON BEING PIXELATED

by EDWARD FORD

Pixelated, adjective: pix·e·lat·ed
    Definition:

1.   displayed in such a manner that individual pixels are discernible
2.   mischievous, prankish, wicked
3.   somewhat mentally unsound

The firm of Oyler Wu willed itself into existence between 2008 and 2012 in an atypical manner, not with house additions but with a series of open structures—installation/exhibition constructions such as Density Fields and the SCI-Arc graduation pavilions. All were more structural frames than enclosures, with not much building envelope and at times no real roof. But what is striking about them is their structural language, which arguably is not about structure at all. All members, usually metal tubes, are typically the same cross section, regardless of their structural load. It is a reappearance of a much older phenomenon, an alternative modernist language that has appeared and disappeared periodically over the last hundred years. It began at the Bauhaus in the tubular metal language of Marcel Breuer's Wassily chair, then Mies van der Rohe's Chaise Longue and Giuseppe Terragni's Sant'Elia chair.

But these three saw it as a language of furniture, not architecture. It broke a lot of architectural rules. To them architecture, even if a lightweight one, required monumentality. It required mass. Architecture required a hierarchy. Some saw it otherwise, and there have been moments in the years since when this linear, tubular language found its way into architecture—in Charlotte Perriand's Alpine hut, in Konrad Wachsmann's *Study of a Dynamic Structure*, in Miralles and Tagliabue's Diagonal Mar Park.

Oyler Wu's version of this furniture/architecture language also breaks a lot of rules:

It invites fragmentation.
It is an architecture of discernable parts, of assembly.
It requires visible joints and an identity of components.
It shows the evidence of making.
There is absence of hierarchy.
There is an equality of elements, in size and apparent function.
There are no columns or beams, girders or joists—the structural units are the same diameter.
Elements are multifunctional and ambiguous.
A column becomes a bench support; a stair rail becomes a table leg.

Early twentieth-century architectural historians like Heinrich Wölfflin argued that the appeal of early Renaissance buildings is their partiality, that they are assemblies of small elements that maintain their individual identity as a part of a whole, and that we respond to them because they are like ourselves. In *Prolegomena to a Psychology of Architecture*, he wrote, "the individual [unit] is a unified community in which all parts work together for a single purpose."[12] That is, the parts have an anthropomorphic quality. I would argue that this anthropomorphic quality is precisely the virtue of the Oyler Wu structures. The architects realized early on that applying this unitized system to larger programmatically driven

12 Wölfflin, Heinrich. *Prolegomena to a Psychology of Architecture* (German, 1886), translated by Michael Selzer. CreateSpace Independent Publishing Platform, Keepahead Press Architectural Theory Texts, Book 1, 2016.

buildings—scaling up the frame and adding a building envelope—would be problematic. This was particularly true in relation to the typology they were beginning to work with, the high-rise apartment building, and the place, Taipei, Taiwan.

Monarch Tower

In the first of their apartment towers to be realized, Monarch Tower (2017), their task was to apply a thin layer of architecture to a predetermined floor plan of apartment units. Beyond the edge of the base plan, they were allowed only five meters at the front and one-and-a-half meters on the side. While this area could contain balconies, it could not be enclosed space. The architects have been candid about the literally superficial mode in which they felt they were working, but the typology of applying a thin layer of architecture to a predetermined floor plan is in truth an all-too-common phenomenon anywhere, particularly for apartment towers. Frank Gehry's 8 Spruce Street in New York and Jeanne Gang's Aqua Tower in Chicago are standard blocks of standard apartment unit plans. Both could be easily wrapped in a completely different architectural expression with no real change to the plan. What makes them a Gehry or a Gang building is a thin layer of applied styling.

In any case, the larger scale of the Monarch Tower required a new strategy—a process the architects call "pixelation." While the linear elements of the earlier work are present, they are a composition of lines, an underlying geometric skeleton rather than a structural reality. The design began with the facade of a twenty-two-by-twenty-two-meter rectilinear block, sixteen stories tall, overlayed with a projected surface at the required distance. Onto this exterior surface a series of tightly spaced vertical, curvilinear lines are drawn. They are not themselves real elements but they locate the real elements, and while clearly visible they are so only by implication. Across the face of the building are a series of unit assemblies, one for each dwelling, that occupy the layer beyond the exterior wall of the apartment. Each unit is composed of three elements with different degrees of transparency: a fragment of a glass bay window, an aluminum mesh screen, and a metal-framed glazed balcony. Like their earlier work, these elements have an individual, anthropomorphic quality. The bay windows in particular bring to mind Auguste Perret's adage, "a window is a man standing."[13]

But while the projecting units are nearly identical, they are not vertically aligned, and slide horizontally. They are, in fact, located by aligning their corners with one of the curvilinear vertical lines. In almost any other apartment of the past two hundred years, traditional or modern, projecting windows or balconies like these would be arranged in vertical stacks. They would be subordinate to a rigid compositional organization. The tower arrangement is far more asymmetrical and far less hierarchical, but articulating the identity of the individual units takes precedent over the creation of a unifying formal order of the totality.

Dunhua Tower

The second Taipei apartment tower, the Dunhua Tower, nearing completion, is seventeen floors high but has a deeper triangular plan and a thinner vertical profile. And again, the design is confined to a narrow layer two meters outside the edge of the apartment proper. The pixelating strategy, with some modification, continues here. There are vertical lines here as well, at times merely implied by the pixelation, while at other times, real elements. There are,

66 8 Spruce Street (formerly Beekman) Residential Tower. Gehry Partners. New York City, New York. 2011.

67 Aqua Tower. Studio Gang. Chicago, Illinois. 2010.

in fact, two facades. The base facade is that of the individual units overlaying the pixelated organization. The second is the common structures they share. Unlike the conceptually subtractive flat plane of the Monarch Tower facade, the Dunhua Tower facade is a series of additive projections serving the individual units. The wall of each apartment unit is in three parts—a massive stone-clad wall behind with deeply recessed windows, metal-framed balconies with patterned glazing, and sometimes but not always a perforated metal screen. The units slide horizontally, creating pixelated lines similar to the Monarch Tower facade. But there is another series of structures recalling Oyler Wu's earlier tubular work. Across the faces of the projecting units, and interpenetrating openings between them, are several tubular metal structures. The first, at the base, is a four-story-tall vertical extension of the ground-floor entry canopy. The second frame traverses the top ten stories, occupying a narrow V-shaped vertical ventilation shaft, holding a series of individual laundry balconies for the adjacent units. Connected to both these frames is a series of unglazed window-like elements, creating yet another layer on the exterior.

Conclusion

To understand the virtues of this architecture, one must compare the Monarch and Dunhua towers with their typological relatives. As in Gehry's 8 Spruce Street and Gang's Aqua Tower, a thin perimeter layer defines the design. In the latter two it is simply curvilinear shapes. In the Oyler Wu towers, however, this layer is one of architectural experiences, a series of differing spaces, not a stylized tack on. These spaces bring to mind a great moment in twentieth-century modernism—the exploration of an architecture of the in-between by Aldo Van Eyck and Louis Kahn—the window that is a little room between interior reality and the world outside.[14]

If we look at 8 Spruce Street, we see the tall, vertical, continuous edges of its curving surfaces. If we look at the Aqua Tower, we see the undulating edges of its floors and the curving geometric envelope they imply. Style and geometry unite all into an identifiable, singular image. They are iconic buildings. In the Oyler Wu towers there is a willingness to risk fragmentation for the sake of individuality. The individual unit, and the parts of the unit, have an autonomy. If we look at the north facade of the Monarch Tower, we see something more fragmented and less unified than Spruce Street or Aqua but something that has far more substance and less styling. We see sixty-eight windows implying sixty-eight apartments. They have a complexity, but not at the expense of unity. If less useful as glib trademarks, they are more profound as serious works of architecture. But within these units is something else: they also have a partiality. They have the quality of an assembly of dependent and identifiable elements that Wölfflin thought created the humanistic qualities in Renaissance architecture.

Oyler Wu's work accepts, even celebrates, the complexity of the modern building. They have found ways to articulate the part without fragmenting the whole. Their pixelated work, like that of their predecessors Perriand, Wachsmann, and Miralles and Tagliabue, is mischievous, prankish, wicked and somewhat mentally unsound, in the very best way.

13 Bruno, Reichlin. *The Pros and Cons of the Horizontal Window: The Perret—Le Corbusier Controversy*. Daidalos 13, September 1984. pp. 56–78.

14 McCarter, Robert William. Aldo van Eyck and Louis I. Kahn: *Parallels in the Other Tradition of Modern Architecture*. ZARCH No. 10, 2018. pp. 44–61.

70 Embedded Volumes, Puzzling Assemblies.
Oyler Wu Collaborative. 2024.

by DAVID ERDMAN

PROGRAM(MING) THE MOTTLE

The distinction between program and programming has been debated in architectural discourse for nearly a century. In a fever pitch of questioning, enthusiasts, practitioners, and academics have contested which dominates which: form or function. While early modernist determinism equated program with function, postmodernism nearly banished the term, and by the late eighties program became a generative tool that is formally indifferent. With the rise of computational technology and the architect's capacity to engage multiple media in the late twentieth century, concepts of program and the act of programming expanded culturally. It was at that transitional moment, during the formative educational years of Dwayne Oyler and Jenny Wu, that programming and its discourse began to include an array of manifestations that eroded the false binaries and campy inner-disciplinary arguments that had pitted form and program against one another and had siloed architects into one tribe or another.

The work of Oyler Wu Collaborative stands on the shoulders of that late period and wisely liberates itself from the confines of being formal or informal, of being for program or against it. Using model-heavy processes (both digital and physical) and reflecting an ethos committed to tacit material understanding, the practice might appear to be a devotee of the formal camp; a cohort historically accused of disregarding program and function in favor of composition and aesthetic beauty. Yet, it is precisely because of their material tenacity and their esoteric processes of making that we can see a heightening, attenuating, and coupling of their design interests with perception, experience, and subtle but important undertones of cultural desire. It is this binding coherence that associates their assemblies with "acts" of puzzling, cutting across scales.

At one scale, "puzzling assemblies" is a perception of the designer, of one who tinkers, one who iterates and assembles and tries to fit things together that are not easy bedfellows. This is a core principle of architectural work and labor: that we attempt to bring coherence to things that otherwise fall apart. That we "puzzle" (verb). To understand what is being invoked at this scale is to understand that an architect is a dualist (at a minimum) and a pluralist (more typically) who sees a multitude of prospective relationships and opportunities in how form and assemblies might be habituated, circumnavigated, and perceived. All of which is to say that there is an underlying suggestion that the drive, thirst, and curiosity of architects lies in their desire to puzzle—not necessarily solve—difficult fits

Certainly this is the innuendo of Oyler Wu's "programming"; that we do not resolve a program but arrange and assemble a set of possible outcomes and interactions. The late twentieth century's discourse on programming culminated in a sectional understanding (largely leveraged by Rem Koolhaas, OMA, and their watershed of practices like MVRDV, FOA, BIG...) that activated the z axis as a third vector for program. In these projects and practices, architects went beyond plan, which is not insignificant. Stacking in particular sets up a vertical array of programmatic interactions that only make sense as one moves through them (often on ramps, lifts, or the proverbial escalator) in section and where plans can appear frighteningly illogical. Take MVRDV's Double House as a case in point.

Oyler Wu Collaborative takes programming beyond section to a new level of engagement and complexity, deploying nested, interlocked, and dovetailed programs, each leveraging methods of joinery as tactical, scalar, programmatic concepts. This swerve of definition enriches the possible behavioral outcomes and interactions in their projects. By going beyond and between xyz into a more quadrilateral space, Oyler Wu understands programming as a fourth-dimensional vector; one that is equally present in material and form, but also may be a void or negative space versus a "positive." This positive and negative, circuitry and volume, steel and wood thread through one another and literally engage the inhabitant—as a prospective space of social condensation and interaction.

In this way we see that "puzzling assemblies" applies not only to the designer, the one who tinkers, but now at the scale of program, the individual user becomes a perceiver and player in Oyler Wu's "puzzling assemblies." The programmatic mix, the prospective chemistry of interactions, and the gauging of how to condense those interactions through assembled programmatic structures and subdivisions of space create the possibility of a variety of interactions and behaviors. Through the inhabitants and their interests, the program and its ecology of potentials contribute to the vitality of the community of folks who interact with it on a regular basis.

One way to describe programming in the work of Oyler Wu is as a foggy, patinated, somewhat messy embodiment of qualities and experiences. What I would call "The Mottle" (pronounced like 'model' but with a "t", and here is used intentionally for its double meaning) is something that is precise, and yet is aware of how a material (or in this case a person and body) impacts the environment in which they interact. From jewelry to furniture to the Exchange pavilion to Monarch, their first completed residential tower, we see dense, ghost-like, overlapping meshes tracing figures and caught in creases. These meshes track circuitry or structure and circumnavigate human and architectural bodies, twisting, reorienting, interlocking, and nesting the sequences, perspectives, and/or relationships we might associate with the spaces we move through and around. The finishes and qualities relate to the programming in imaginative ways. The projects have an unearthed, aged quality and can appear similar to archeological findings—as if parts of some larger organism have been

71   Double House. MVRDV Winy Maas, Jacob van Rijs, Nathalie de Vries. Utrecht, Netherlands. 1997.

reassembled. Materials can transform over time, changing sheen, patina, or texture. The vibration between scales, between solids and voids, between circuitry and volume, between perimeter and interior each have their versions of nesting and interlocking. And finally, none of Oyler Wu's projects are polychromic. They are muted, often gray, white, in some cases wood, or a combination of the three. Their matte and/or rough patinated finishes further reinforce a tactility that provokes discovery, a textural and sensual Braille captivating our attentiveness beyond sight, or seen into the haptic and felt.

Each of these scales and attributes, from the molecular to the macro, further deepens the idea of puzzling, assembling, and how they cohere into programmatic effects. Oyler Wu assembles each element to promote interaction, between inside and outside, between upstairs and downstairs, between seen and sensed. They evoke a third space that is the hazy substance within or between these joints, details, or creases. Oyler Wu's programming is mottled. It is both inclusive and adaptive, leveraging the activities between object and void, between elements to amplify social and environmental interaction and engagement. It taps into our desires as inhabitants and designers and provides a subtle but important conversation around climate: that you let the environment seep in. This idea of cohabitation with the outside, while not explicit in the work, is present. The concepts of interlocking and nesting go beyond traditional detail terminology and Oyler Wu's amplified programmatic tactics, expanding into ecological opportunities: to let water in, to "nest," and interlock site with building.

Oyler Wu Collaborative's contribution to the discourse of programming is perhaps that it is future and past, that it is the surrounding environment and the interior, that it is what is felt more than seen. It is exciting to look back across the projects and also to imagine how their expanded programmatic approach will continue to shape the discourse in the years ahead.

72 Physical Model. Intersphere. Oyler Wu Collaborative
Helsinki, Finland. 2024.

THE CONSTRAINTS OF SECTION

by PAUL LEWIS

In simple terms, a section is a vertical cut. As such, it can reveal fascinating attributes of objects and buildings. It can equally and indiscriminately expose the mundane. This is particularly the case if the cut is taken after a building has been designed primarily in plan. Yet even if there is great attention given to the development of the section in the design, there are three constraints that dominate most contemporary buildings.

First, the relentlessness of flat floor plates—and their direct alignment with capital measured in square feet—limits the development of vertical space in a building. Vertical spaces or voids are carved out of those stacked plates, and the loss of square footage must be commercially justified. For example, an atrium's value as a spatial feature must be argued against its own expense as well as the removal of that very floor area. Prior to the development of reinforced concrete and steel assemblies, a building's section was much more constrained by gravity, limiting vertical spatial articulation largely to ceilings (domes, arches), or articulations of the ground (amphitheater, step wells). While concrete and steel construction are capable of cantilevers, volumetric exploits, and other extraordinary formal feats, these materials are predominantly deployed as repetitive slabs used to maximize Floor Area Ratio and profit. The efficiency enabled by slab construction has produced its own constraint, such that creatively stacking them has become one means to produce section, however limited. The efficiencies of slab construction have consumed volume as our primary building component, and the qualities of section suffer as a result.

Second, if the effects of a section are concentrated on the interior, and produced through articulations of a horizontal slab, the exterior elevation is often separate from these logics. While intensifying a building's section can be a way to resist conceiving of the building as an object, creating occupiable interior qualities, these may not be legible on the exterior.

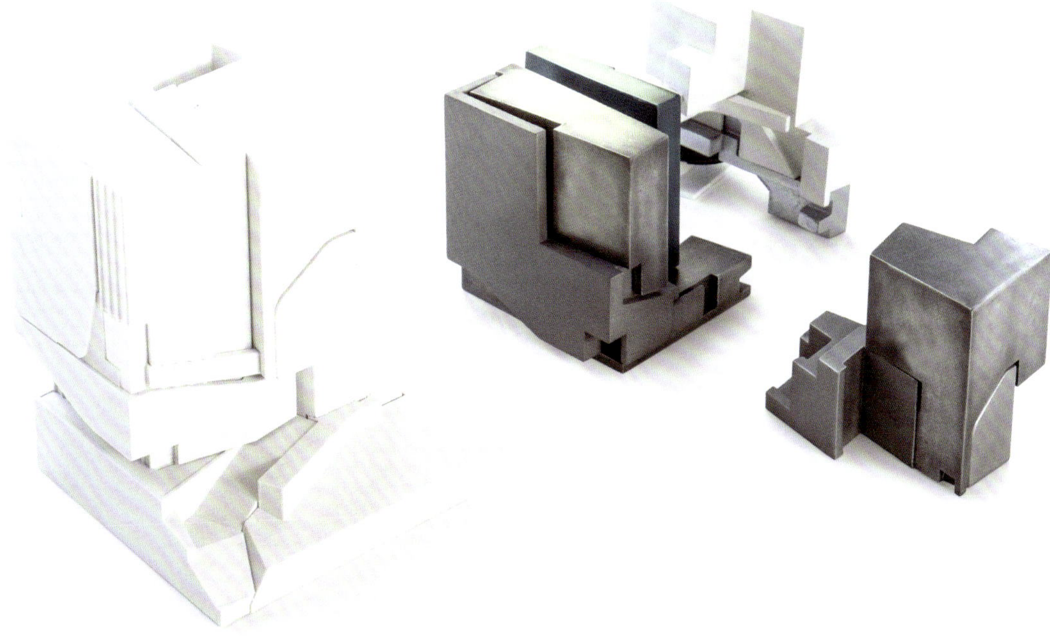

There are multiple buildings that avoid this problem by simply turning the section into an elevation, often by exposing the slab on edge with glass infill between. Alternatively, one can divorce the interior from the exterior and clad the building in other terms.

Third, most buildings that exhibit extraordinary interior spaces through their section can nonetheless be revealed through a single cut. Despite comprising some of the most iconic building sections from the past hundred years, the majority of the buildings in our book *Manual of Section* repeat, if not extrude, a single sectional strategy.[15] The predominance of a single sectional strategy over so many iconic examples indicates the difficulties of building fully three-dimensional spaces.

Oyler Wu Collaborative's work manages to elude all three of these constraints. Indeed, their project of *Puzzling Assemblies* prioritizes the intricate volume over the flat slab; celebrates the complexity of the interior in dialogue with the articulation of the exterior; and is the result of multiple vertical cuts, each of which reveals a richness of formal and spatial exploration. This obsession presents itself in projects like the Ivanhill Residence, where the volumetric intricacy of the spaces defines both the exterior appearance and the internal organization. Unlike most residential projects, none of the houses are defined by their floors; they are immersed in a complex nesting of forms interlocking throughout the building's mass, such that no single section can reveal the richness of this interaction. In this project, and throughout Oyler Wu's work, the section is not just a vertical cut, reinventing its logic and in the process disposing its constraints.

15 Lewis, David; Lewis, Paul; Tsurumaki, Marc. *Manual of Section*. New York City, New York: Princeton Architectural Press, 2016.

REORIENTING THE CITY

by MARCELYN GOW

Puzzling implies a process of reorientation. It involves the discovery of precise alignments of incongruous parts that will allow them to interlock, thereby creating shared seams. These reorientations may operate on a formal level, they may suggest alternative ways of moving through space and establishing connectivity, or they may produce adjacencies between different spatial qualities. Puzzling confounds a straightforward reading of something in favor of eliciting multiple ways of understanding a whole. Working through a puzzle involves persistence and a process of discovery. The formal differentiation between pieces of a puzzle may be accompanied by continuities that are established through a careful deployment of pattern, coloration, material shifts, or textures, depending upon the scale at which the puzzle operates. On a small scale these continuities may be established through an interlocking of components, whereas on a larger scale connections may be constituted by passages, streets, city blocks, and other urban forms.

An artifact that embodies the logics of a puzzle at the scale of the city is the document produced by Guy Debord and Asger Jorn in 1957 entitled *The Naked City: Illustration of the Hypothesis of Psychogeographical Turntables*. This alternative map of Paris presents its user with what could be construed as an urban-scale puzzle, drawing attention to distinct, localized qualities within the fabric of the city rather than presenting a coherent whole. The puzzle pieces, which were characterized by Debord as "unities of ambiance," are fragments that have been excised from a map of Paris and arranged on a white ground. The collaged fragments reveal areas of the city where orientations shift, and multiple organizational logics coalesce. Red, tapering, and curving arrows emanate from each segment of the urban fabric presented. These arrows refer to the action of "plaques tornantes" or turntables for reorienting movement.[16]

From afar, the archipelago of map fragments presented in *The Naked City* resembles pieces of a jigsaw puzzle that have been strewn across a blank sheet of paper. The diverse shapes of the pieces resist aligning to form a unified whole. Gaps between each of the pieces invite speculation as to how one might move from one area of the map to the next. The swerving arrows act as vectors of deviation from the axiality of the boulevards. The directives offered by the map suggest ways in which we might move counter to the established grain of the city to perform alternative circulation patterns. The document invites its user to imagine and enact multiple versions of the city as known. The alternative orientations, implied ways of moving, and attention to local context that are inherent to *The Naked City* as a tool for reimagining the city are advanced and extended in the urban-scale projects of Oyler Wu Collaborative.

16   Debord, Guy; Jorn, Asger. *THE NAKED CITY–Illustration de l'hypothèse des plaques tournantes en psychogeographique* (1957). La société du spectacle. Paris, France: Buchet/Chastel, 1967.

In Oyler Wu Collaborative's work we discover entanglements between urban-scale forms that embrace the logic of a multidimensional puzzle. Space for public access is distributed vertically throughout interlocking volumetric assemblies, enabling the contours of districts within an urban-scale proposal to overlap and interact with one another. This creates an admixture of shared spaces within buildings, but also between them.

Oyler Wu Collaborative provocatively reimagines how urban public space can be designed so that it is activated in multiple dimensions and has the capacity to reorient possibilities for collective gathering and the production of civic space. The part-to-part reciprocities that exist in the urban-scale massing of Oyler Wu Collaborative's work also characterize the engagement between individual buildings and the grounds with which they are in conversation. In the Cold War Veterans Memorial, for example, the notion of ground becomes manifold. Grounds operate as puzzled ramps and circulation paths that interlock precisely with the massing of the building to actively shape the civic experience. Puzzled grounds are designed to encourage multiple forms of movement, intertwining through building masses and producing varying degrees of porosity within them. This logic enables a multiplicity of both indented and elevated grounds with specific qualities and features to appear throughout the building form. The puzzling assembly logic of grounds in the Cold War Veterans Memorial promotes the possibility for infrastructural, landscape, and architectural form to interlock and entangle in ways that produce multivalent identities for each.

Within an assembled puzzle, part-to-whole relationships are, in most instances, designed to resolve into a cohesive entity. A tight-fit logic often exists between individual pieces. The urban constructs of Oyler Wu Collaborative deploy both close-fit and loose-fit strategies to allow for the presence of voids that suggest complementary relationships with adjacent parts. The gaps that exist between the puzzle pieces in Debord and Jorn's map are perplexing in a productive way as they liberate the geo-graphy, the writing of the city, to enable multiple urban narratives. Likewise, the loose-fit strategies in Oyler Wu Collaborative's work are deliberately and precisely deployed to produce a more vibrant urban whole. Just as Debord and Jorn's map celebrated the heterogeneity of the city and the spontaneous encounter between diverse entities in the urban fabric, so too does the work of Oyler Wu Collaborative invite us to discover the activating and engaging qualities of puzzled urban constructs.

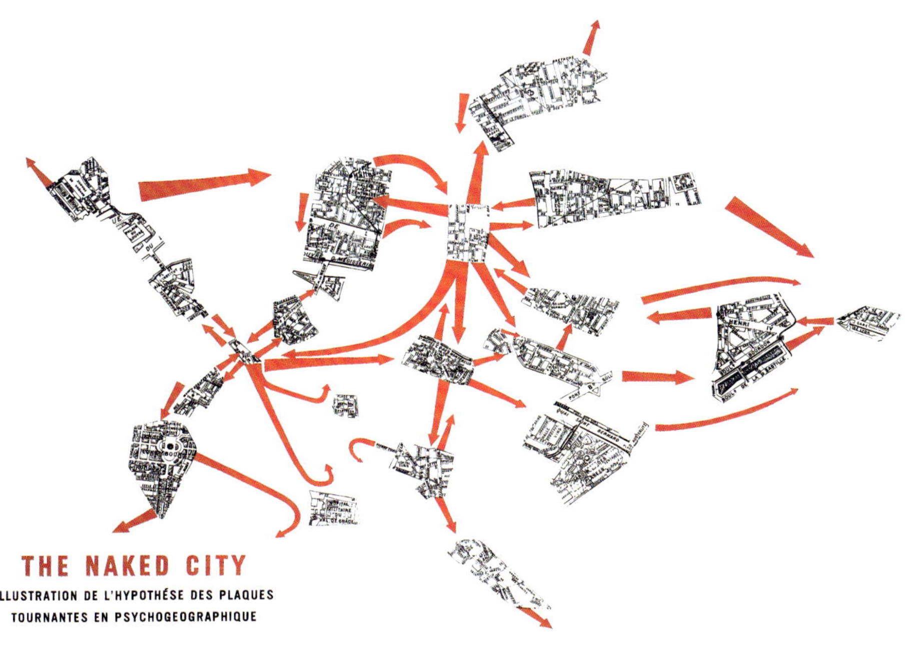

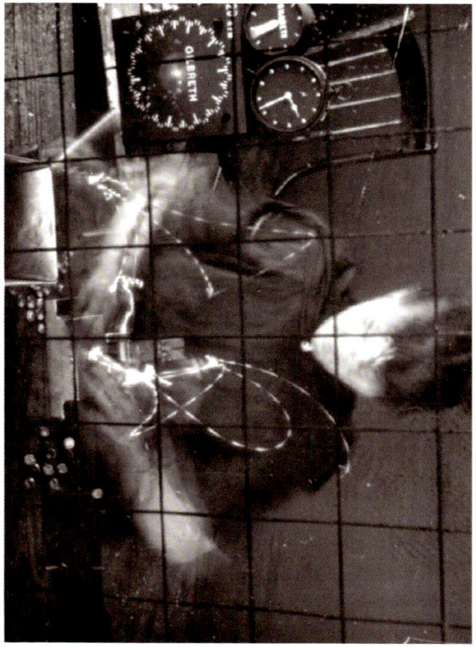

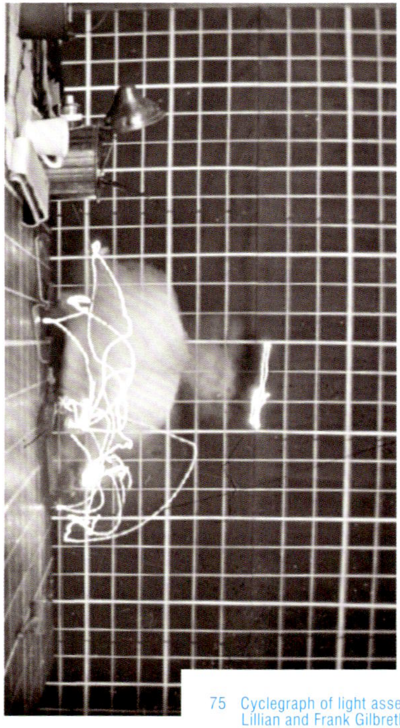

75 Cyclegraph of light assembly work. Motion Efficiency Study.
Lillian and Frank Gilbreth. c. 1914.

76 Cyclegraph of assembly in front of gridded background.
Motion Efficiency Study. Lillian and Frank Gilbreth. c. 1914.

A BUILDING.
BUILDING A...

by ANNA NEIMARK

The term "building" is not straightforward. A building with the article in front of it, is a noun. It is a fact. Something finite. A building is the first thing that comes to mind when thinking about the work of the Oyler Wu Collaborative. Buildings are the things that they work on. Period.

By contrast, building followed by the article a, becomes something different, something more enigmatic. It is not quite a noun but a gerund, which is ostensibly a verb turned noun, a verb that is caught in the middle of action. A gerund is not an object, it is insufficient by itself and cannot be followed by a period. Building a dot dot dot is no longer a fact, but a task about to be realized; its practice is wrapped up in all sorts of projections, instructions, and specifications. It is rather open-ended or puzzling, to use an Oyler Wu term.

Building-as-fact sublimates the process of building. And building-as-gerund sublimates the objecthood of building. We must hold both definitions in focus to appreciate the projects presented in this book. After all, the double meaning of building in architecture—as a spatial object and as a temporal process—is at the core of Oyler Wu's academic practice. Three-dimensional puzzles play an instrumental role in representing both space and time. They are small-scale pedagogical devices that represent the bigger problems encountered on a site of construction, the site of building a building. The puzzling mechanism demands careful attention and fine motor skills. In studio, Oyler Wu's students are often seen picking locks and solving Hanayama puzzles, appearing to be planning a heist. In fact, they train on sliding parts, swiveling wheels, hinging joints, and rotating axes, to develop their technical intuition in design. This training brings studio culture to its essence—an abstract space where visual, tactile, and conceptual ideas coalesce into experiential learning.

77 Design Study by Wan-Yu Chen & Yiyu Zhou. Puzzling Assemblies Studio at SCI-Arc taught by Jenny Wu, 2021.

78 Los Angeles Natural History Museum at Taylor Yard Proposal, by Faris Ahmed and Jordan Scheuermann. Puzzling Assemblies Studio at SCI-Arc taught by Dwayne Oyler, 2021.

Zeynep Çelik Alexander described this approach, popularized by the first-year preliminary course (Vorkurs) at the Bauhaus, as kinaesthetic knowing.[17] The compounded term, composed of two roots, kinetic and aesthetic, binds formal training to bodily experience. Learning through movement and familiarization brings the students into a close relationship with the objects at hand; they become intimately linked with the mechanisms' controls. Undoubtedly, their hands change shape over the course of the semester, as they build their finger muscles and tactile intelligence.

Learning through tuning the body may remind us of another pair, Lillian and Frank B. Gilbreth, a psychologist and industrial engineer who developed powerful techniques for applying scientific management to industry. In a series of motion studies, they documented workers performing time-based tasks, such as welding, typing, or stitching. With a long camera exposure, the Gilbreths captured the continuous motion of laborers' bodies following a bright point that moved during their fulfillment of a task. The resulting curve, against a gridded background, disclosed the smoothness and efficiency of operation in measurable terms. What is pertinent to Oyler Wu is not the goal of efficiency but a similar practice of visualization, a depiction that can be reflexive and instructional through its representation. Learning to depict motion through time in spatial terms holds a similar function for any student seeking spatial knowledge.

Drawing puzzles produces representational problems: interlocking mechanisms move in and out of pictorial view. Chunks must be exploded along orthographic axes to reveal the techniques of assembly, held together by dashed vectors, pointed arrows, and annotated texts. These signs instruct us on how to put the puzzle together with our eyes and in our minds. The exploded isometric drawing is not just a fact. It is an instrument that can be tuned: because it has a hinge, it can be folded; because it has an axis, it can be spun. It is possible to intervene in this drawing and to change the course of construction, the order of assembly, the hierarchy of joined parts, the smoothness and efficiency of operations. Such documents convey rules of assembly as well as pedagogical intent. They are instructions that instruct—studio devices that train a generation of students on the representational power of building a building.

17   Alexander, Zeynep Çelik. *Kinaesthetic Knowing: Aesthetics, Epistemology, Modern Design*. Chicago, Illinois: The University of Chicago Press, 2017.

Making and physical experimentation are central to the way we practice architecture. And while we've been actively involved in the hands-on fabrication of much of our full-scale work, we've also dedicated significant swaths of time to working on things with a profound, yet less direct relationship to the final form. These tend to be object-like and abstract in nature. They are pseudo-architectural in their formal and spatial character, and free of scalar signifiers. In most cases they aren't connected directly to a single project, rather they intended to extract principles that find broad application across multiple projects.

They are neither pure artistic inspiration, nor are they architectural models in the conventional sense of the word. The interest in making these things isn't just about craft, material, or even tectonic resolution, although those are certainly valuable byproducts of the investigations. Our objective is to leverage forms of making in order to expand our design thinking, to interrogate ideas, and to open up creative territories that simply wouldn't be imagined otherwise. These investigations are an essential bridge between the conceptual synthesis of ideas and their architectural outcome—which is not only critical to the development of the project, but to the strengthening of the ideas.

For us, they are a time to think about relationships large and small, and to jump fluidly between different scalar ideas like site relationships, programmatic elements, and building components. The objects and experiments are a test bed for interrogating possibilities that aren't yet fully restrained by the preconceptions of an architectural outcome, yet they are forced to reckon with a set of formal, organizational, and spatial qualities that will ultimately serve as a vehicle for the architecture's key qualities.

Throughout this section we explore several different types of investigations that come at the idea of puzzling from different vantage points. The studies include an extensive series of primitive assembly studies from basic hinges to mechanical latches. We work through various formal possibilities, like spheres, cubes, and rectangles. The introduction of wire frames then presents those ideas in a very different light—volumetrically and perceptually. The objects are studied in both isolation and in relationship to one another. And with each of the studies, there is an intense emphasis on highlighting the essential relationships between parts that are key to their upcoming architectural translation. With this extensive, yet by no means exhaustive, set of object studies, we hope to shine a light on the remarkable territory found in the assembly of parts, as well as the richness of this kind of design thinking.

INVESTIGATIONS

SECTION 2

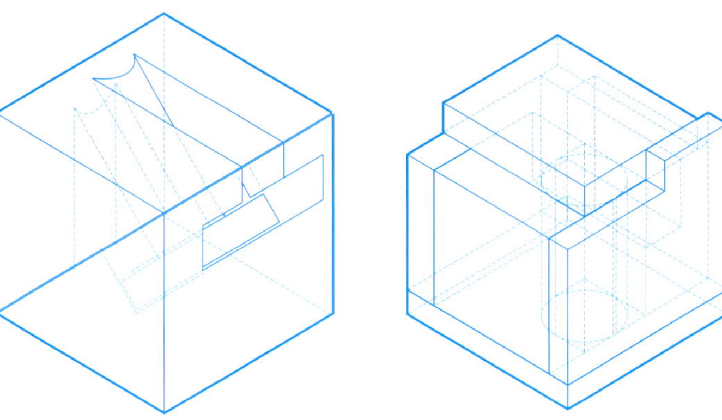

PRIMITIVES

We began by operating on a series of primitive cubes as a way to explore the basic interactions between parts. Each study focuses on a single type of connection, exploring systems like hinges, pivots, slides and swivels, fastened and fitted joinery, and locks. Using geometries specific to the required assembly method of each cube, parts are shaped as direct product of simple maneuvers, distilling their features into shapes that are emblematic of how they operate. The geometric input is pure and straightforward, introducing no foreign geometries into the system.

The primitive shape introduces a degree of abstraction, selectively concealing and revealing the key features of the connection method. Additionally, the primitive operates as a tool for revealing a set of movements in space, leaving only the gaps and seams necessary for the operation of the puzzle.

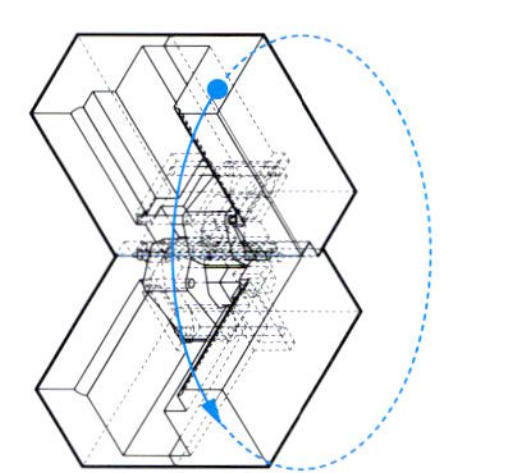

BUTT HINGE (MORTISE HINGE):
Butt hinges utilize interfacing plates joined by a pin or rod to provide rotational movement around an axis.

BARREL HINGE (PIVOT HINGE):
Barrel hinges consist of two guiding channels with a cylindrical barrel to allow rotational movement around an axis.

CONTINUOUS HINGE (PIANO HINGE):
Continuous hinges run the entire length of interfacing components for smooth rotational movement around an axis.

CENTER PIVOT HINGE:
Center pivot hinges use a single pivot point located at the center of interfacing objects, allowing the attached object to pivot around its axis.

OFFSET PIVOT HINGE:
Offset pivot hinges use a single pivot point located off-center of interfacing objects, allowing the attached object to pivot around its axis, while partially or fully overlapping each other.

KNIFE PIVOT HINGE (PIVOT SETS):
Knife pivot hinges use a single pivot point located at the ends of interfacing objects, allowing the attached object to pivot around its axis, to fully overlap each other.

BEARING PIVOT:
Bearing pivots use ball bearings or roller bearings housed in a pivot mechanism to allow for low-friction rotational movement.

FRICTION PIVOT:
Friction pivots use friction or resistance to control the rotational movement of two components.

DETENT PIVOT:
Detent pivots incorporate a detent mechanism, a spring-loaded roller at the end of a cylindrical rod, to hold two objects into place.

Hinges and Pivots allow for rotational movement around a fixed point or axis.

HINGES & PIVOTS

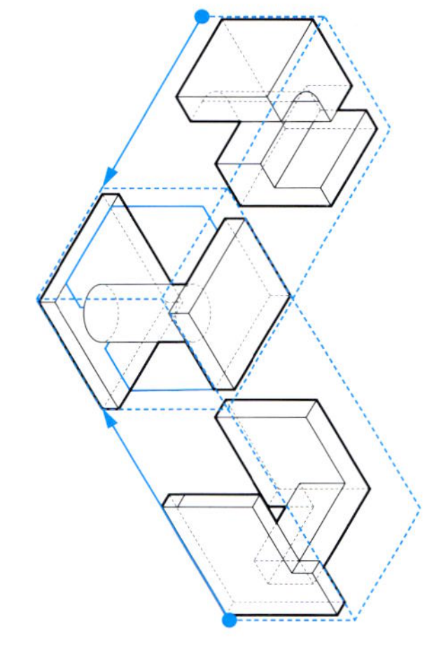

PLATE SWIVEL:
Plate swivels consist of two plates connected by a central pin allowing one plate to rotate relative to the other to provide 360-degree rotation.

BALL BEARING SWIVEL:
Ball bearings consist of two circular plates connected with interlocking ball bearings, allowing one plate to rotate on top of the other allowing low-friction rotation.

BALL JOINT SWIVEL:
Ball joint swivels use a ball joint mechanism to allow rotational movement in multiple axes.

SOCKET AND PLUG SWIVEL:
Socket and plug swivels consist of a socket and plug to allow for rotational movement.

UNIVERSAL JOINT (U-JOINT):
Universal joints are couplings that allow for rotational movement between two shafts at an angle to one another.

SLIDE CHANNELS:
Sliding channels create a linear path of movement along a track or groove, allowing compatible fitted parts to extend, retract, or slide.

TAPERED CHANNELS:
Tapered channels create a linear path of movement along a track or groove, but limit their compatible parts to extend, retract, or slide.

Swivels allow for uni-directional rotational movement around a fixed point or axis, and slide mechanisms allow bilateral movement along a linear direction.

SWIVELS & SLIDES

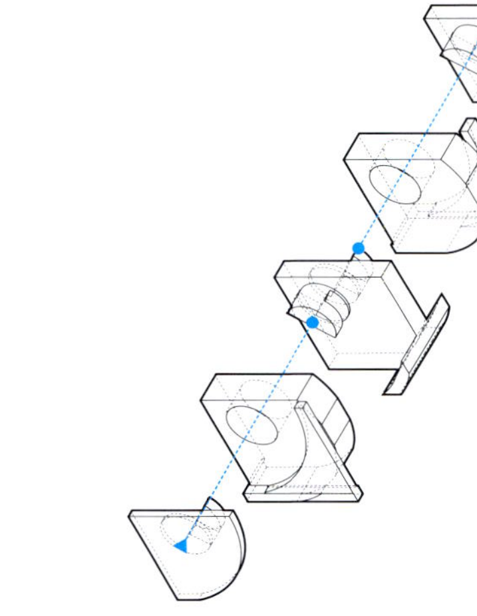

THREADED FASTENERS:
Threaded fasteners connect objects through their tightly fitted juxtaposition to join together.

PINS:
Pins are components placed in unfixed parts that fill the gaps or voids between their features to create a joint.

MORTISE AND TENON:
Mortise and Tenon joints consist of a protruding 'tenon' that fits into a corresponding cavity or 'mortise' on another.

TONGUE AND GROOVE:
Techniques for tongue and groove joinery use shaped parts to interlock with each other, preventing lateral movement between the interconnected pieces without the need for additional fastening.

DOVETAIL:
Using interlocking wedge-shaped projections, or 'dovetails,' parts fit into corresponding slots on another piece.

CLAMPS:
Clamps hold materials together by exerting pressure to ensure a tight and secure bond between the joined components.

SNAP-FIT:
Snap-fit connections use interlocking features, or 'snaps,' that are pliant enough to fit together, joining two or more pieces of material without the need for additional fasteners.

RATCHET JOINT:
Ratchet joints feature incremental stops or notches to create resistance and stability at specific positions of transformed parts.

Techniques for joinery are methods used to connect two or more pieces of material together using mechanical or pressure joints.

PINS & JOINERY

CAM LOCKS:
Cam locks use a rotating object or 'cam' to fit into a slot or groove to exert pressure to secure it in place against another piece.

BAYONET MOUNTS:
Bayonet mounts use a combination of pins and grooves to secure two pieces together with a twisting motion.

ZIPPER:
Zippers consist of splines with interlocking teeth or coils that slide together to fasten two parts.

SLOT AND TAB:
Consisting of protruding 'tabs' of one part that fit into corresponding 'slots' on another, the interlocking of the two is pressure-fit to secure them together.

Locking and interlocking connects two or more pieces of material together using compatible or corresponding features to fix their movements into place.

LOCKS & INTERLOCKS

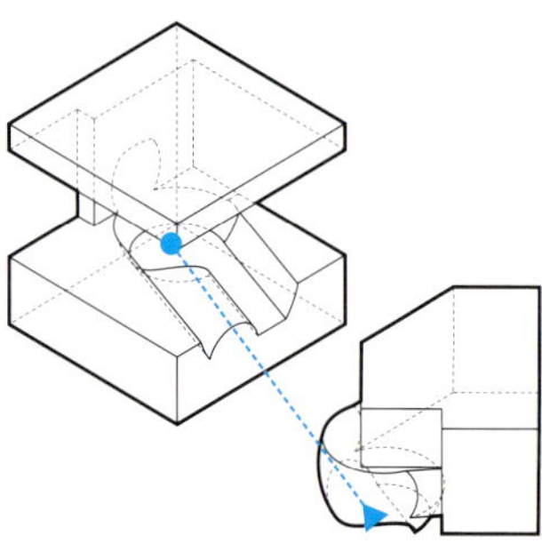
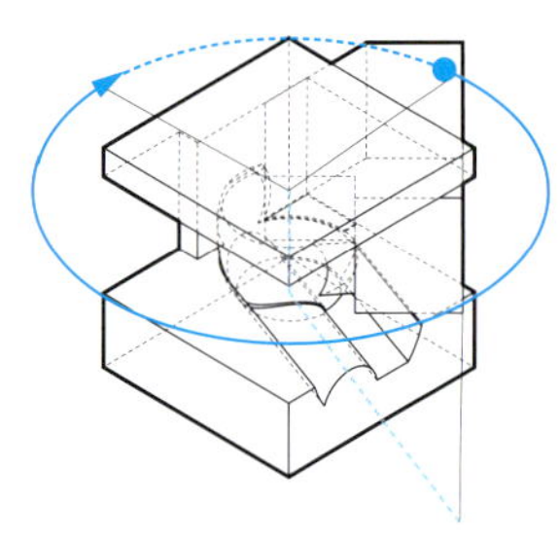
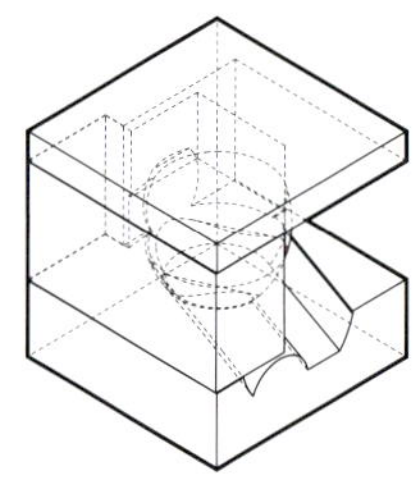

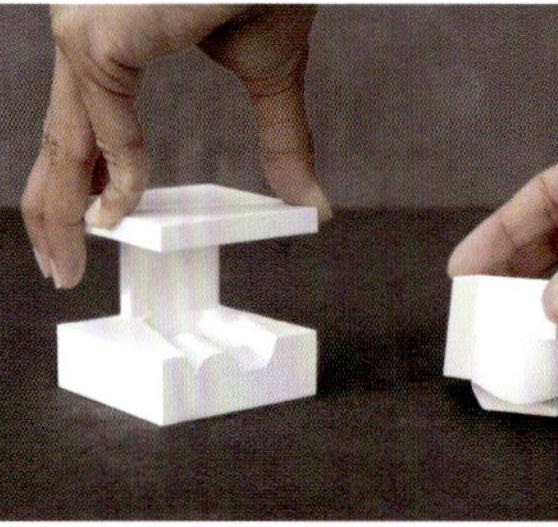

CB.02

CHISEL PIVOT

Slide pin into socket. Pivot parts until their outermost edges meet.

Slide skewed part into groove until faces
meet. Turn to align exterior faces.

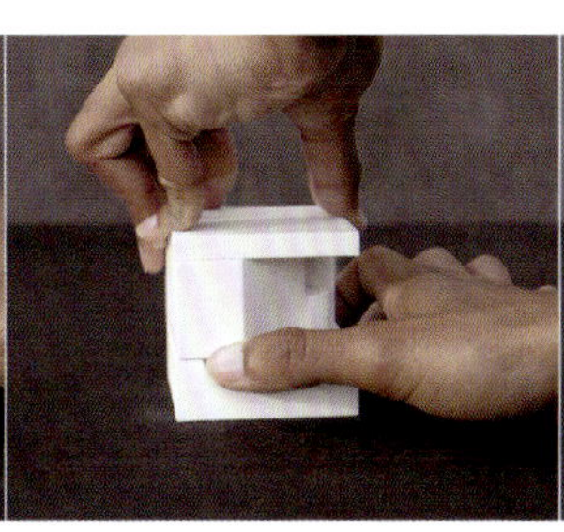
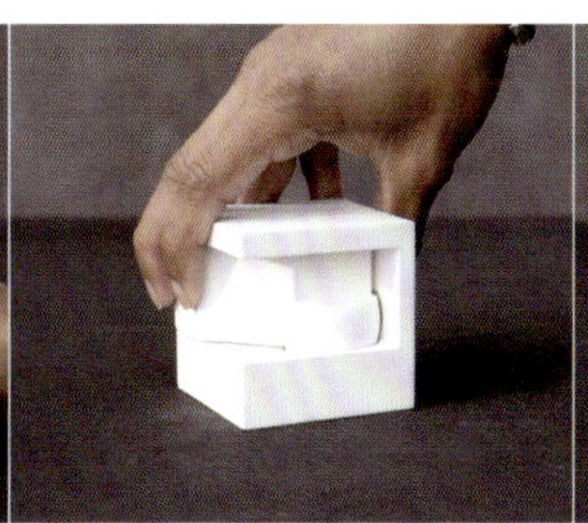

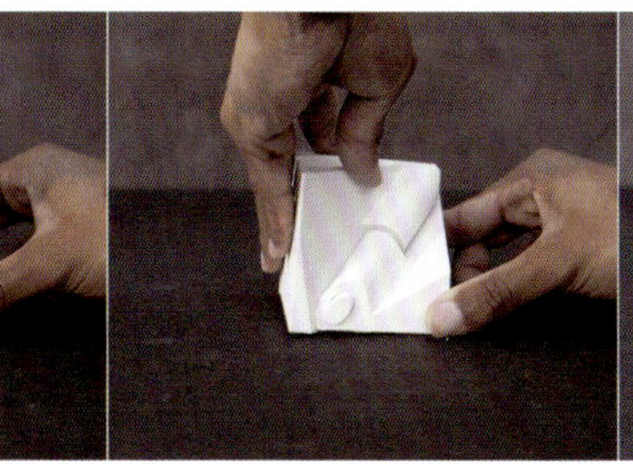

03

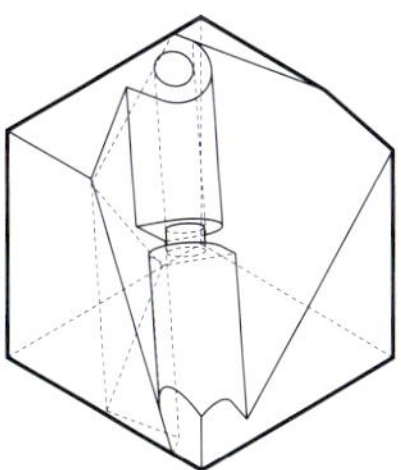

02

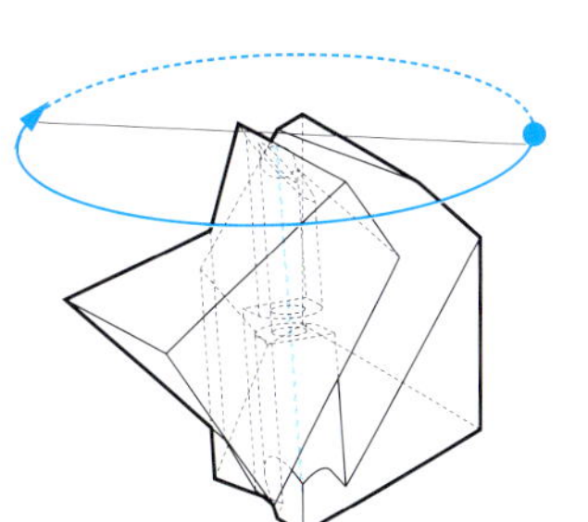

01

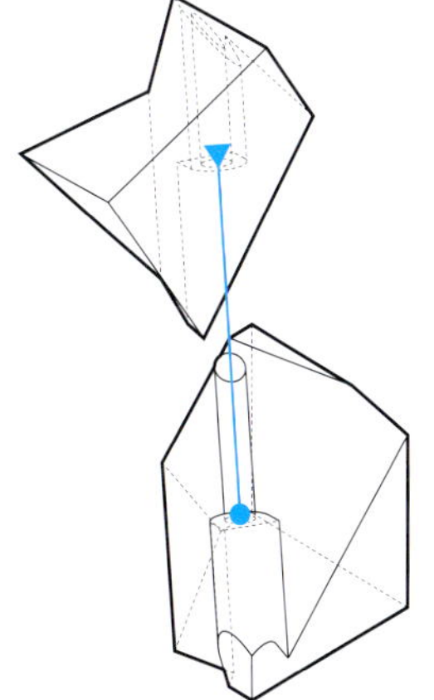

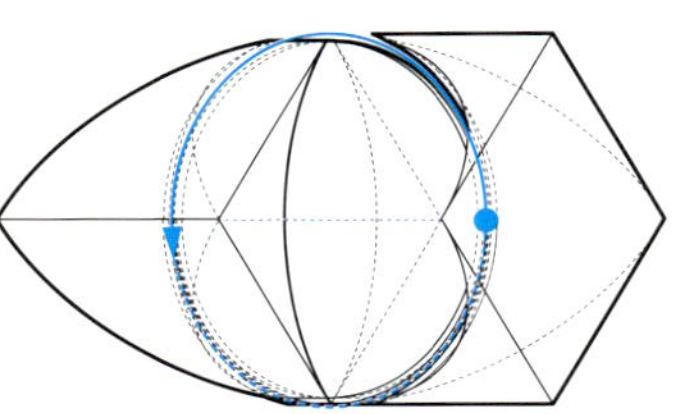
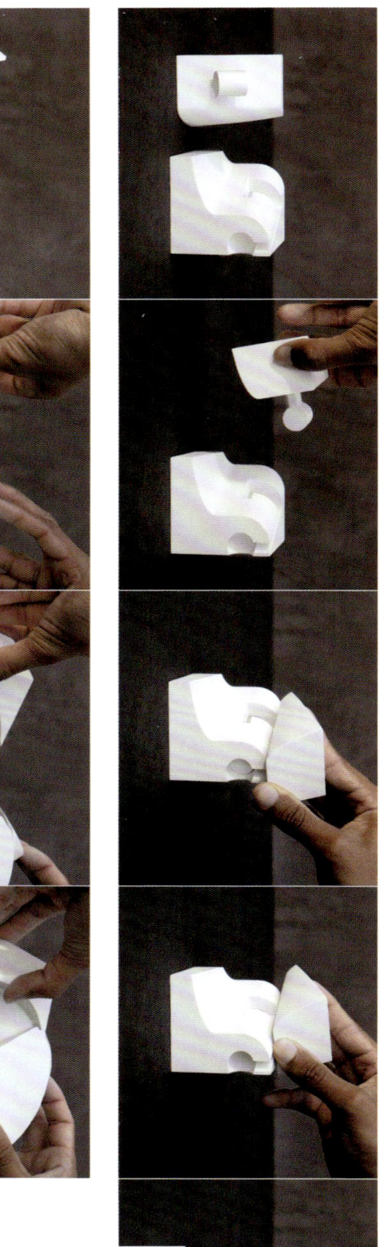

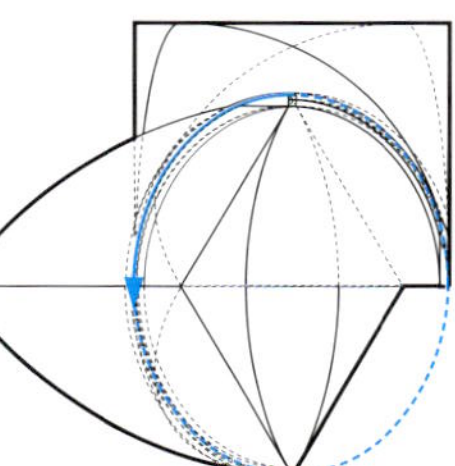
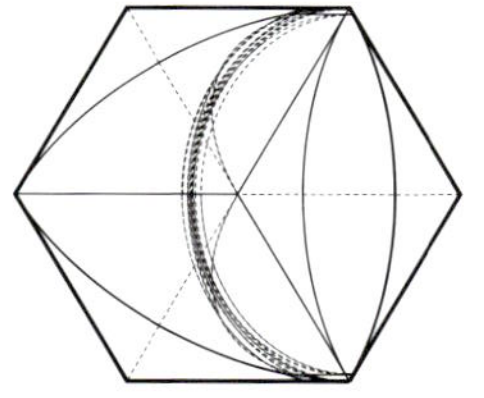

01

02

03

CB.03

SPIN-LOCK

Align tab with channel. Slide through so faces meet.
Rotate to create shifted cube. Shift to lock into place.

CB.04

SURFACE HINGE

Face parts obliquely at corners. Slip channel into grooved surface. Turn until interior surfaces are flush.

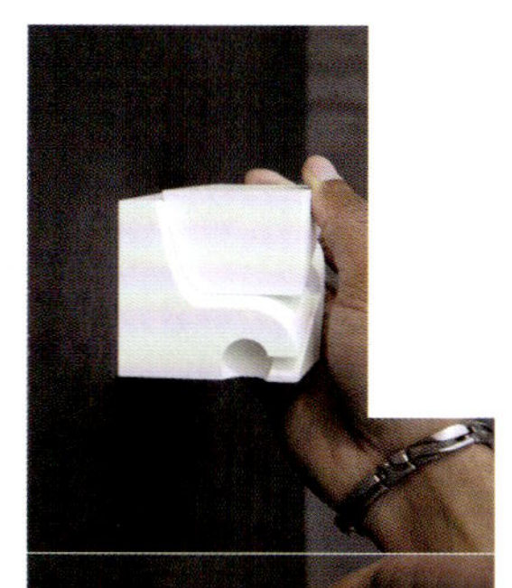

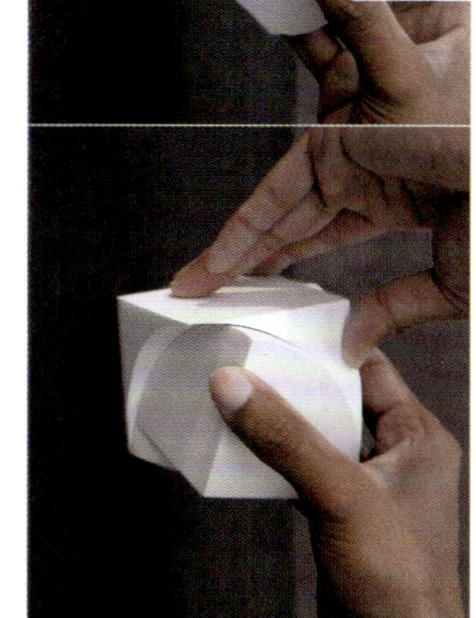

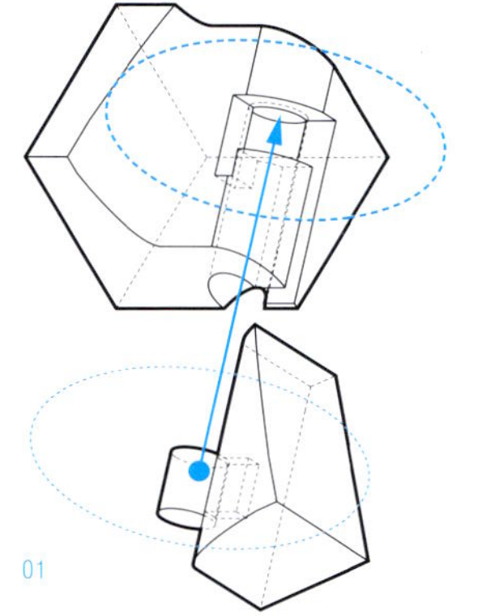

01

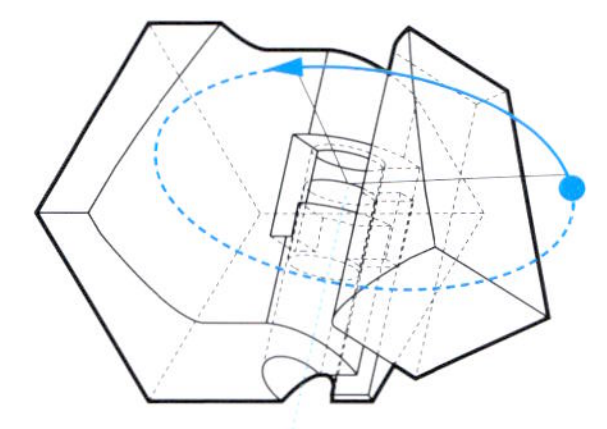

02

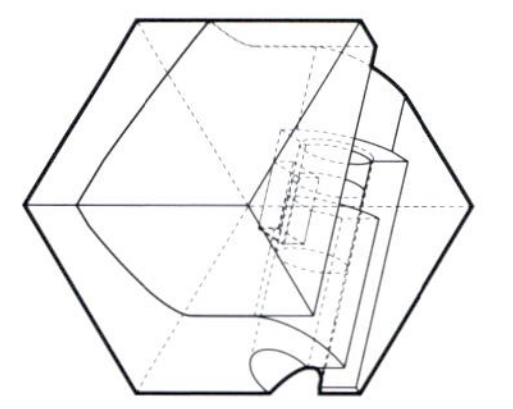

03

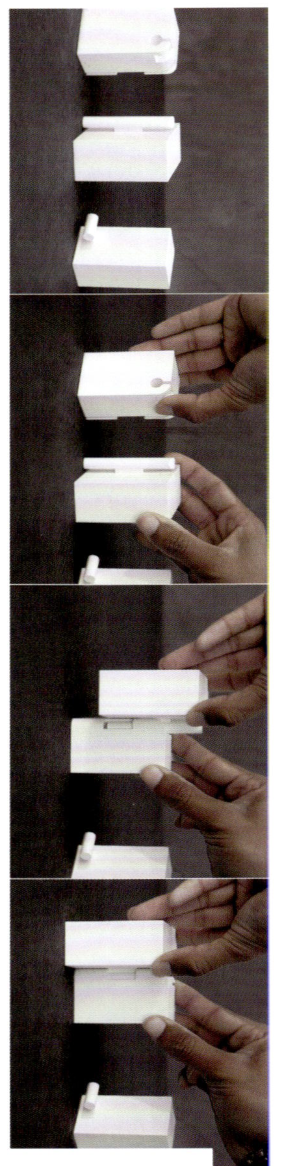

01

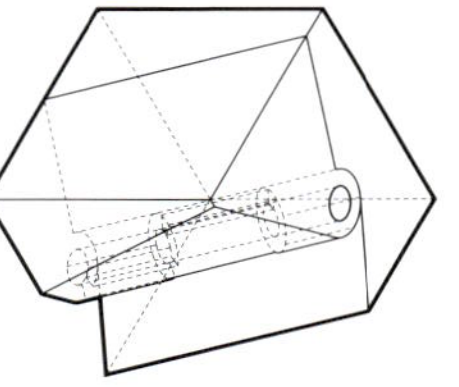

02

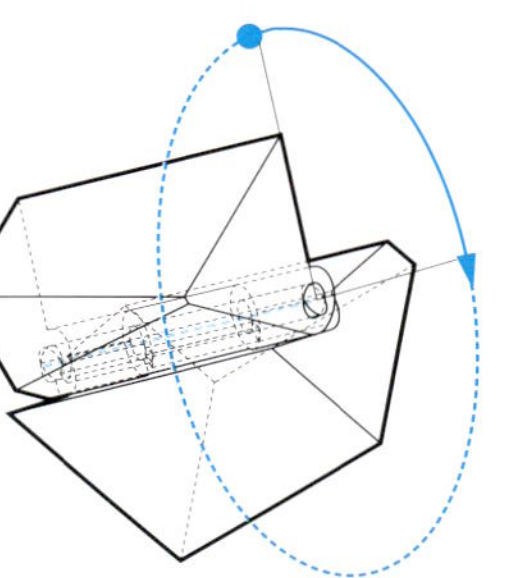

03

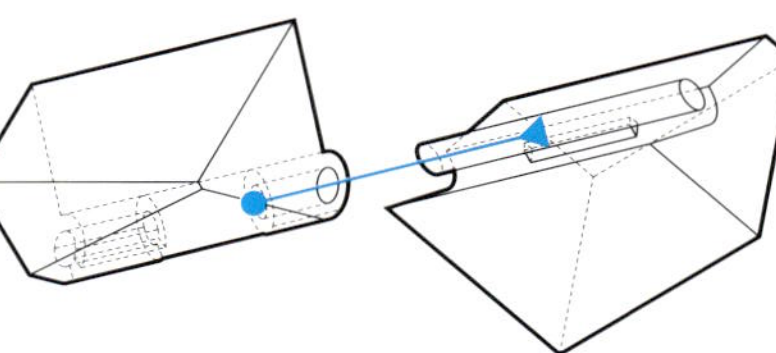

CB.05

SCRAPED HINGE

Slide socket over pin until exterior faces align. Rotate
until angled faces meet and outside face is flat.

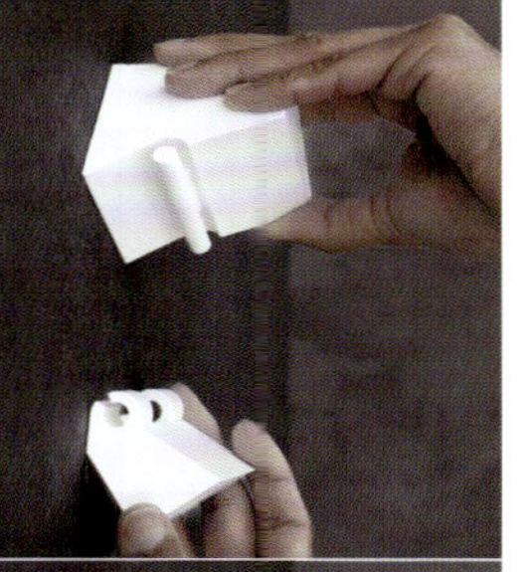
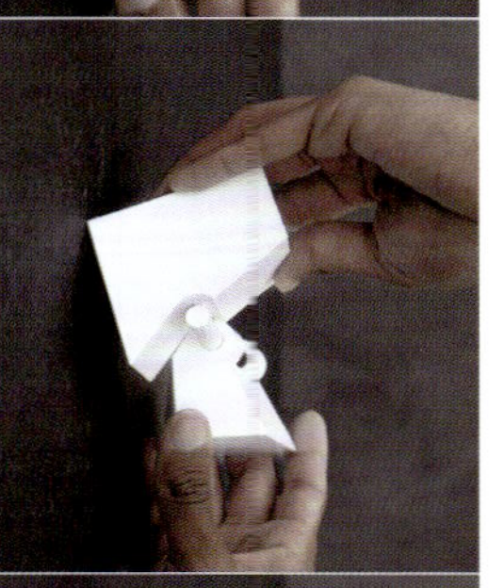

CB.06

ROTATING PIN

Slip tab into groove. Turn in x and y axis.
Slip tab into groove. Turn in y and z axis.

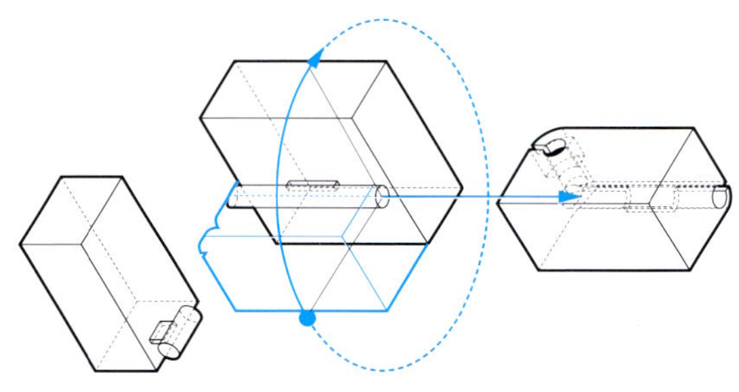

03

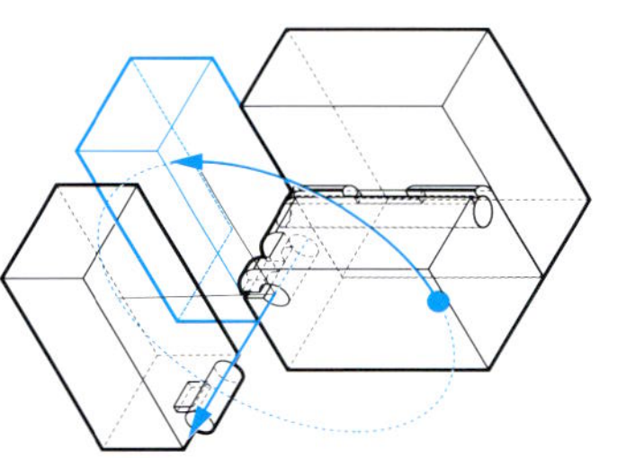

02

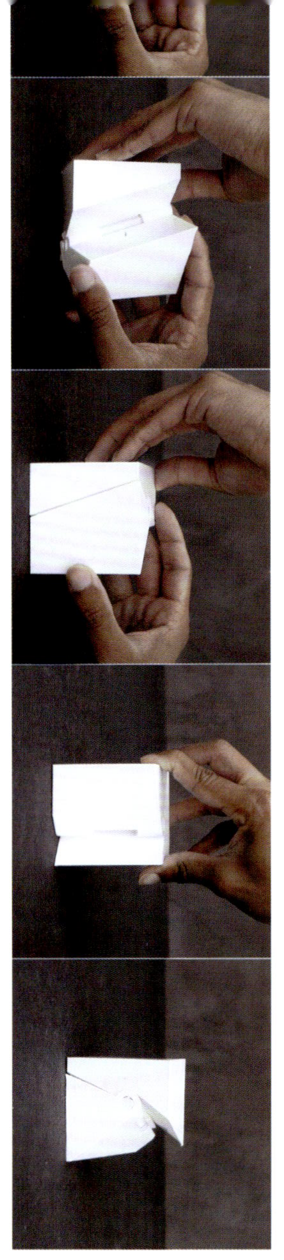

01

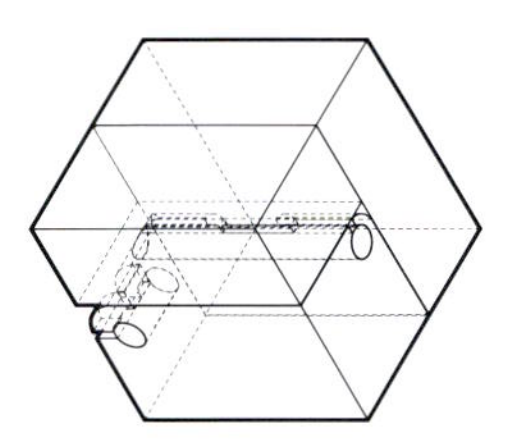

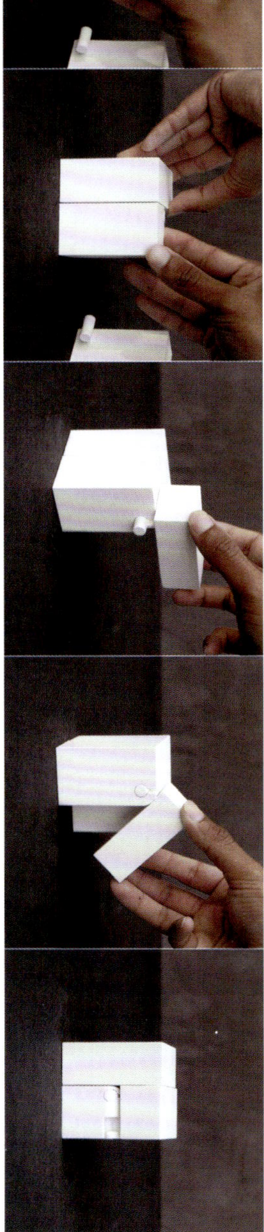

CB.07

TURNTAB

Align parts at 90 degrees along their angled faces. Slide parts together along that face to slot the tab into the channel. Turn parts to lock into place.

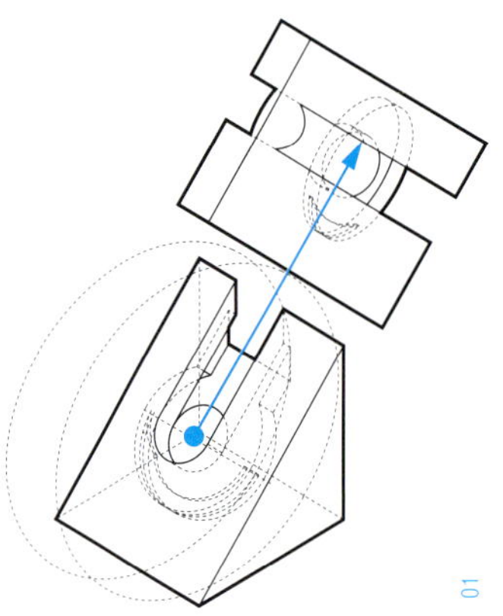

01

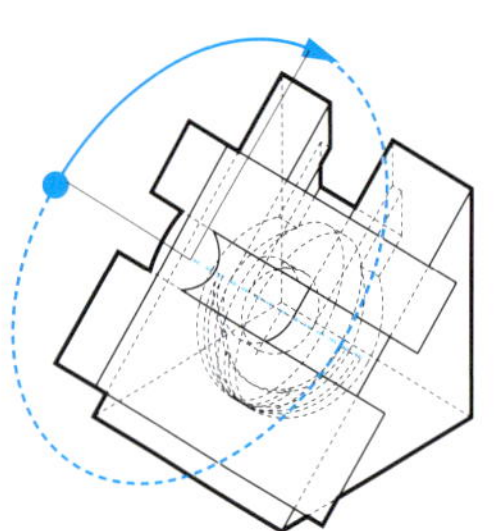

02

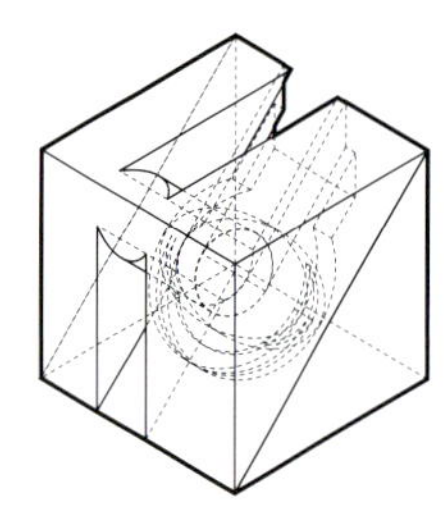

03

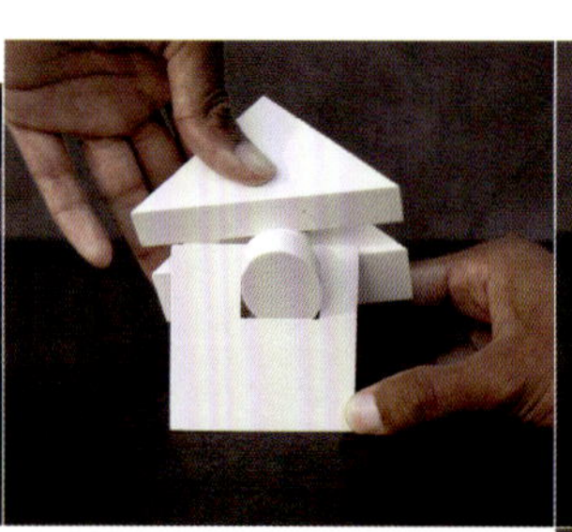

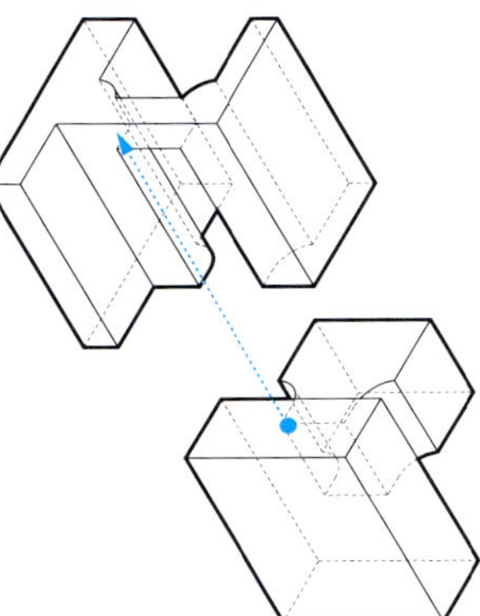

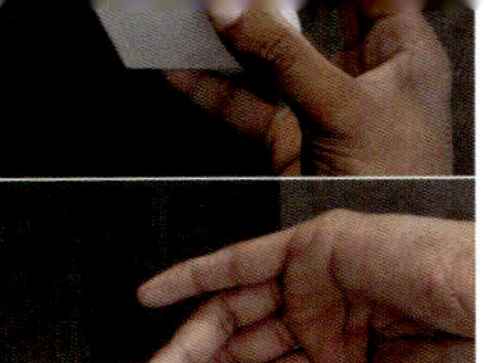

01

02

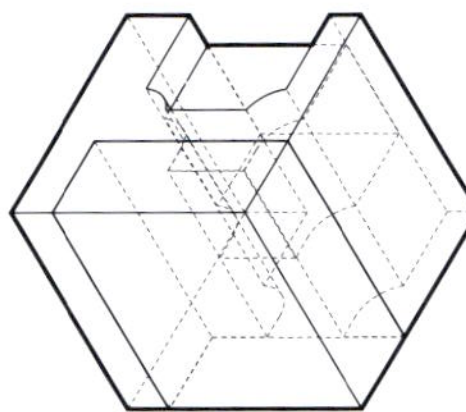

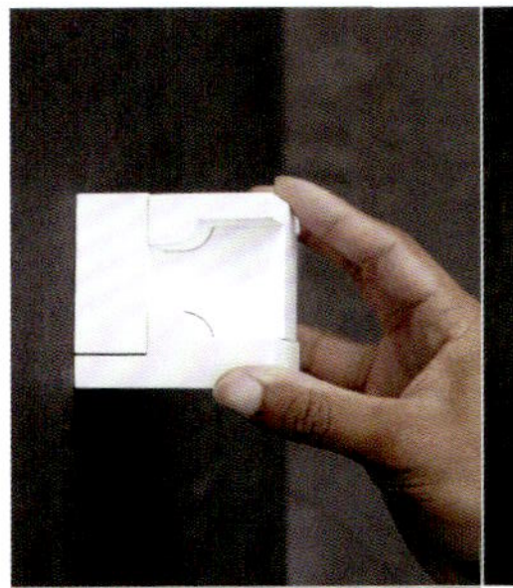

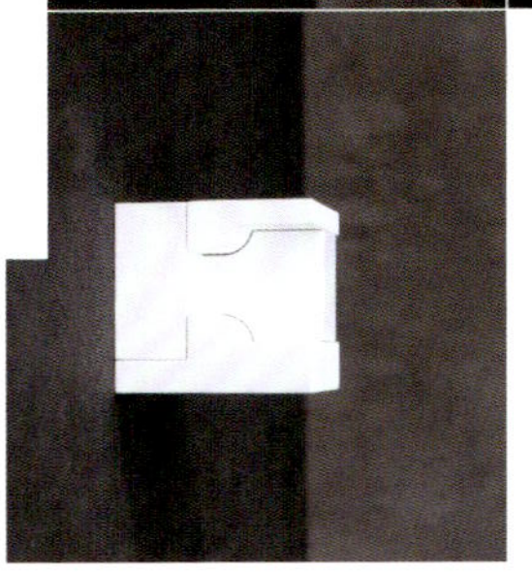

CB.08

SLIDE LOCK

Align tab to gap in opposite part. Slide through
grooved channel until exterior faces align.

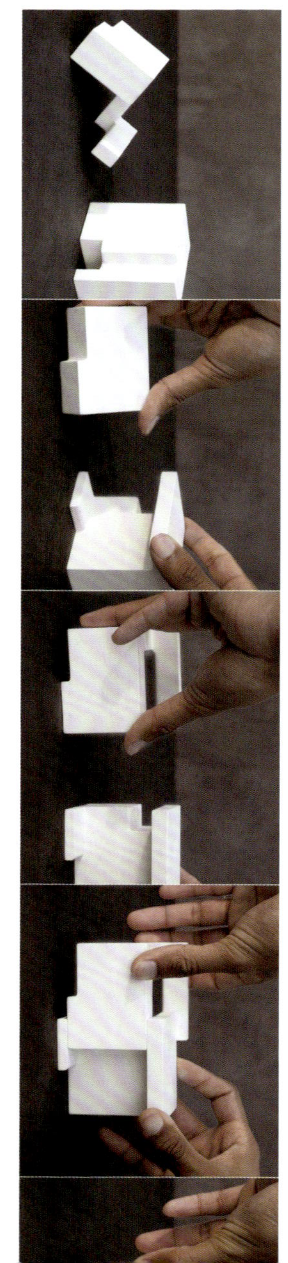

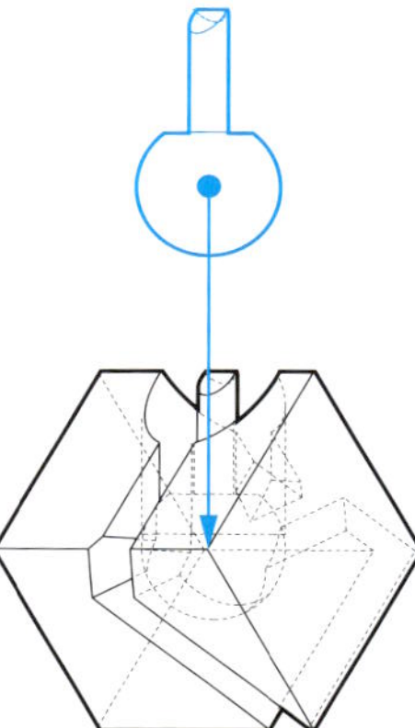

01

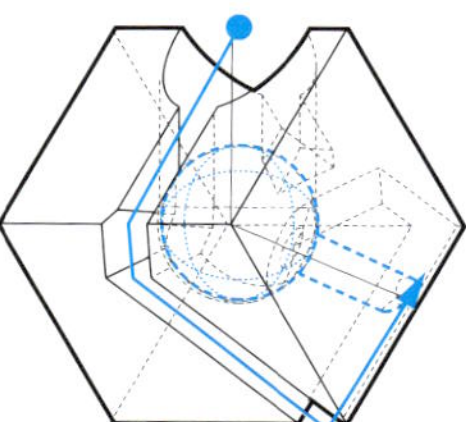

02

CB.09

BALL SWIVEL

Slot pin into opening. Swivel pin end along groove until pin edge meets end face of solid.

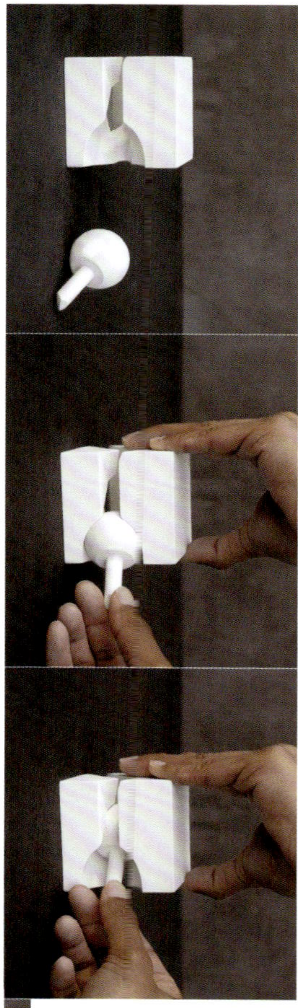

CB.10

Align void area with gap in solid part. Slide wrapping part into gap. Shift to click into place.

02

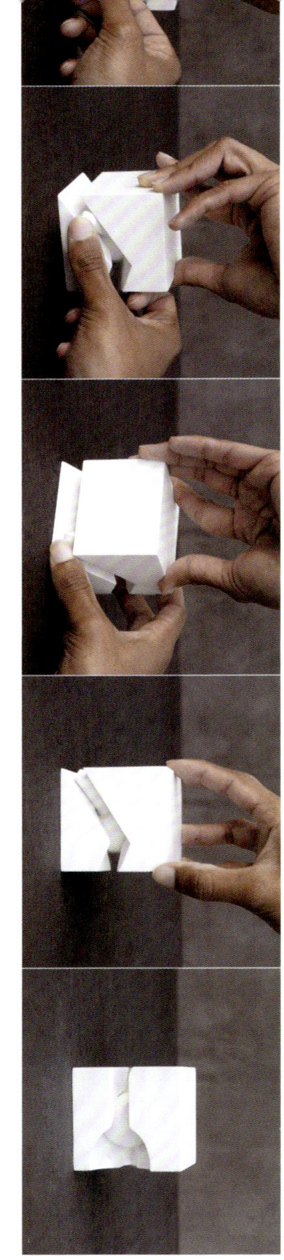

01

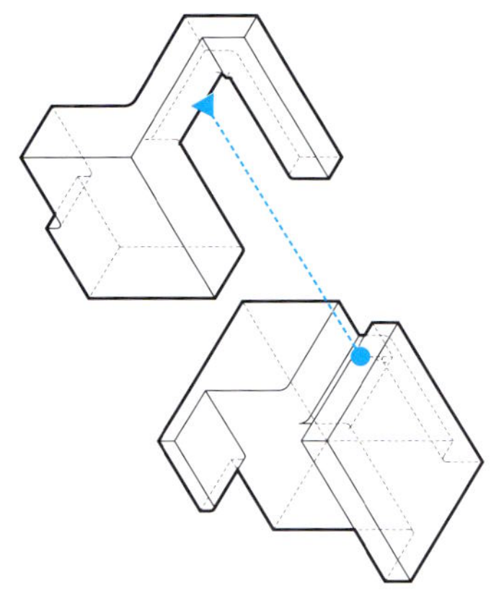

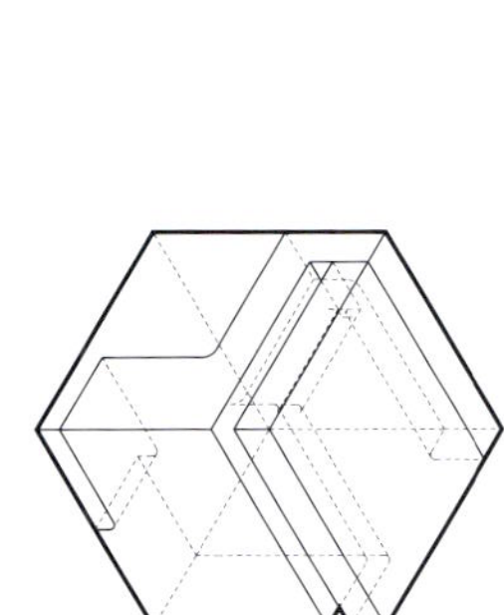

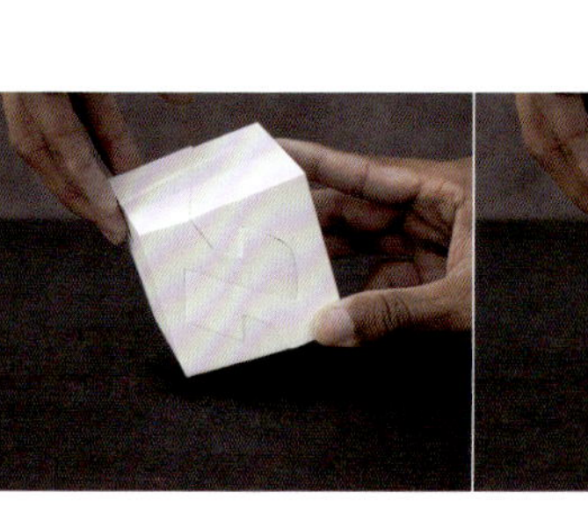

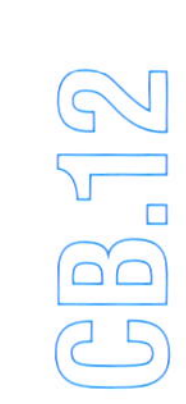

CB.12

SCREW PIVOT

Orient parts inversely so center spline is aligned.
Pivot one part until all internal laces meet.

CB.11

SHELL CAP

Align parts so diagonal edges face the same direction.
Sleeve parts until flush to interlock solid and void.

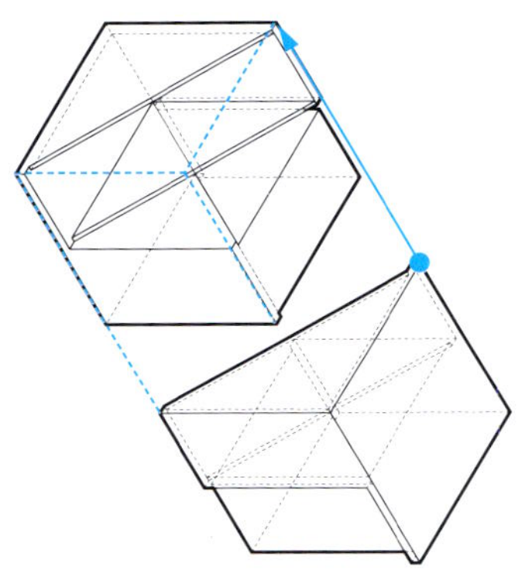

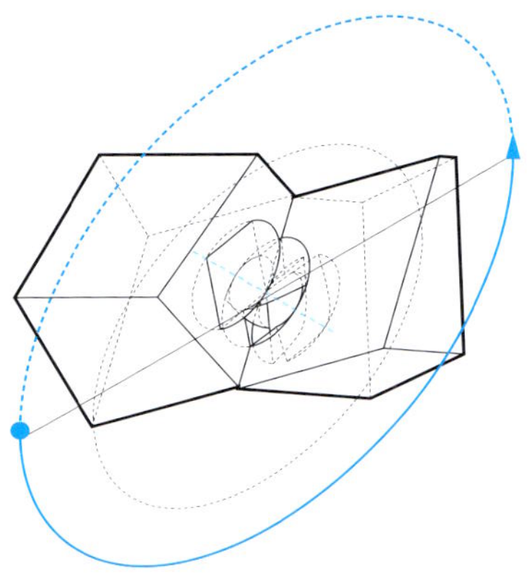

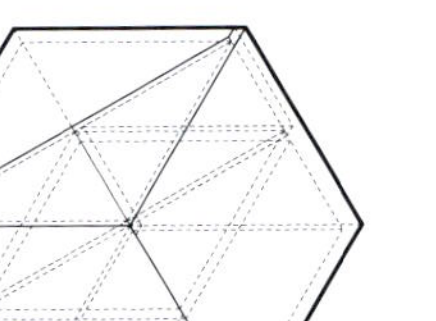

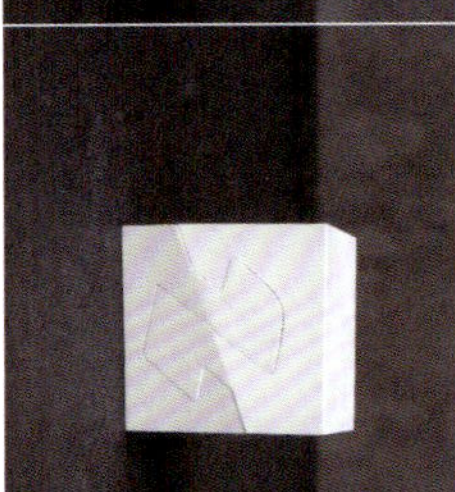
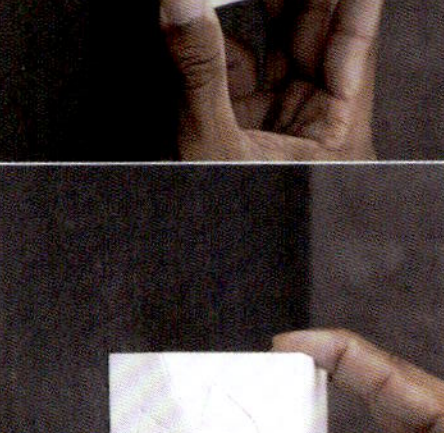

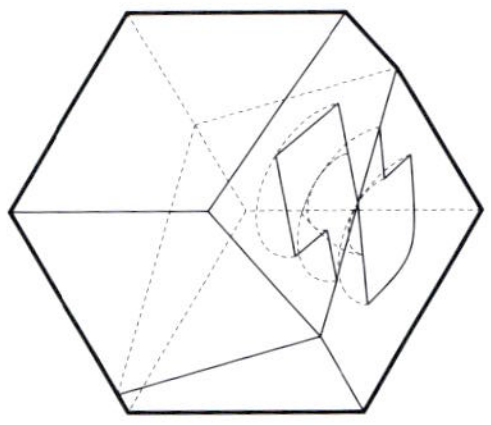

02

01

02

01

CB.14

SURFACE PIN

Overlap parts at channel. Slide grooved surface
through channel to lock into place.

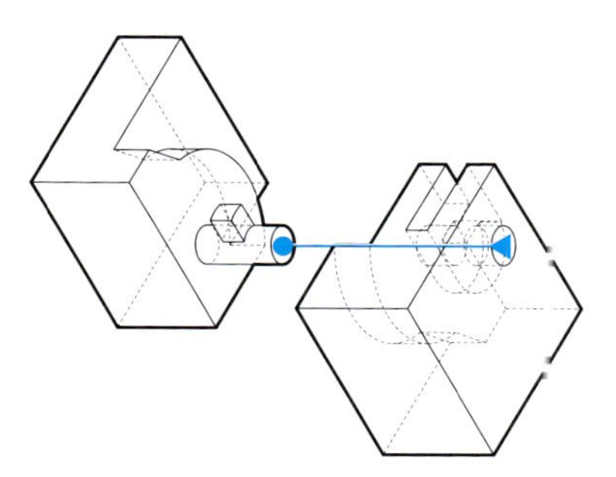

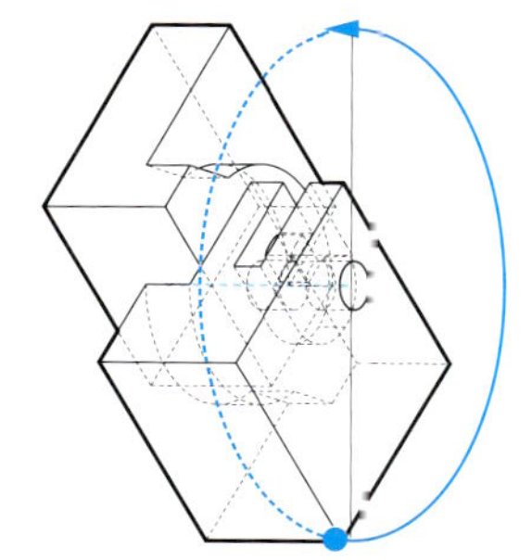

01

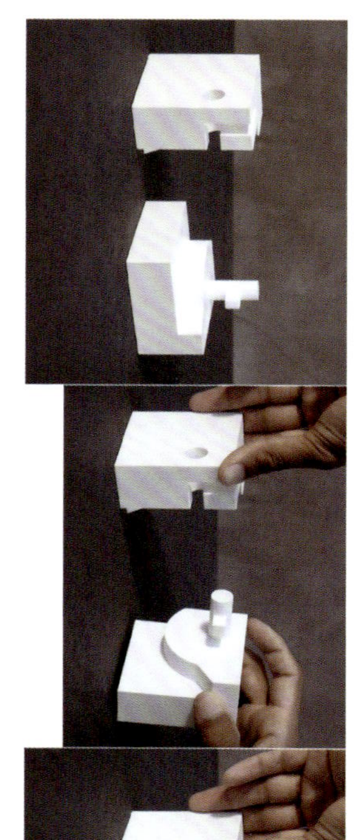

02

02

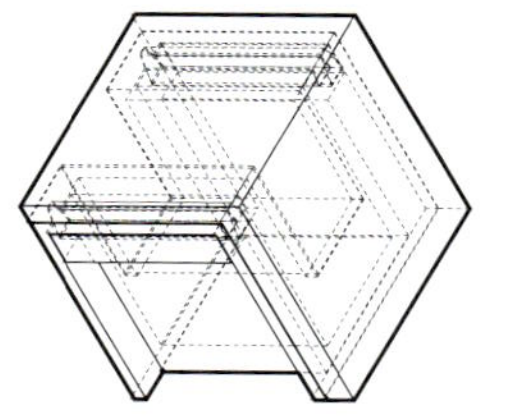

CB.13
PIN TURN
Place pin into hole and slide past tab. Turn part until exterior faces are flush to lock into place.

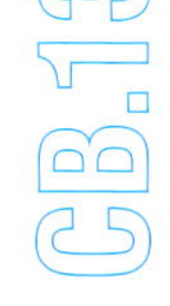
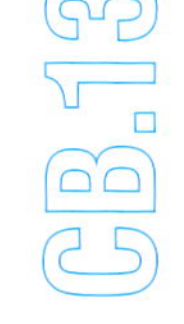

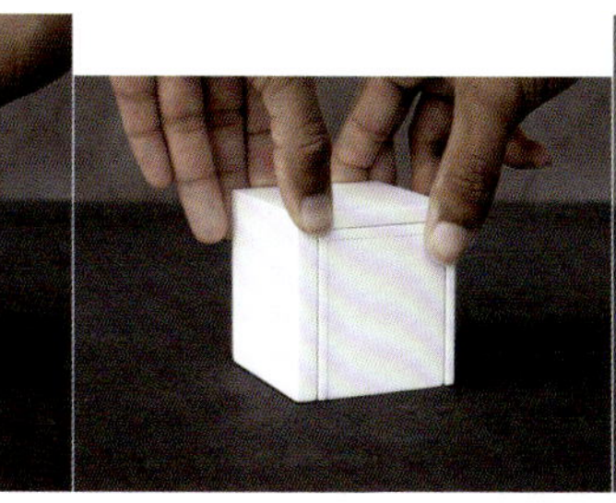

01

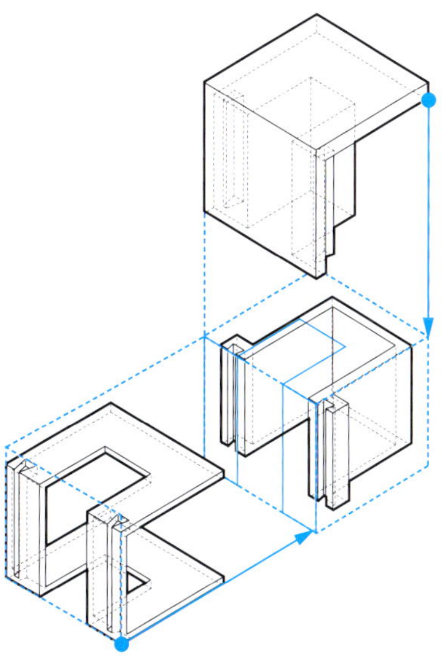

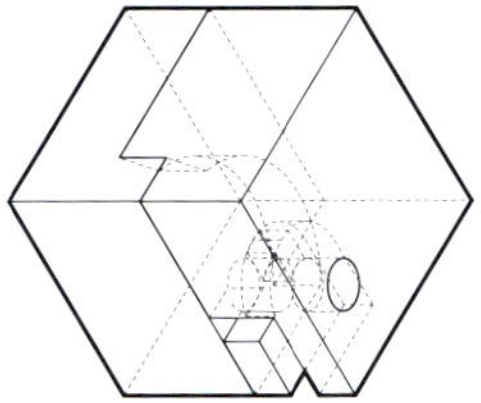

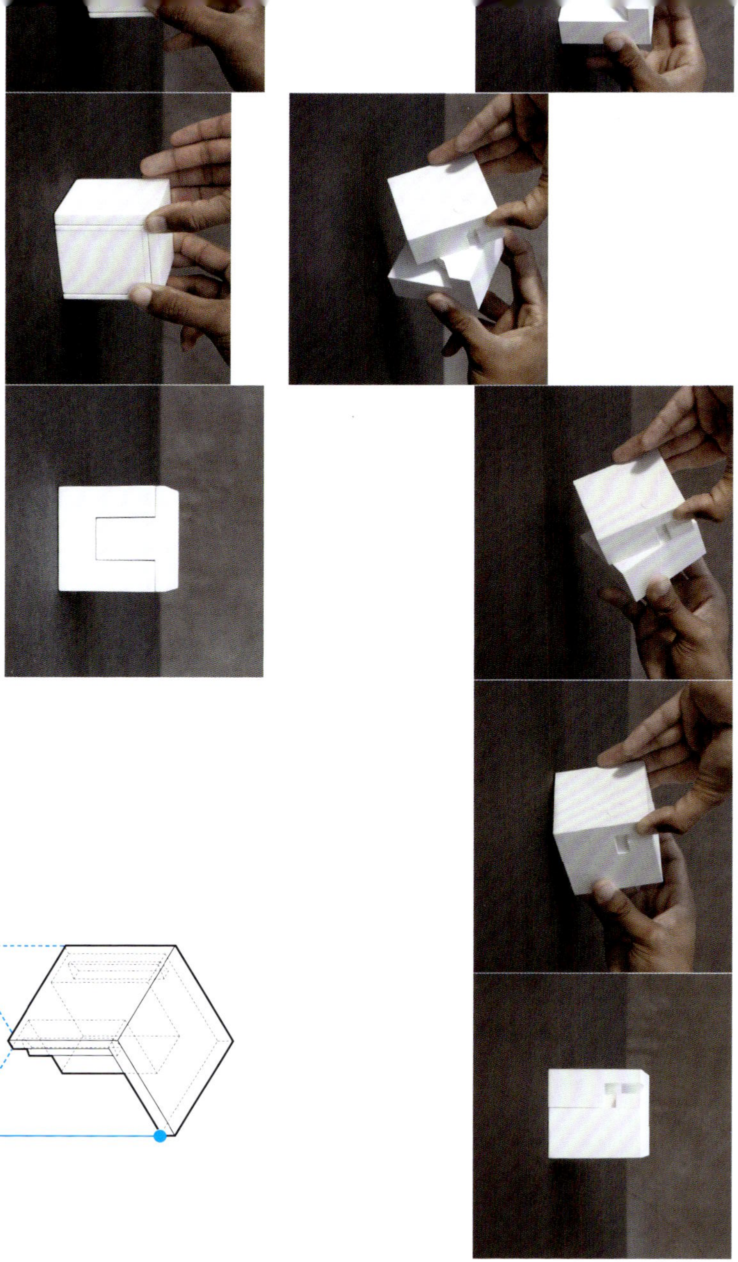

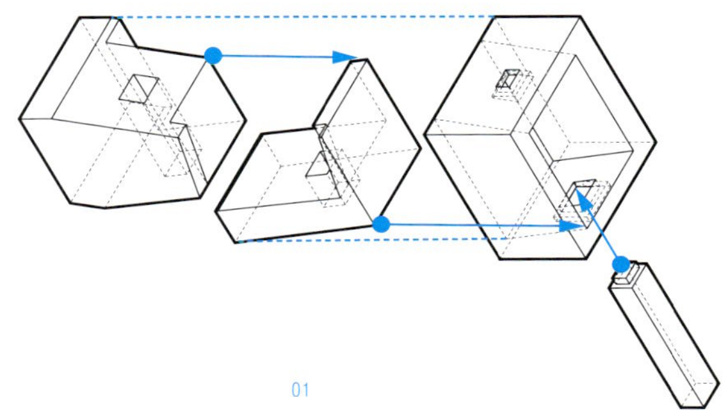

01

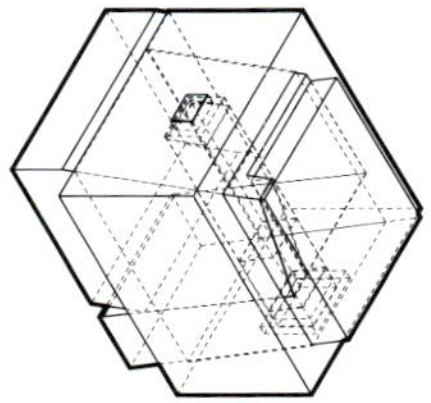

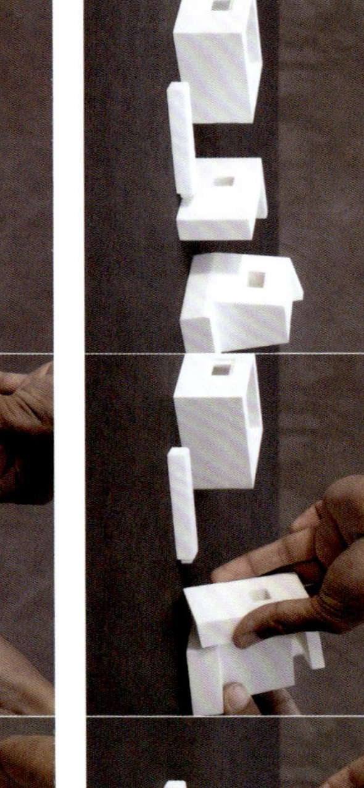

02

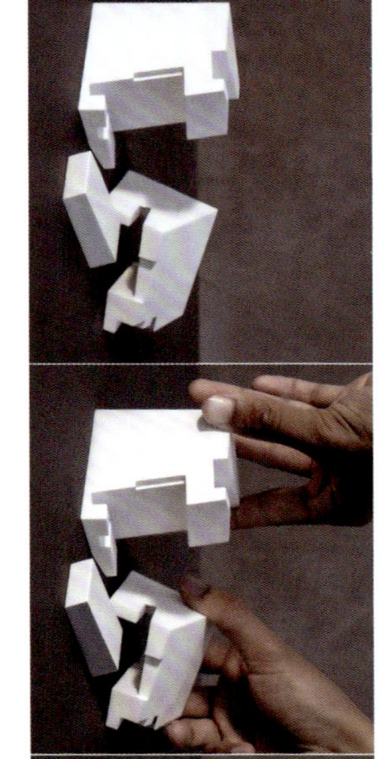

CB.16

ECCENTRIC GROOVE

Solid parts groove to fix along two directions.
Pin slips through the gap to create tight fit.

CB.15

CAPTURE PIN

Layer solid parts on their angled faces. Capture
layered parts with ring part to fix them together.
Slide pin through aligned openings to lock.

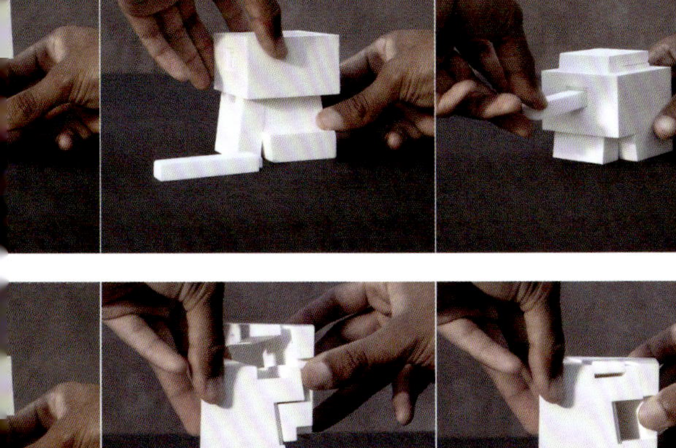

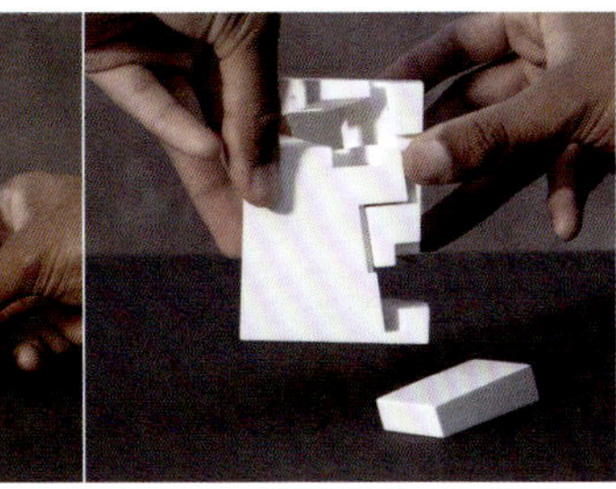

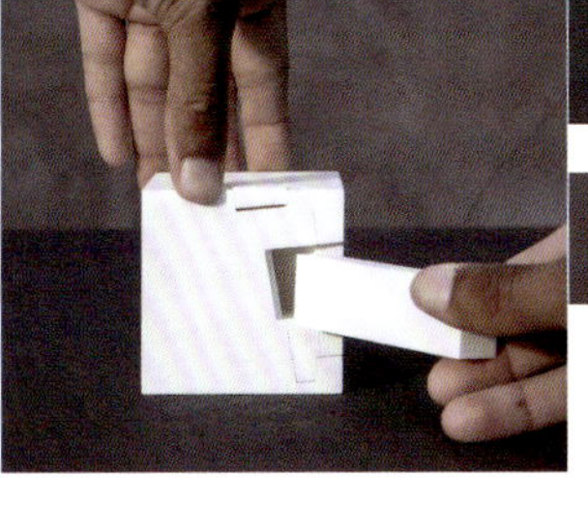

01

02

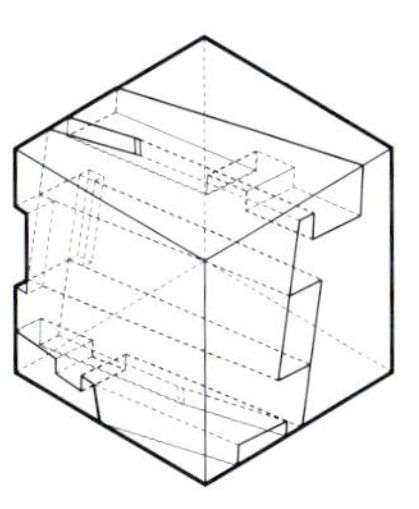
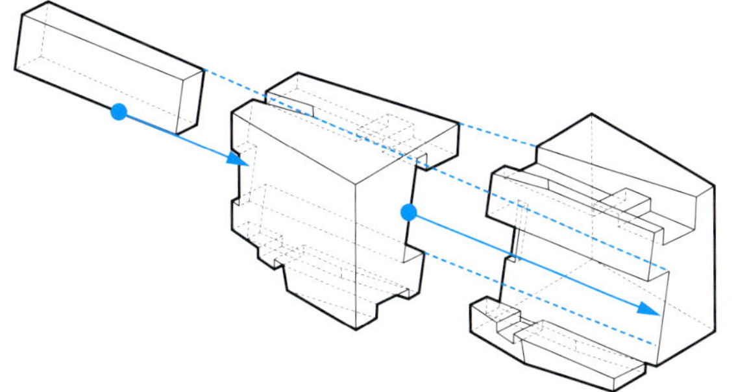

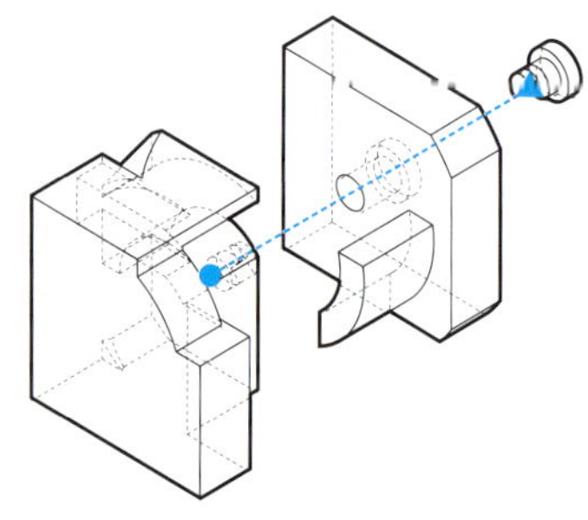
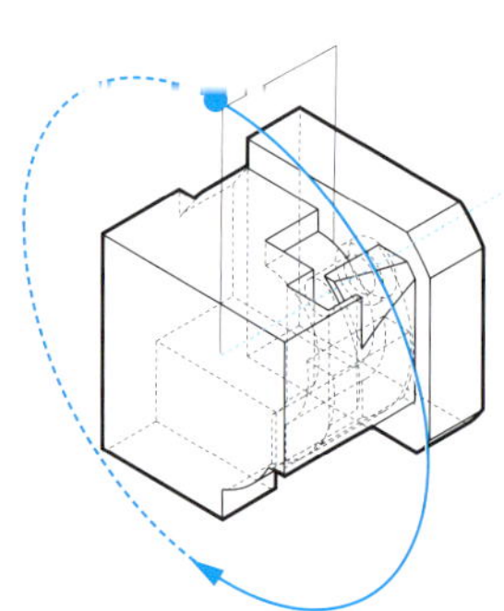

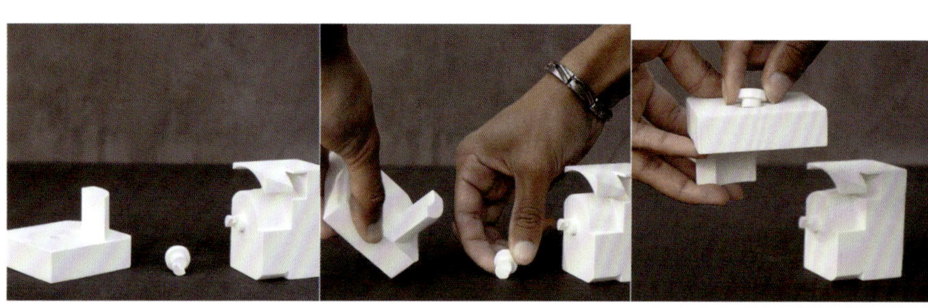
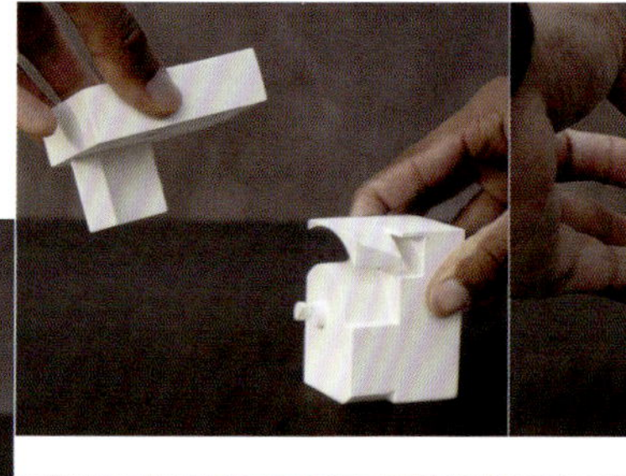
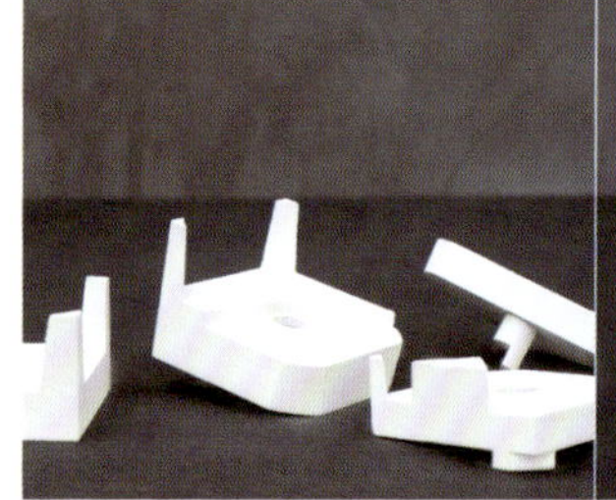
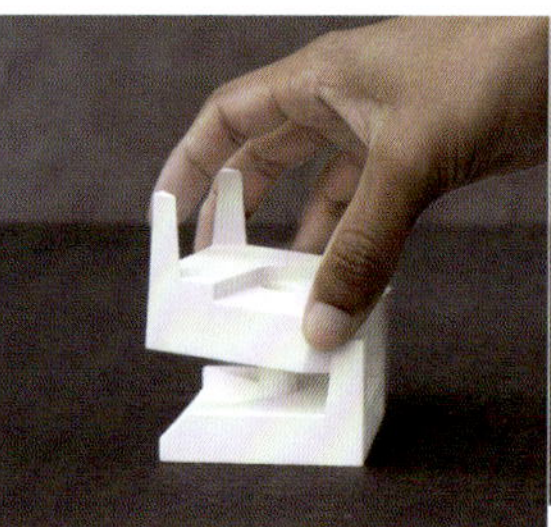
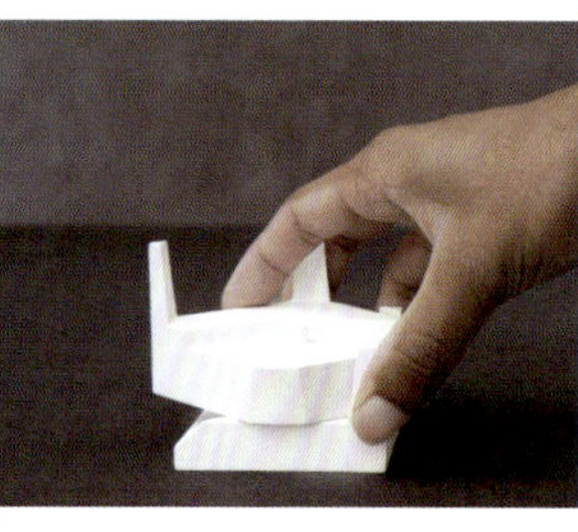
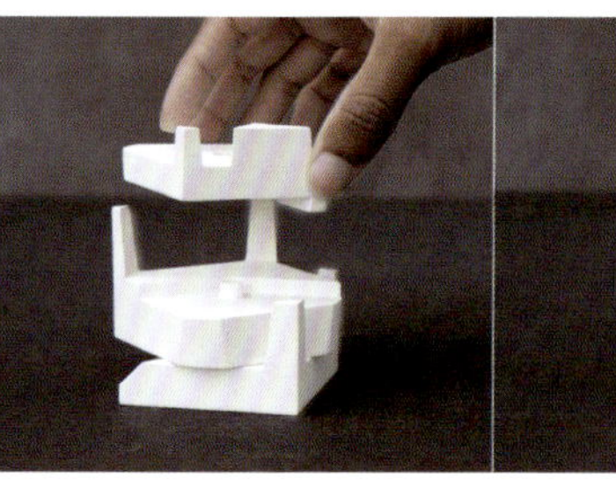

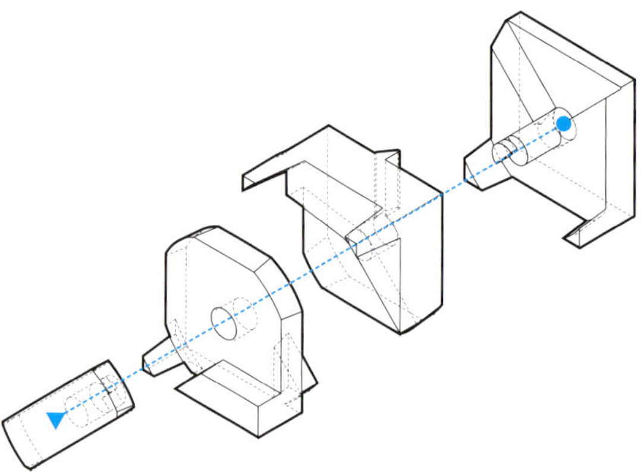

INVESTIGATIONS

CB.18

PINNING LOCK

Layer parts so that all features point in the same
direction. Orient the pin part to align with the openings
of the layered parts. Slip pin through openings.
Turn pin tab to spin and lock parts together.

02

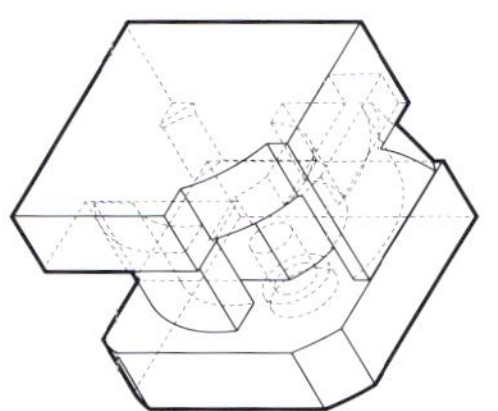

03

CB.17

PIN KEY LOCK

Place pin part into opening until flush with
exterior face. Hold in place, and slide pin of
solid part on the opposite side. Holding pin in
place, turn solid part to lock parts together.

03

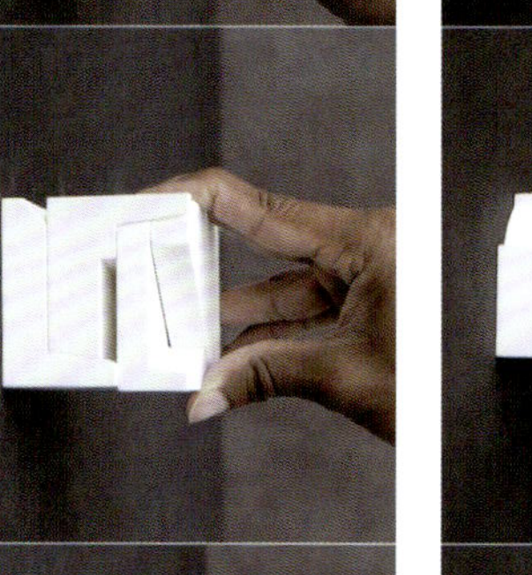

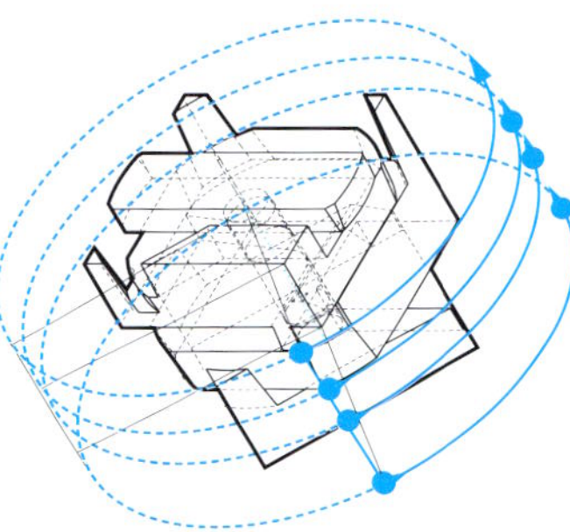

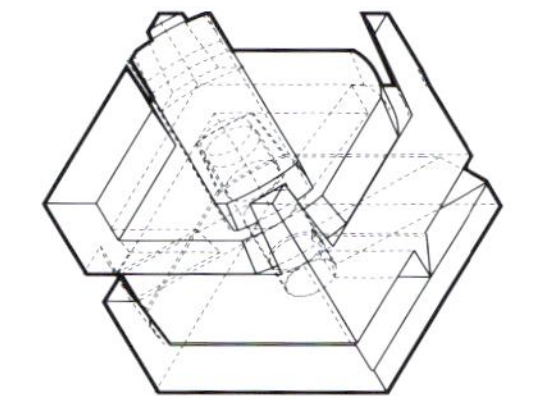

CB.20

GROOVE PIN

Align grooves of each part at corners. Slide part through groove until exterior faces are flush.

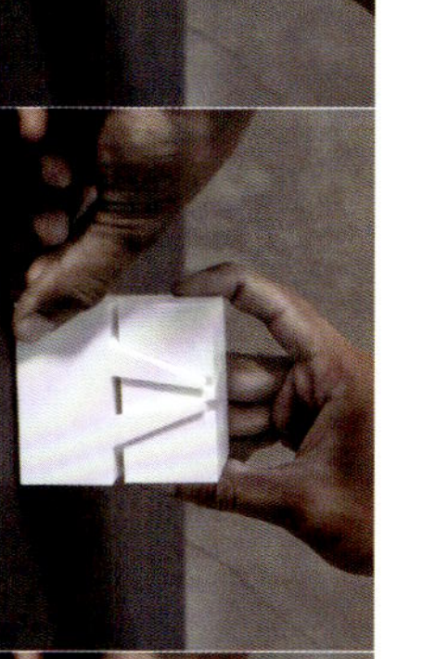

01

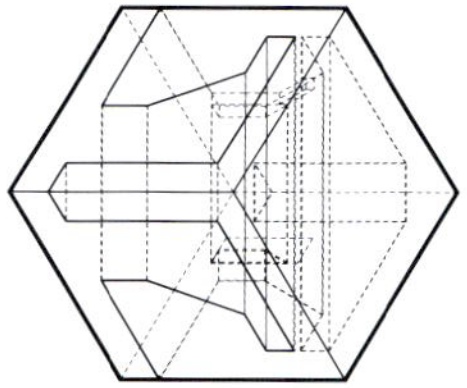

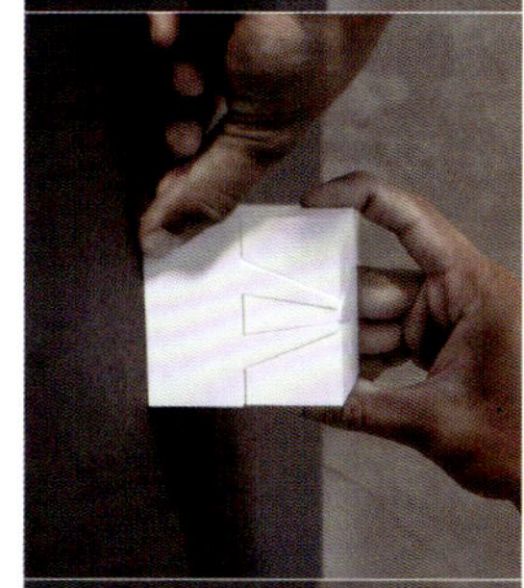

02

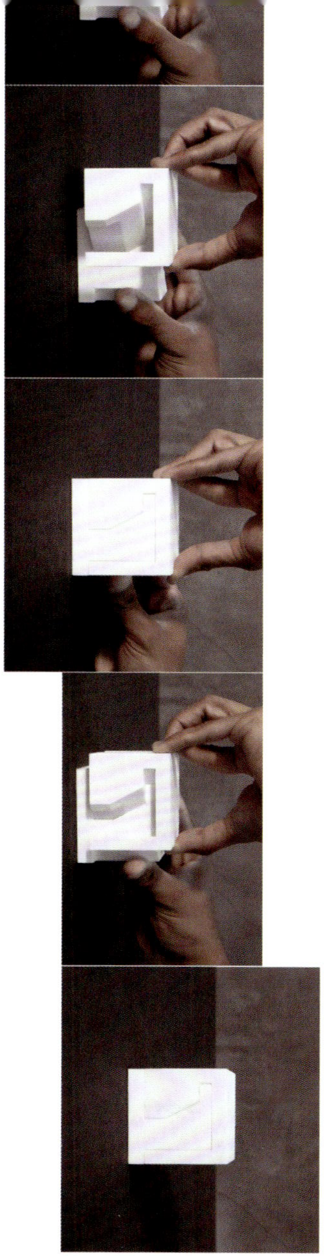

CB.19

DOVETAIL

Orient parts to face inversely. Slide parts together through grooves until exterior faces are flush.

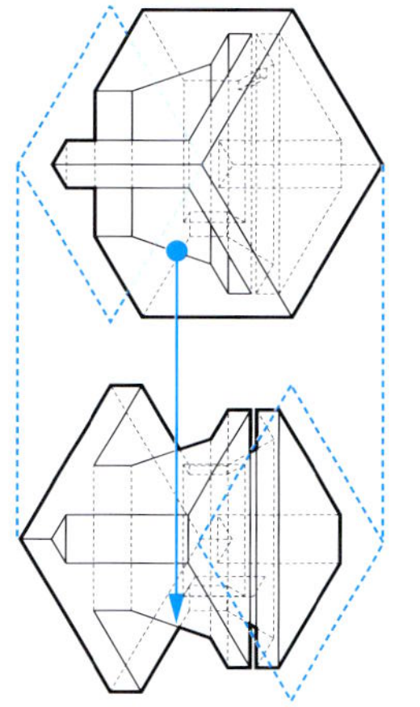

01

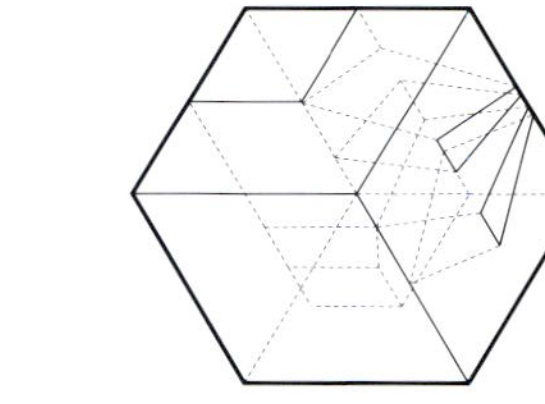

02

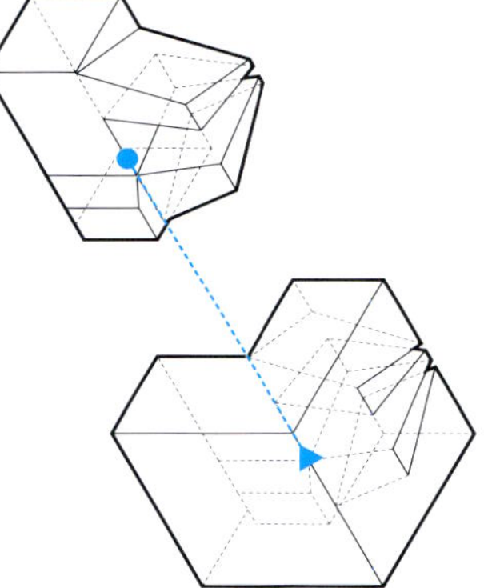

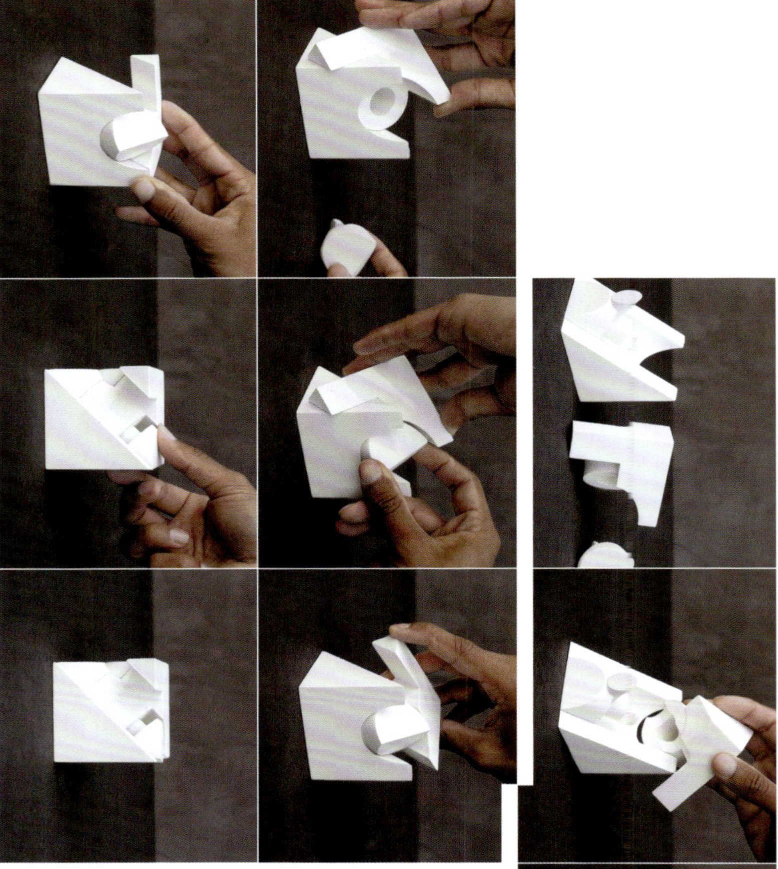

01

02

03

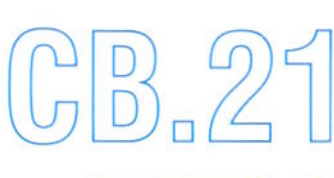

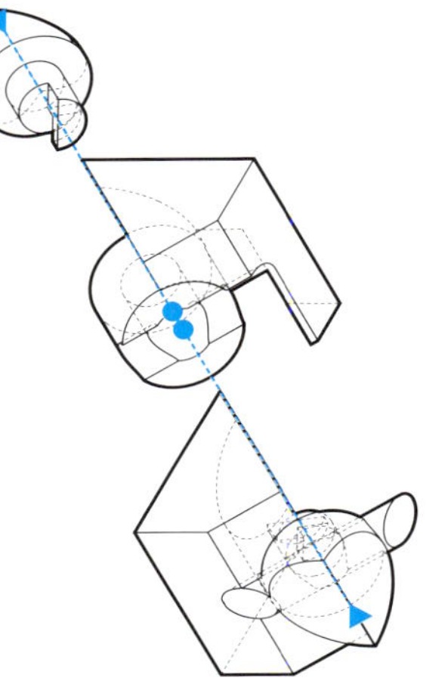

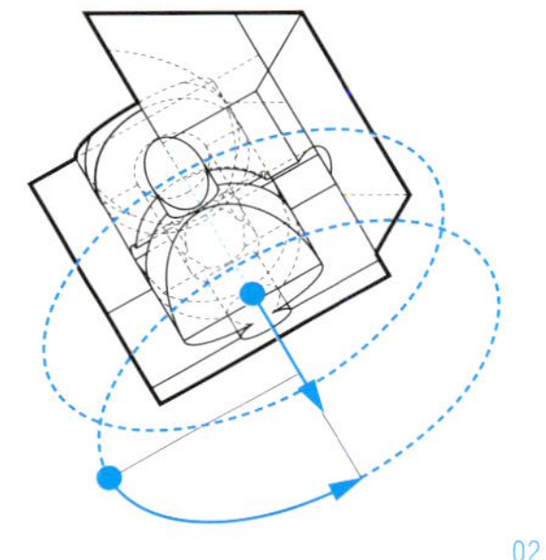

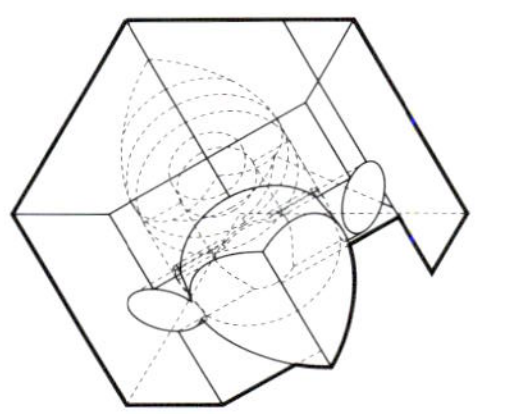

CB.21

INTERLOCKING PIN

Orient opening of pin along angled face. Slot pin into opening. Slide pin part into connected parts. Spin captured part 45 degrees so exterior edges meet. Turn pin part to interlock all parts together.

CB.22

HIDDEN LOCK

Slide surface tab into opening of inversely shaped part. Press pin part into opposite side of combined part. Spin pin part to lock into place.

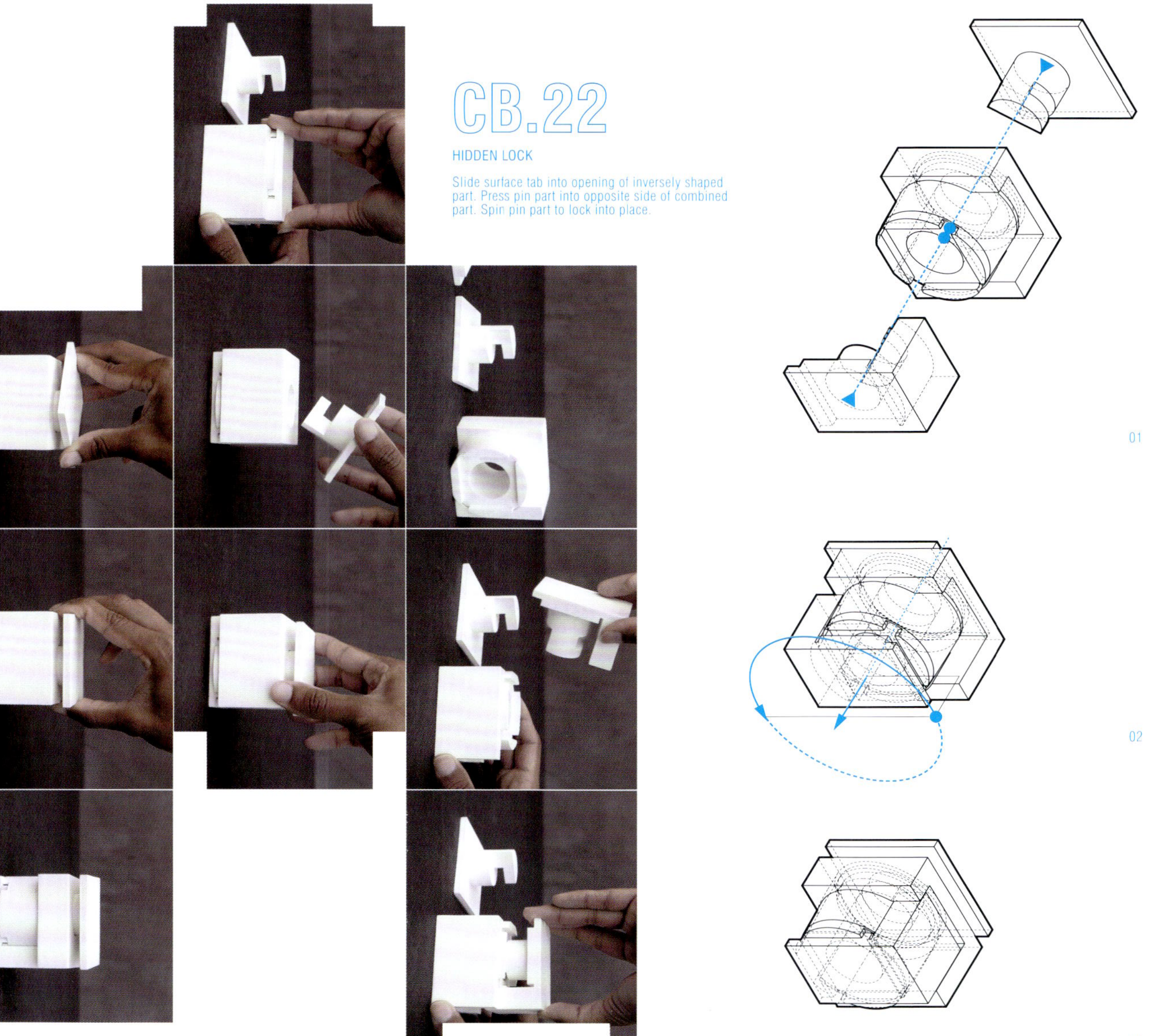

CB.23

ECCENTRIC LOCK

Slide pin into opening of solid part. Turn pin part 90
degrees to fit into grooves in solid part to lock into place.

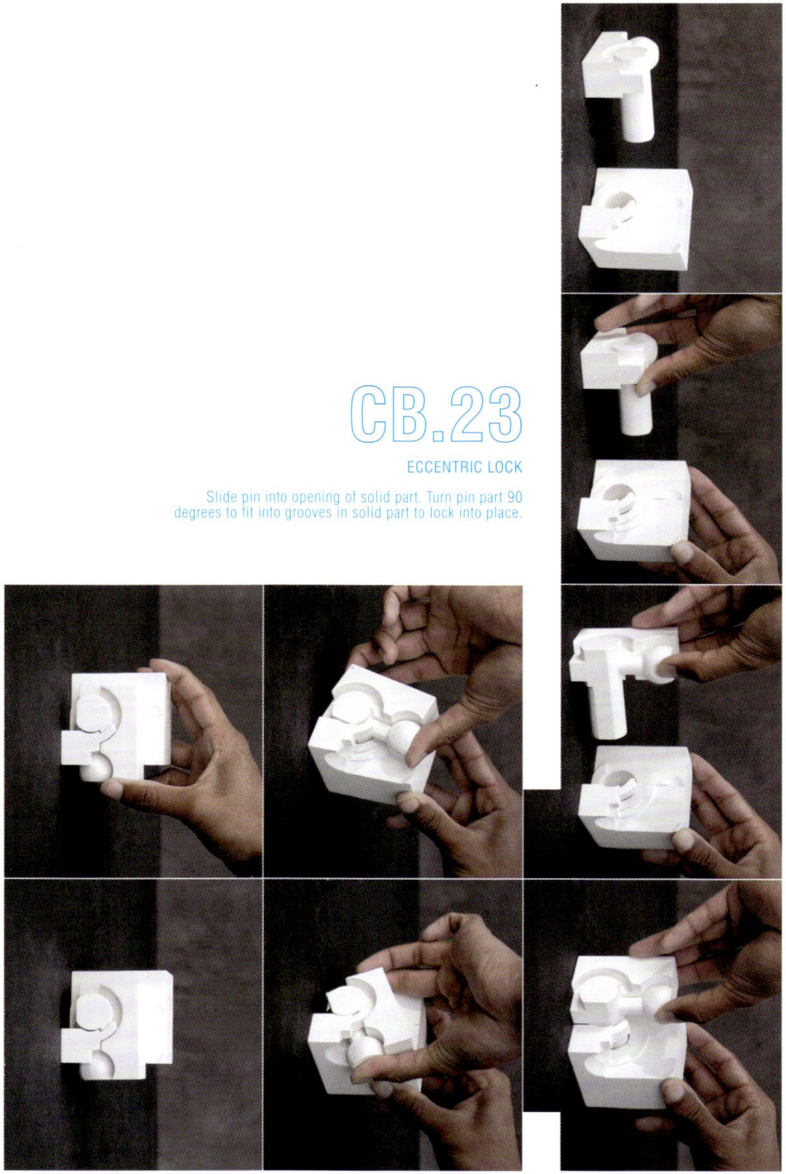

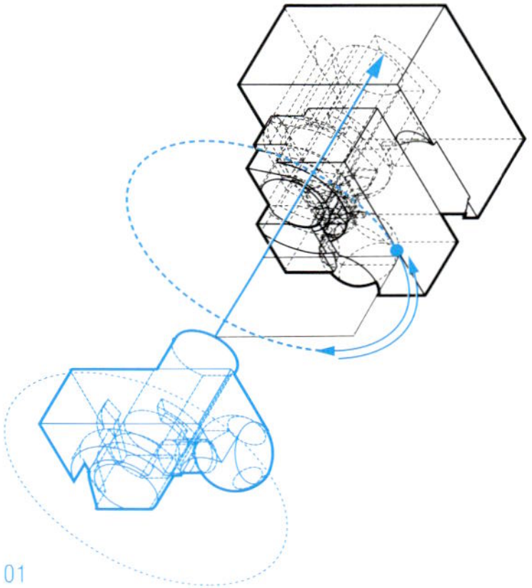

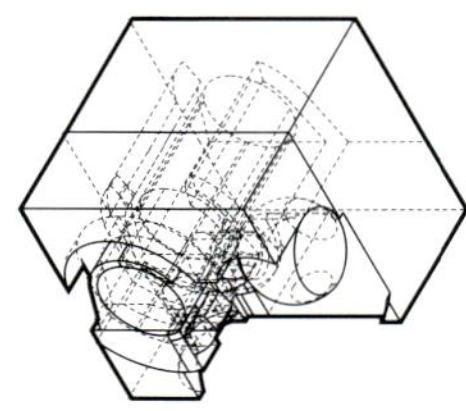

01

02

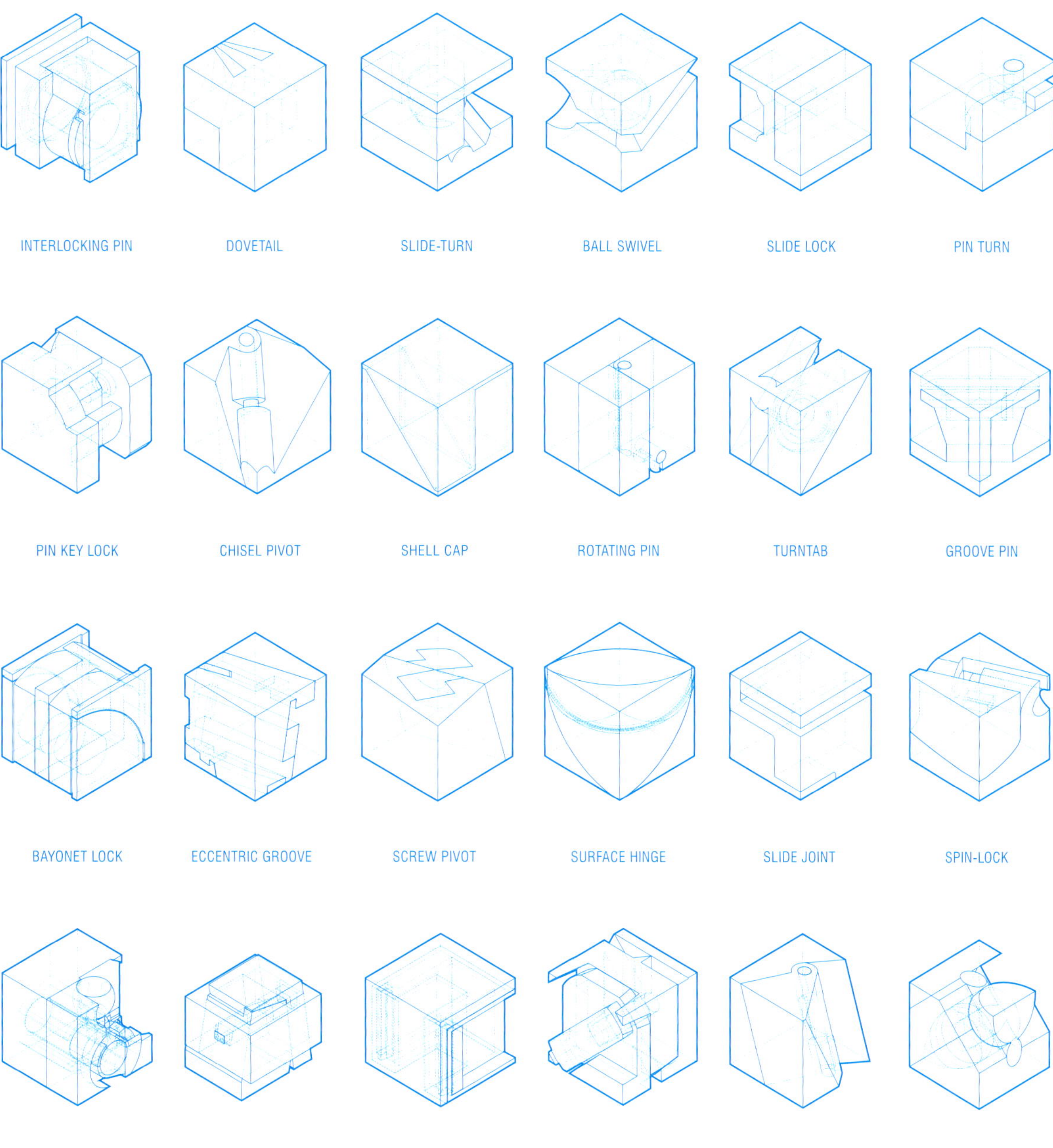

INTERLOCKING PIN
DOVETAIL
SLIDE-TURN
BALL SWIVEL
SLIDE LOCK
PIN TURN
PIN KEY LOCK
CHISEL PIVOT
SHELL CAP
ROTATING PIN
TURNTAB
GROOVE PIN
BAYONET LOCK
ECCENTRIC GROOVE
SCREW PIVOT
SURFACE HINGE
SLIDE JOINT
SPIN-LOCK
ECCENTRIC LOCK
CAPTURE PIN
SURFACE PIN
PINNING LOCK
SCRAPED HINGE
HIDDEN LOCK

PUZZLES ARE MADE OF INTERLOCKING PARTS. FROM RELATIVELY SIMPLE DESIGNS WITH ONLY A FEW PIECES, TO A VOLUMETRIC MATRIX OF COMPONENTS, THE DIVERSE SHAPE AND DESIGN OF EACH PIECE OF A PUZZLE IS CAREFULLY FORMED TO CREATE A FITTED CONNECTION.

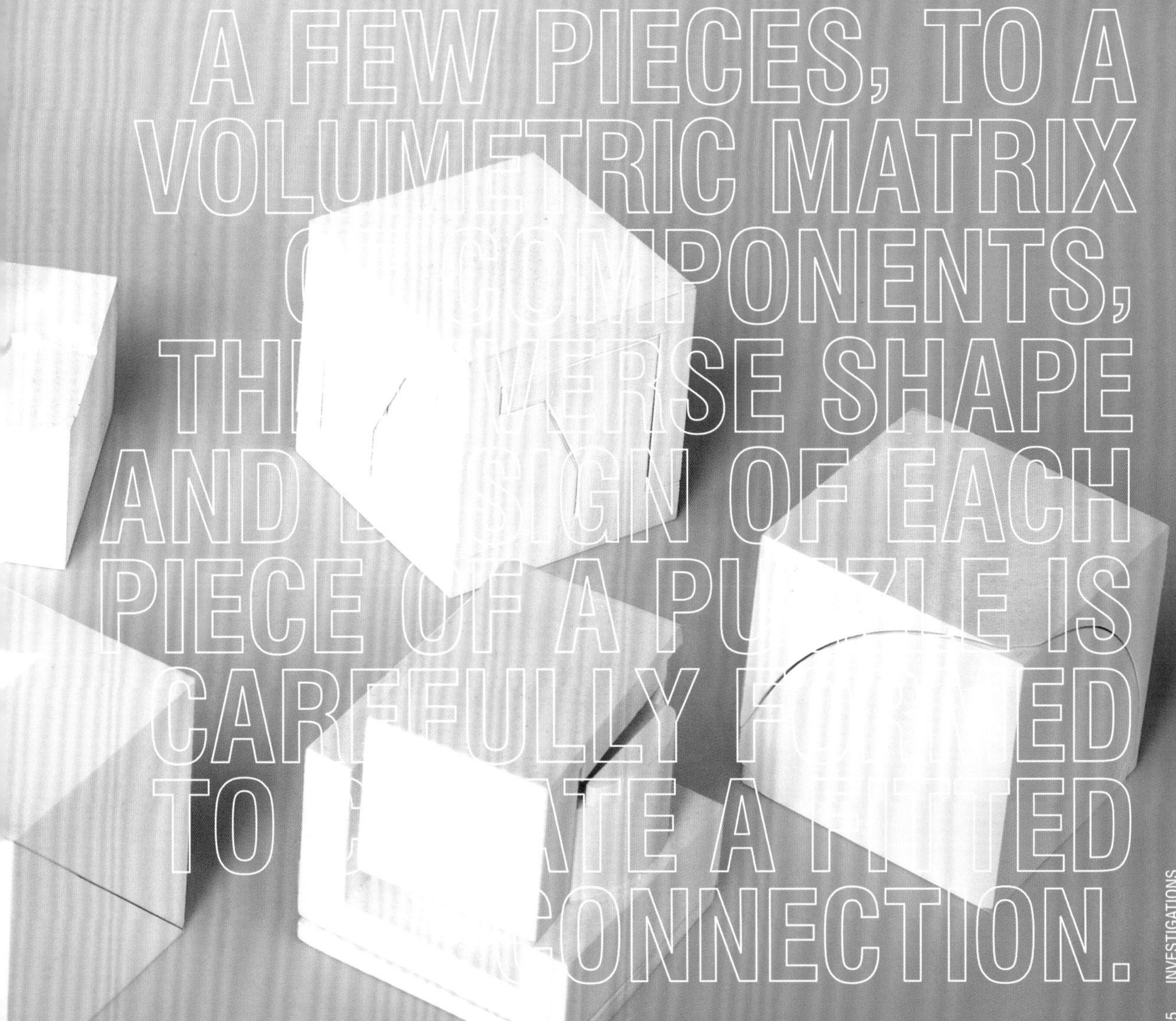

SPHERICALS

Within our Primitive cube studies, interactions are revealed by a dynamic yet basic set of visual clues. Their operation is relatively intuitive, and their x, y, and z axes provide an orientation that helps decode the inner workings. Spheres remove that sense of orientation, resulting in a more constant and three-dimensional interrogation of each part's relationship to the whole.

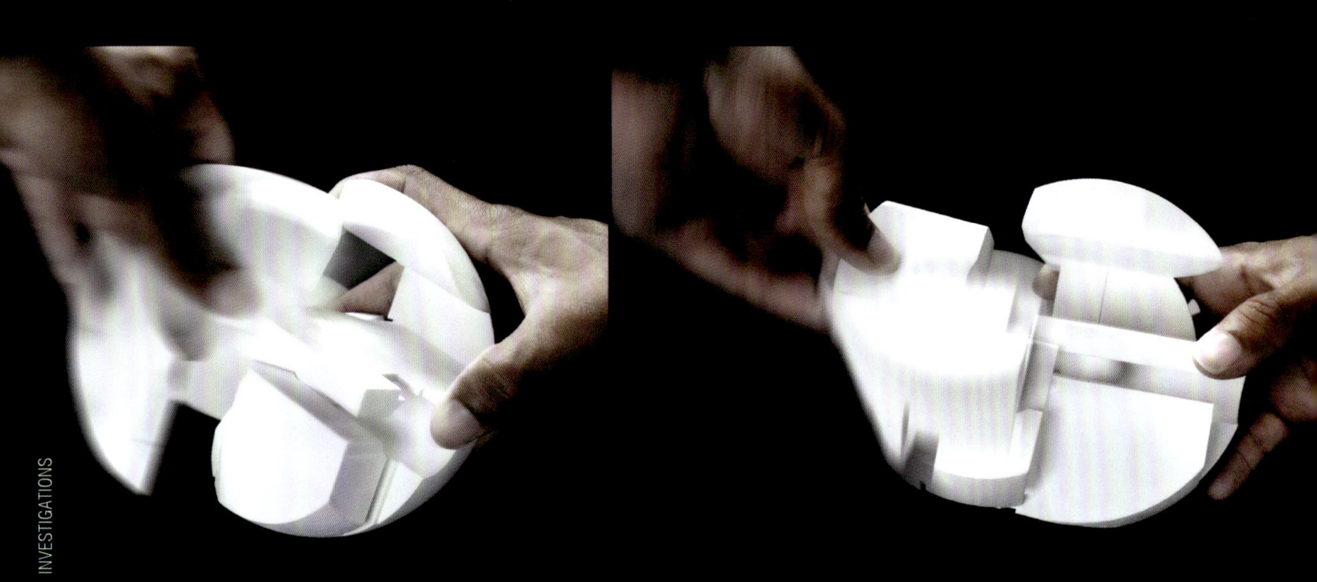

01
02

SP.A

Comprised of only a few parts,
they fit together by slipping
through internal voids, nesting to
complete the full geometry.

01   NESTLED PARTS

Shaped masses are a result of
how the parts are assembled, as
gaps and openings give indication
to the perceived movement
of each against the other.

TECTONIC FIGURES   02

Though much of the puzzled form
is shaped by how parts interact,
the key feature that binds them
visually and geometrically lies in
how the overall assembly finds
completeness in a fixed state.

03   RECOMPLETION OF FORM

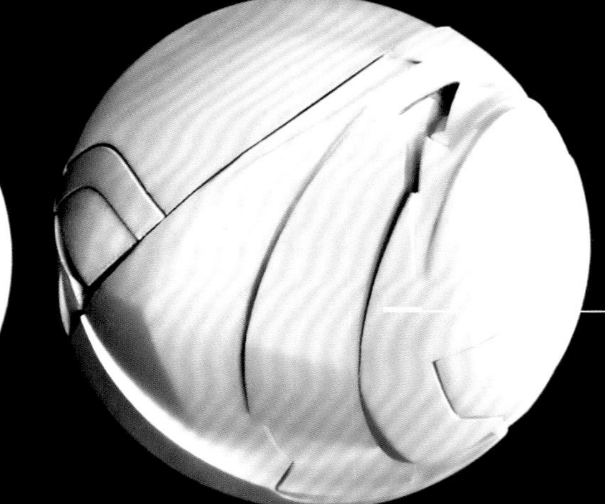

ARCING JOINT   04

As multiple parts come together,
the figures overlap. They find a fit
along a joint that arcs with the shape
of the exterior form of the sphere.

06   INTERNAL REVEALS

The reading of the form depends
on the observable features that
punctuate the internal dialogue.

CO-CENTRIC SHAPING   05

Every part is shaped by the
spherical volume, crafted to fit
in co-centric juxtaposition.

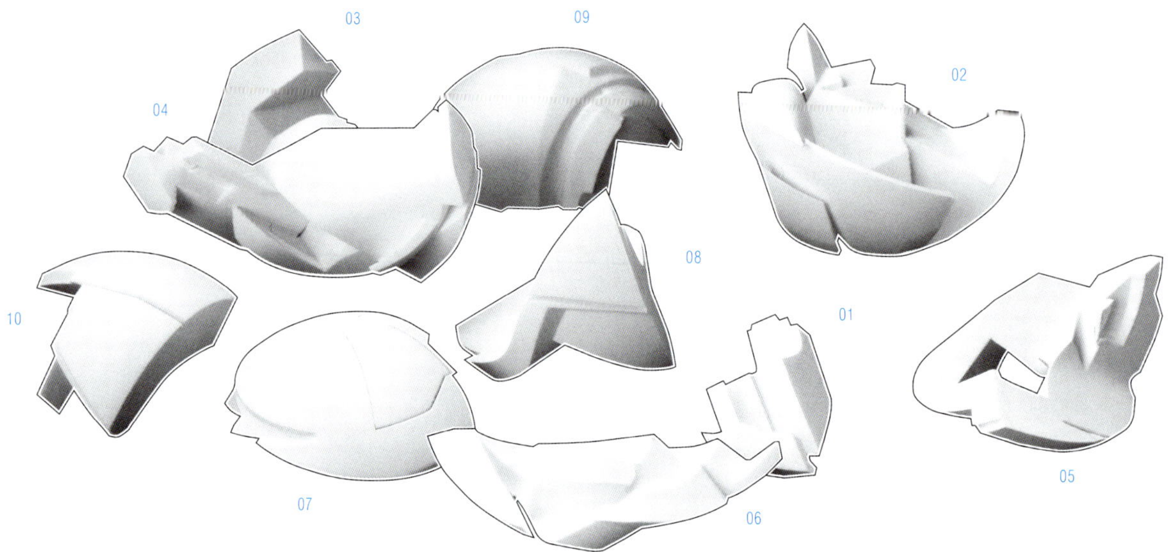

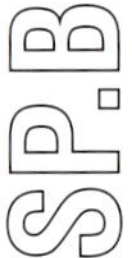

As with the primitive cubes, Sphericals offer operational clues through the distinctive geometric cuts and carves that differentiate those necessary for assembly from those of the primitive host. This is especially true in the case of linear movements that introduce rectilinear geometries into the predominantly curvilinear field. However, for the sake of these studies, we've also introduced rotational movement into the puzzle. This operation produces a proliferation of curvilinear geometry that conflates the recognition of the outer surface with the operational movements of the puzzle, effectively increasing the degree of difficulty necessary to assemble and disassemble the puzzle.

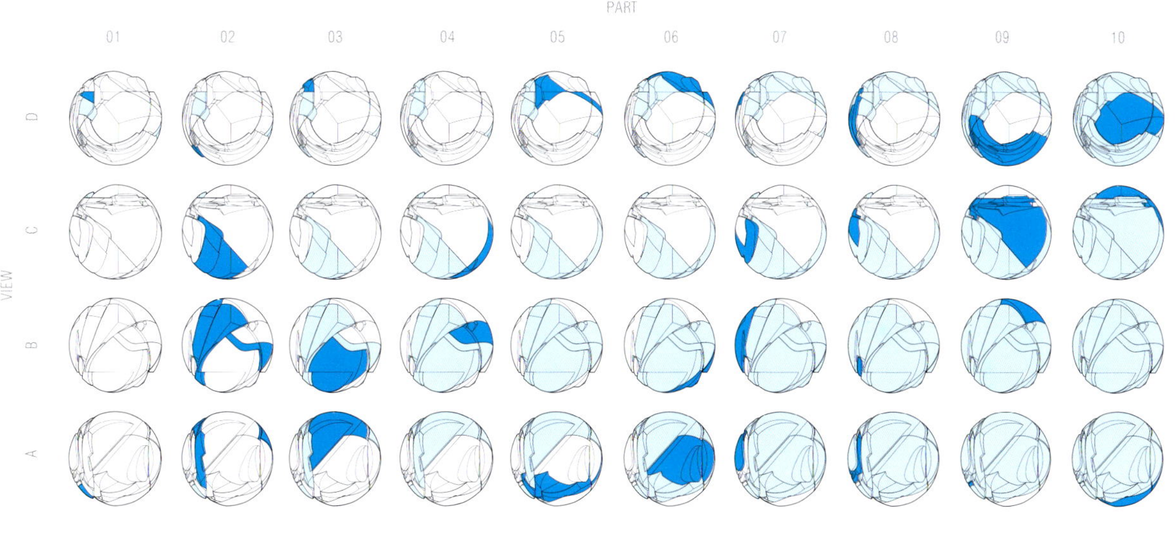

PART
01 02 03 04 05 06 07 08 09 10
VIEW
D
C
B
A

PUZZLES RELY ON CAREFUL EXAMINATION AND ACTIVE ENGAGEMENT.

PUZZLES REQUIRE AN INVESTIGATION OF THE SHAPE AND STRUCTURE OF THEIR PARTS THROUGH PROGRESSIVE TRIAL AND ERROR. IT IS THE PROCESS OF ASSEMBLY THAT ILLUMINATES A SENSE OF DISCOVERY.

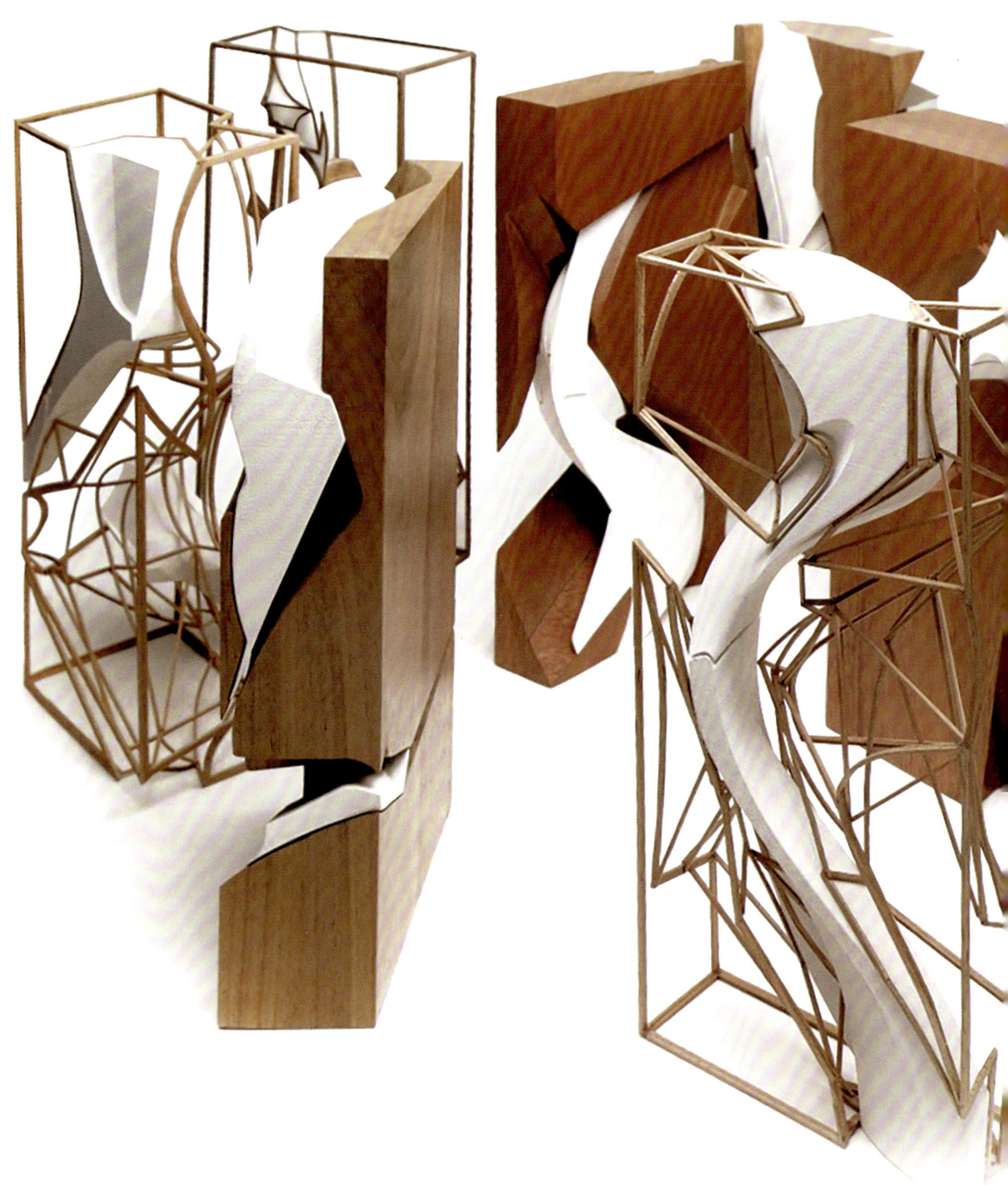

ACTIVE INLAYS

"Inlay" typically refers to a thin surface material that is embedded into another with outer surfaces that expressively coincide, commonly consisting of a primary three-dimensional object and a relatively thin secondary material. By exploiting the ambiguity of this definition, the Active Inlay studies challenge this hierarchy, and investigate the possibility of a more interwoven set of geometries.

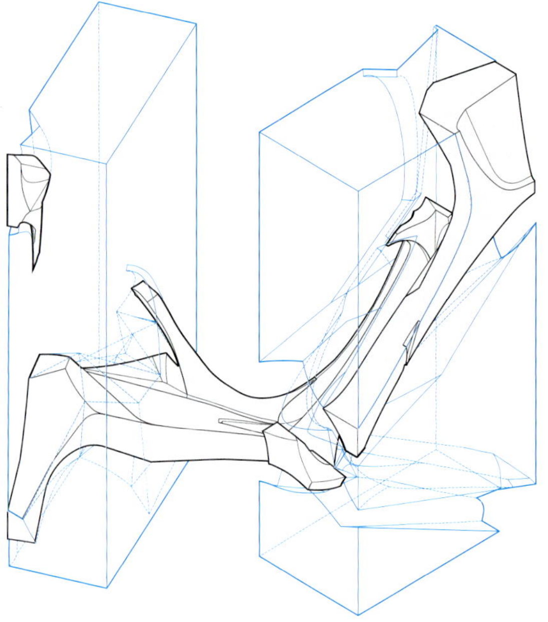 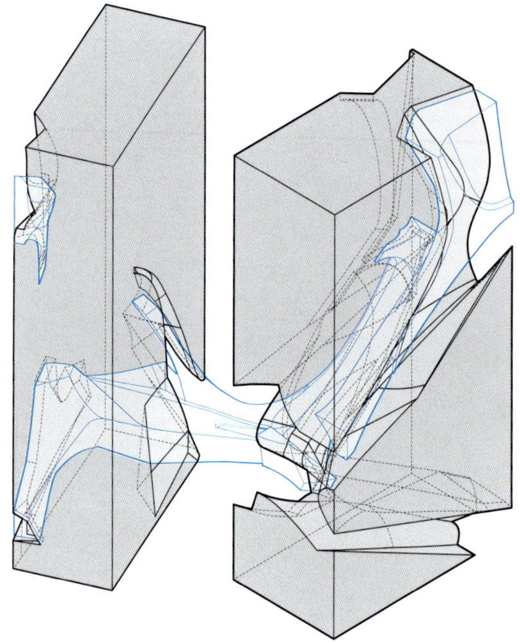

In Active Inlays, rectilinear "hosts" contain an interplay of eccentric geometric objects that reveal themselves in curious ways, creating an uncertainty about the true nature of their three-dimensional interconnectedness. At times, the objects suggest a conventional surface inlay—thin, isolated, and two-dimensional. At other times, they reveal themselves to be part of a larger, interconnected, three-dimensional network. This perceptual uncertainty about implied and literal continuities has particularly relevant architectural applications when considered in relation to ideas of facade, internal spatial and organizational continuities, and the relationship between the two.

As in our Primitives studies, spaces and seams are key to understanding the three-dimensional relationship between parts. They reveal that in some places the inner objects are tightly fit to the host geometry, while at other locations they express a loose-fit relationship. These loose fits suggest a jostling for space—as though the two entities are in close dialogue with one another, yet not entirely in sync. The voids and seams produce an aesthetic tension and also introduce spatial qualities—making the studies especially useful in their potential for translation into architecture.

AI.01

SHAPED SURFACES   01

Subtle and expressive surfaces carve voids in solid
volumes, shaping their formal features with objects that
interact in ways that suggest an embedded logic.

SECTIONAL FIGURES   02

In the shaping of the overall volume, unexpected figures are produced
on the surface. These clearly reveal sectional qualities that are more
diverse, yet leave their full three-dimensional properties ambiguous.

EMBED-HOST RELATIONSHIP   03

'Host' volumes remain rectilinear in their overall shape,
like a section cut of a larger series of expressively inlaid
interactions. This creates a dialogue between solid and void.

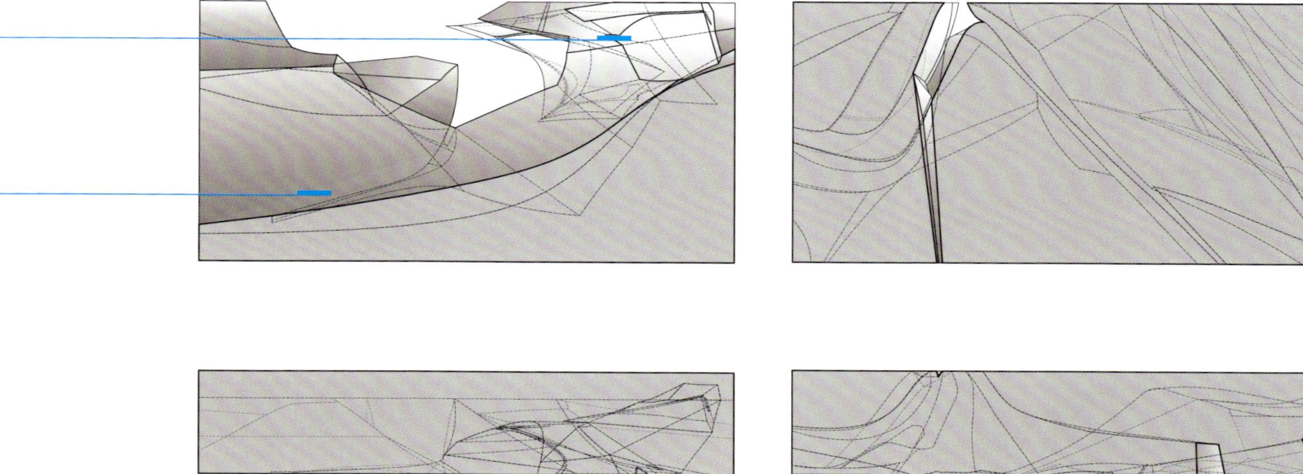

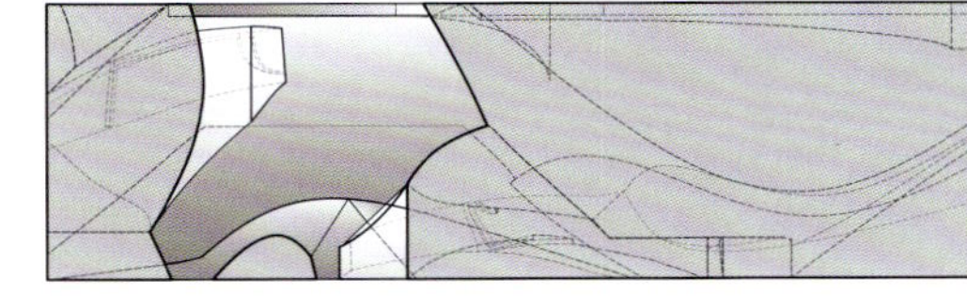
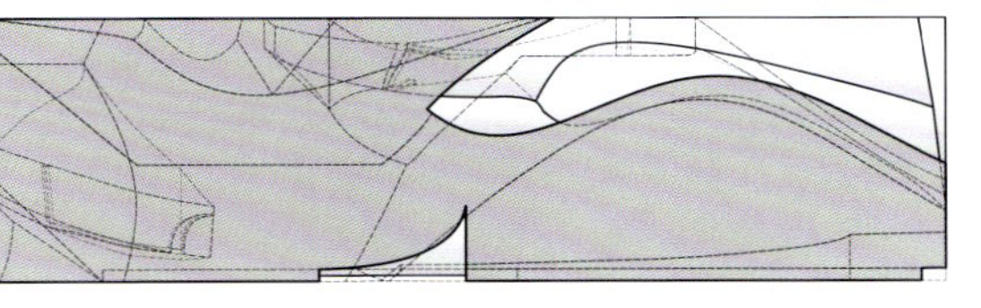
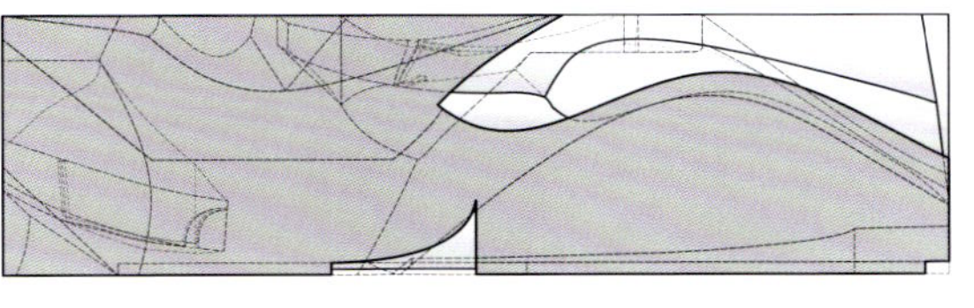

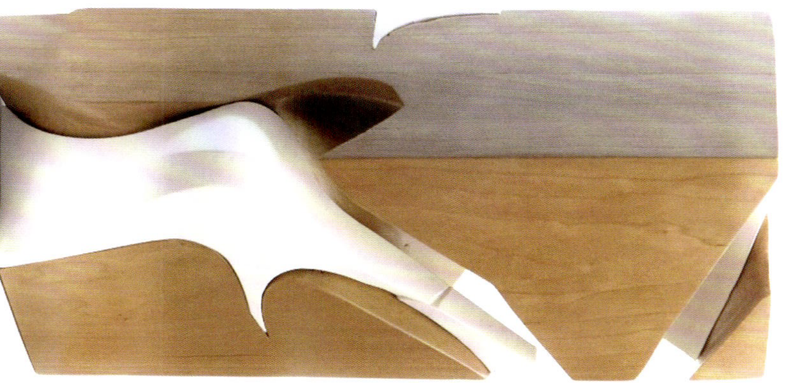

Rather than concealing the joints between each object, or placing them in conventionally logical juxtapositions against one another, the seams that are created in their interactions float freely across surfaces to reflect an internal dialogue.

SEAM STRATEGIES   04

Rather than mere juxtaposition, the objects engage to confront the contrasting languages of their solid shape. Finding fixed positions in regard to one another is a process of establishing formal relationships that use the eccentricities of the objects as what gives character to how they are resolved in space.

ECCENTRIC POSITIONING   05

There are moments where the embedded objects are presented in their fragmented form, not fully revealed, but suggest readings of continuity in how those geometries extend to shape the solids around it.

AUTONOMOUS ELEMENTS   C6

AI.03

SHAPED SURFACES   01

Subtle and expressive surfaces carve voids in solid
volumes, shaping their formal features with objects that
interact in ways that suggest an embedded logic.

SECTIONAL FIGURES   02

In the shaping of the overall volume, unexpected figures are produced
on the surface. These clearly reveal sectional qualities that are more
diverse, yet leave their full three-dimensional properties ambiguous.

EMBED-HOST RELATIONSHIP   03

'Host' volumes remain rectilinear in heir overall shape,
like a section cut of a larger series of expressively inlaid
interactions. This creates a dialogue between solid and void.

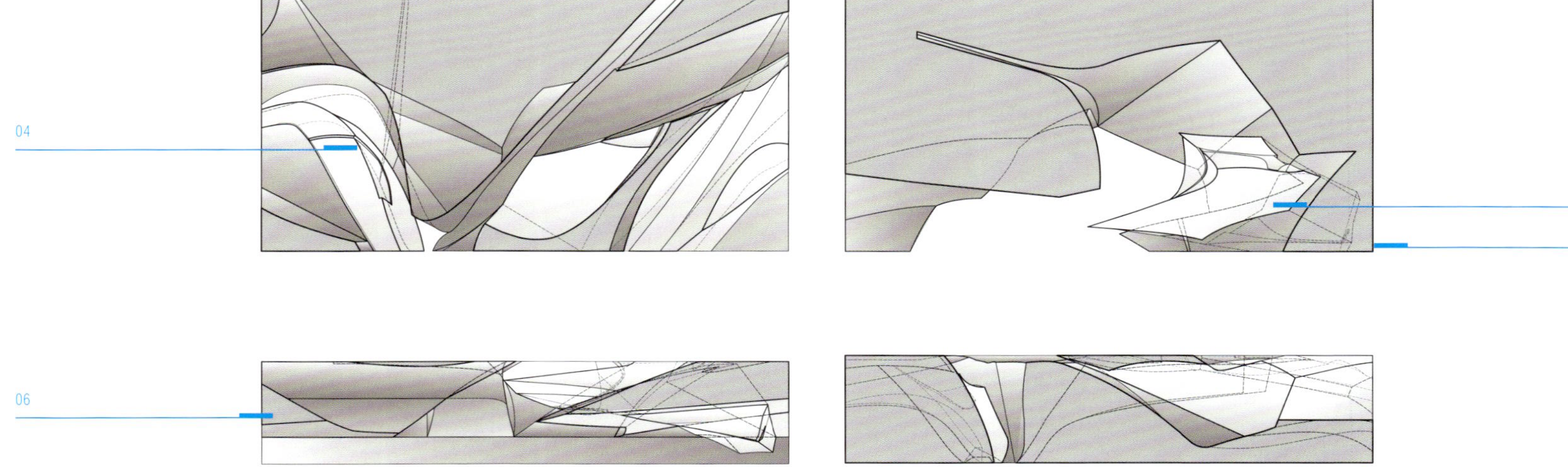

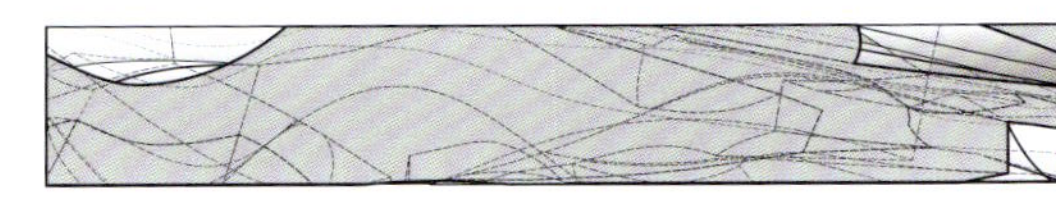

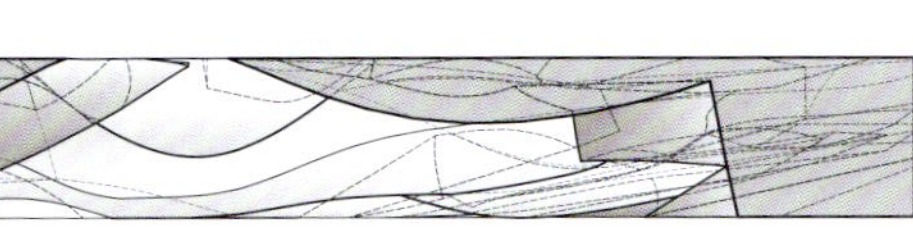

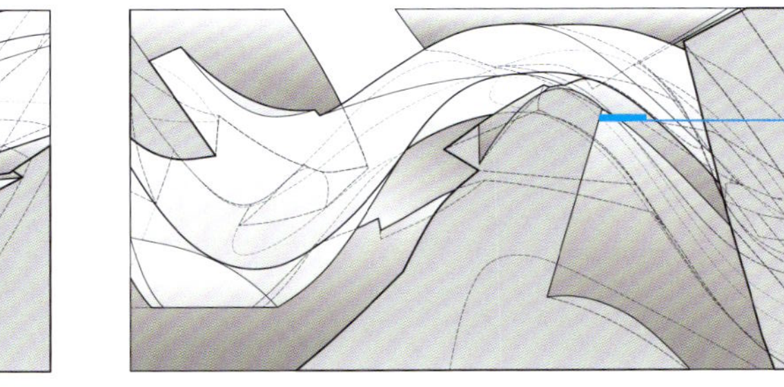

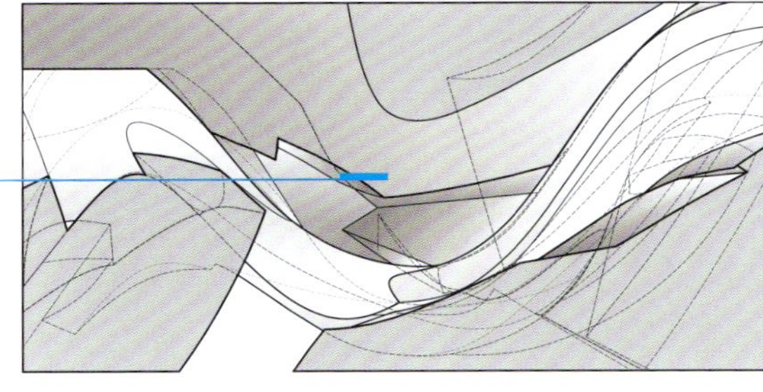

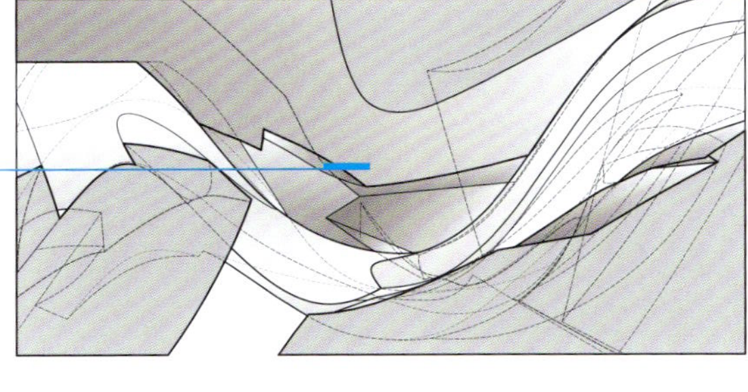

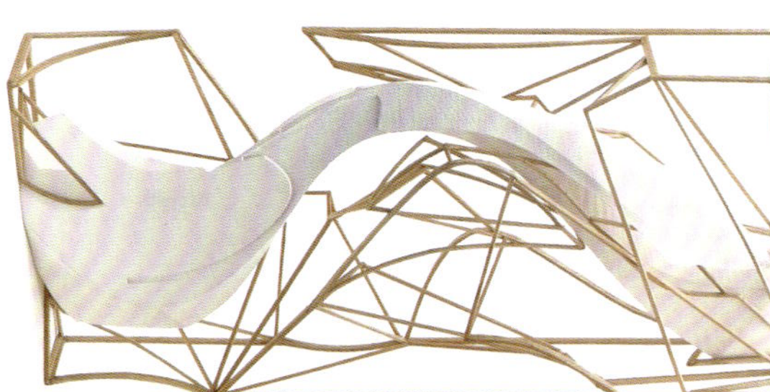

Rather than concealing the joints between each object, or placing them in conventionally logical juxtapositions against one another, the seams that are created in their interactions float freely across surfaces to reflect an internal dialogue.

SEAM STRATEGIES   04

Rather than mere juxtaposition, the objects engage to confront the contrasting languages of their solid shape. Finding fixed positions in regard to one another is a process of establishing formal relationships that use the eccentricities of the objects as what gives character to how they are resolved in space.

ECCENTRIC POSITIONING   05

There are moments where the embedded objects are presented in their fragmented form, not fully revealed, but suggest readings of continuity in how those geometries extend to shape the solids around it.

AUTONOMOUS ELEMENTS   06

AI.04
AI.04.1

AI.05
AI.05.1

SHAPED SURFACES 01

Subtle and expressive surfaces carve voids in solid volumes, shaping their formal features with objects that interact in ways that suggest an embedded logic.

SECTIONAL FIGURES 02

In the shaping of the overall volume, unexpected figures are produced on the surface. These clearly reveal sectional qualities that are more diverse, yet leave their full three-dimensional properties ambiguous.

EMBED-HOST RELATIONSHIP 03

'Host' volumes remain rectilinear in their overall shape, like a section cut of a larger series of expressively inlaid interactions. This creates a dialogue between solid and void.

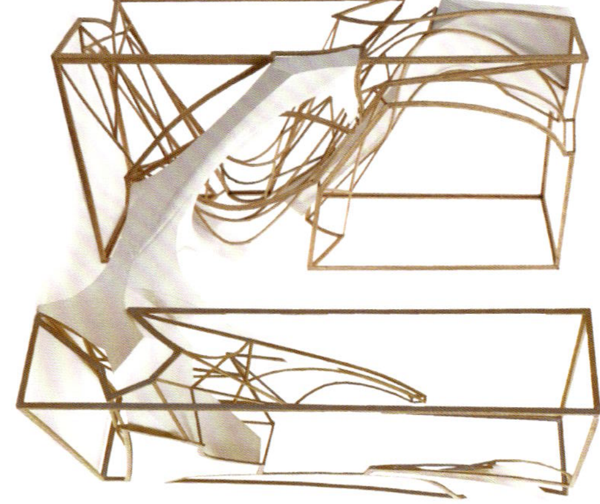

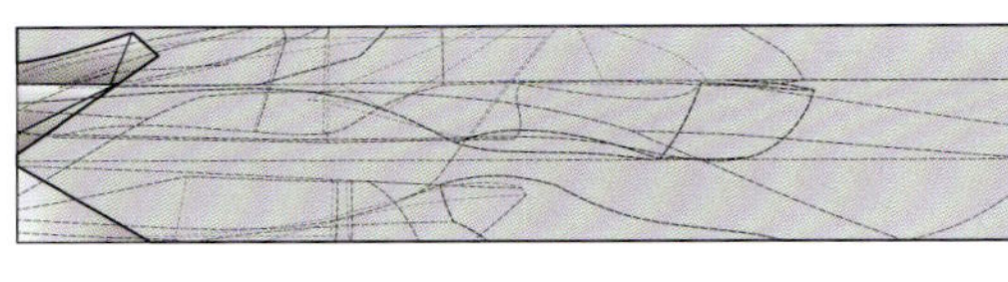

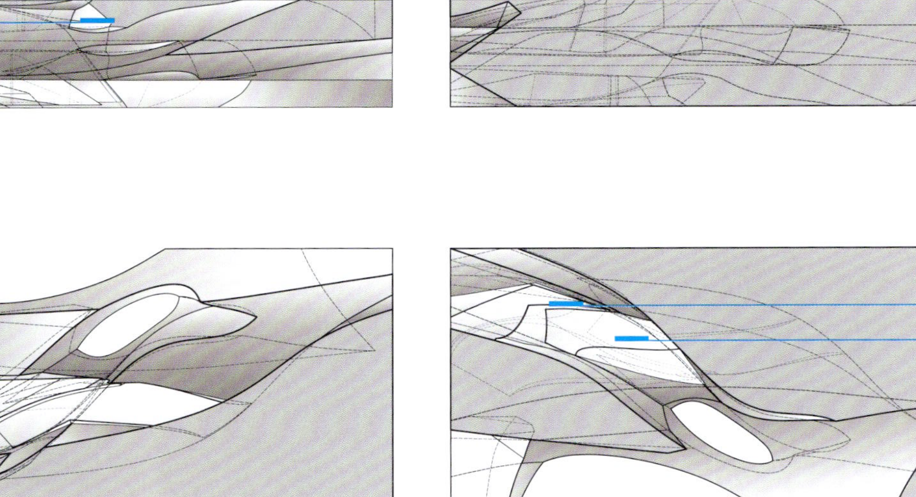

Rather than concealing the joints between each object, or placing them in conventionally logical juxtapositions against one another, the seams that are created in their interactions float freely across surfaces to reflect an internal dialogue.

SEAM STRATEGIES   04

Rather than mere juxtaposition, the objects engage to confront the contrasting languages of their solid shape. Finding fixed positions in regard to one another is a process of establishing formal relationships that use the eccentricities of the objects as what gives character to how they are resolved in space.

ECCENTRIC POSITIONING   05

There are moments where the embedded objects are presented in their fragmented form, not fully revealed, but suggest readings of continuity in how those geometries extend to shape the solids around it.

AUTONOMOUS ELEMENTS   06

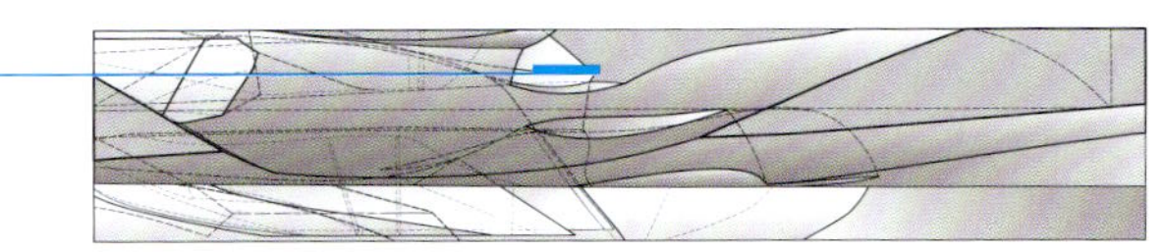

AI.06

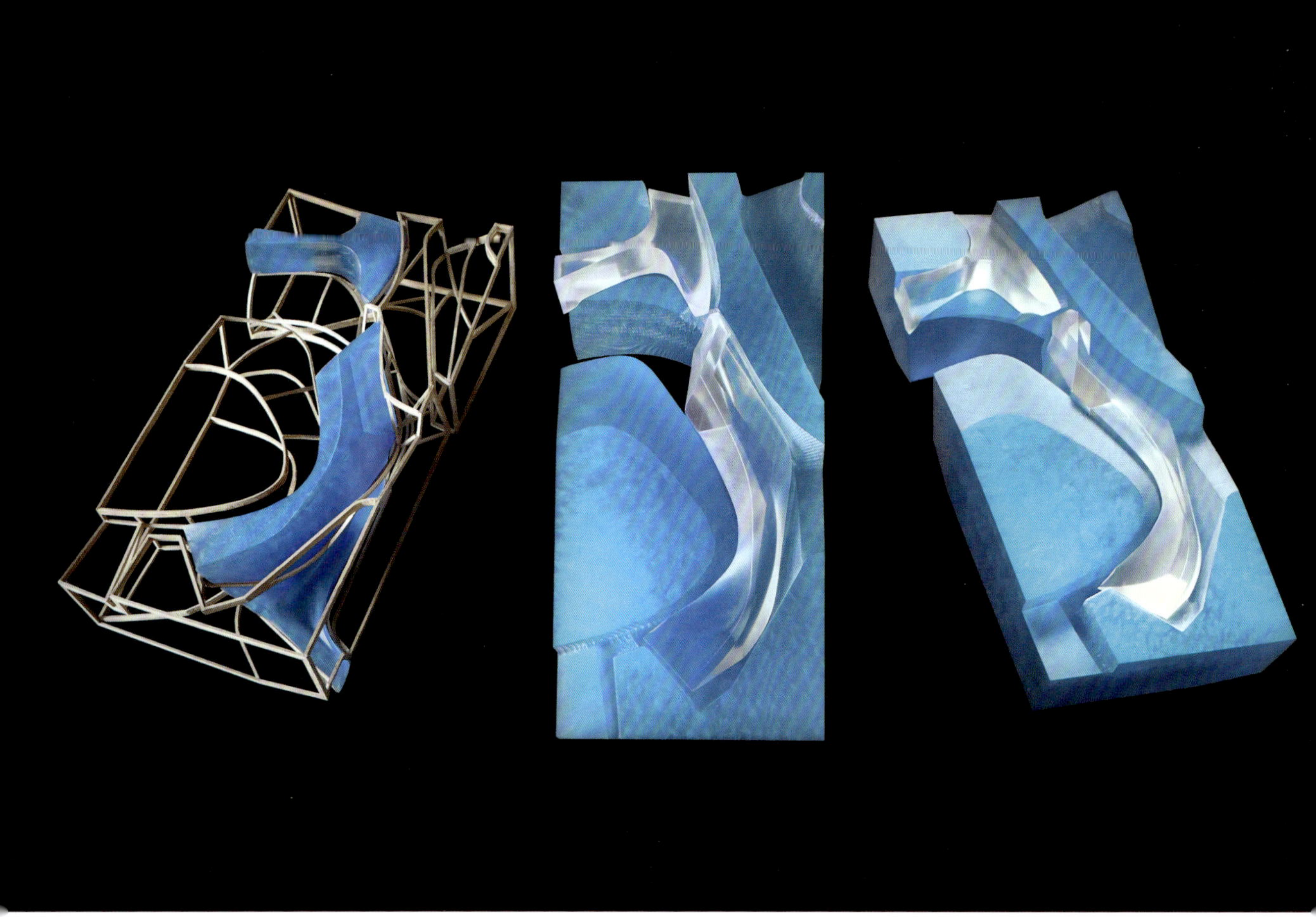

  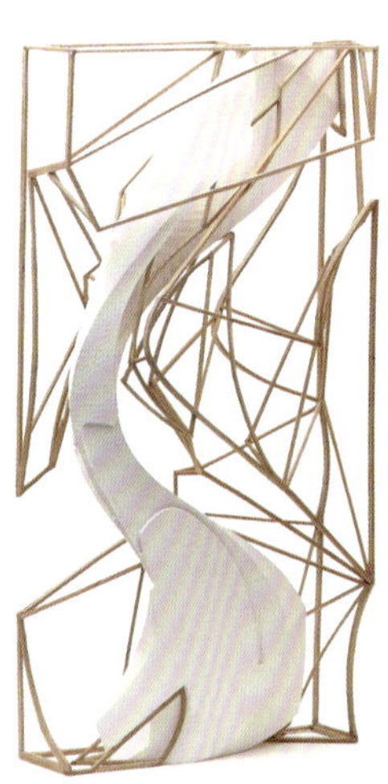 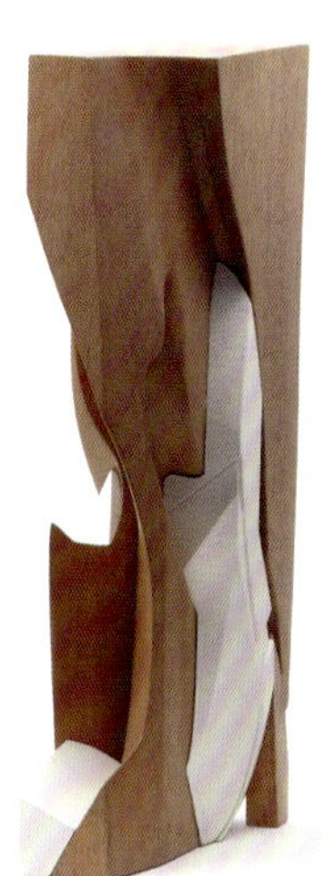 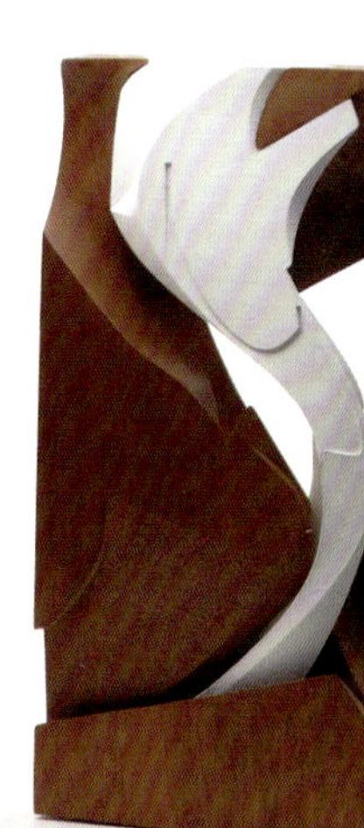

Conceived of as being part of a larger contiguous field of rectilinear volumes (now removed from their original location and proximity to others), the studies also include external markings that invite geometric dialogues. These exterior markings or voids are suggestive of missing, relocated, or shifted elements. This strategy also exists at a much smaller scale as seams on the internal objects, constricting and expanding in width, suggesting geometric relationships. Viewed in isolation, the surface treatments found at the various scales may appear to be simple markings, but they find greater resonance when considered collectively as part of a larger set of dialogues.

The full collection of *Active Inlay* studies includes the exploration of translucent materials and frame-based volumes that reveal the true inner workings of the elements.

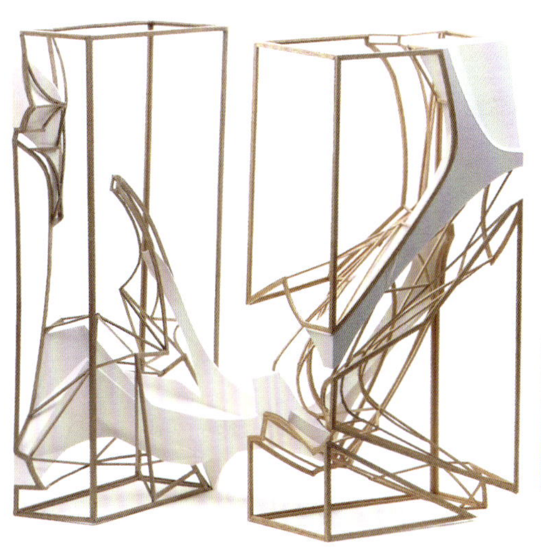

INLAY
FIELD

Building on the work of Active Inlays, Inlay Field considers a more interrelated and expansive network of elements. Analogous to a set of urban relationships, the investigations explore the ways in which an adapting and transformative network of connections might be placed in dialogue with a volumetric field. The idea is to maintain a repetitive space between volumes of various sizes, with eccentric volumes puncturing, carving, penetrating, or nestling as they find their place in the overall collection of parts.

Each object that intersects the field is three dimensional, but is consumed, obscured, and disrupted as a result of its movements from one volume to the next. These encounters create eccentric geometries and overlapping conditions where ambiguities of solid and void can come into view, and where subtle dialogues between parts are ever-present. Comprised of both linear frames and solid volumes, the objects swirl and twist as they move through the field, embedding themselves into carved volumes that fix them in a state of dynamic repose.

PUZZLES STRIVE FOR A SENSE OF COMPLETION. PARTS OF A PUZZLE ARE INTENTIONALLY DESIGNED TO PROVIDE JUST ENOUGH INFORMATION TO REQUIRE ENGAGEMENT BETWEEN THEM, AND YET REMAIN ELUSIVE.

BRICKS & TOTEMS

Expanding on the discoveries of our Primitive cube studies, and learning from the scaleless interactions of Active Inlays, Bricks & Totems explore a focused yet expansive approach to connected parts through rectilinear "bricks" and "totems." These complex, three-dimensional puzzles explore a range of connection techniques that spin, turn, jostle, pocket, click, and lock to articulate their assembly methods.

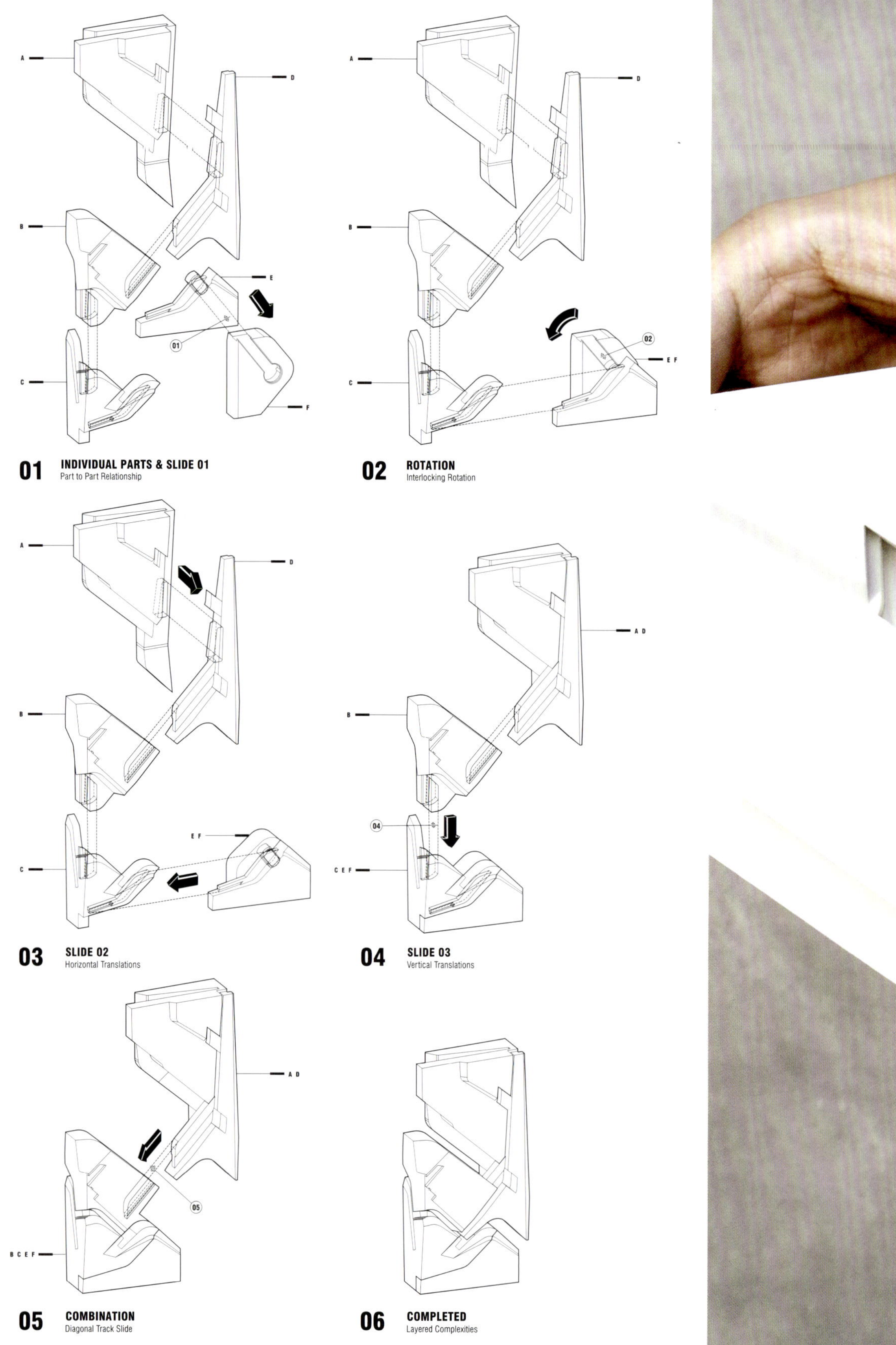

01 **INDIVIDUAL PARTS & SLIDE 01**
Part to Part Relationship

02 **ROTATION**
Interlocking Rotation

03 **SLIDE 02**
Horizontal Translations

04 **SLIDE 03**
Vertical Translations

05 **COMBINATION**
Diagonal Track Slide

06 **COMPLETED**
Layered Complexities

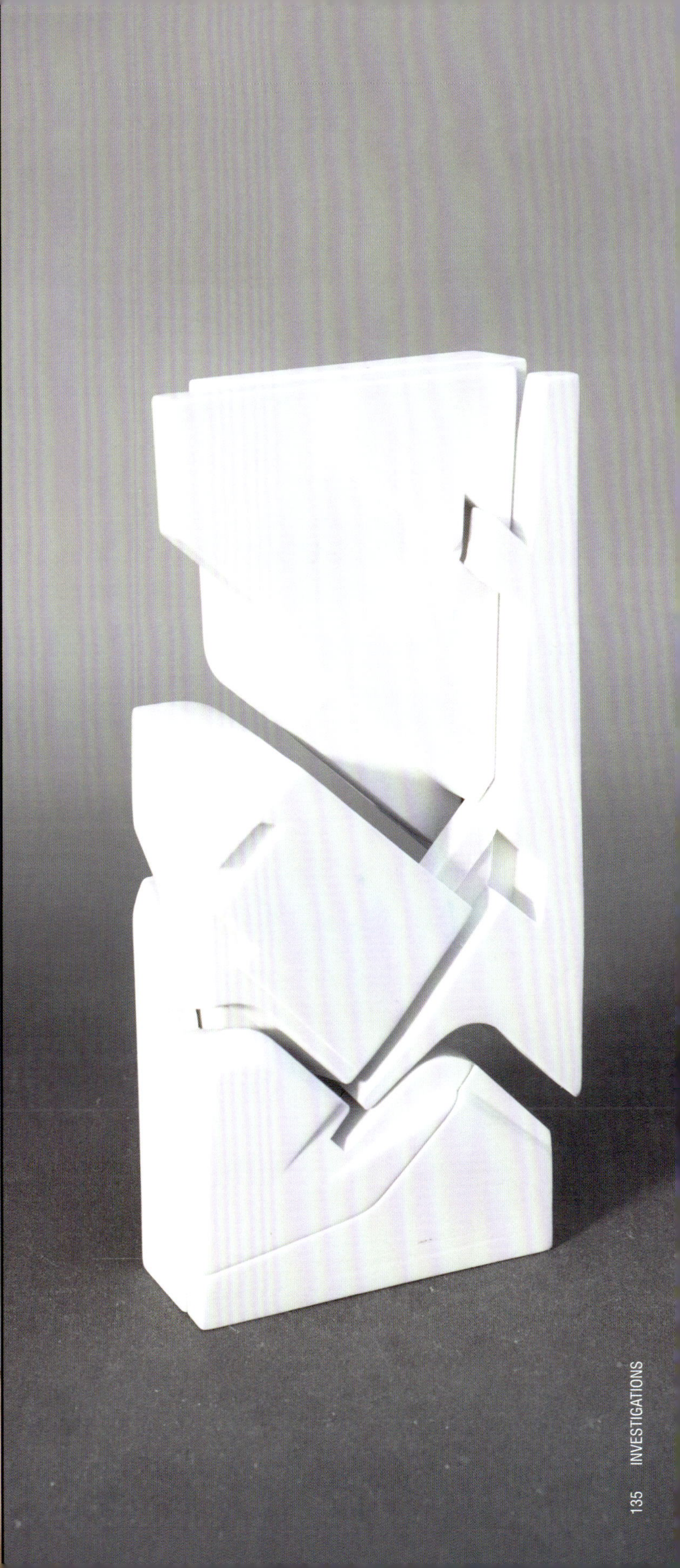

PZ.02

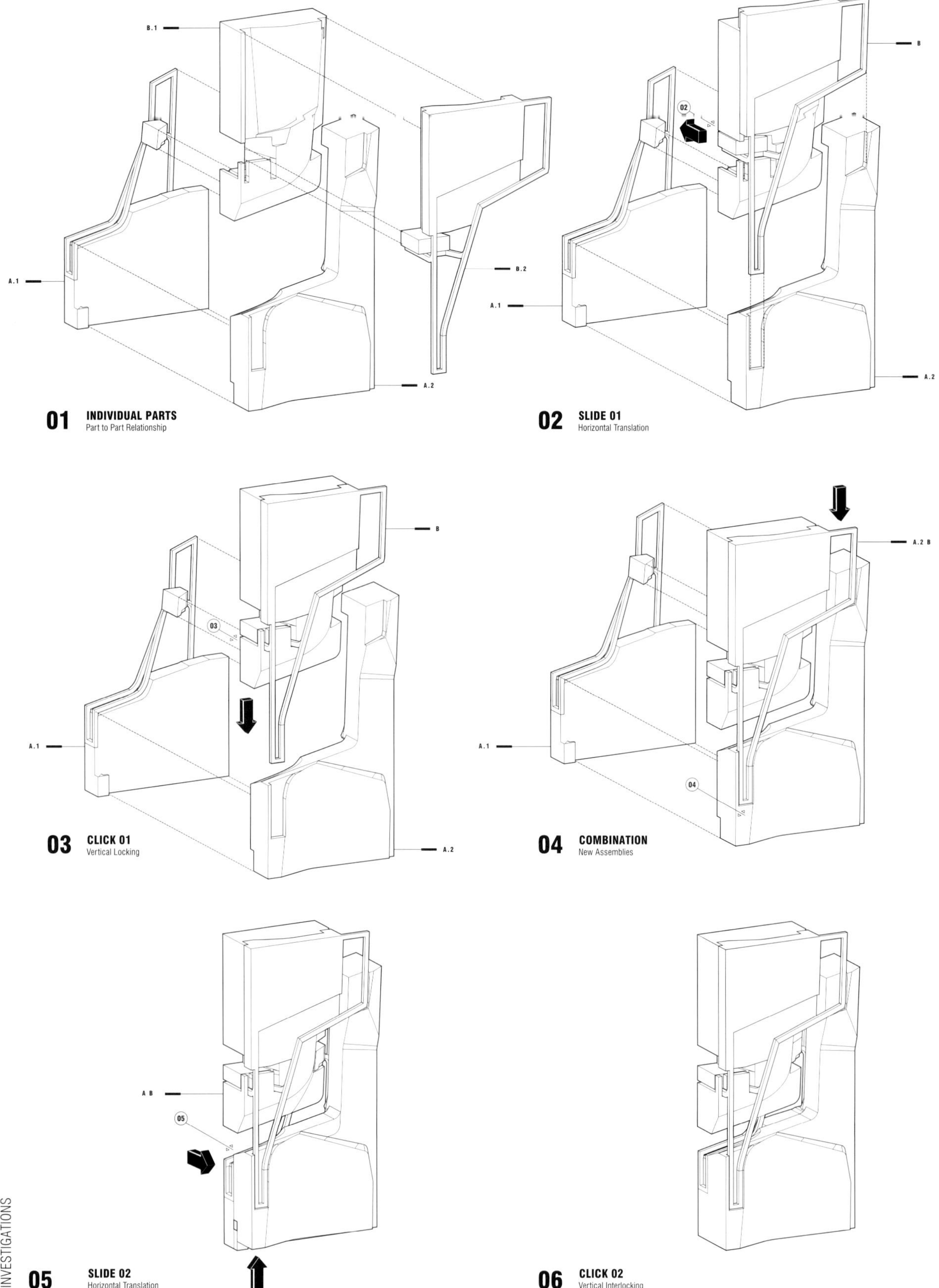

01 **INDIVIDUAL PARTS**
Part to Part Relationship

02 **SLIDE 01**
Horizontal Translation

03 **CLICK 01**
Vertical Locking

04 **COMBINATION**
New Assemblies

05 **SLIDE 02**
Horizontal Translation

06 **CLICK 02**
Vertical Interlocking

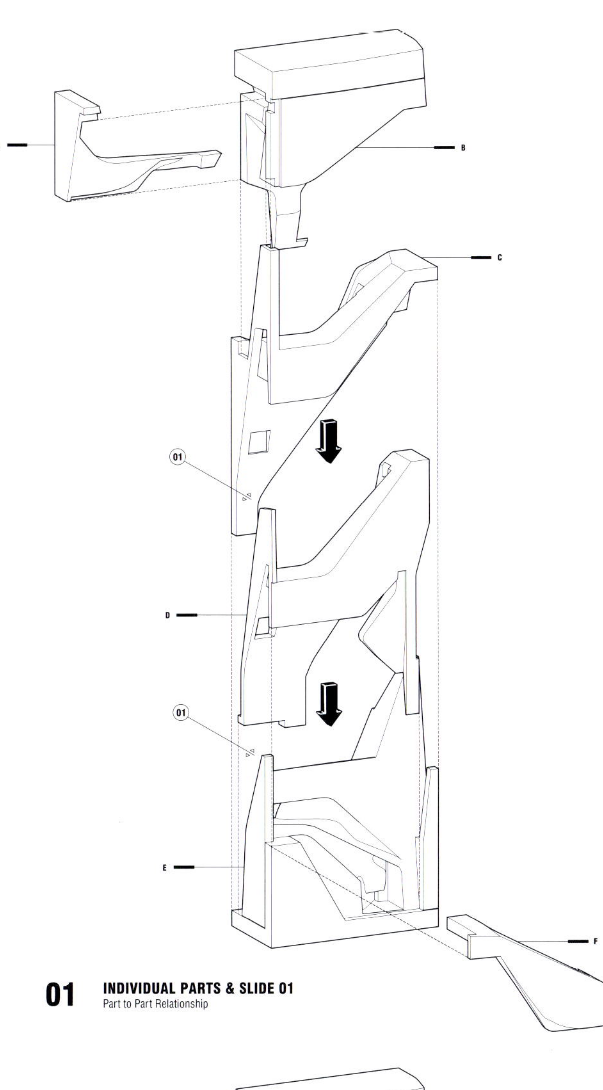

01 **INDIVIDUAL PARTS & SLIDE 01**
Part to Part Relationship

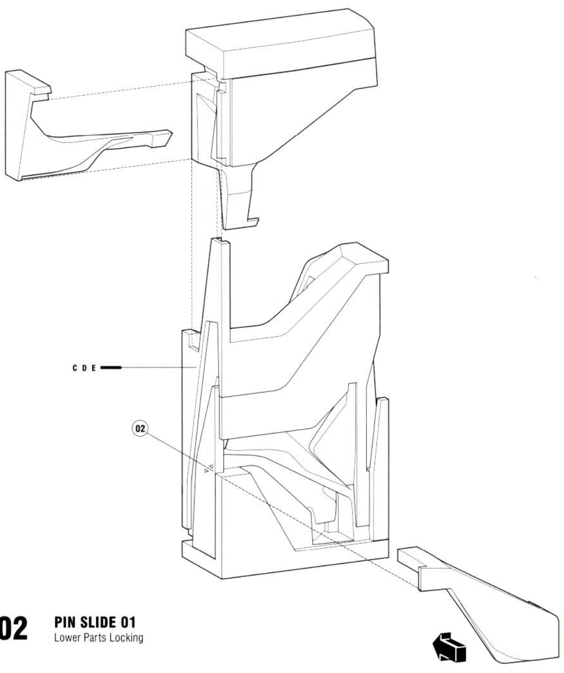

02 **PIN SLIDE 01**
Lower Parts Locking

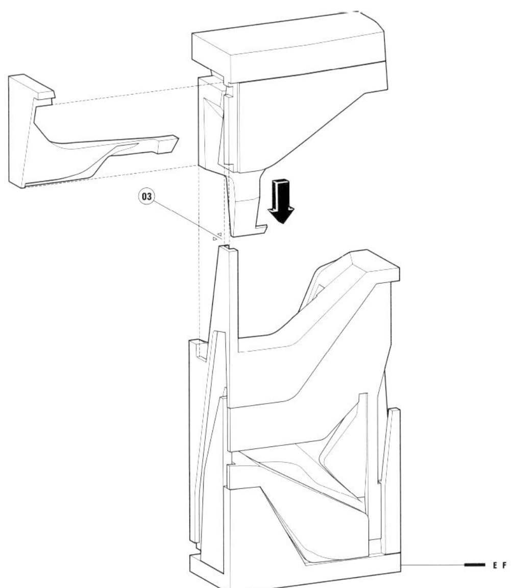

03 **SLIDE 02**
Vertical Translation

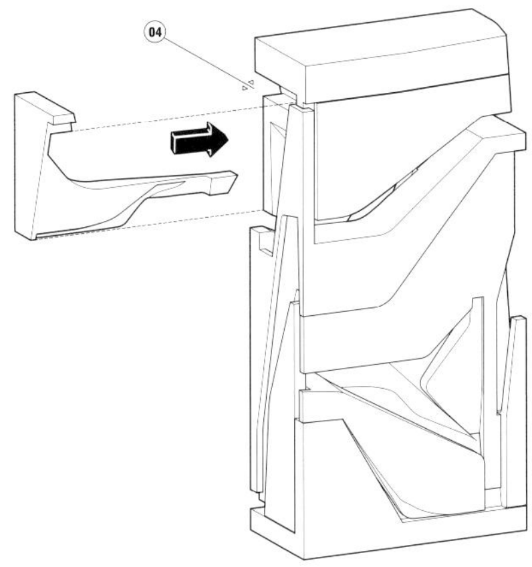

04 **PIN SLIDE 02**
Vertical Locking

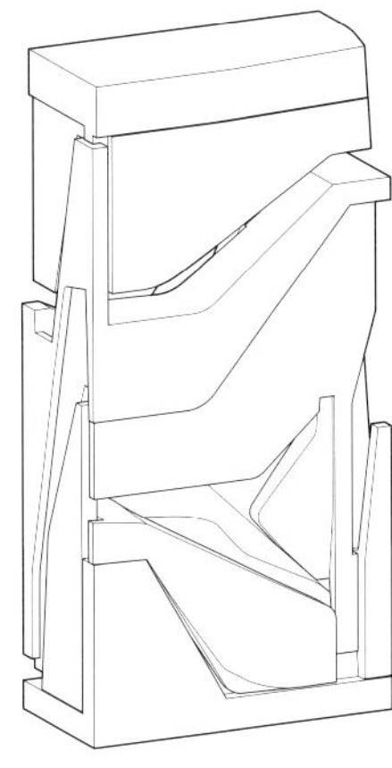

05 **COMPLETED**
Layered Complexities

Because each study is produced with the intention of being constructed and dismantled, the characteristics of each face suggest both the method of assembly as well as the nature of its individual parts. In some cases, seemingly completed or interconnected parts are in fact extensions of formal traits from secondary, tertiary, or unlinked movements of others. The spatial qualities registered on the outer faces of the completed object prompt a physical engagement that reveals unexpected movements and strategically hidden alignments.

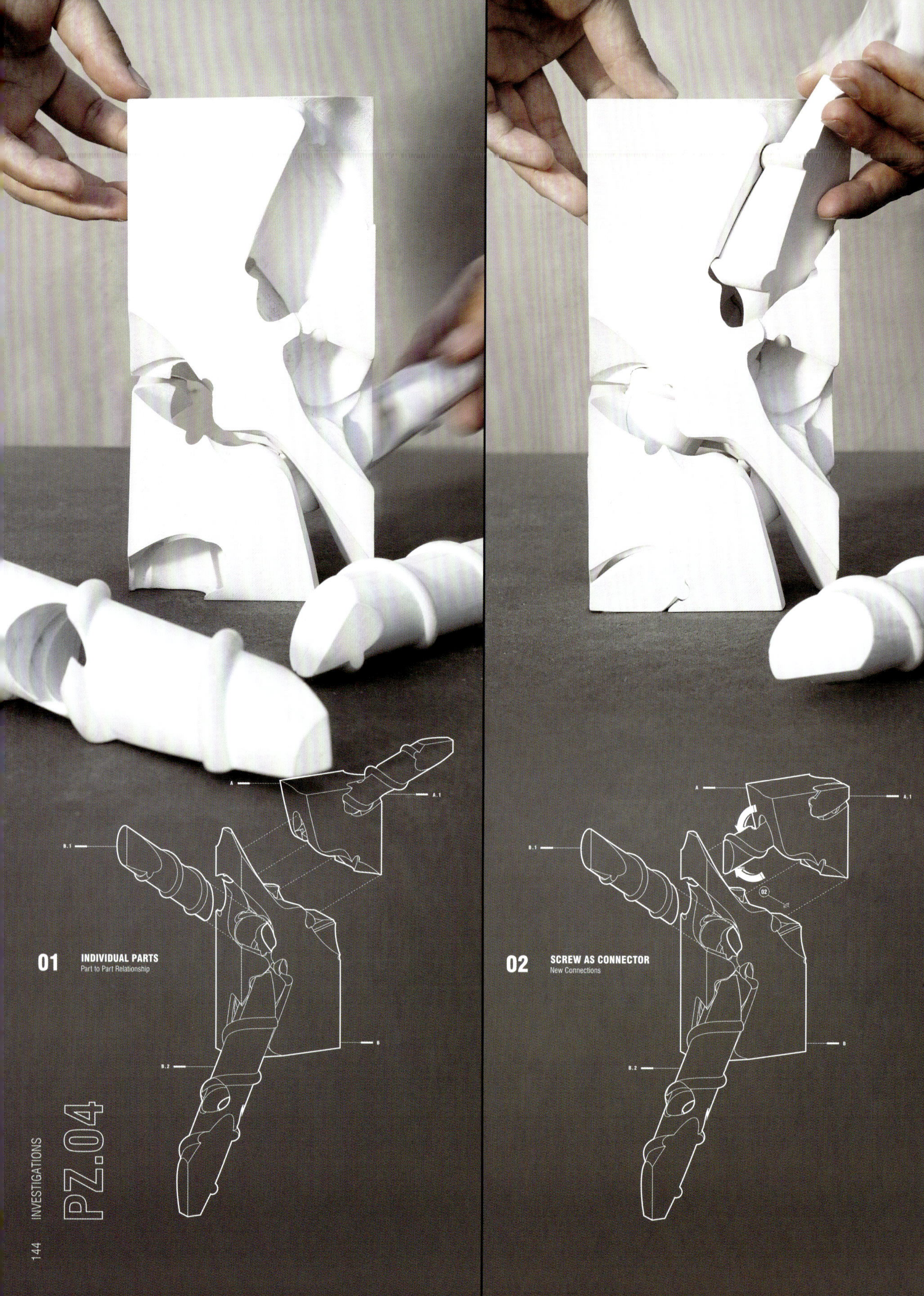

PZ.04
INVESTIGATIONS
144
01
INDIVIDUAL PARTS
Part to Part Relationship
A
A.1
B.1
B.2
B
02
SCREW AS CONNECTOR
New Connections
A
A.1
B.1
02
B.2
B

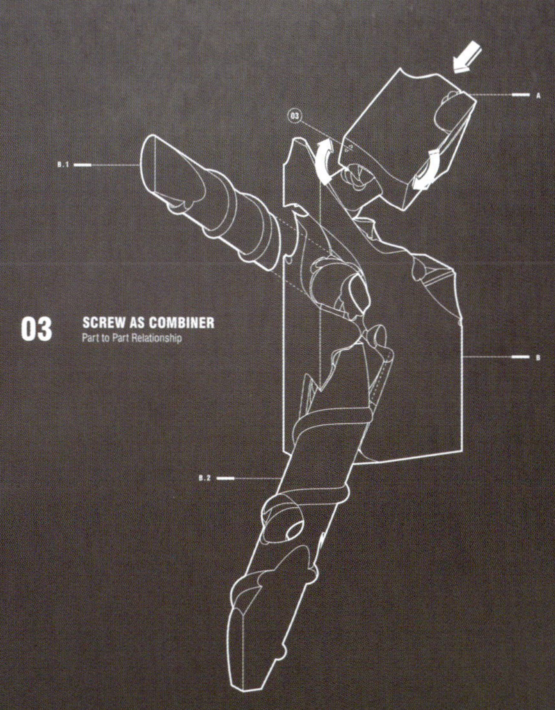

03 SCREW AS COMBINER
Part to Part Relationship

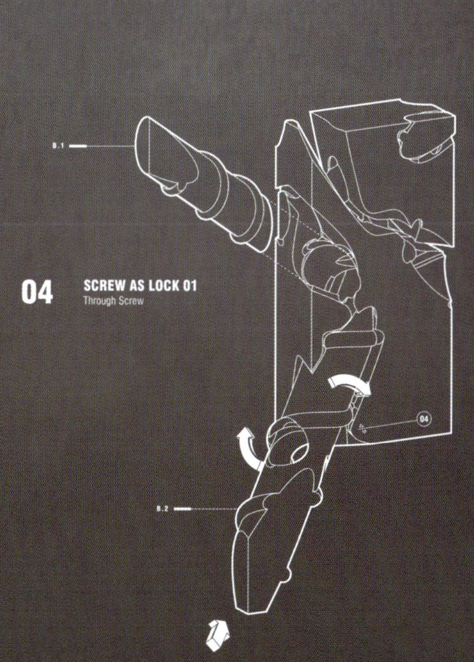

04 SCREW AS LOCK 01
Through Screw

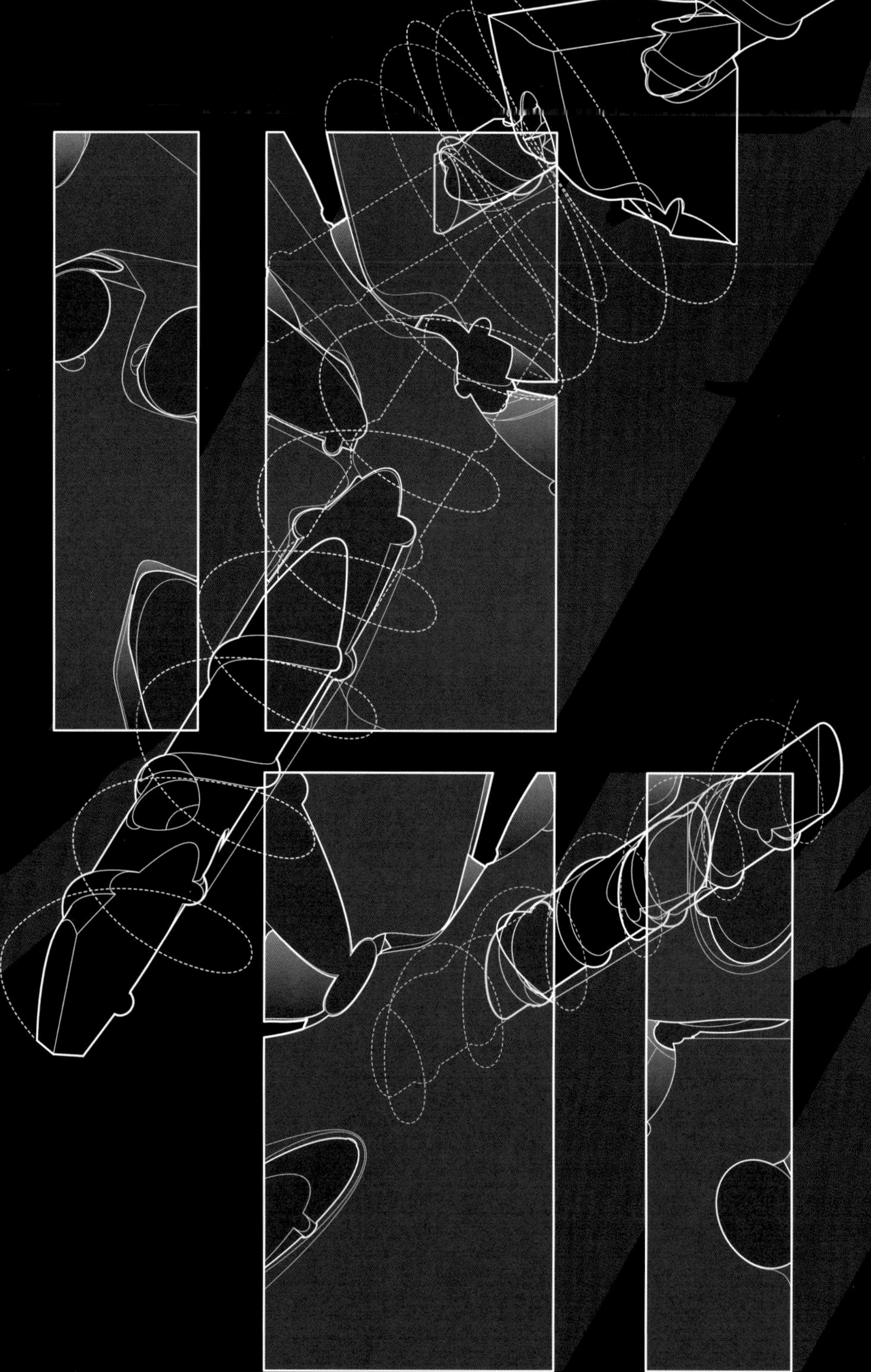

PUZZLES ARE DESIGNED TO CONCEAL THEIR PROCESS OF ASSEMBLY.

THEY EVADE AN IMMEDIATE UNDERSTANDING, AND CONSEQUENTLY ARE SLOW TO REVEAL THEIR ASSEMBLY LOGIC.

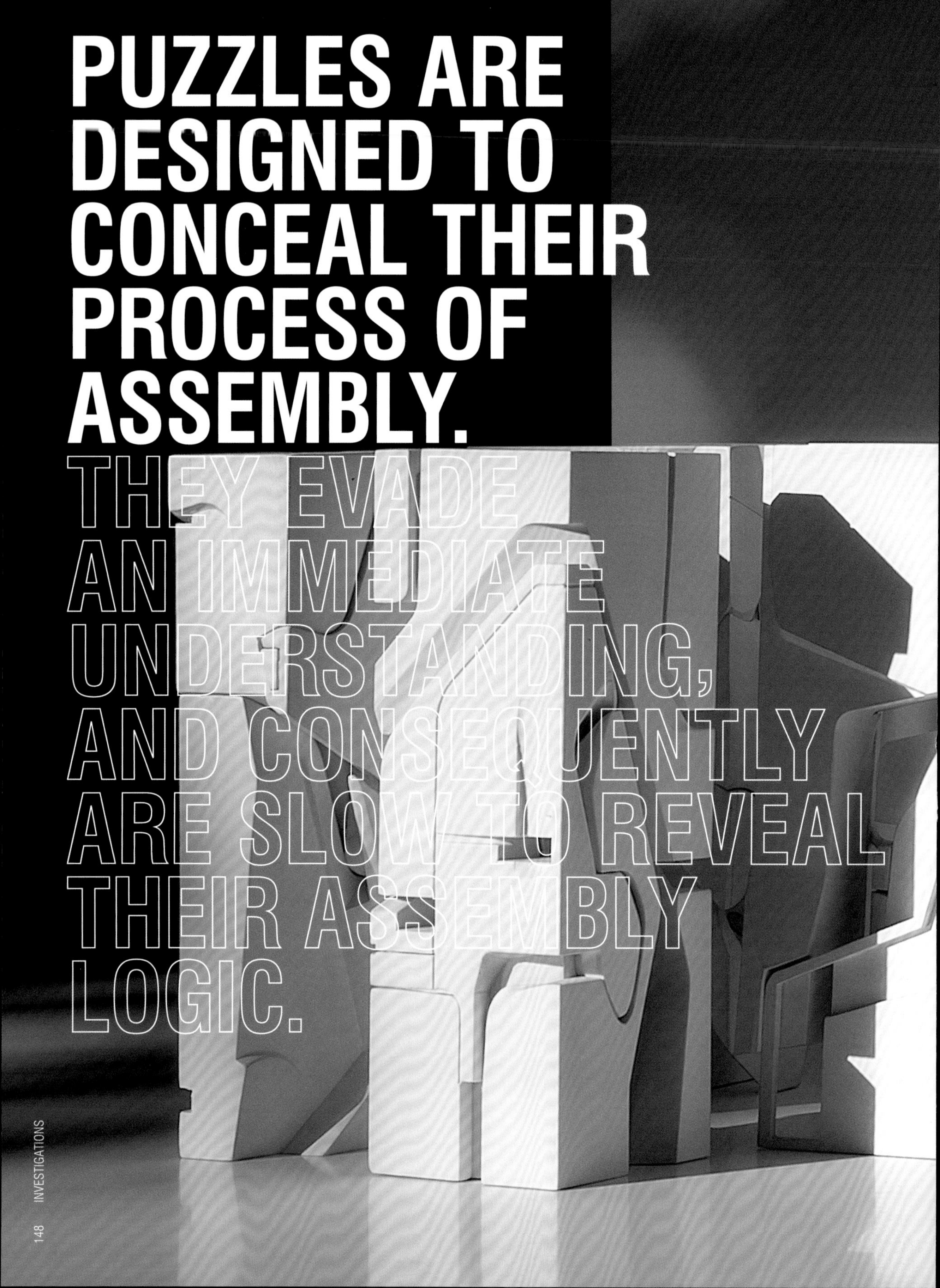

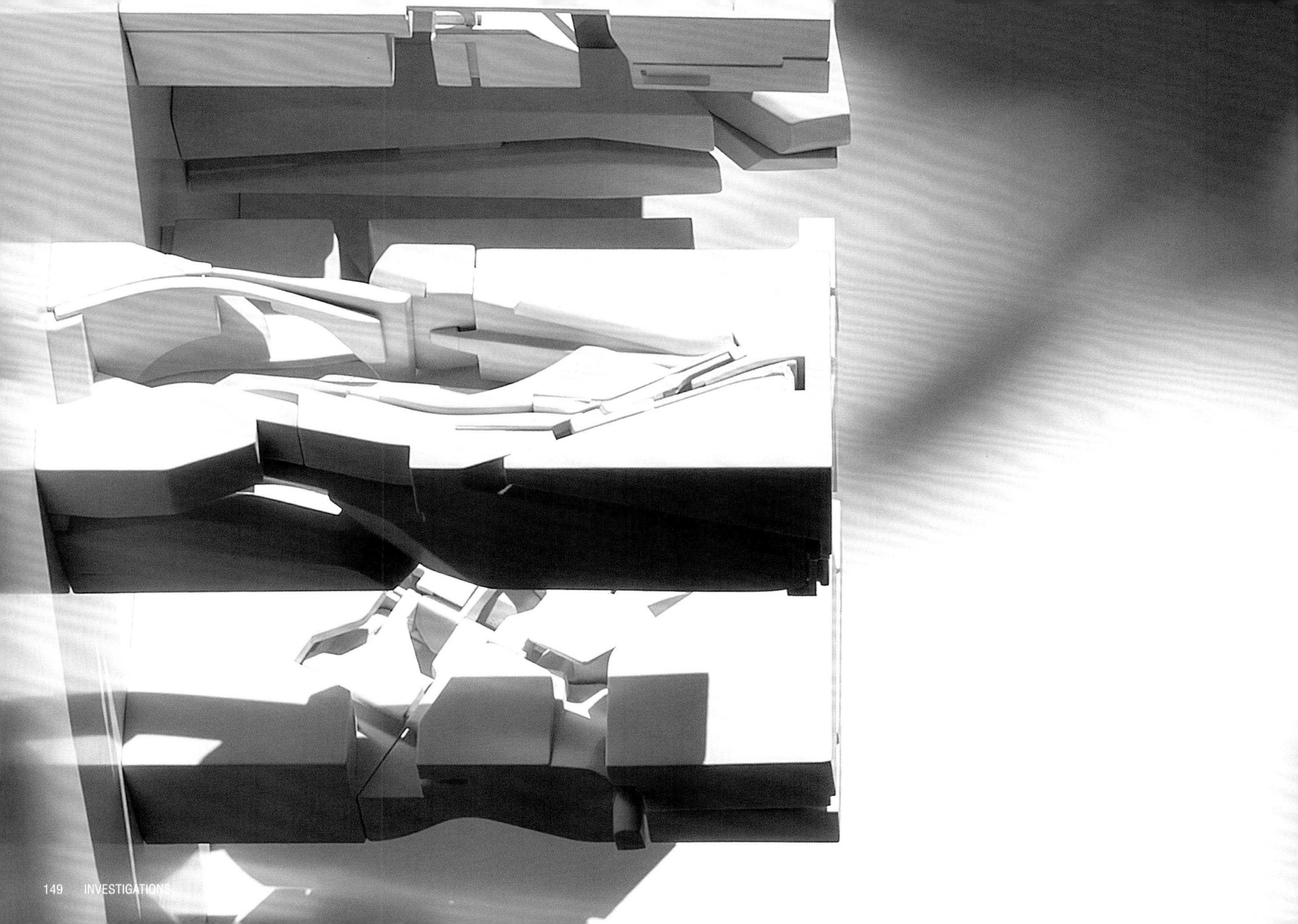

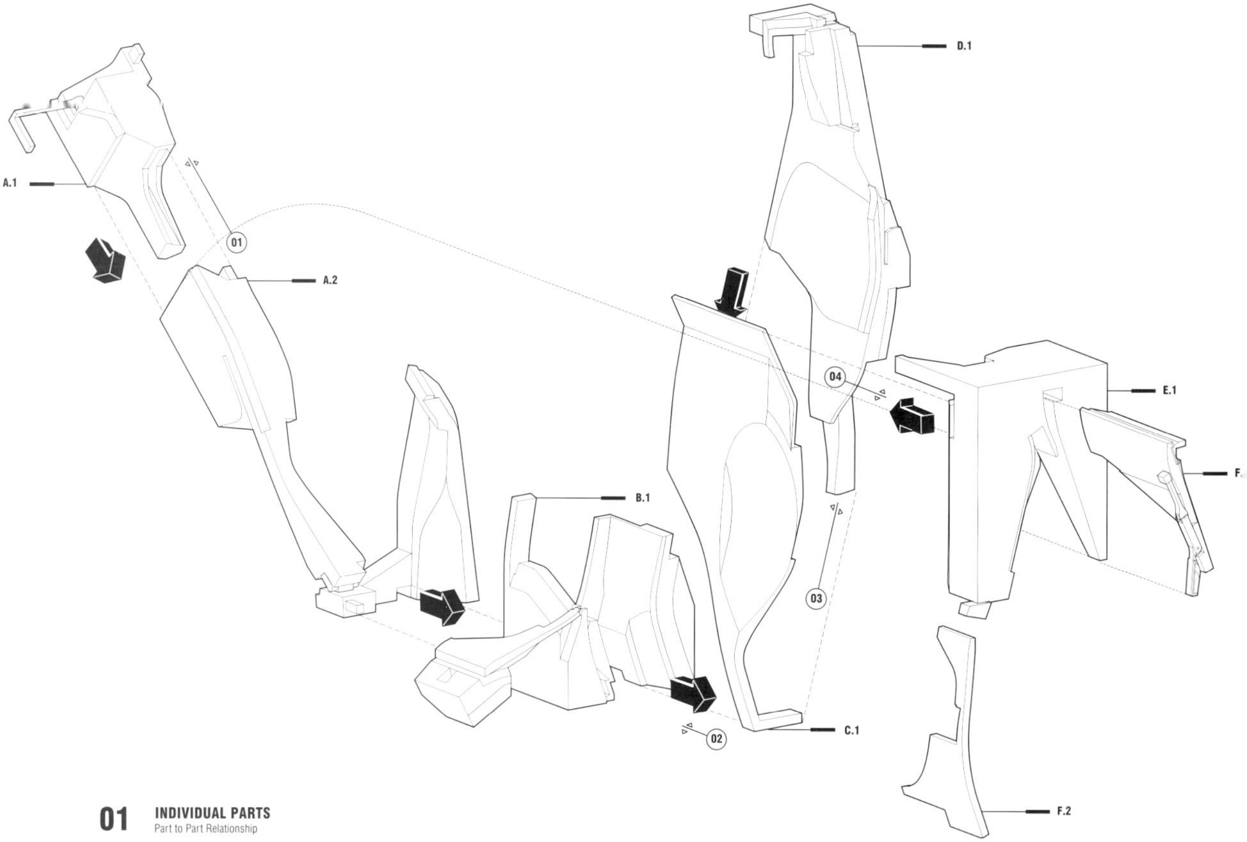

PZ.05

01 **INDIVIDUAL PARTS**
Part to Part Relationship

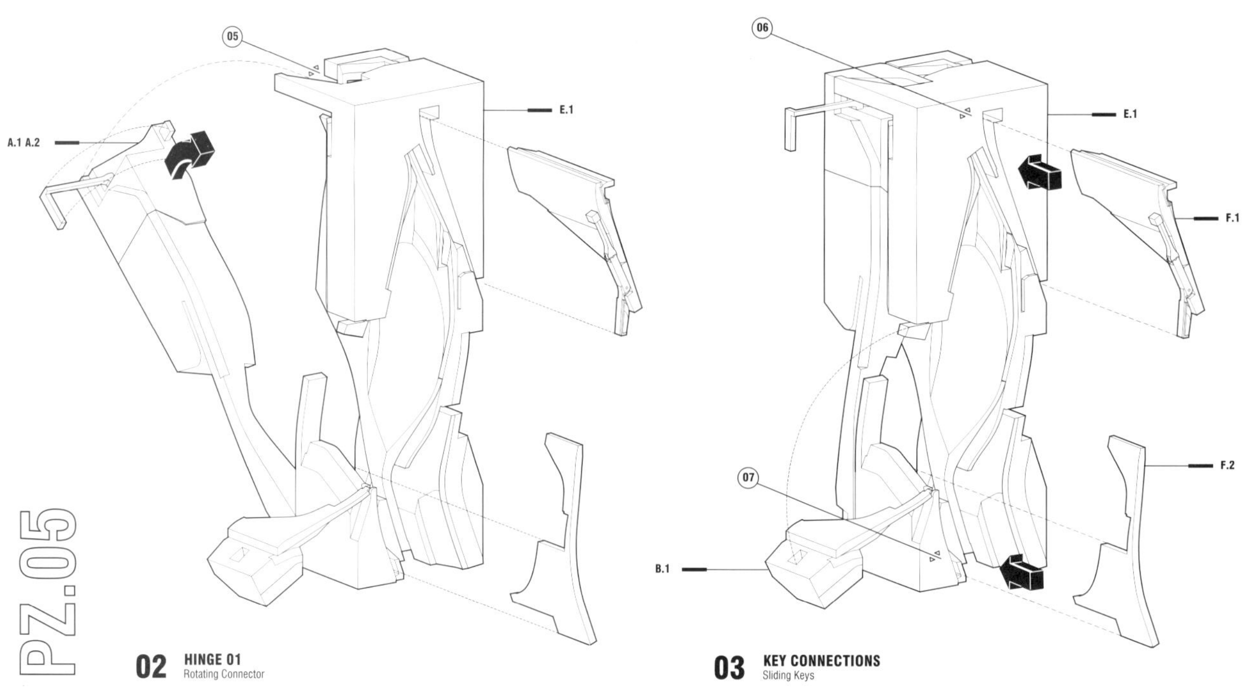

02 **HINGE 01**
Rotating Connector

03 **KEY CONNECTIONS**
Sliding Keys

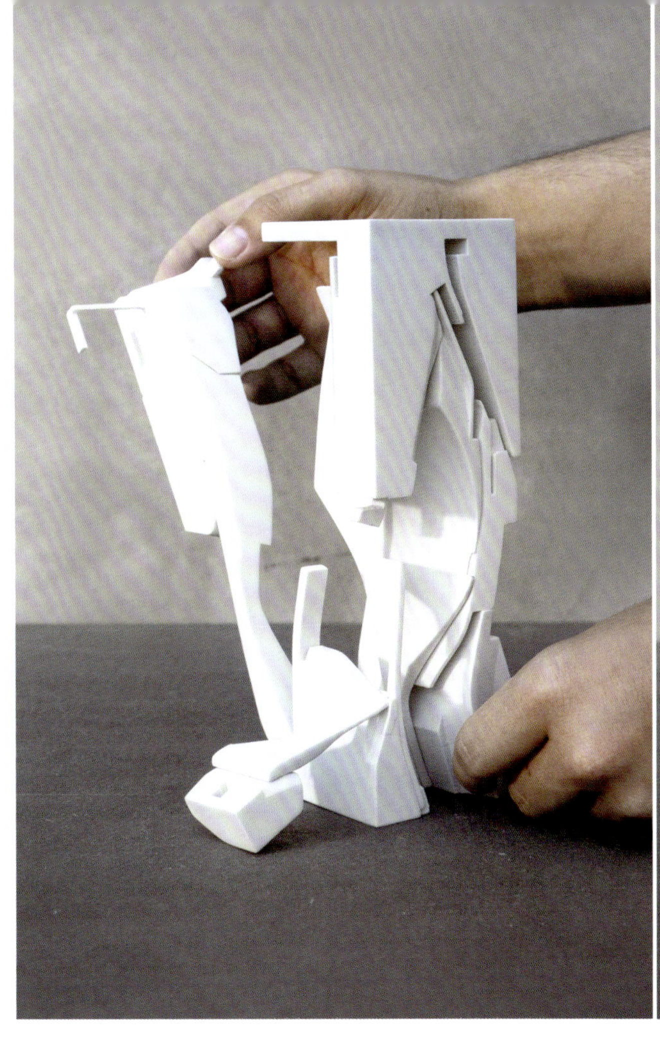

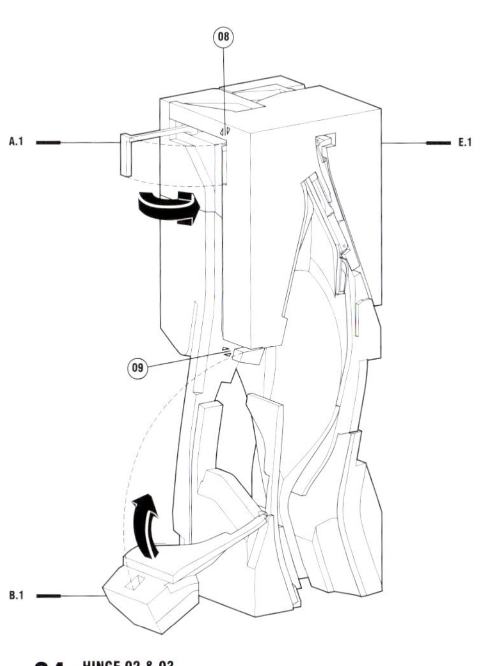

04 **HINGE 02 & 03**
Rotating Connector

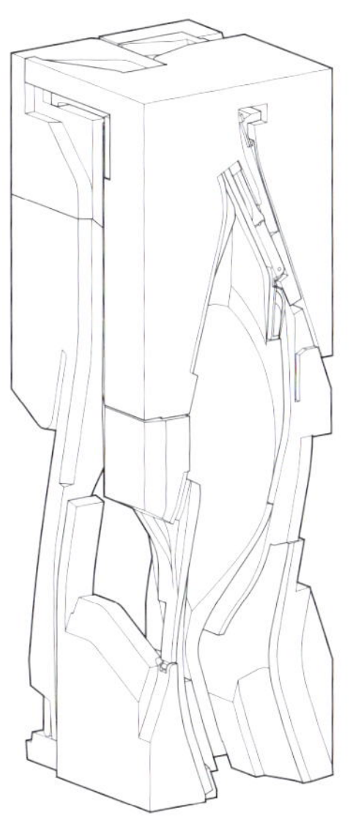

05 **COMPLETED**
Mechanical Inlay

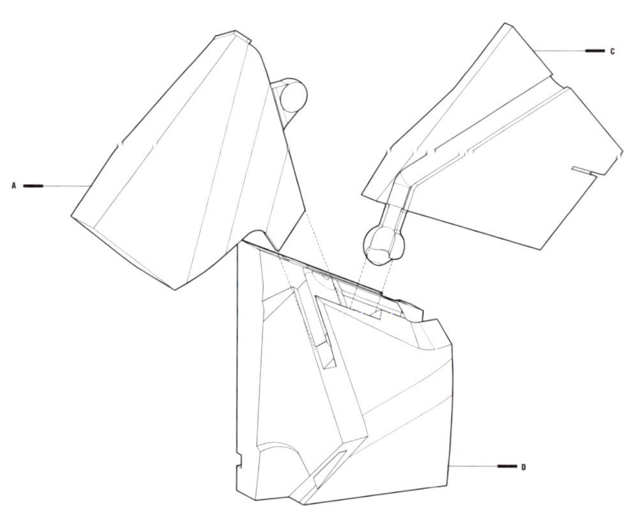

01 **INDIVIDUAL PARTS**
Part to Part Relationship

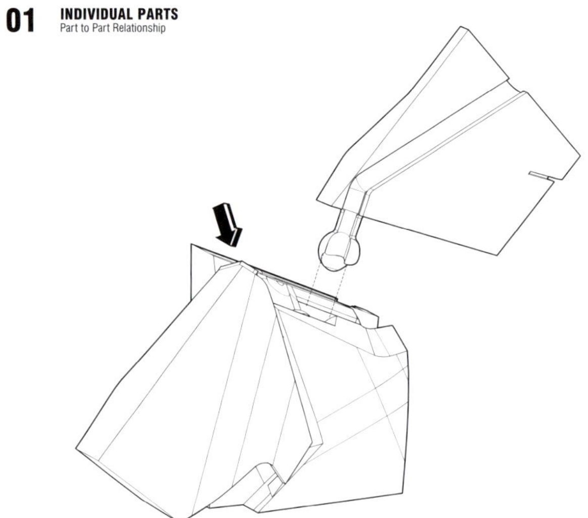

03 **CLICK 01**
Vertical Locking

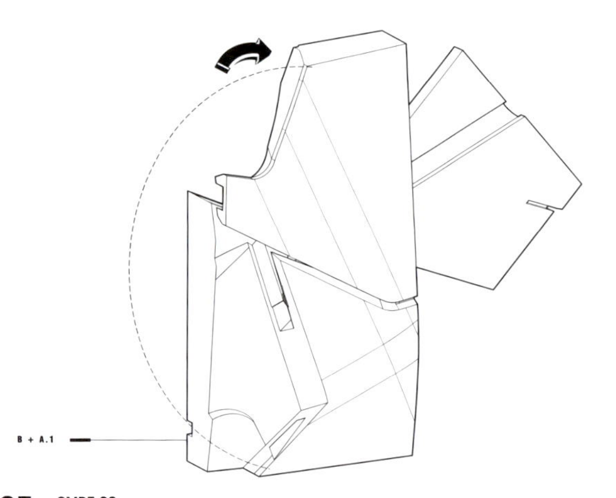

05 **SLIDE 02**
Horizontal Translation

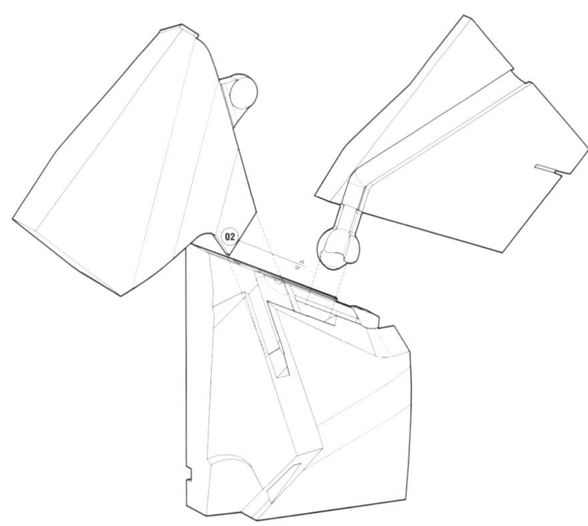

02 **SLIDE 01**
Horizontal Translation

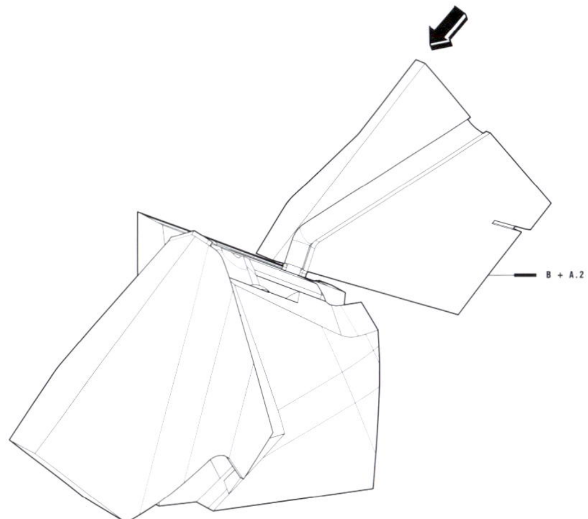

04 **COMBINATION**
New Assemblies

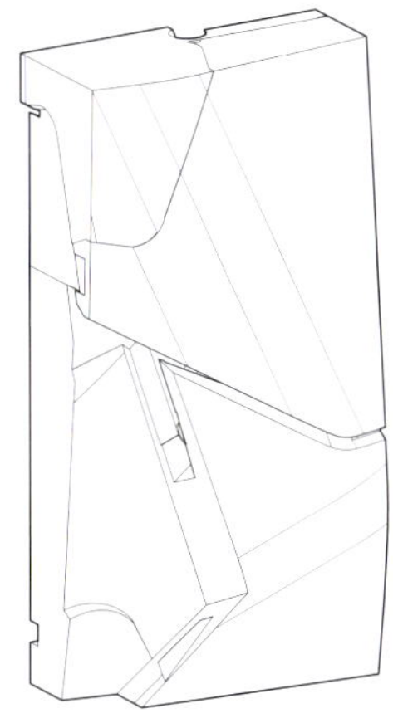

06 **CLICK 02**
Vertical Interlocking

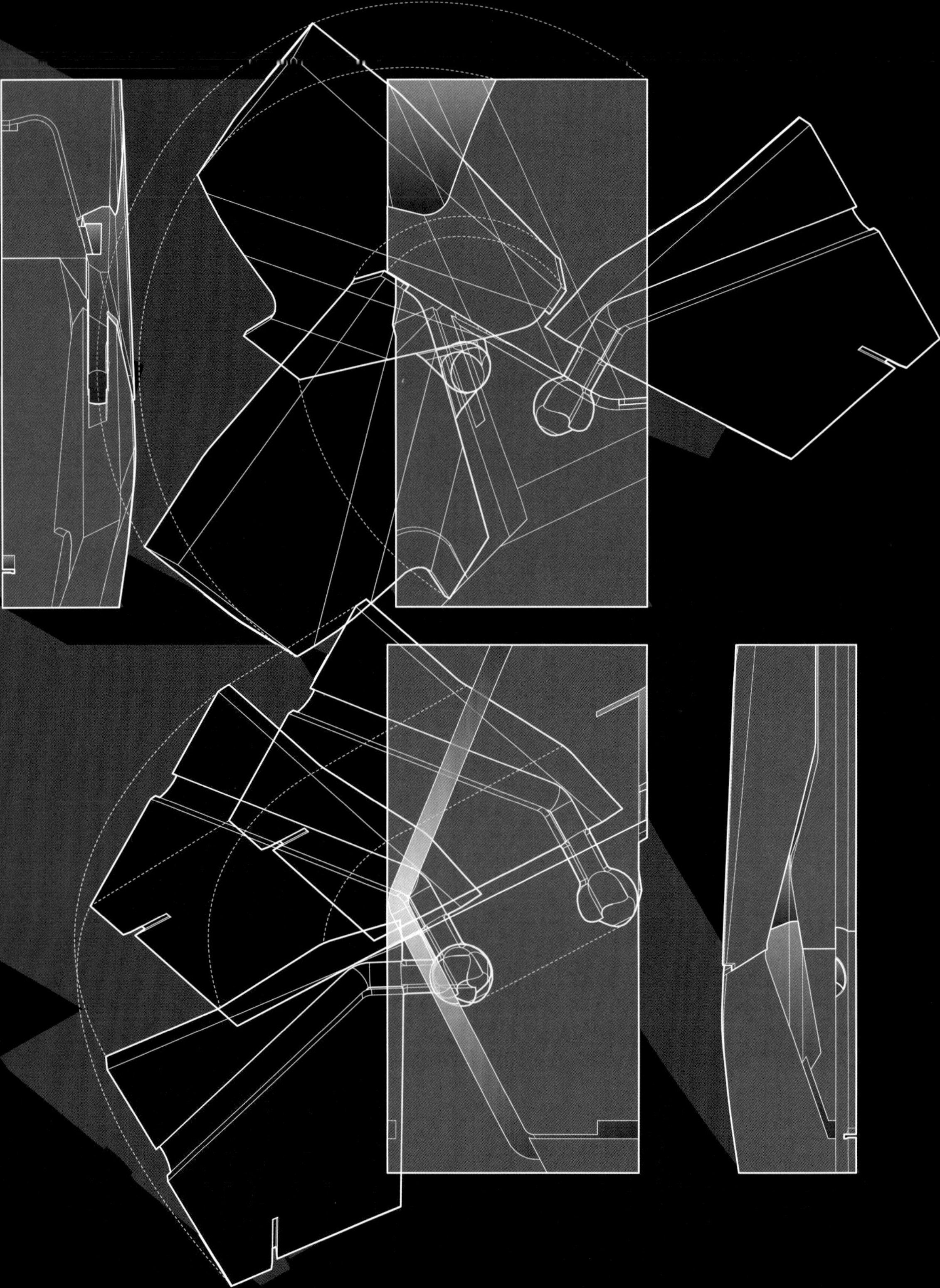

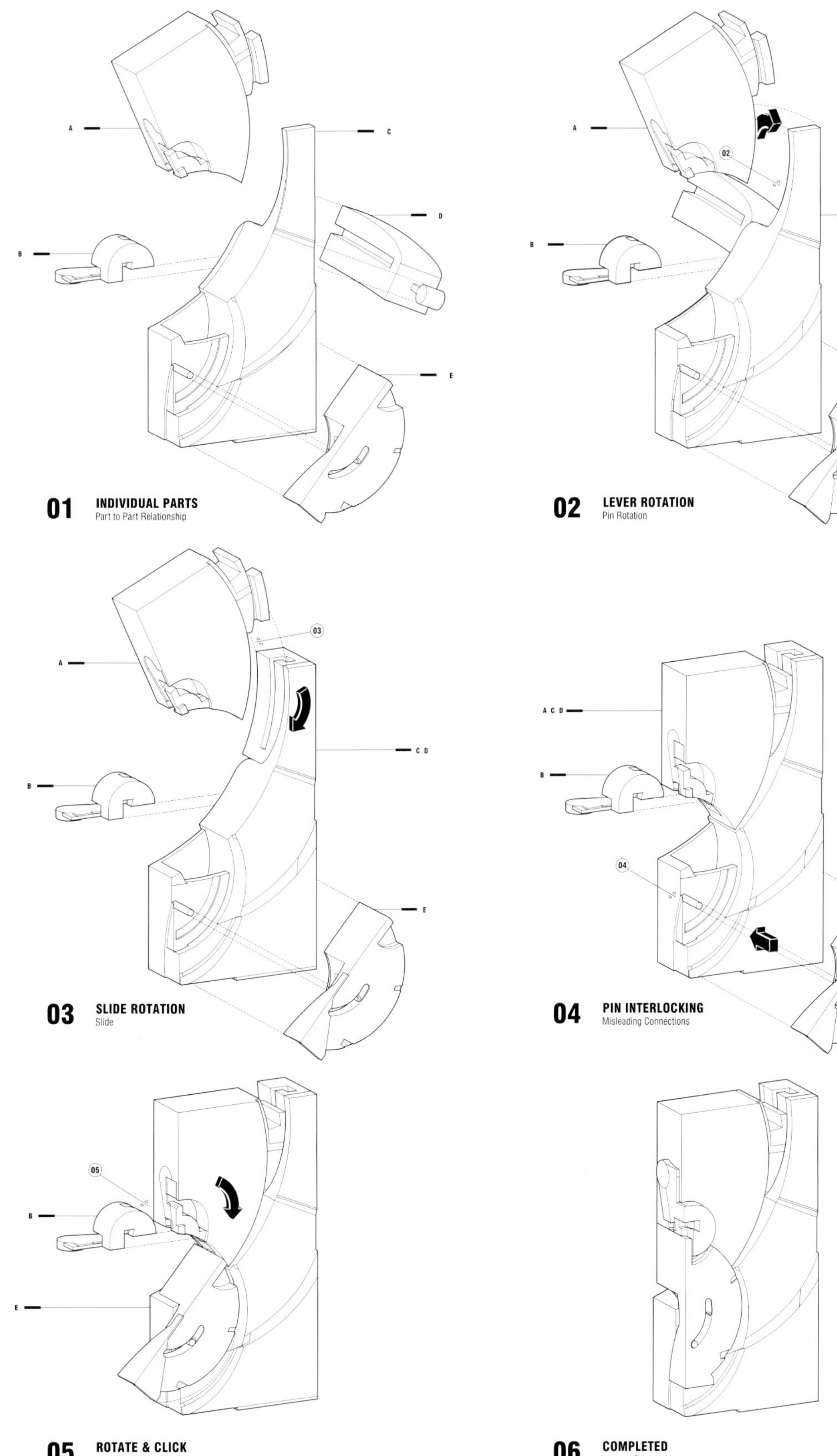

A
B
C
D
E
01 INDIVIDUAL PARTS
Part to Part Relationship
A
B
02
C D
E
02 LEVER ROTATION
Pin Rotation
A
B
03
C D
E
03 SLIDE ROTATION
Slide
A C D
B
04
E
04 PIN INTERLOCKING
Misleading Connections
B
05
E
05 ROTATE & CLICK
New Alignments
06 COMPLETED
Layered Complexities

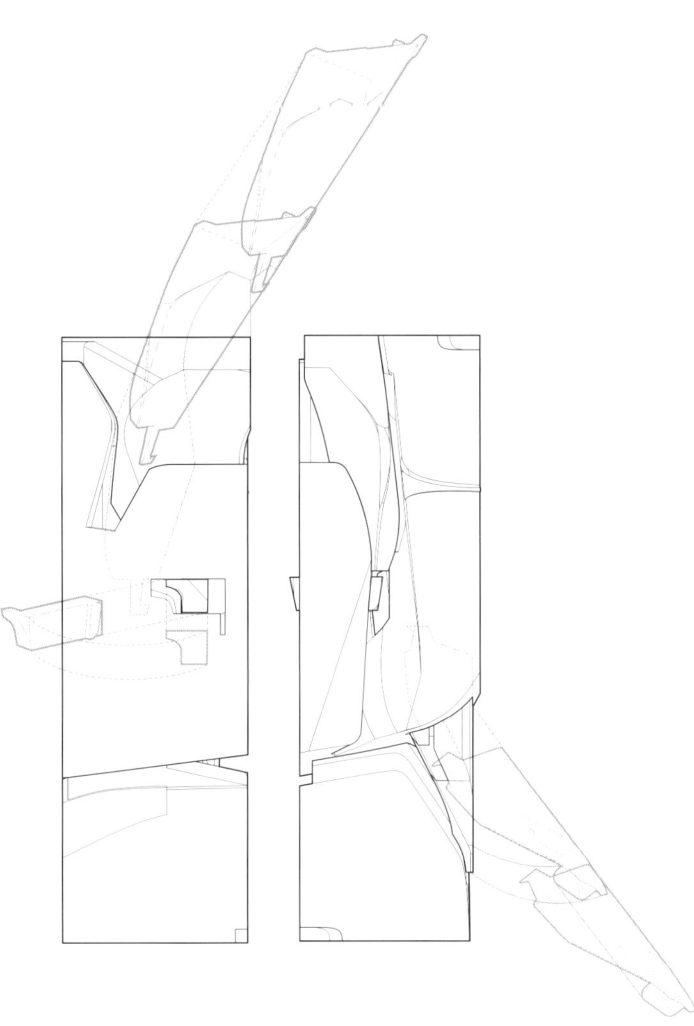

Each puzzle is evaluated not just as a form, but as an ideology—how it expresses both the part and the assembly, and how those readings contribute to engagement with the puzzle. The embedded logic in each individual shape subtly conveys continuities, connections, and volumetric combinations, yet delays the full understanding of the puzzle in order to produce an enlightening interaction.

PZ.08

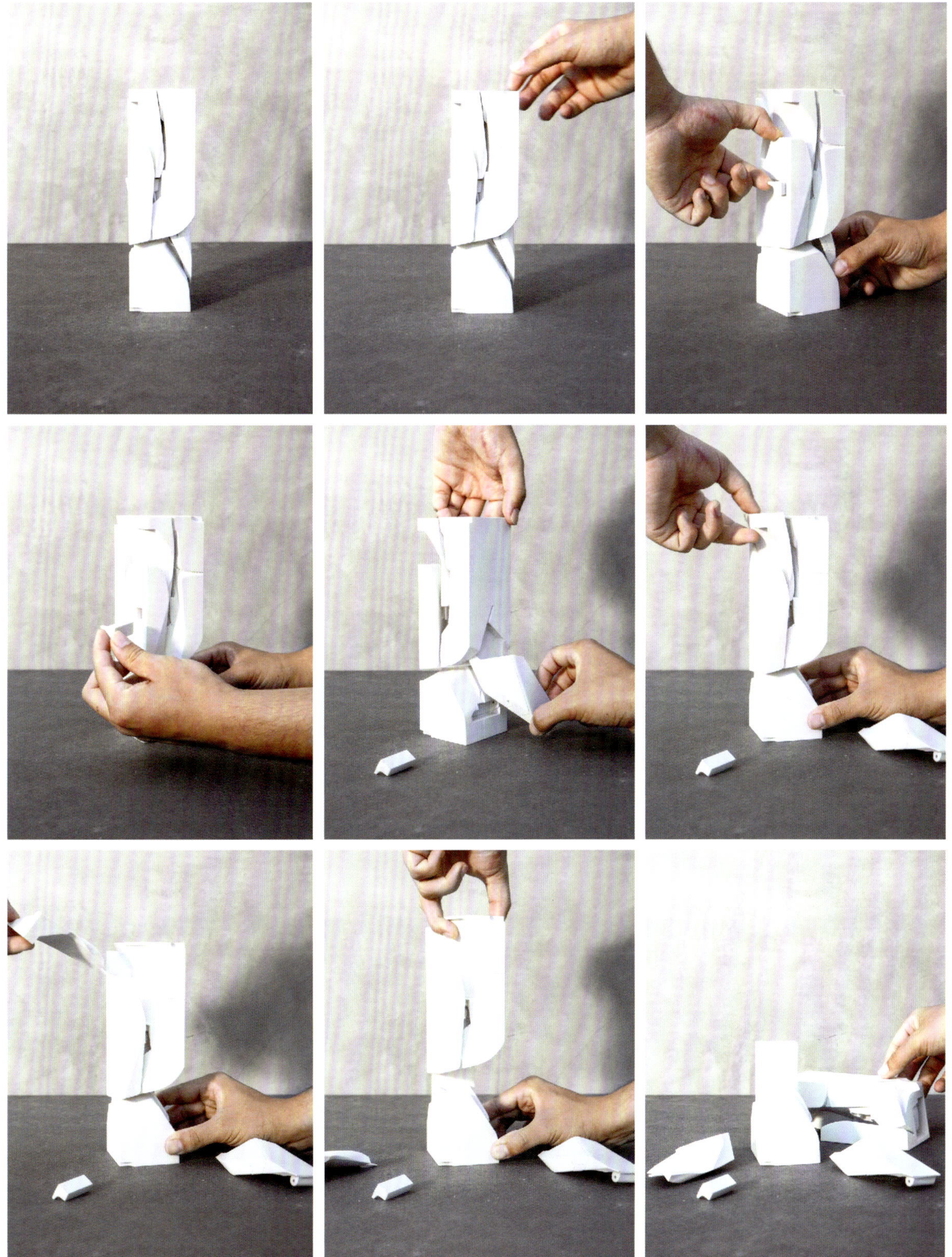

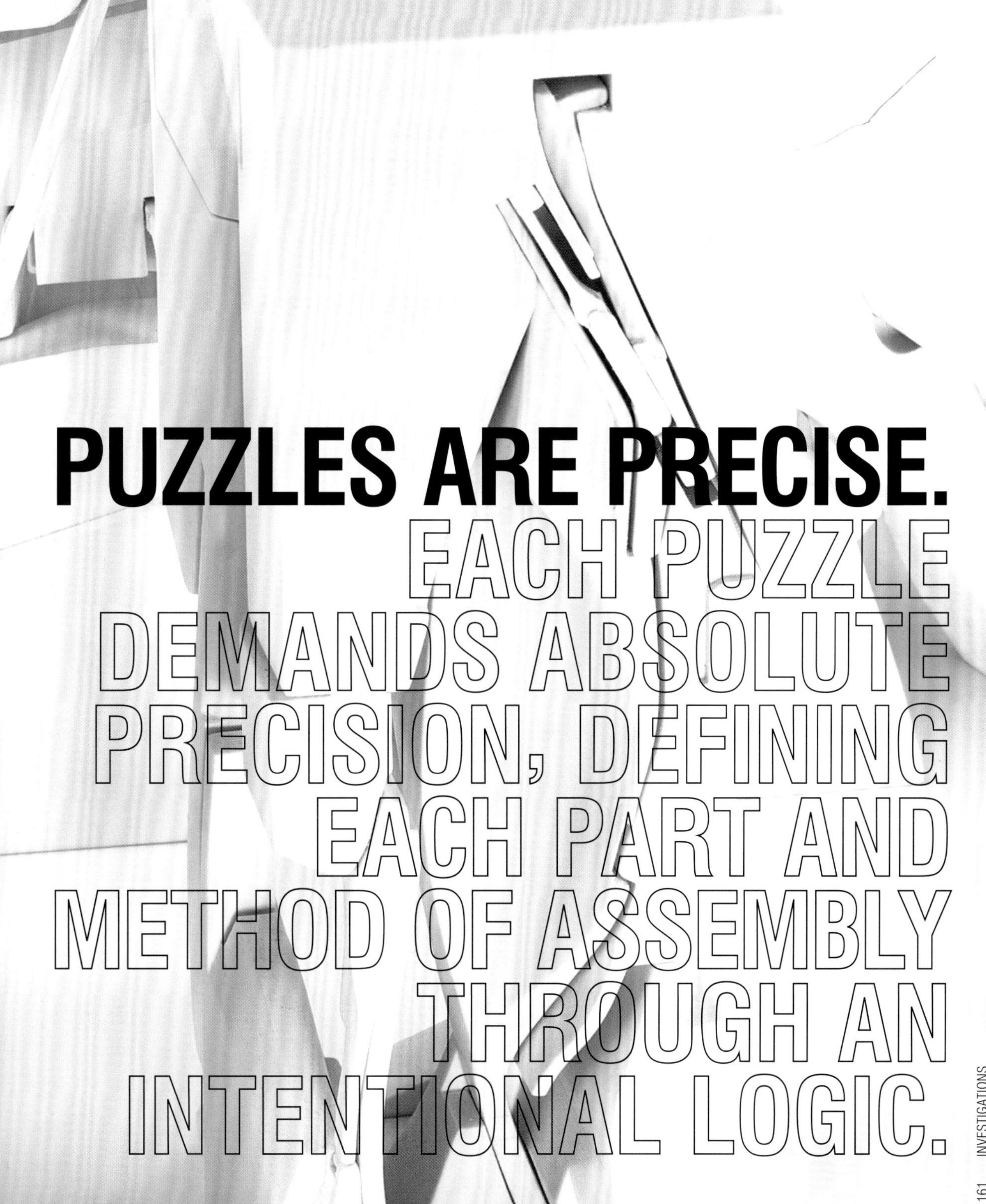

PUZZLES ARE PRECISE.
EACH PUZZLE DEMANDS ABSOLUTE PRECISION, DEFINING EACH PART AND METHOD OF ASSEMBLY THROUGH AN INTENTIONAL LOGIC.

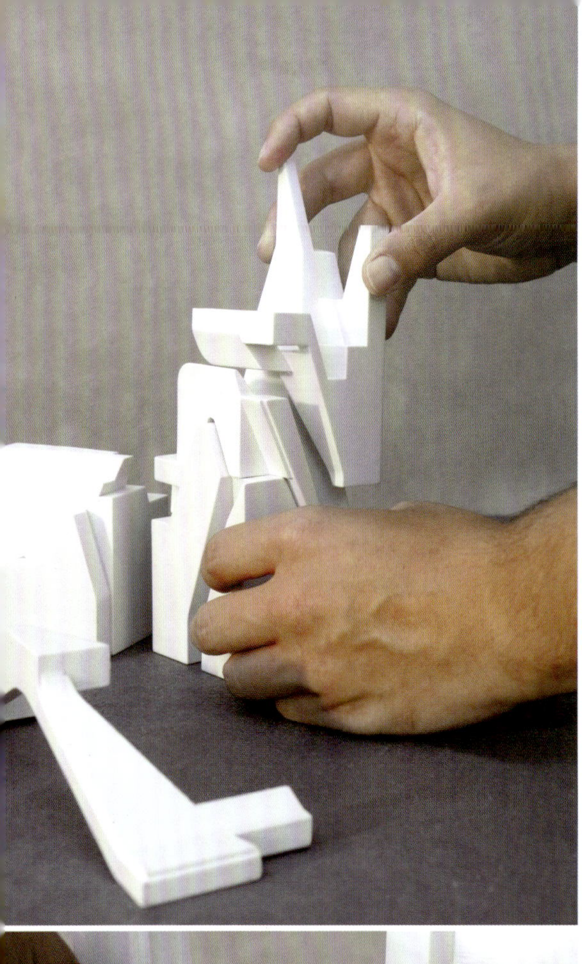

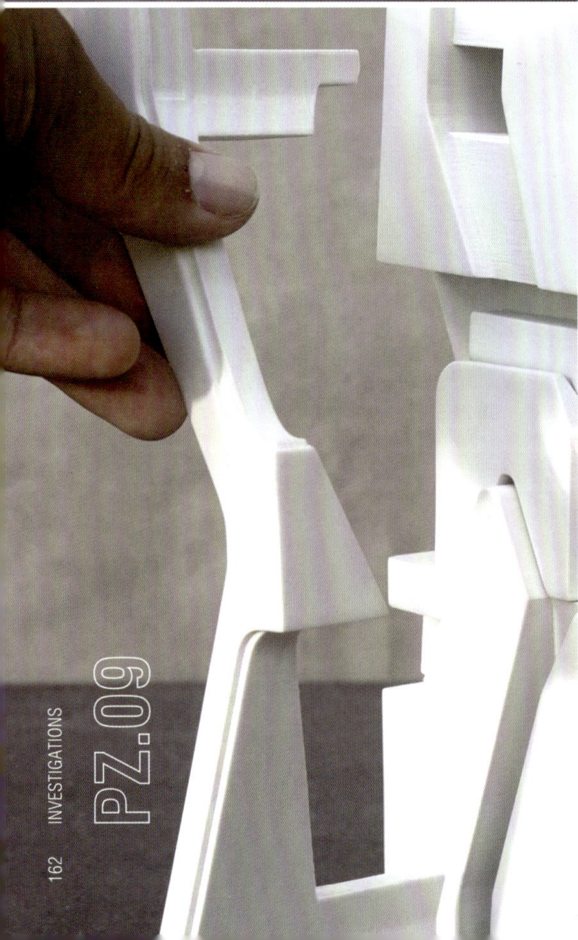

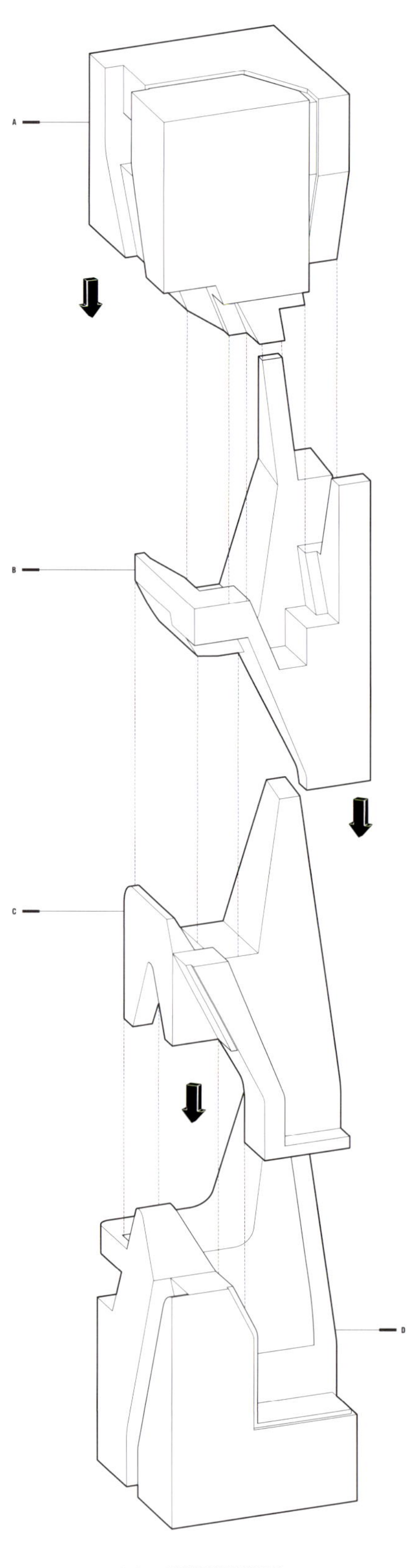

01 **INDIVIDUAL PARTS**
Part to Part Relationship

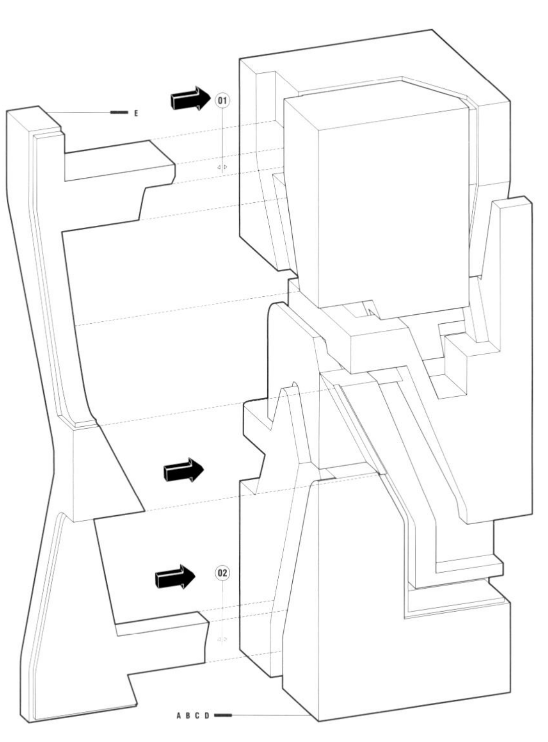

02   **PIN INTERLOCKING**
Hidden Pins

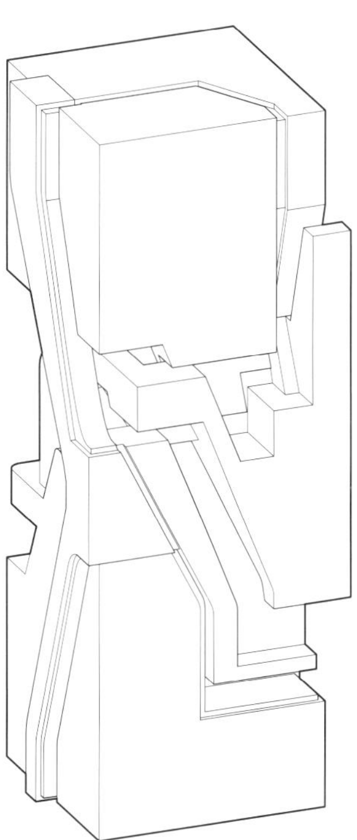

03   **COMPLETED**
Secure Loose Fit

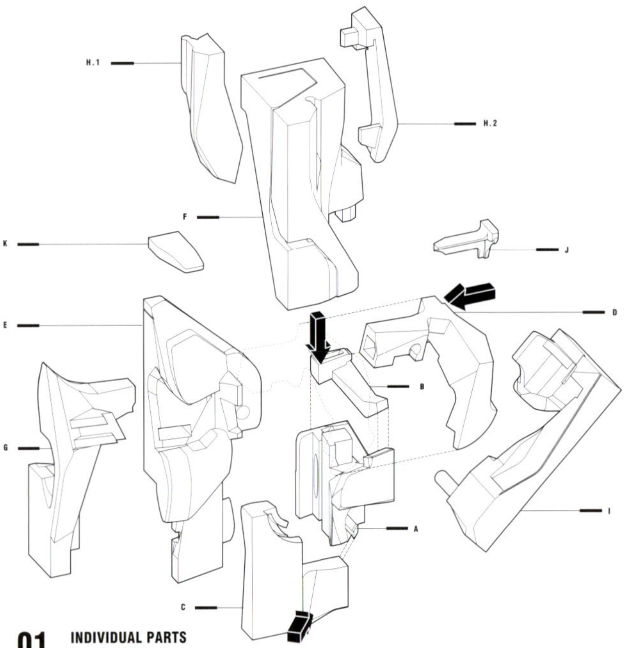

01 INDIVIDUAL PARTS
Part to Part Relationship

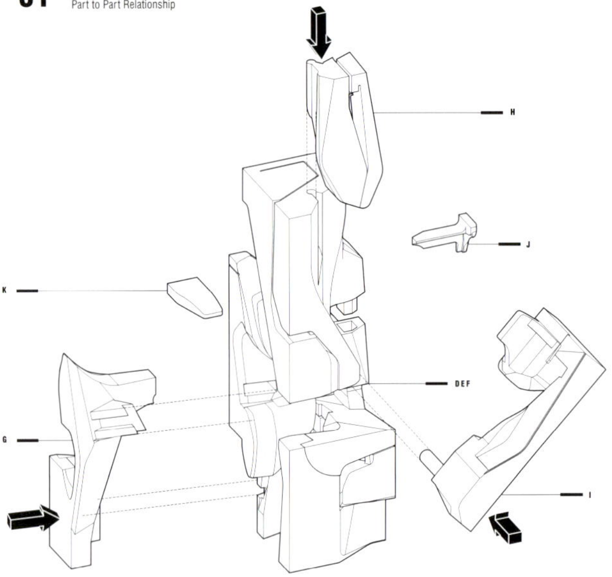

03 MOVE 8–10
Slide Along Rails

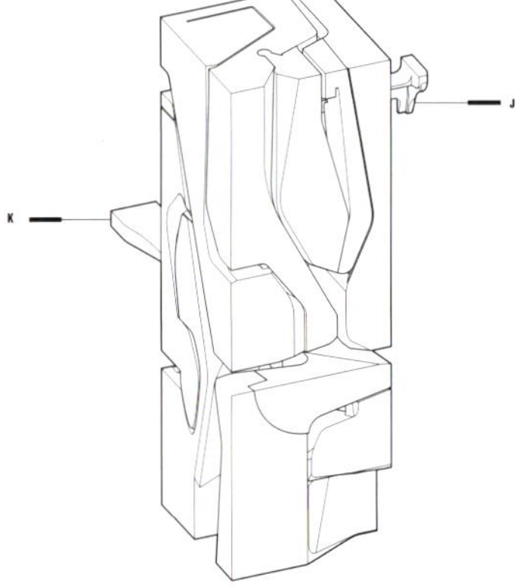

05 LOCKING PINS
A Puzzling Start and End

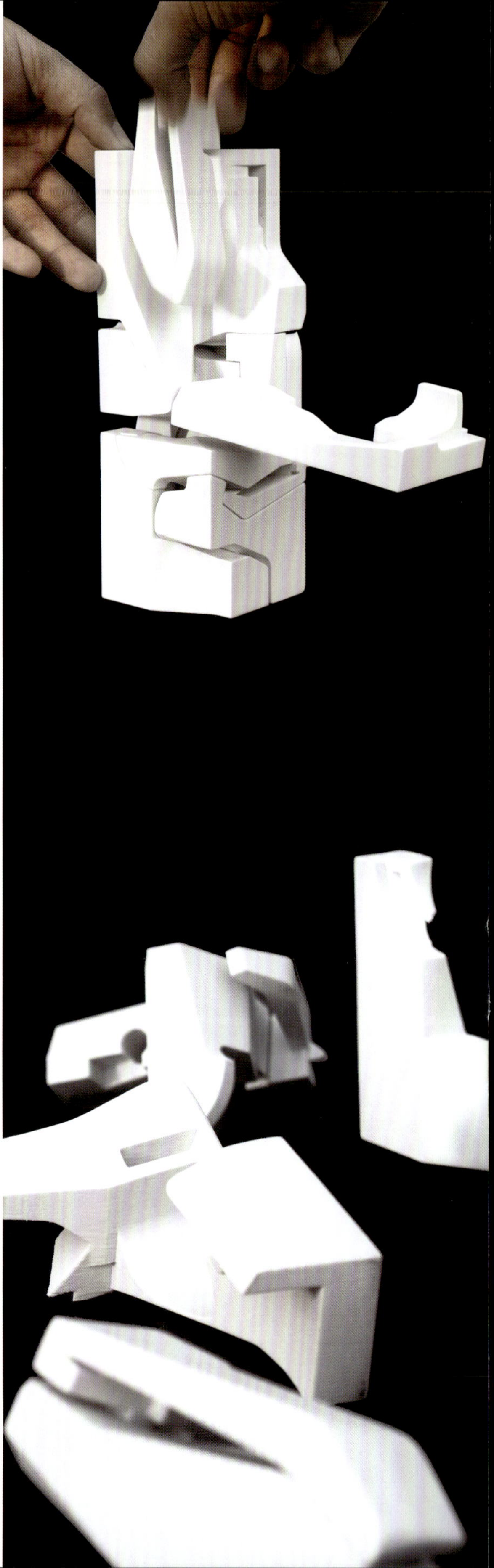

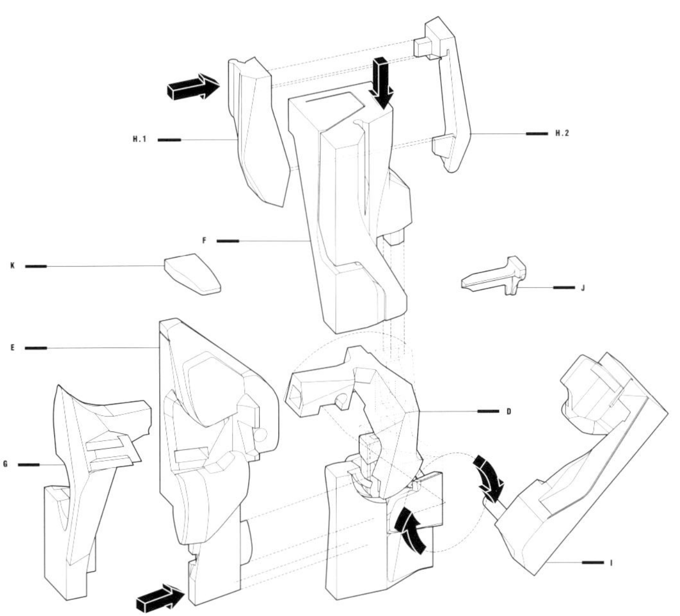

02 **ROTATION & SNAP**
Consecutive Locking with Mortise and Tenon

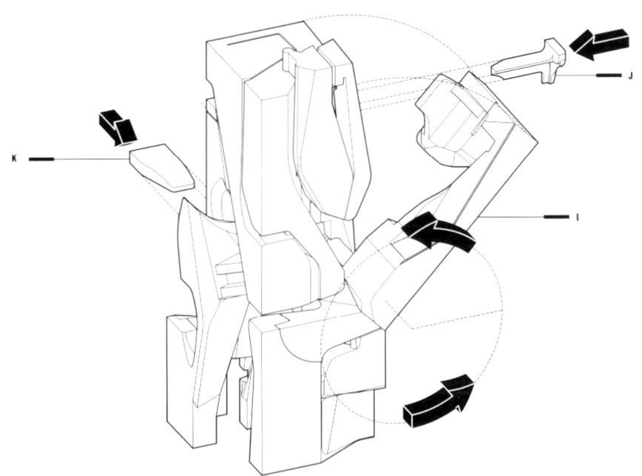

04 **MOVE 11–13**
Rotate to Clamp

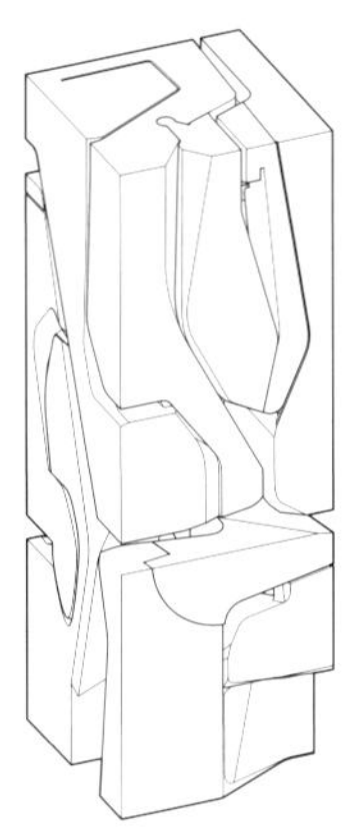

06 **COMPLETED**
Part to Whole Relationship

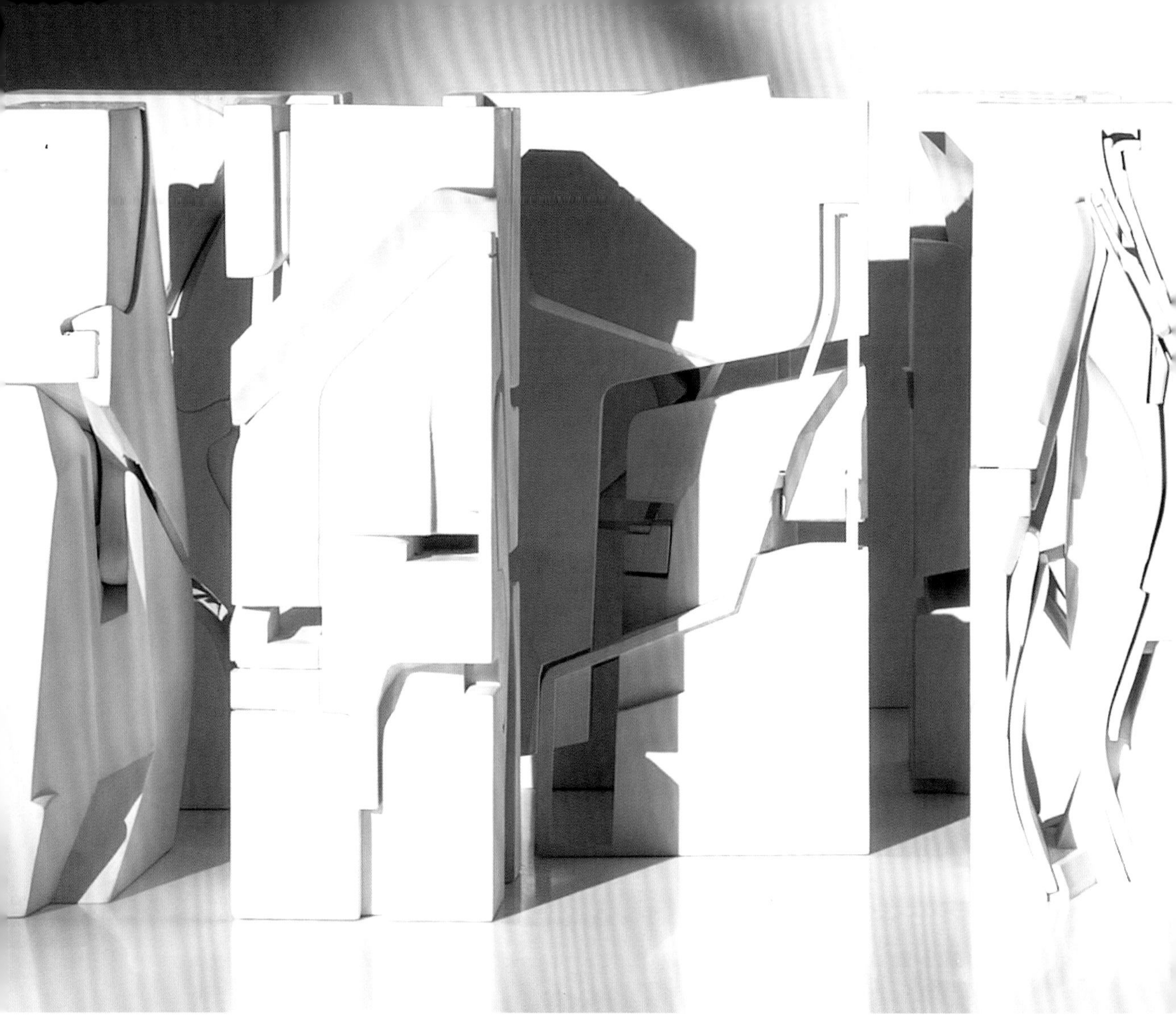

In keeping with the logic of puzzles, these studies include a proliferation of seams, notches, and voids that conflate purely geometric articulations with the key operational features of its assembly and disassembly. The lessons learned in the maneuvers and interactions, both operational and non-operational, can inform the development of more complex assemblies at the scale of architecture—in everything from the small-scale material reveals, to programmatic organizations, to the siting of a building.

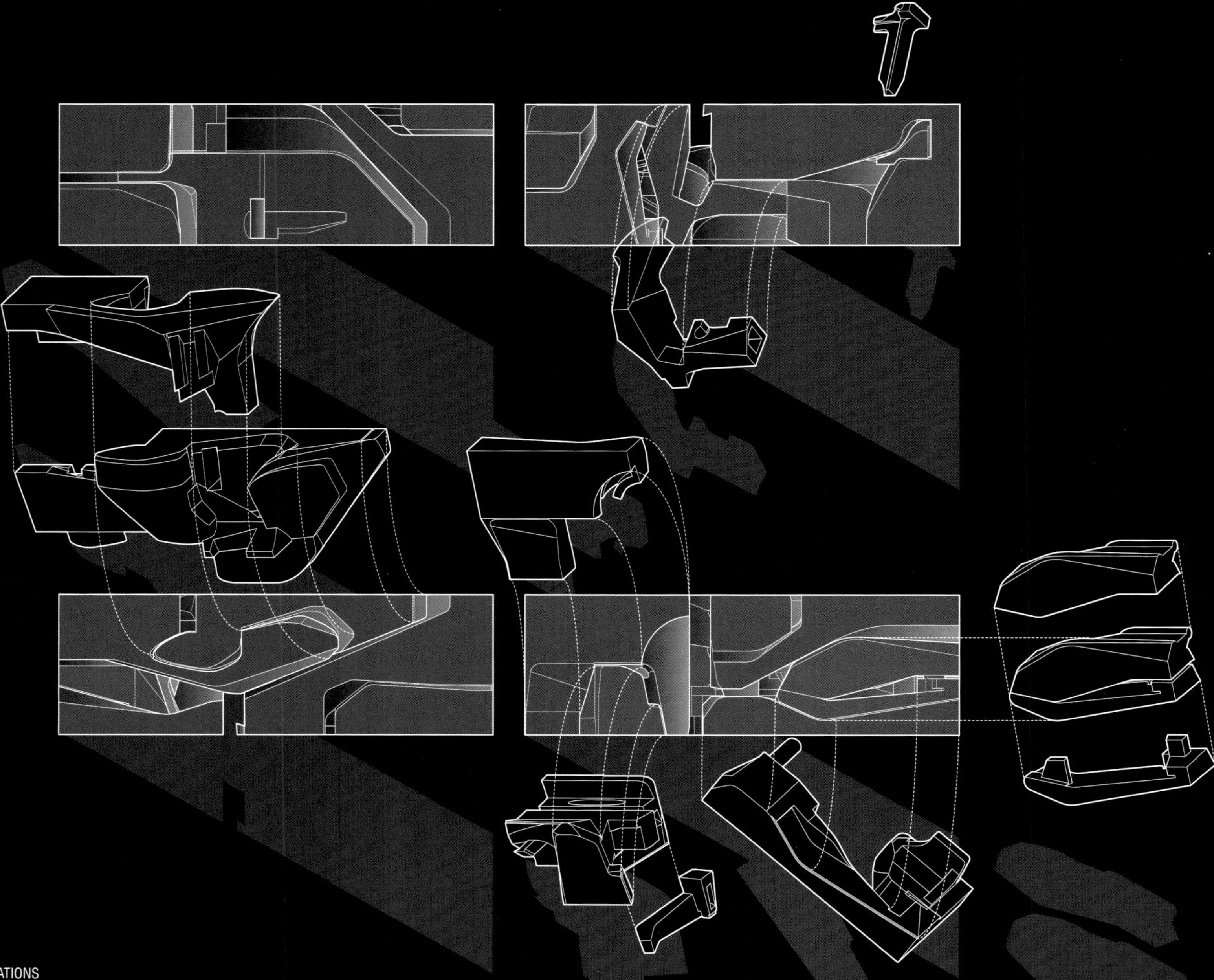
ATIONS

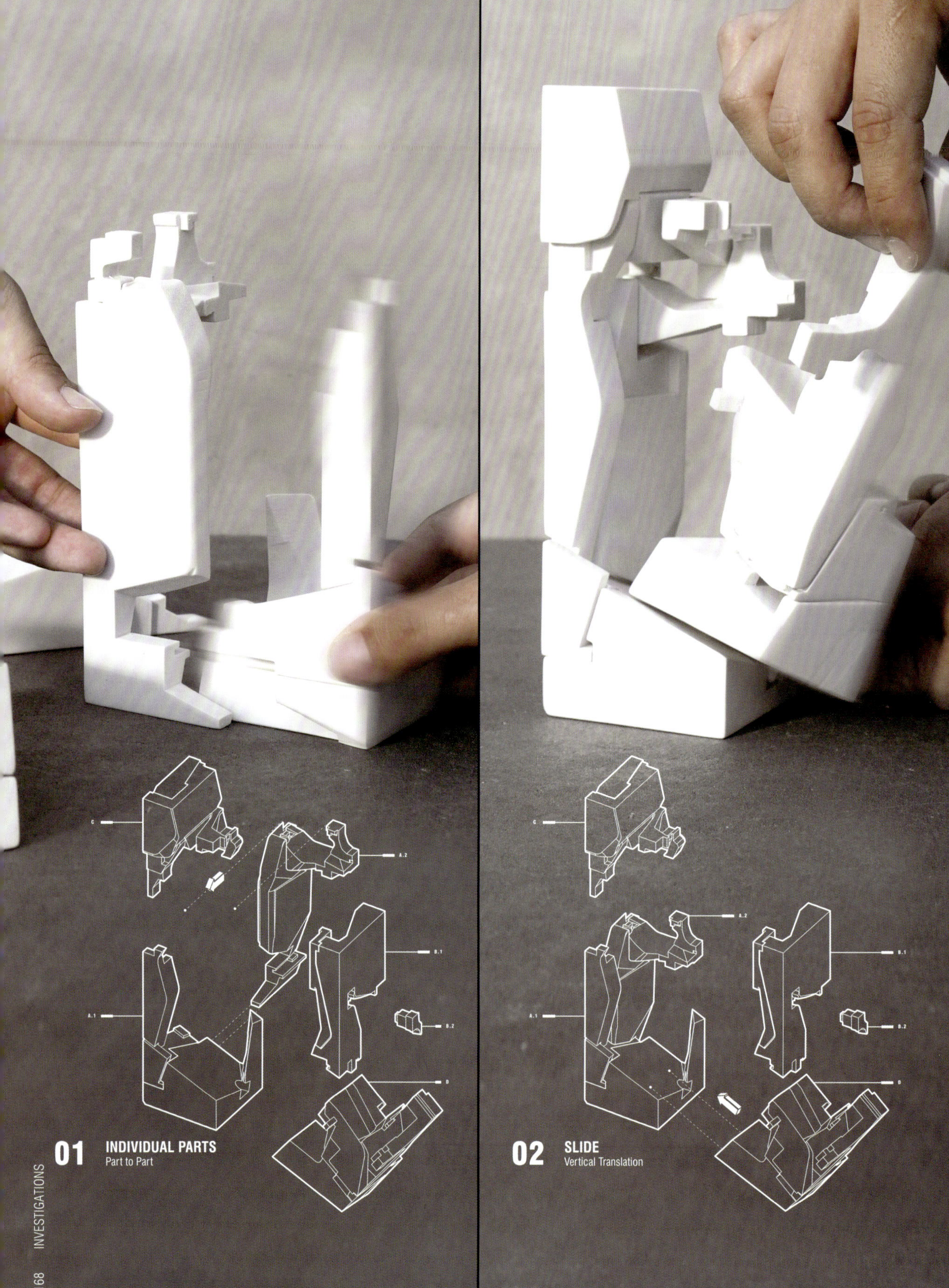

01 **INDIVIDUAL PARTS**
Part to Part

02 **SLIDE**
Vertical Translation

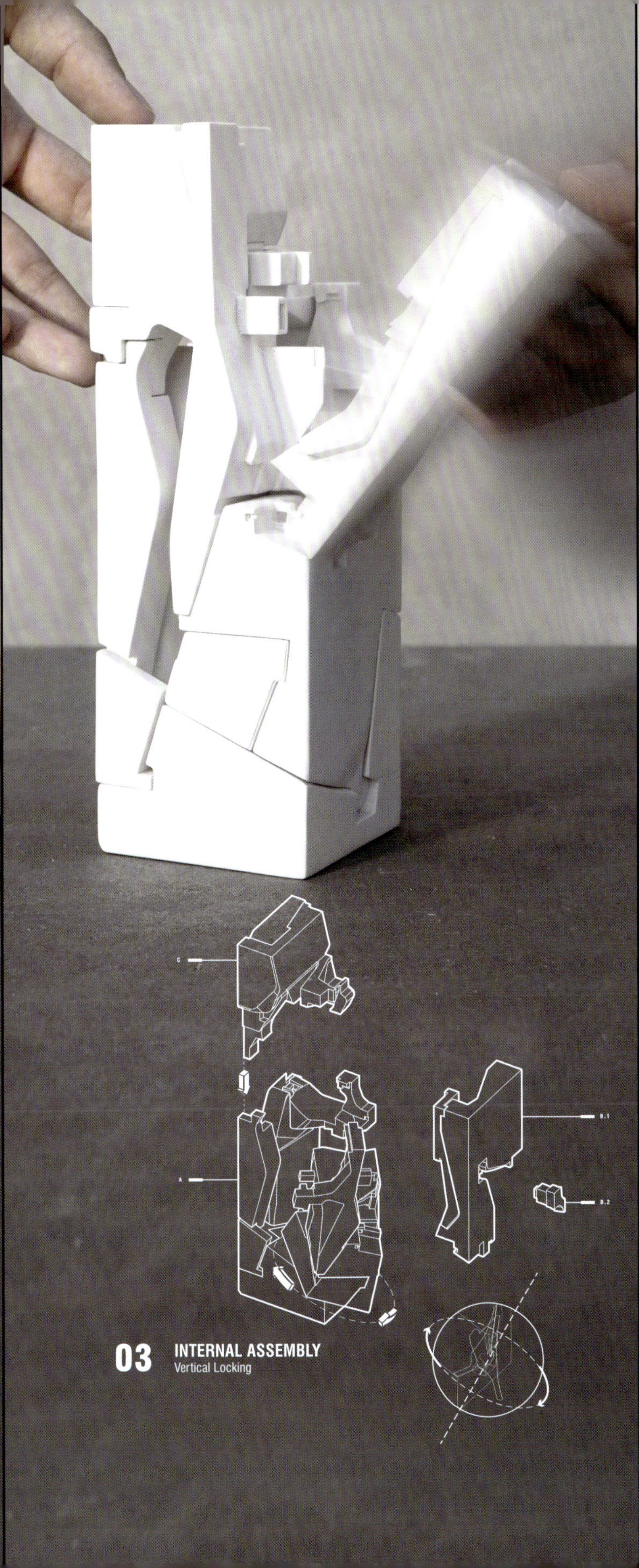

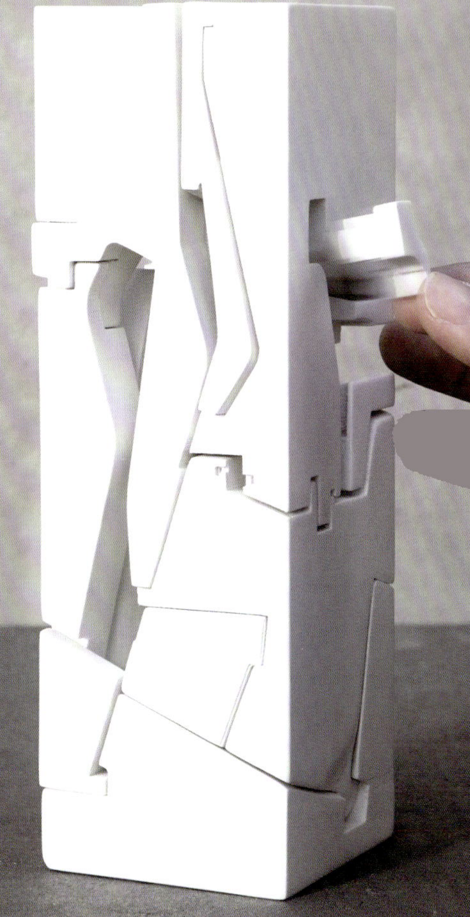

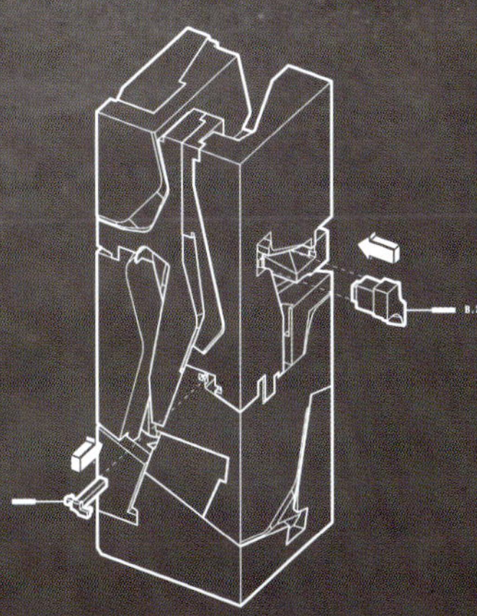

03 **INTERNAL ASSEMBLY**
Vertical Locking

04 **LOCKING**
Rotate to Lock

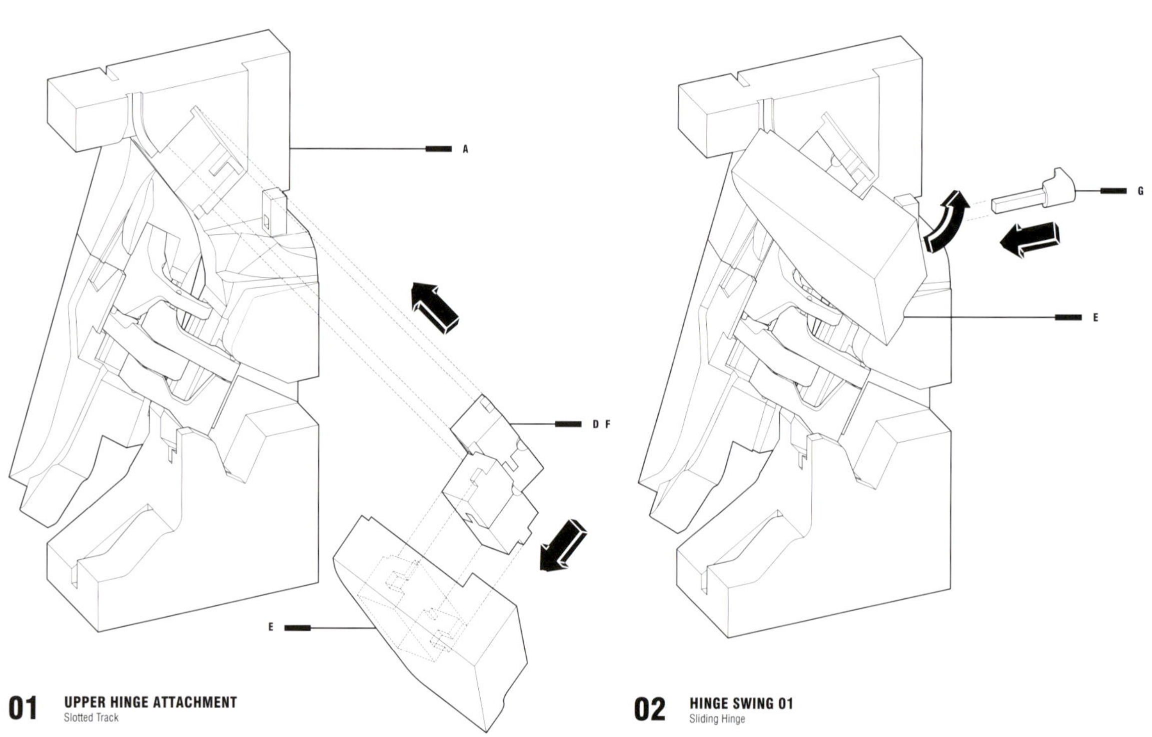

01 **UPPER HINGE ATTACHMENT**
Slotted Track

02 **HINGE SWING 01**
Sliding Hinge

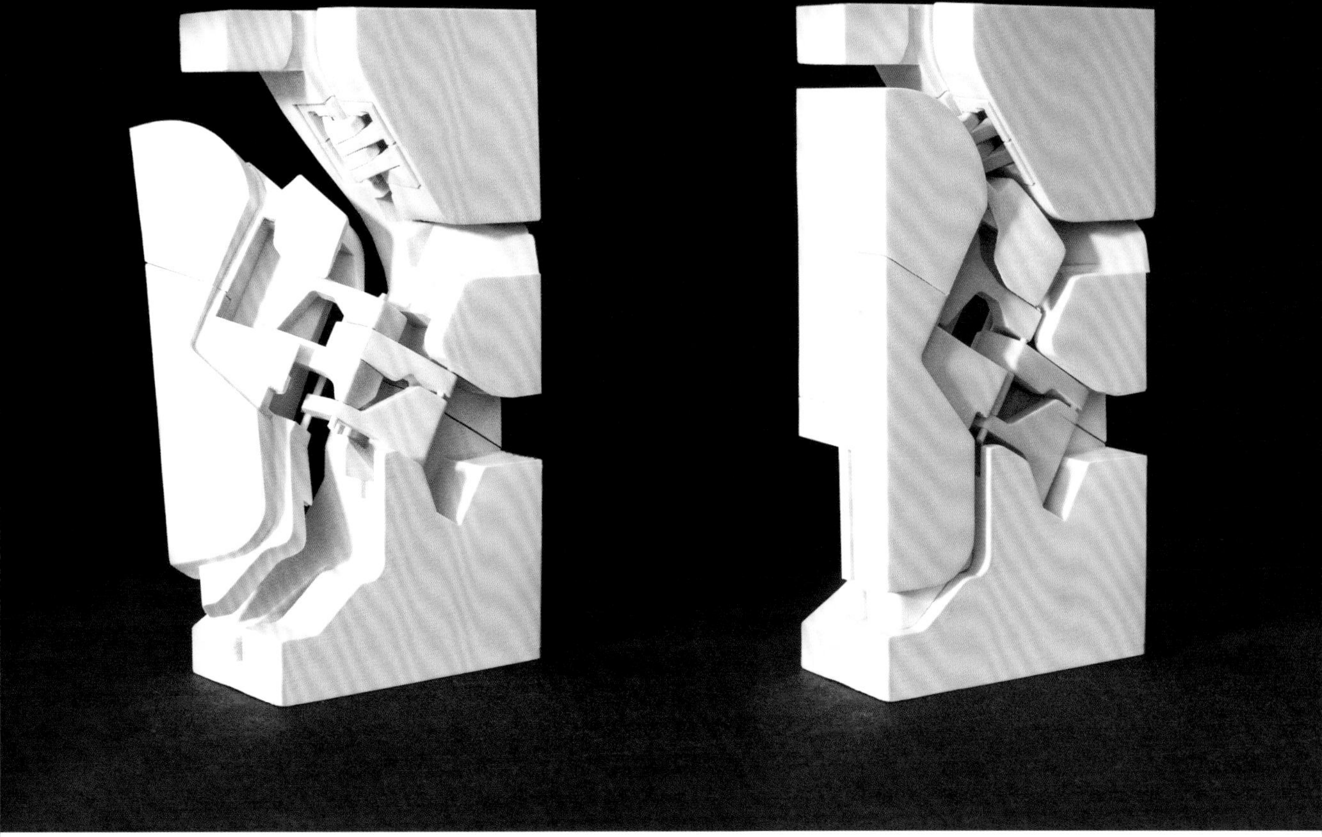

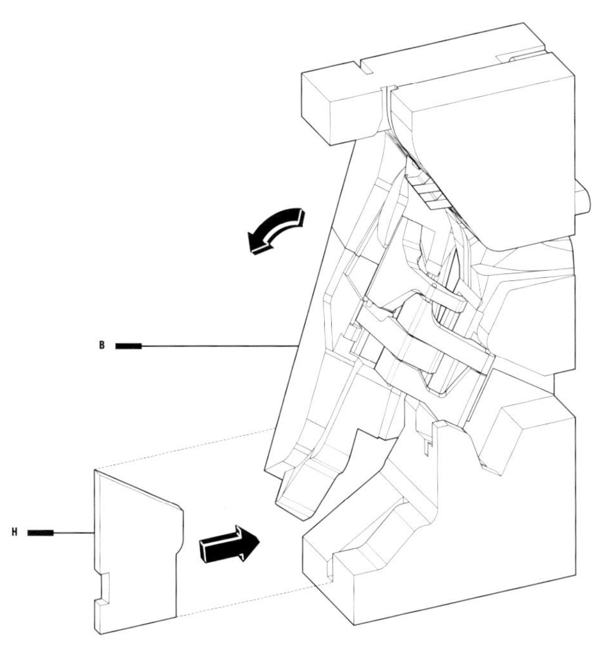

03 **HINGE SWING 02**
Sliding Hinge

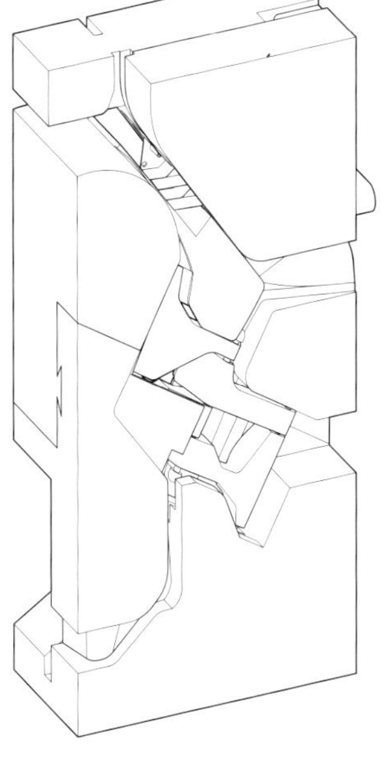

04 **COMPLETED**
Internalized Mechanism

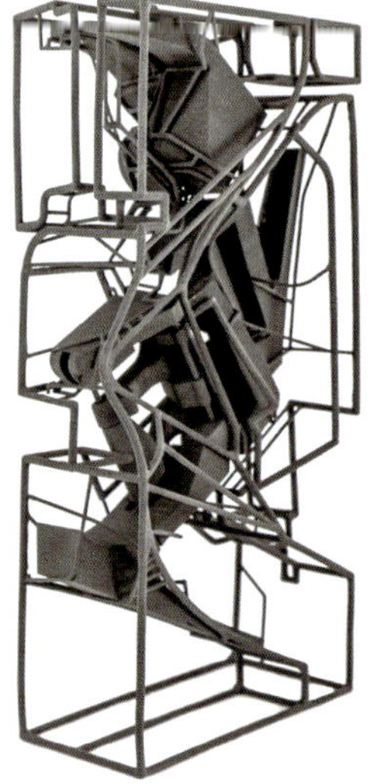  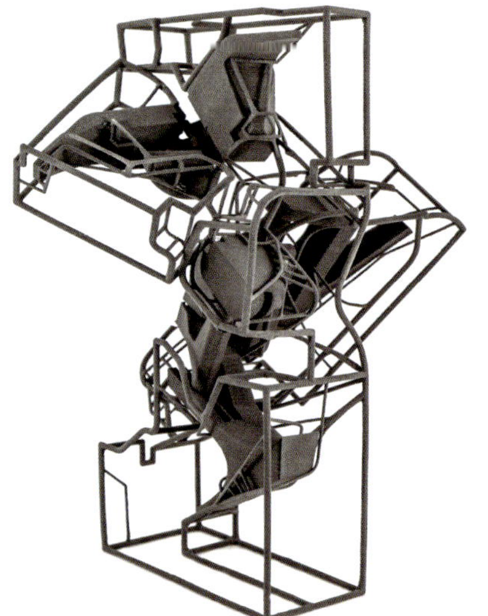 

HYBRIDS

Hybrids further our investigation into puzzling assemblies through an interwoven combination of both volumetric solids and linear frames. This combination exposes the interaction of the key internal features of each puzzle, revealing the essential forms of interlock necessary for its operation. While the skeletal frames still clearly suggest the sense of the whole, the reading is shifted toward the individual parts, their relationships, and their tendency to meander freely through the system.

Hybrids consider the frame boundary as a dynamic lens that simultaneously defines space, while also allowing related geometric volumes in the background to be recognized. This instantaneous oscillation between frame and solid, foreground and background, is a powerful perceptual tool that doesn't exist in quite the same way in solid volumetric puzzles. Because it hypothetically allows the frames of implied volumetric elements to become literally interlocked, it also compels a deeper visual investigation in order to confirm the true nature of their relationships.

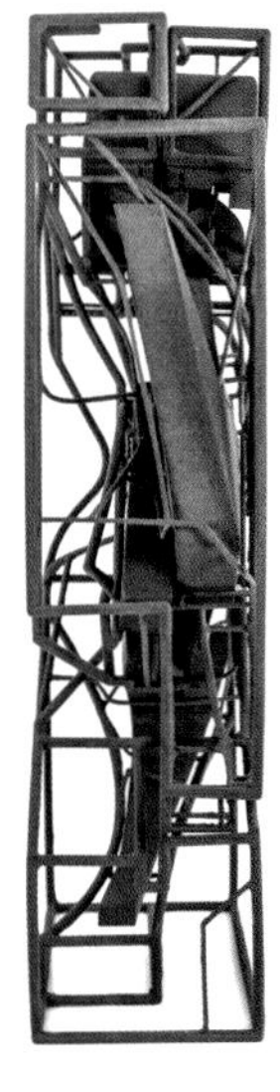
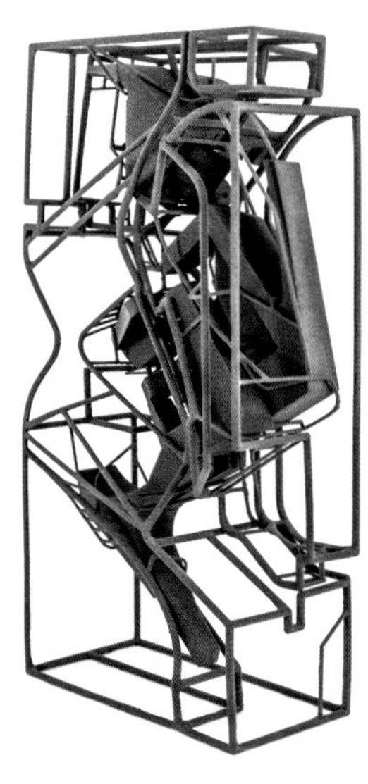

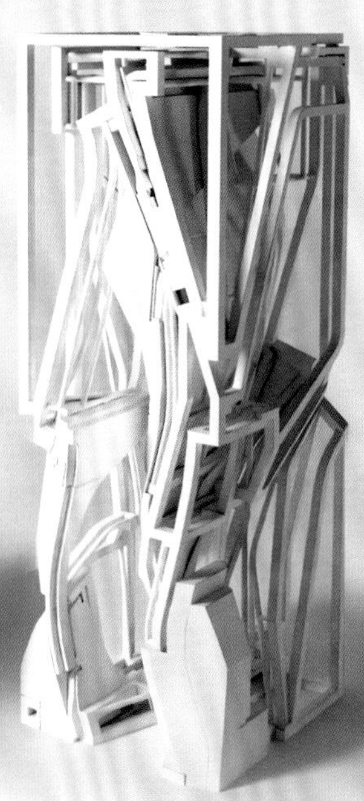

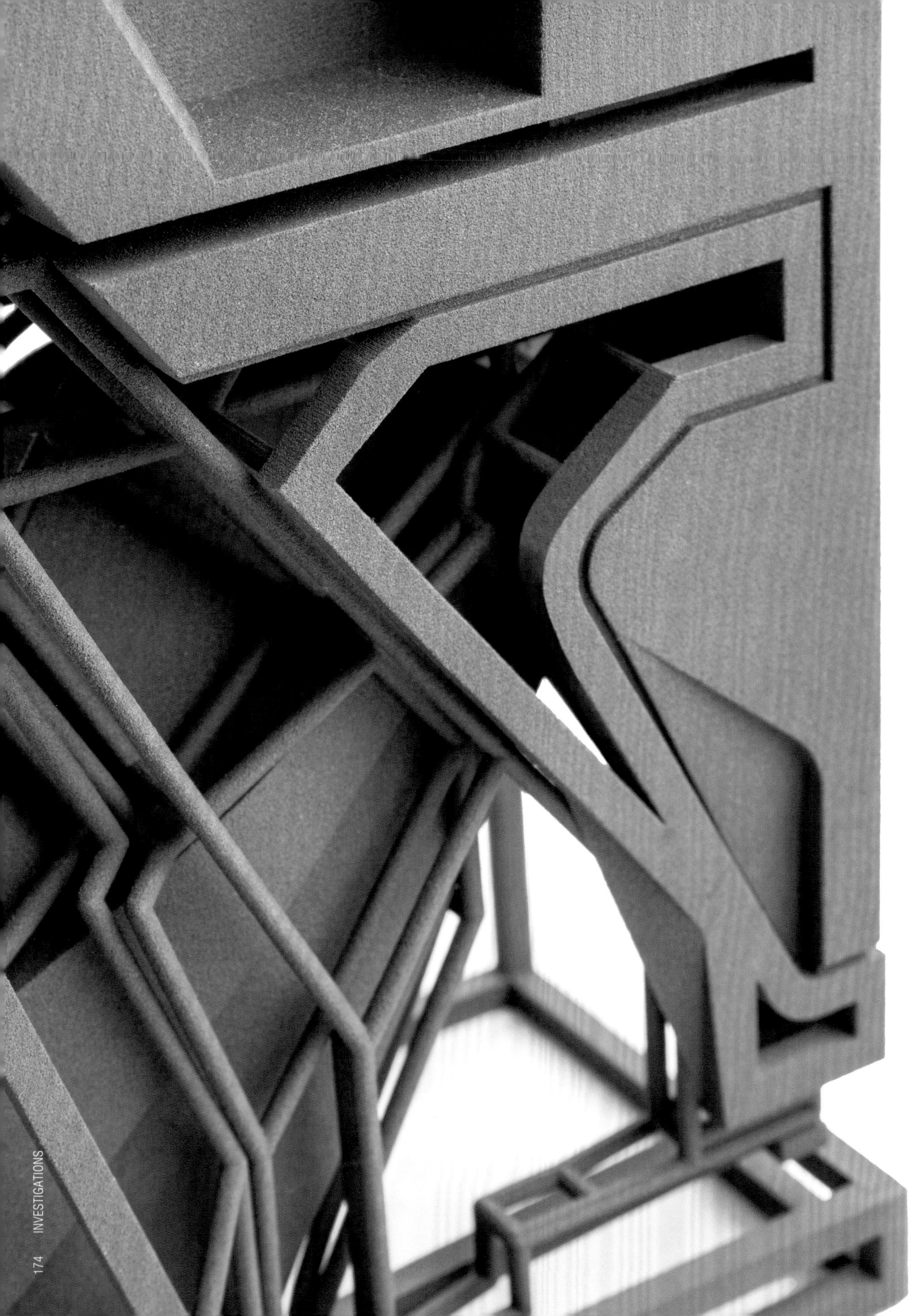

PUZZLES ARE INHERENTLY COMPLEX. PUZZLES OFTEN USE A PROLIFERATION OF GEOMETRY IN BOTH THEIR EXTERNAL AND INTERNAL FORM.

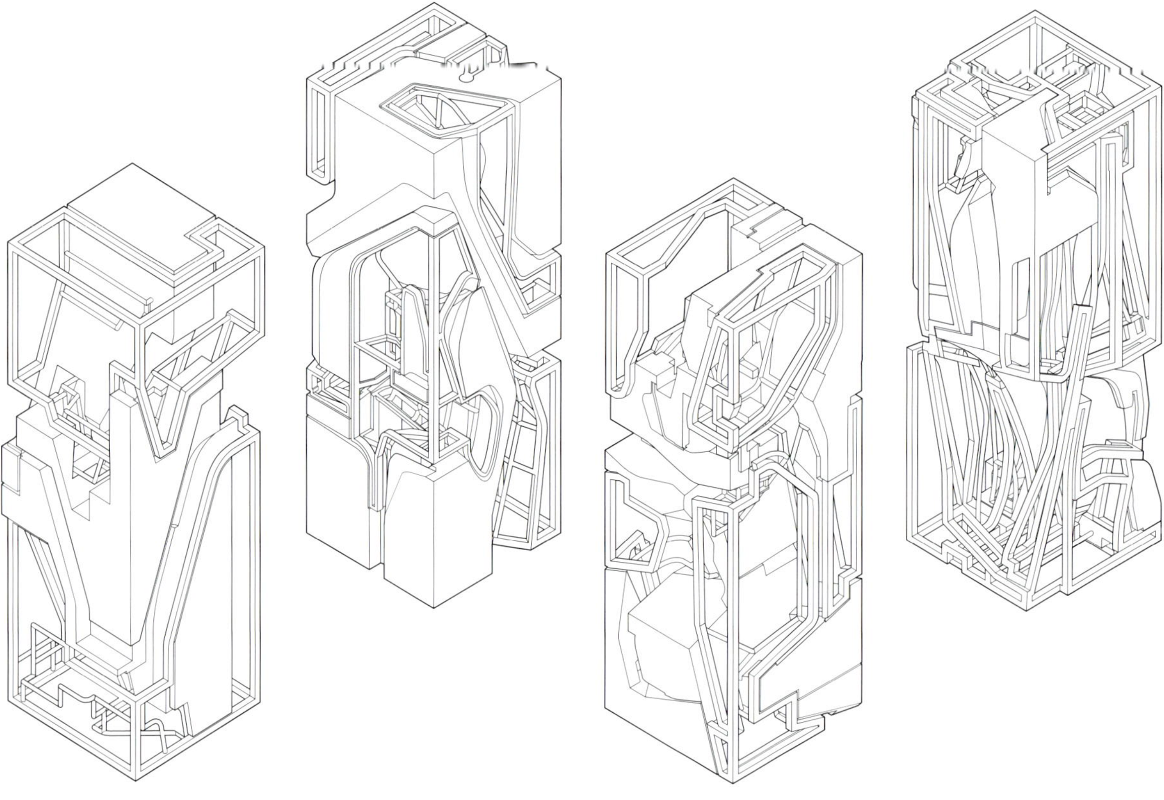

Like all of our previous investigations, Hybrids are designed for assembly and disassembly. However, unlike those previous studies, they stray from some of our puzzle definitions in key ways. By revealing their inner workings, they uncover many of the mysteries that are essential to puzzle logic. They also open up greater amounts of space and rely more on implied readings and tenuous connection systems. The intention here is to push the limits of our definition, and to lean into the characteristics that make them especially suitable for architectural applications.

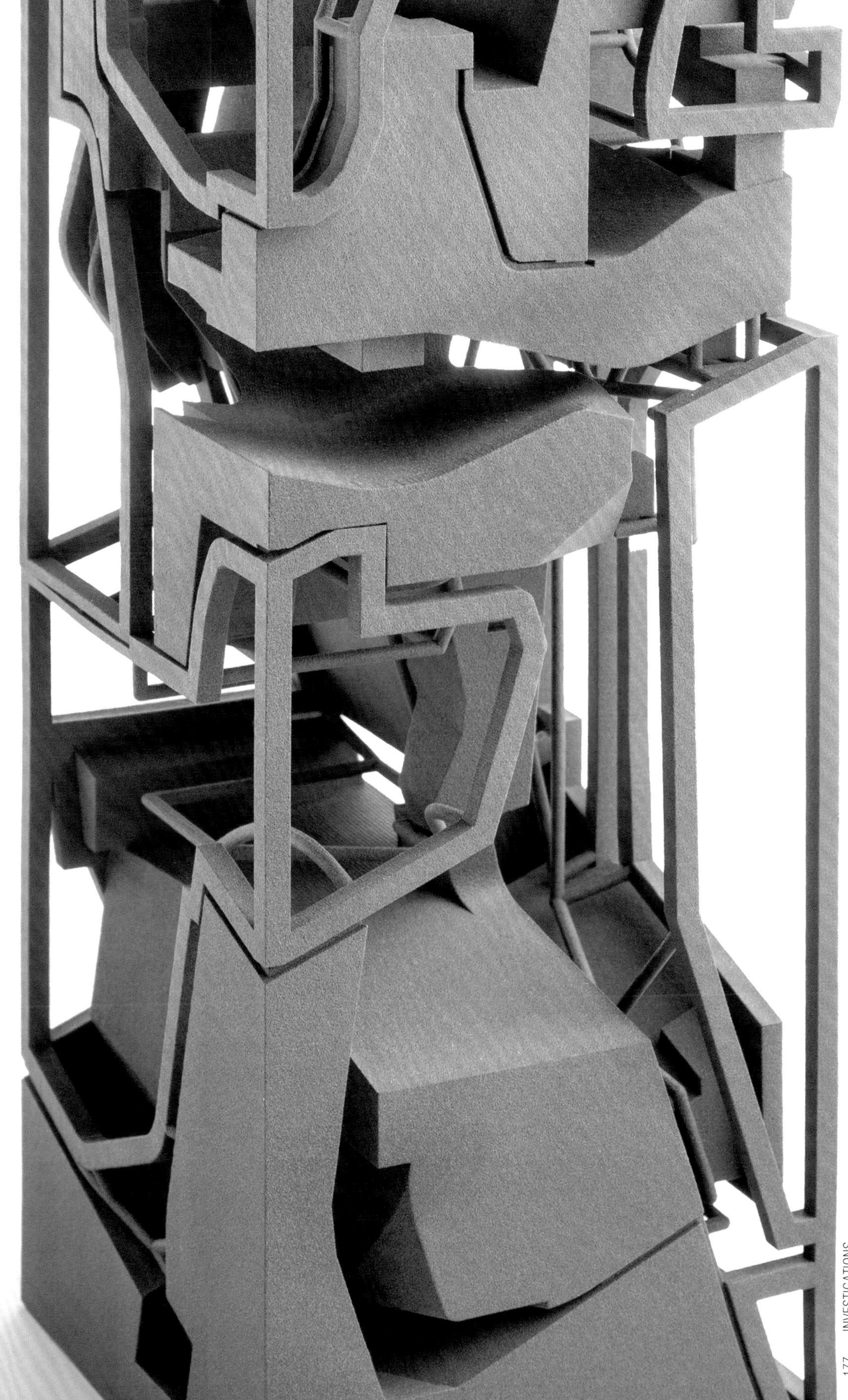

PZ.10.1

FRAMED VOLUMES 01

In the same manner as fully solid relationships, a framed volume highlights the external shaping of objects, but it also simultaneously is expressed as objects that encapsulate space.

EXPOSED INTERACTIONS 02

Using the external boundaries of a volume, the relationship between the parts is more exposed, where the spatial aspects that relate one to another are tied to how they are compatibly formed.

INTERNAL CONTINUITY 03

With volumes of both solid and frame, the internal faces of parts are revealed, positioned in their fixed position, creating continuity between parts.

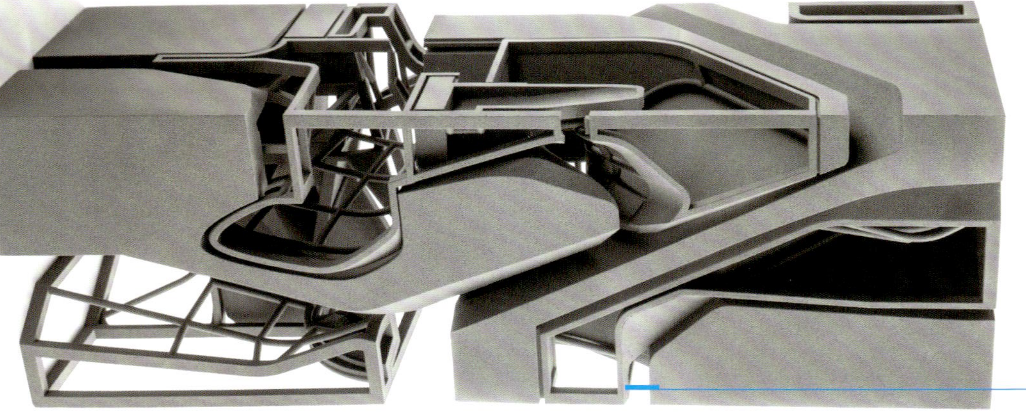

01

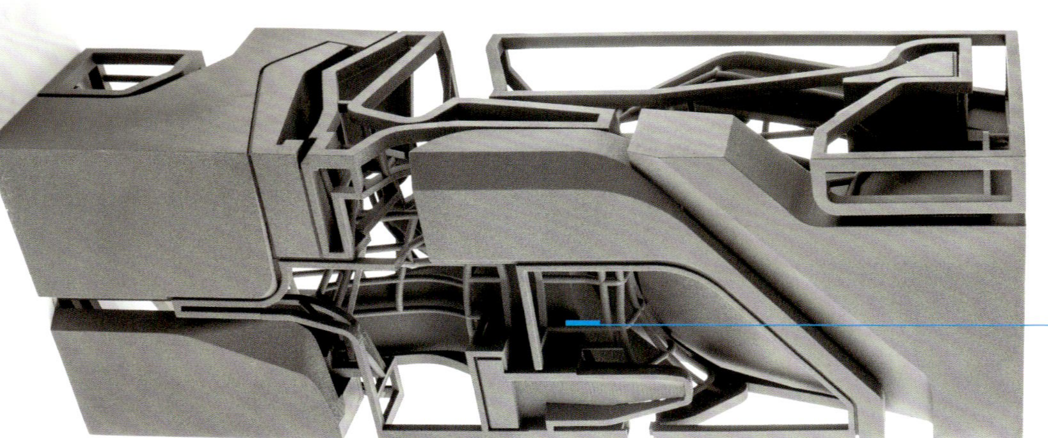

03

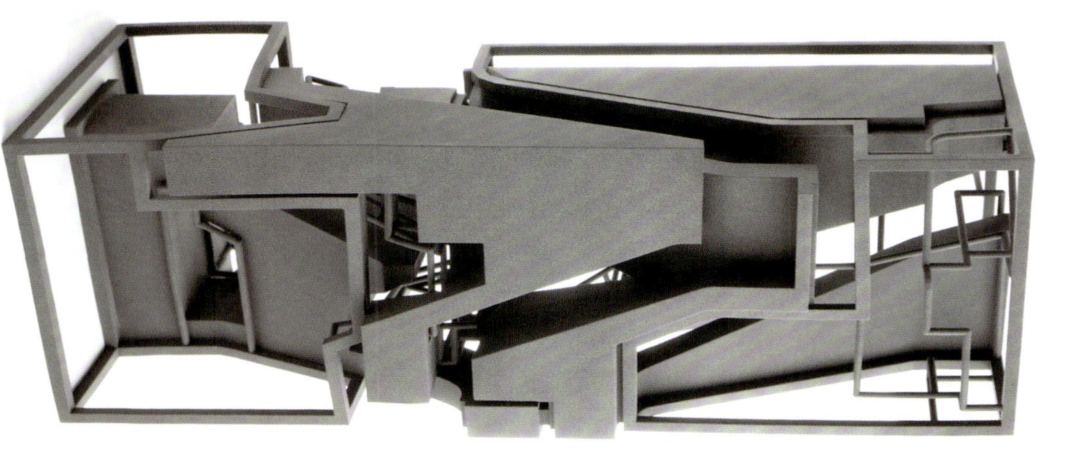

As larger areas become more open, the volumes can be understood comprehensively, where their solidity is more clearly represented in dynamic balance with the frame as being figurally interlocked.

FIGURAL SECTION 04

As frames, the linear puzzled parts read as geometric volumes with a shared system of connection.

LINEAR CONTINUITY 05

Every aspect of the geometries interact to fit together. Framed volumes turn solid to void, leaving their boundary as a physical element to reveal the internal spaces between parts.

VOID OBJECTS 06

PZ.09.1

PZ.10.2

FRAMED VOLUMES   01

In the same manner as fully solid relationships, a framed volume highlights the external shaping of objects, but it also simultaneously is expressed as objects that encapsulate space.

EXPOSED INTERACTIONS   02

Using the external boundaries of a volume, the relationship between the parts is more exposed, where the spatial aspects that relate one to another are tied to how they are compatibly formed.

INTERNAL CONTINUITY   03

With volumes of both solid and frame, the internal faces of parts are revealed, positioned in their fixed position, creating continuity between parts.

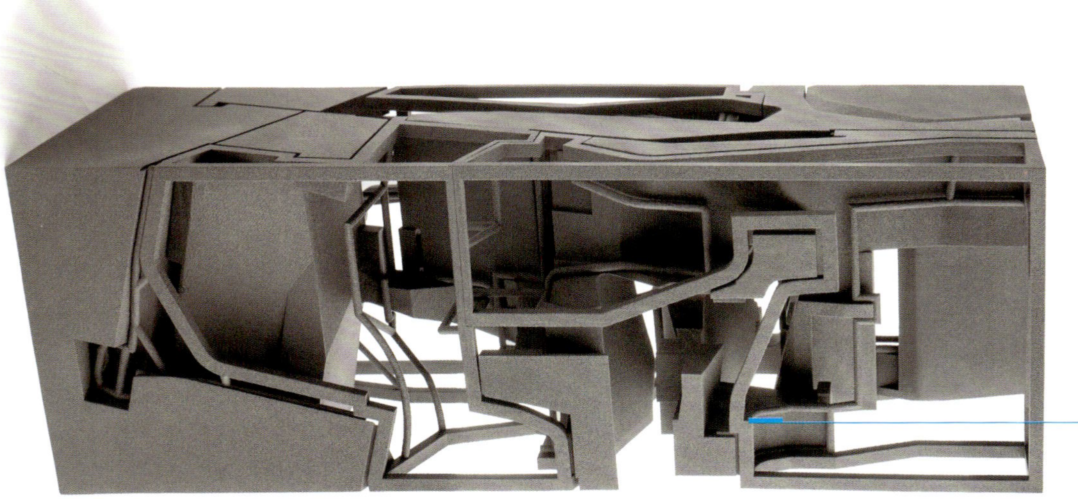

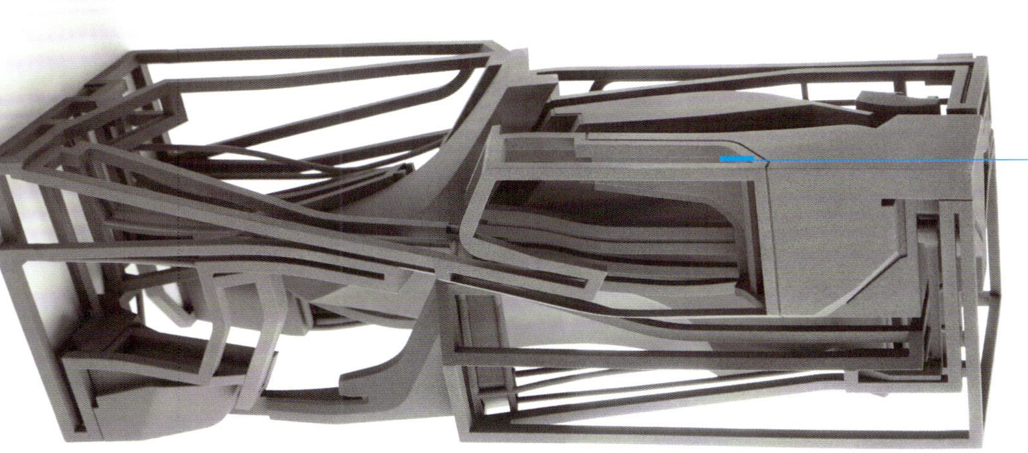

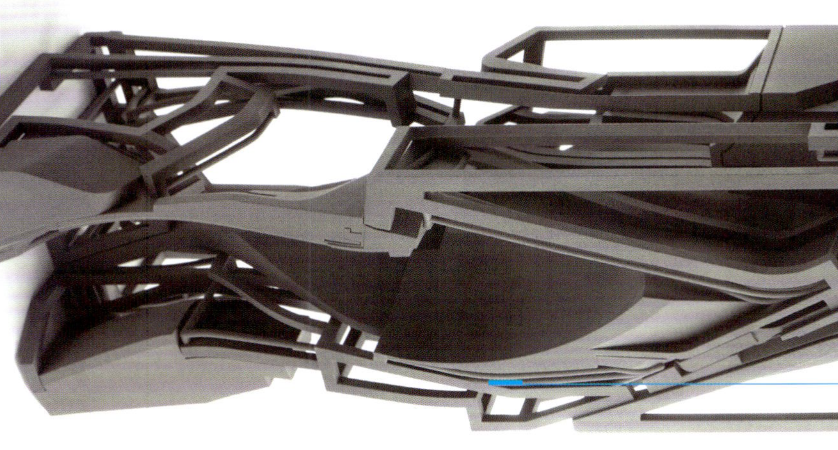

As larger areas become more open, the volumes can be understood comprehensively, where their solidity is more clearly represented in dynamic balance with the frame as being figurally interlocked.

FIGURAL SECTION 04

As frames, the linear puzzled parts read as geometric volumes with a shared system of connection.

LINEAR CONTINUITY 05

Every aspect of the geometries interact to fit together. Framed volumes turn solid to void, leaving their boundary as a physical element to reveal the internal spaces between parts.

VOID OBJECTS 06

PZ.05.1

Assessing how parts fit together requires identifying similarities. Framed volumes expose inner alignments, giving more context to their shape. They also intentionally play with this legibility to both reveal and obscure assembly.

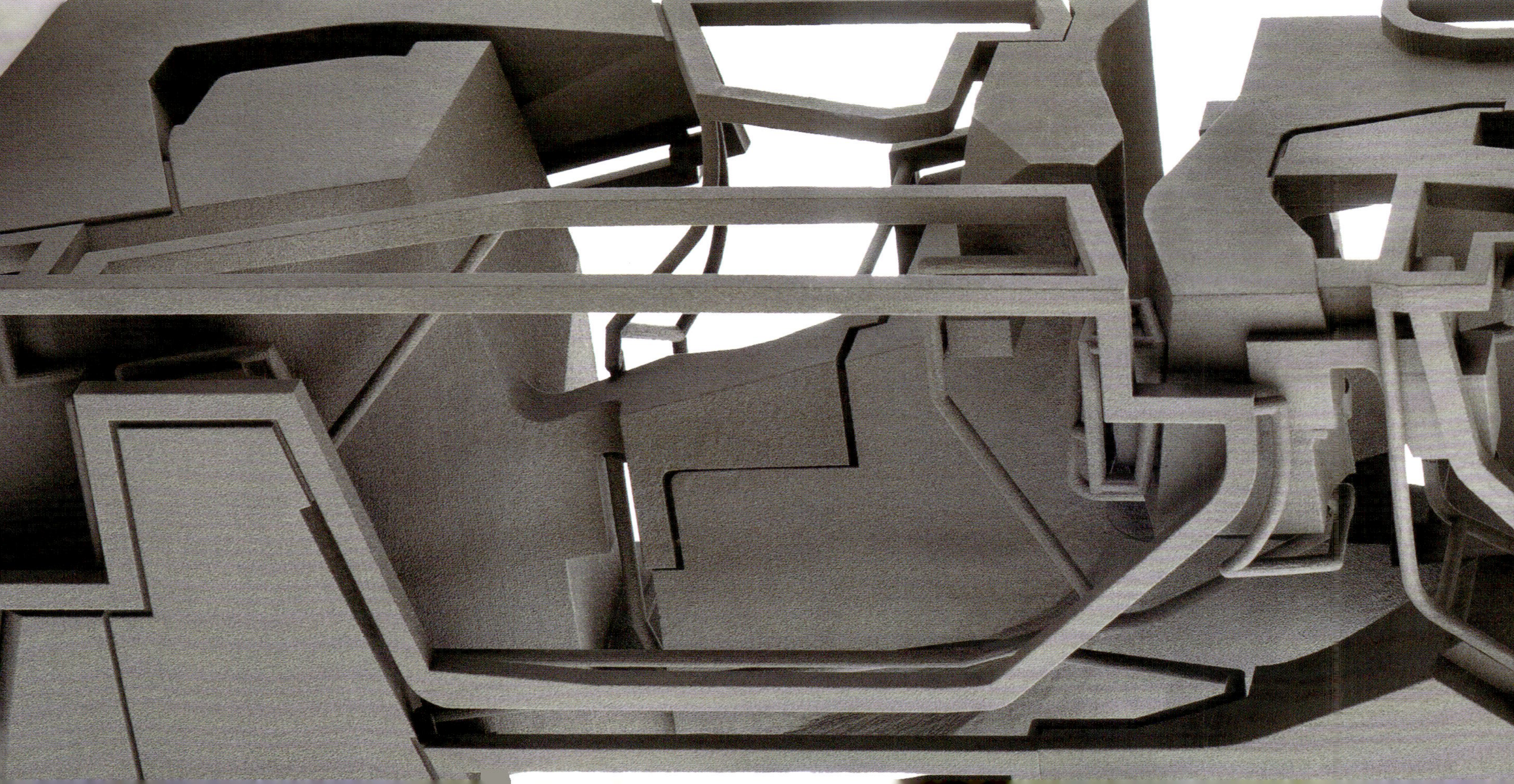

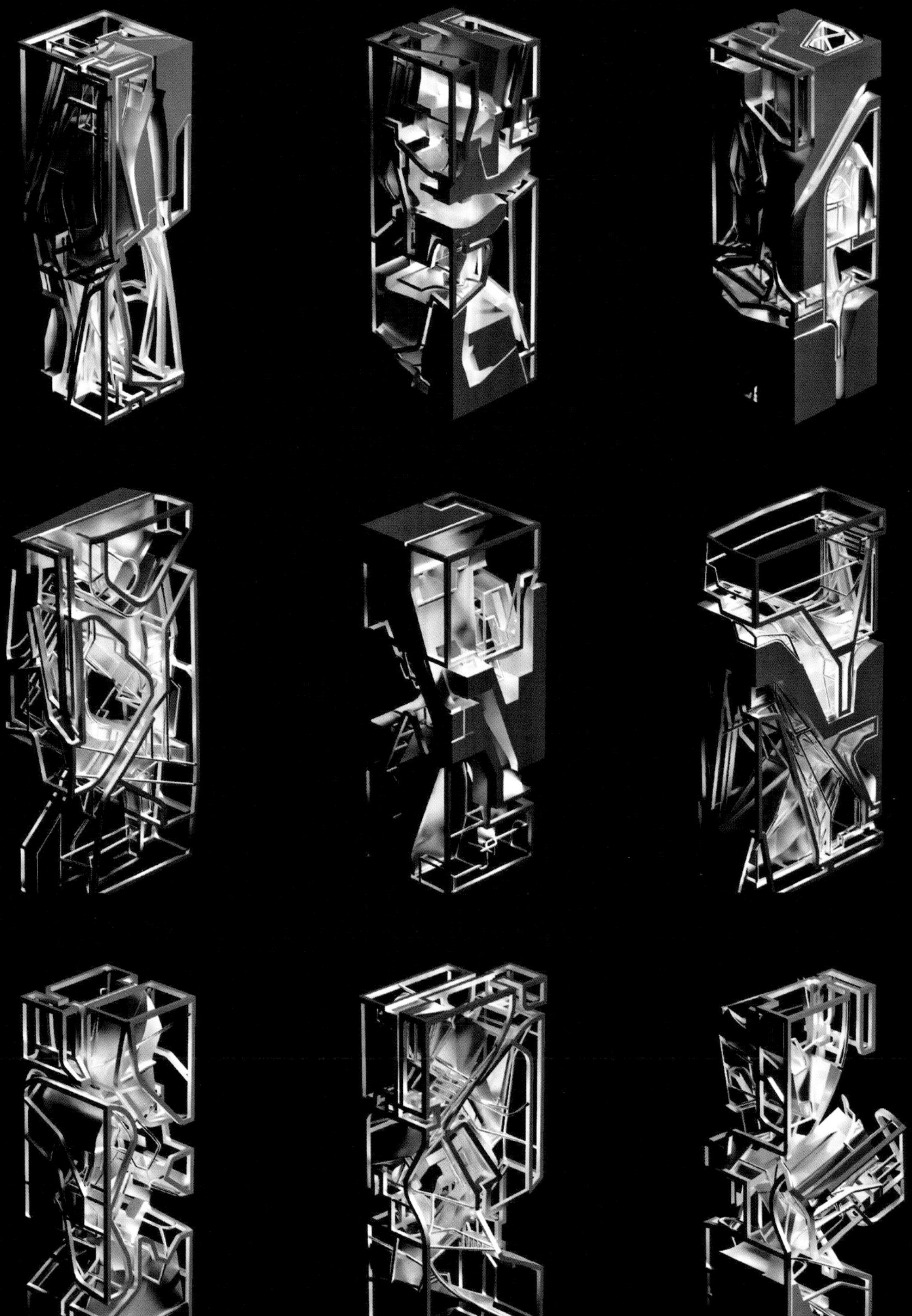

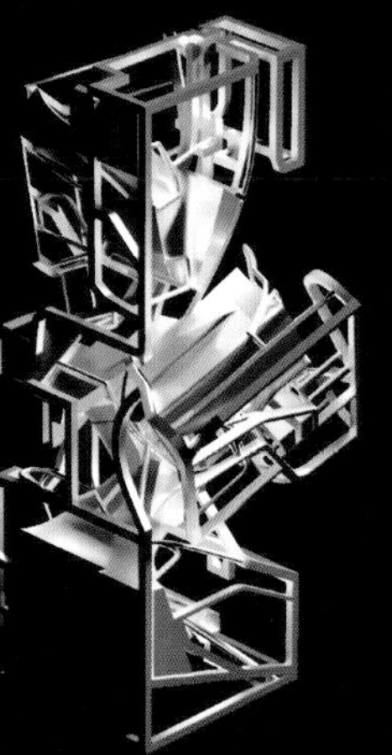

We've intentionally selected the projects in this section for their diverse range of scales and approaches to puzzling assemblies: jewelry, furniture, architectural installations, large-scale buildings, and projects both built and unbuilt. From early projects like Live Wire in 2009 to more recent projects like Monarch Tower in 2017, some works predate our focus on volumetric geometries as a key driver of formal language but nevertheless present the tactics and expressive qualities in alignment with these newer interests. Our hope is to demonstrate the cross-fertilization of design ideas that move between projects—and convey the many ways that this back-and-forth is realized.

Though we've defined a clear set of design approaches in the previous section, it's important to recognize that unlike design investigations, each project does not follow a consistent formula for how it is implemented. We're also keenly aware that architecture and design objects don't come with a set of instructions, and ultimately are developed in consideration with factors that resist formal procedure. Each project presents different constraints and opportunities, and as a result, tends to synthesize our approaches in ways that make this more prominent—sometimes manifesting in tectonic connections, program development, or overall effect for example.

Our interest lies in the development of sensibilities that emerge from this dynamic investigation, and explores the fascinating potential they have to guide the design of projects at many scales. The development of each project is then seen as a way to integrate additional layers of design thinking into architectural ideas of assembly.

PROJECTS

SECTION 3

LACE

LACE marries line-based geometry with intricately woven elements in wearable forms. Through innovative 3D-printing processes, the complex designs avoid mechanical connections, and express formal and spatial properties at an intimate scale.

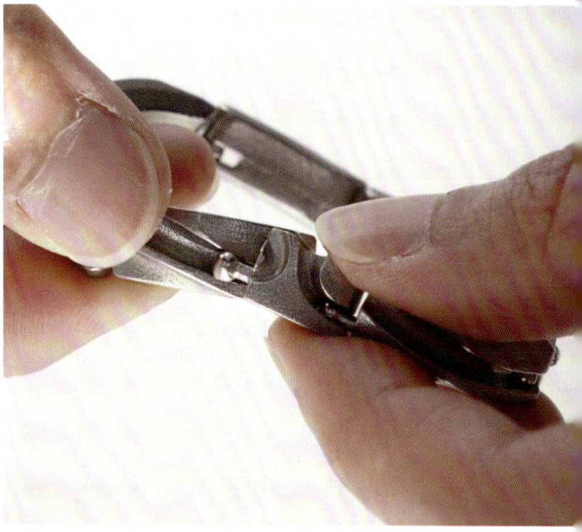

Designs engage functional features as embedded characteristics of their design, shaping their form and appearance. *Chain Earrings in Rose Gold, Andante Pendant in Stainless Steel Bronze, Link Bracelet in Stainless Steel, L Ring in Stainless Steel Bronze.*

Highly attuned to the interaction of parts, the Link Bracelet features a logic of puzzling that transforms its shape language to slide and lock together. In a rhythmic sequence, each module is shaped to connect using grooved surfaces, capturing the connecting components into fitted channels. Each piece is crafted to examine the elegant movement and versatility of the physical line, configuring the outer surfaces with precision and clarity.

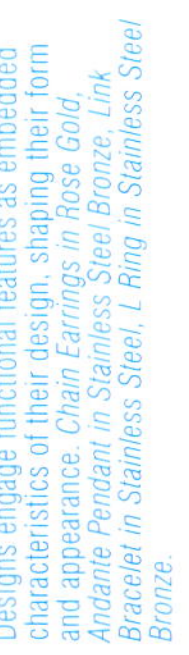

Many pieces are designed to be paired together, integrating parameters of evolving 3D-printing techniques with geometries that can adapt to the ever-changing metrics and methods of manufacturing. Reinterpreting joinery in the design of each piece, the techniques for creating a seamless assembly merge technical and qualitative aspects of how linear elements interact. At a glance, the three-dimensional formations engage each other in seemingly simple ways. However, even in a subtle gesture, the conjoining and splicing of physical lines is explored in depth.

With linear volumes that turn and twist, each piece explores their fit on the body as well as in relation to one another, often sharing compatible features of how they can be worn in combination. *Nocturne Pendant in Stainless Steel, Mobius and Papilio Rings in Stainless Steel, Prelude and Interlude Necklaces in Rose Gold, Amor and Amos Rings in Sterling Silver, Papilio Light in Stainless Steel Bronze, Mobius Bold in Sterling Silver.*

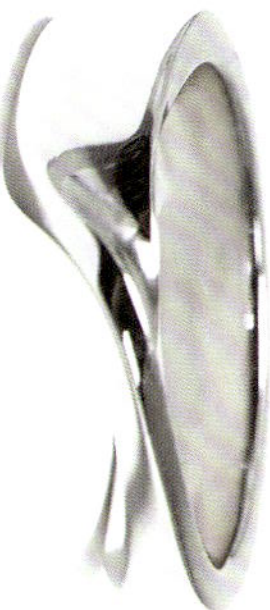

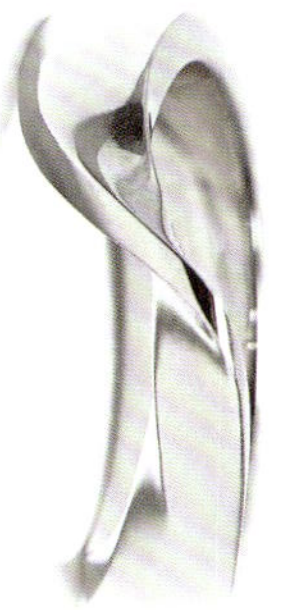

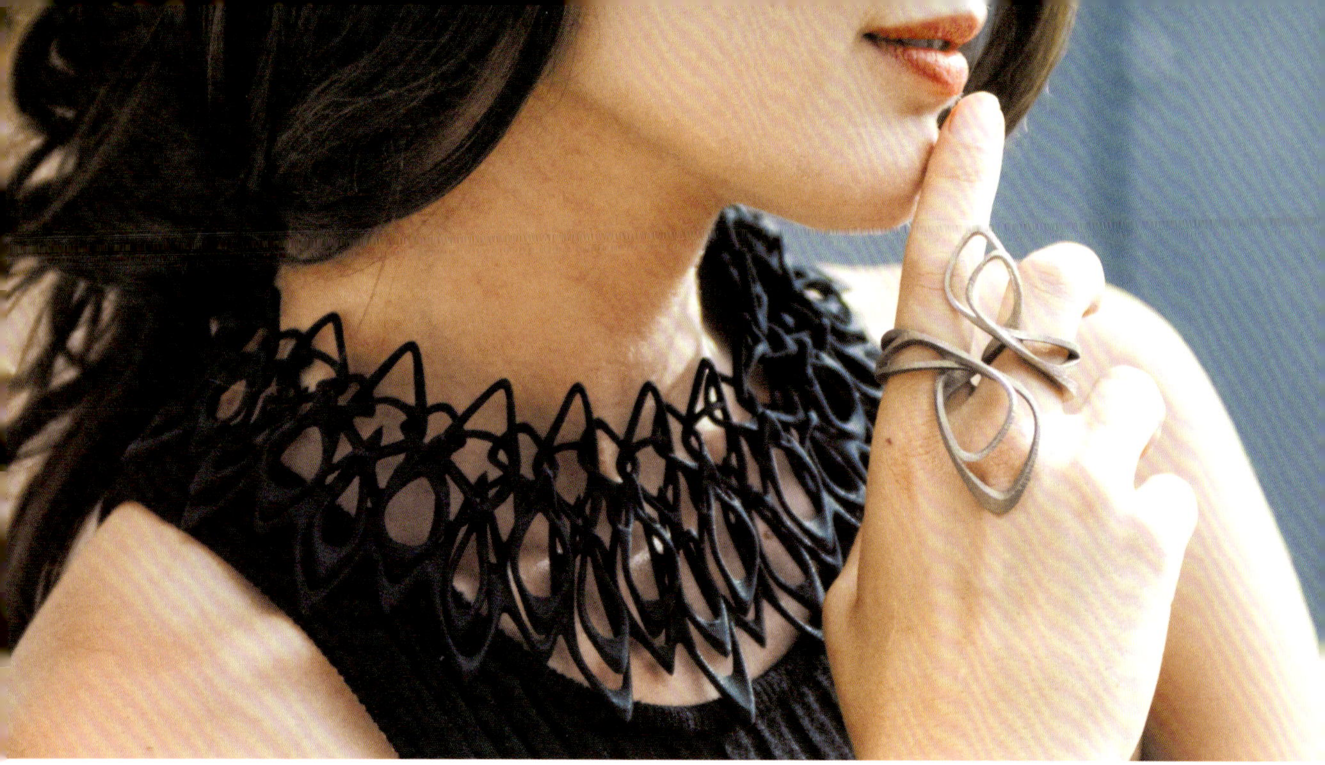

As assemblies, they are conceptually and procedurally linked in overall appearance: tectonically complex in function and aesthetic. Finding unique signatures in jointed figures, elliptical petals, loosely knotted splines, and threaded curvatures, pieces deliberately resolve fitted relationships that engage the body. This idea extends to their presentation as well, where the pieces are displayed in milled panels that echo their continuous features with terrain-like forms.

Stria in Black Nylon, Mobius Light and Bold Rings in Stainless Steel Bronze, Papilio Bold in Sterling Silver, Amare Diamond Ring in White Gold.

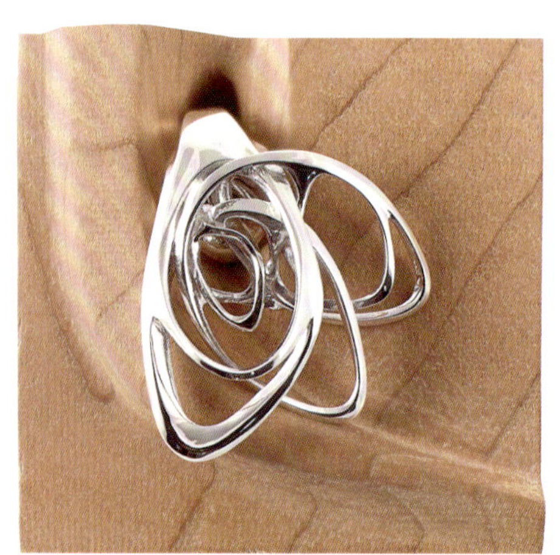

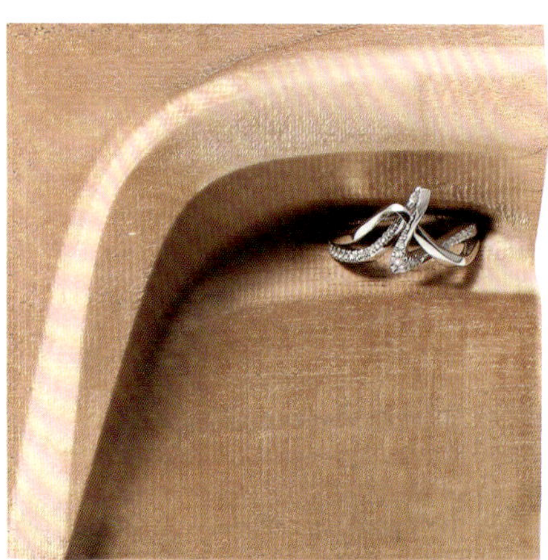

Jenny Wu

The pieces provoke a curiosity for how they are made and fit together, embedding a formal logic that balances the expression of their form with material properties. Creating designs that convey a high level of digital refinement and human engagement, LACE distills the elemental qualities of assembly into imaginative geometries.

Featuring overlapping geometries, many pieces elegantly articulate gestures of their companion piece, fitting in ways that are loosely intertwined. *Rhea Diamond Ring with Solitaire Setting in Platinum, Hera Diamond Wedding Band in Platinum, Amare and Sera Rings in Rose Gold, Amare and Sera Diamond Rings in Platinum.*

INLAY
FURNITURE

Developed as a series of refined prototypes, Inlay Furniture is an array of tectonically considered objects and assemblies that investigate details, materials, and production for high-end furniture. Exploring design techniques primed for larger architectural works, this series uses the figural elements of wood and steel craftwork to articulate elegantly jointed details and expressive volumetric form.

Resolving the complexities of functional design with only a few components, the part-to-part assembly of planar surfaces appears volumetrically related. Scraping and cutting both wood and metal creates impressions on the bench surface that subtly ripple and splice. Flat profiles of the support structure act as inlays in the solid masses of the seat with figural features, highlighting the compatibility of their geometries.

Crafted to express the assembly methods of solids and surfaces, the characteristics of the design reconfigure seating and support as sculpted elements.

SLIPJOINT TABLE

Developed as two tables with compatible forms, this piece captures volumetric space through the tectonically shaped edges of solids and structural surfaces. Using break-form bent steel panels and CNC-milled mahogany, the surfaces fold in three dimensions to brace the sculpted masses, creating an implied connection between the two tables. As functional objects that can be rearranged, the tables can groove, slide, and sleeve into one another, creating a tiered tabletop.

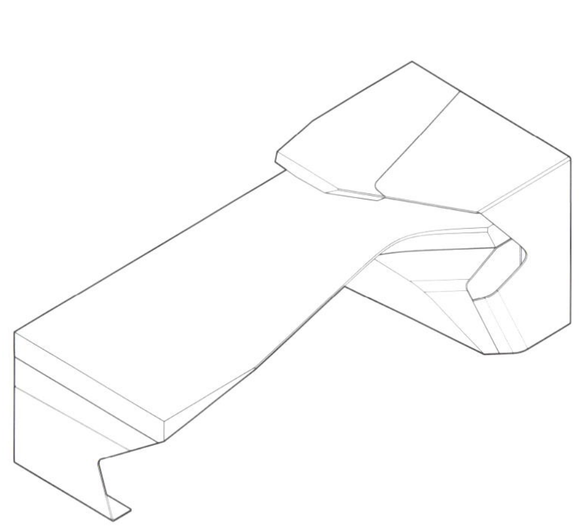

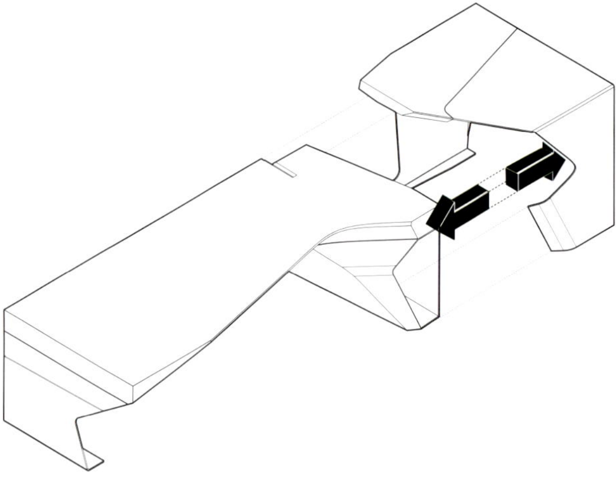

Rather than creating a fixed furniture piece, the table slips apart into two separate tables —aligning along a joint to conceal its individual parts.

JACK & JILL
CHAIRS

Designed in tandem, Jack & Jill chairs pair two interlocked figures that negotiate functional ergonomics with asymmetry, variation, and curious part-to-whole readings. Designed for children, the individual chairs consist of delicate stainless-steel frames and wood masses that are subtly shaped to produce curvature at the seat and backrests. When combined, the chairs unexpectedly nest together, expressing a pure rectilinear volume punctuated by a system of suspended solids.

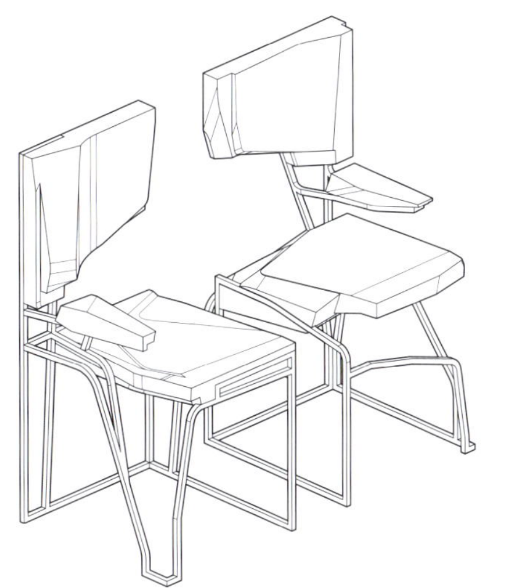
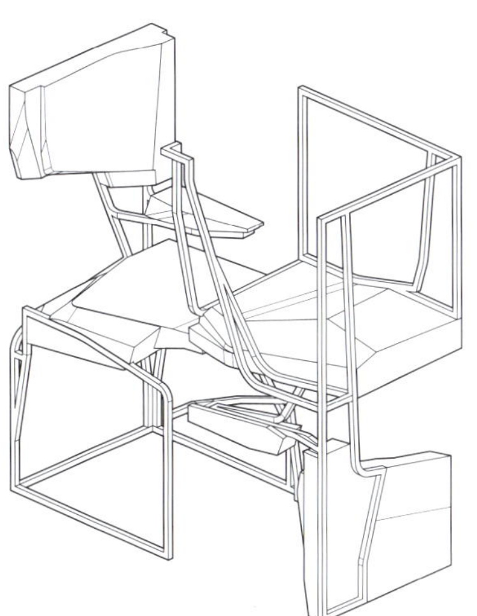
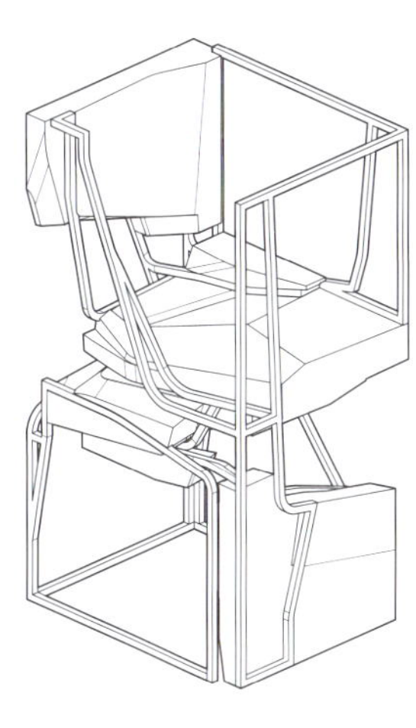

Designed for children, the chairs are representative of the client's desire to commemorate his close bond with his brother. Conceptually sharing this idea, the chairs act as functional totems that highlight how they comfortably interlock.

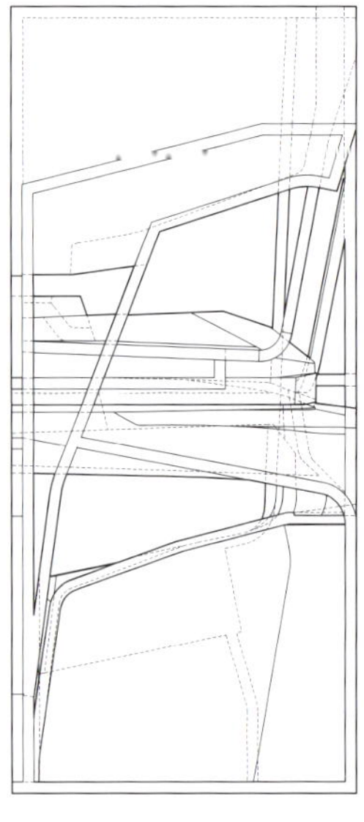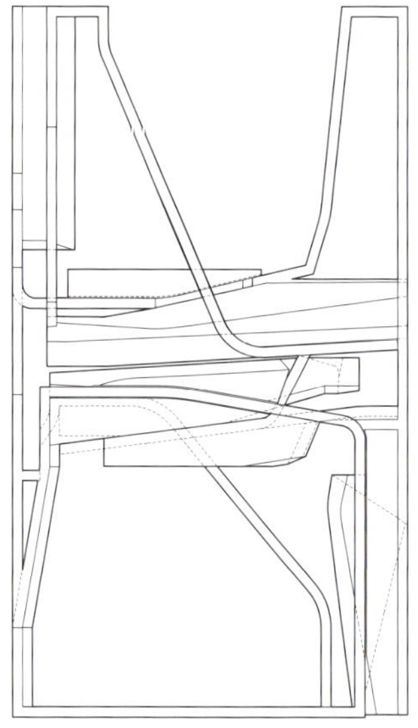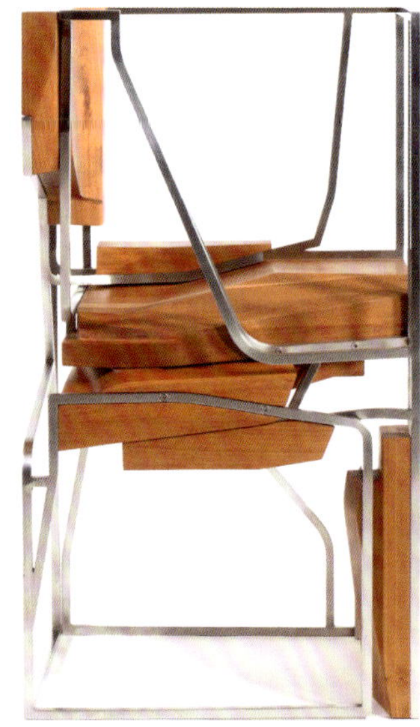

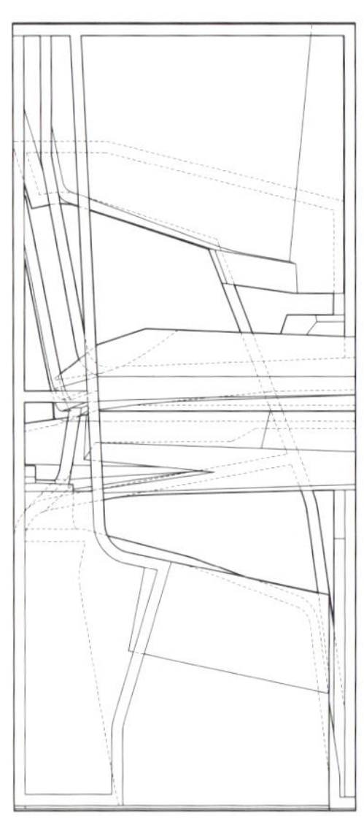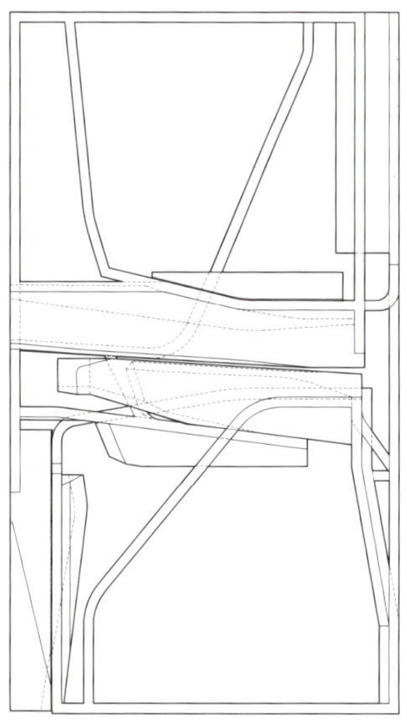

Detailing of the chairs was guided by a set of principles that both ensure an engaging form of interlock, and effectively mask the individual reading of each chair when puzzled together. In order to maintain the purity of the volumes at the outer perimeter, the stainless-steel frame is inlaid into the wood solids, and curious notches in each chair allow for a comfortable fit of the companion chair. The asymmetry of each chair, along with the tight-fit relationship of various parts, is essential to delaying the individual reading of the chairs.

MISSION ROCK
TABLE

Designed to accommodate a myriad of interactions, this assembly uses inlay techniques to combine parts to fit the multifunctional purposes of urban furniture. Using a formal lexicon of street furniture in a layered configuration, its conjoined parts create contoured backrests, adaptable seating elements, and stylized benches in fixed arrangement. From individual seating to large tables for six to eight people, the overall shape of the table gestures to accommodate the diversity of uses, offering a mixture of social interactions.

Balancing structural requirements with highly crafted connections, the table uses custom details to interlock Corten steel and milled hardwood. Creating an armature of interfacing features that join and fasten, surfaces wrap and fold in space to embed with grooved solids. Shaped to the proportions and positions of the solid pieces, the planar elements interact in three dimensions, giving figure to their parts and combining individual features into a connected form.

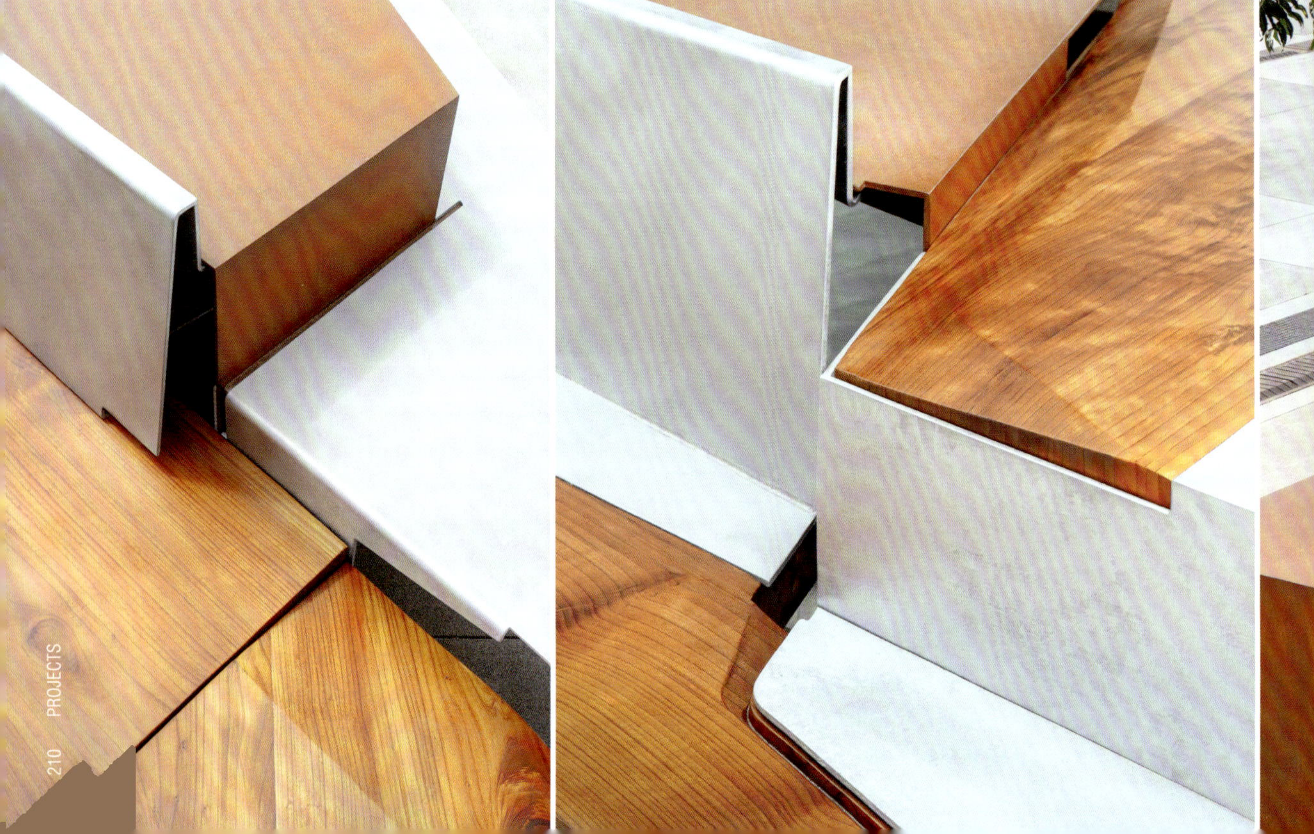

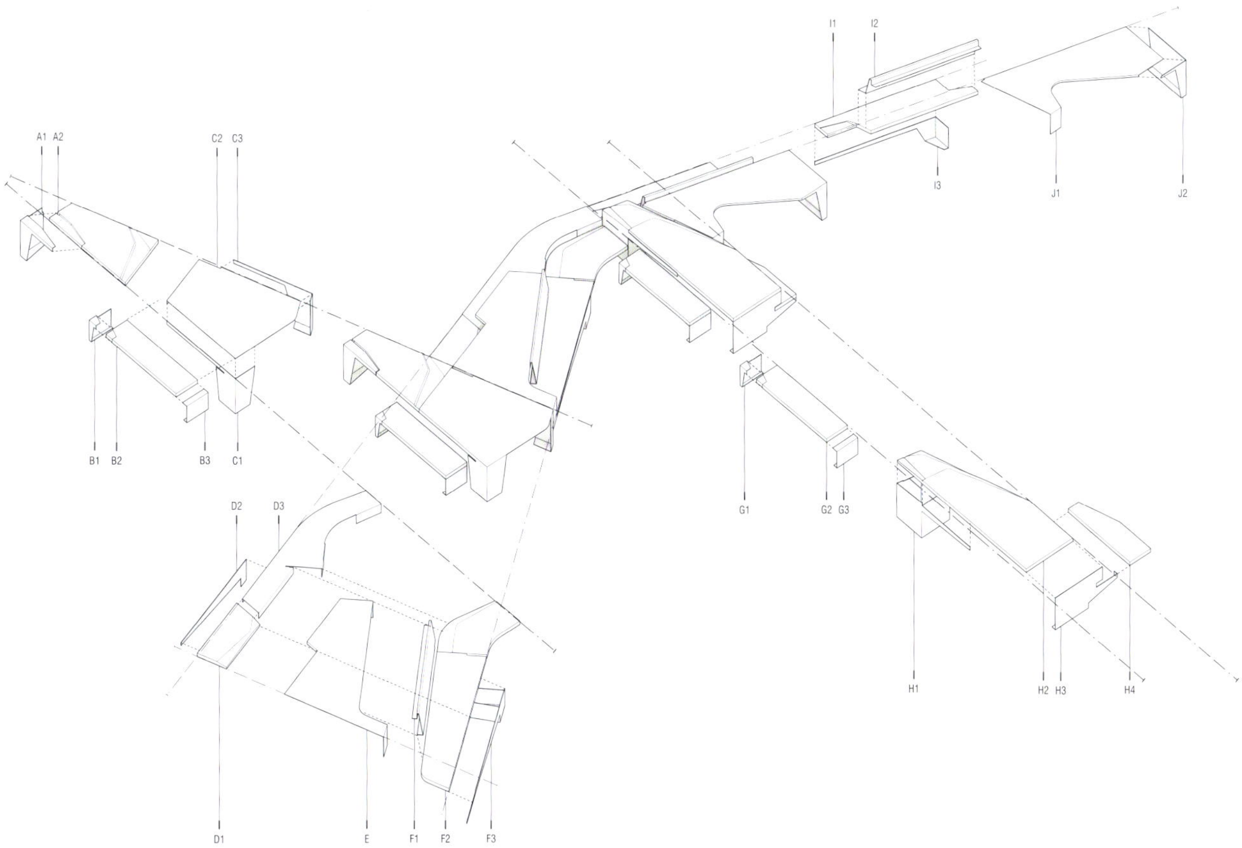

A1 A2
C2 C3
I1 I2
J1
J2
I3
B1 B2
B3 C1
D2 D3
G1
G2 G3
H1
H2 H3
H4
D1
E
F1 F2 F3
PART ASSEMBLY

LIVE WIRE

Live Wire examines what separates designed assemblies from strictly functional systems through the continuous merging and constant transformation of one detail to the next, resulting in a unified architectural expression.

In conventional vertical circulation systems, numerous components are assembled together, with each performing a specific function: guardrails along the perimeter of an elevated space, a handrail attached to adjacent walls, treads and risers for stepped surfaces, and larger structural supports. These individual components often act independently as purely functional systems devoid of architectural experience, or as tectonic relationships that might collectively form from these parts in combination.

Focusing on a highly functional architectural element, the design elaborates on the nature of assembly through the use of a single structural system of one-inch-diameter aluminum tubes. At times bundled into joined branches, and seemingly winding through one another, the metal tubes bend and connect in three-dimensional configurations. In coordinated movement, they create risers that flow into a sloping banister, which then flows into the handrail, and back down to become the nosing of the tread. This directionality merges features of the stair into a uniform system, yet blurs its aesthetic and spatial perception, challenging the structural reading of these elements as part of the tectonic language of the assembly.

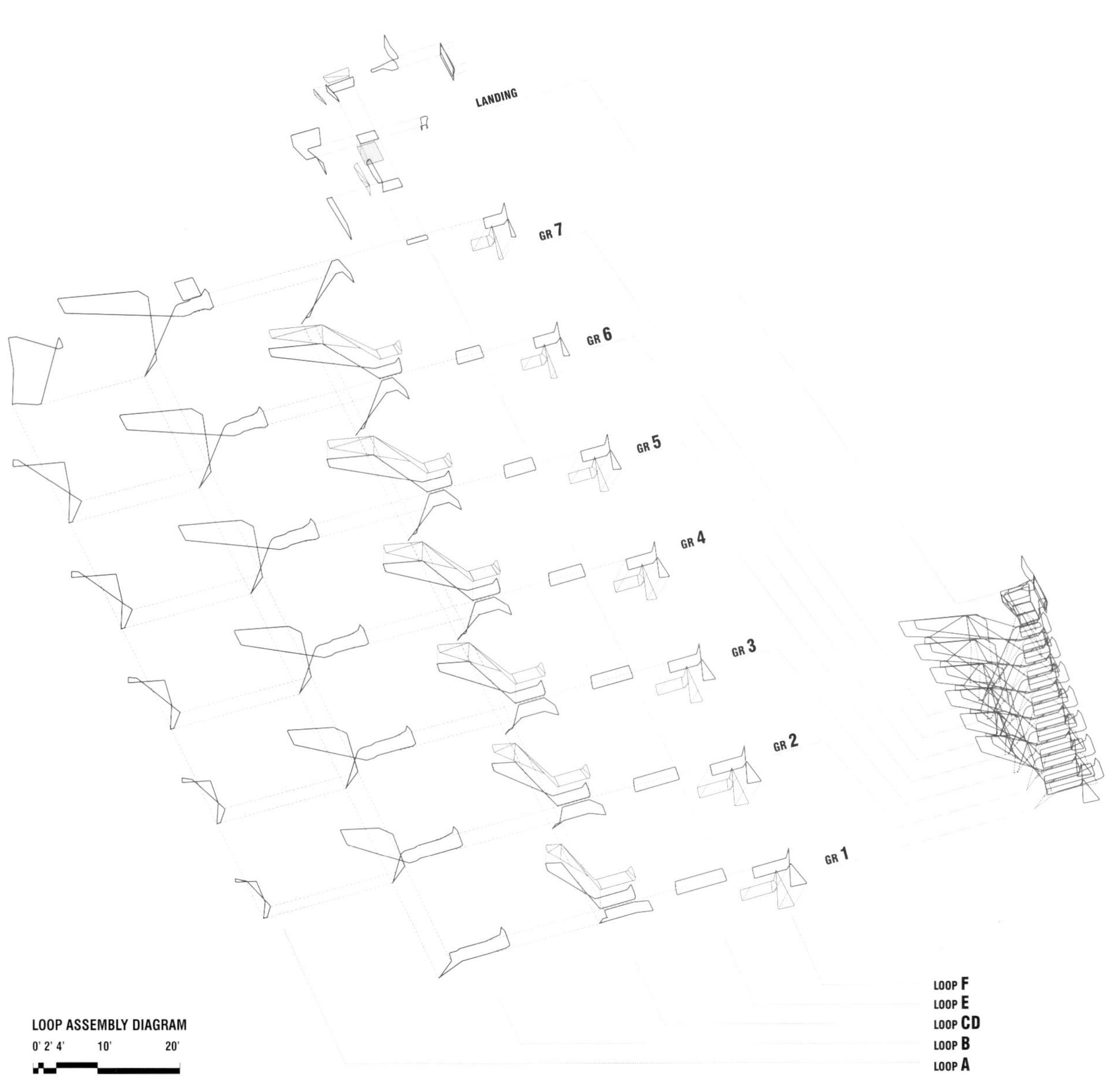

LANDING
GR 7
GR 6
GR 5
GR 4
GR 3
GR 2
GR 1
LOOP F
LOOP E
LOOP CD
LOOP B
LOOP A
LOOP ASSEMBLY DIAGRAM
0' 2' 4'   10'   20'

Occupying the space between floors, Live Wire expands the functional language of a stair more comprehensively into a systematic and uniquely tectonic architectural space. Linking the floor level of the gallery to the catwalk above, the stair details expressively contrasting qualities, from lightweight to heavy, from compact to monumental, from ephemeral to permanent.

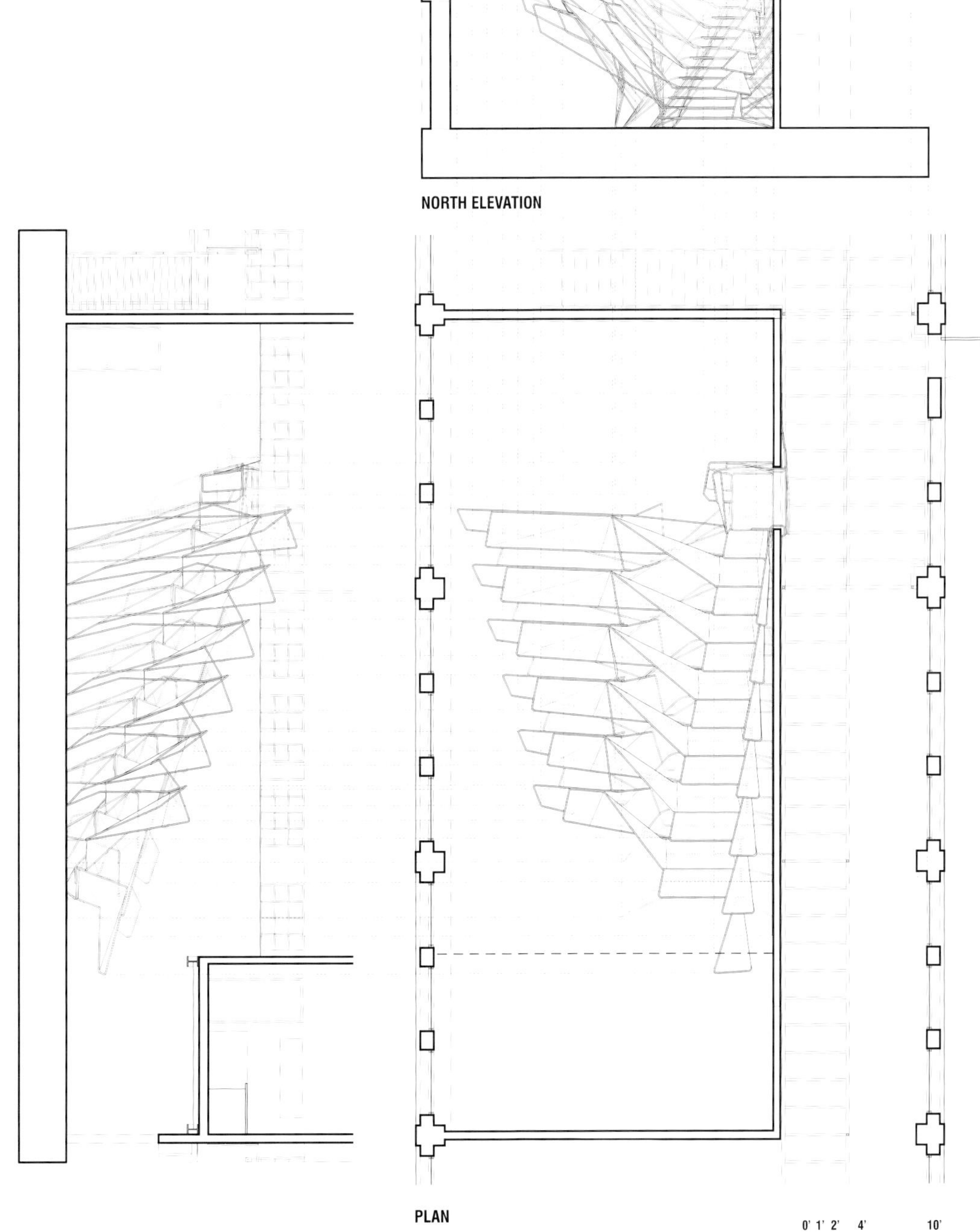

LOOP A TUBE FORMATION

LOOP D TUBE FORMATION

PERFORATED ALUMINUM FORMATION

PERFORATED ALUMINUM FORMATION

LOOP E FORMATION

FORMATION DIAGRAM

0' 1' 2'   4'   10'

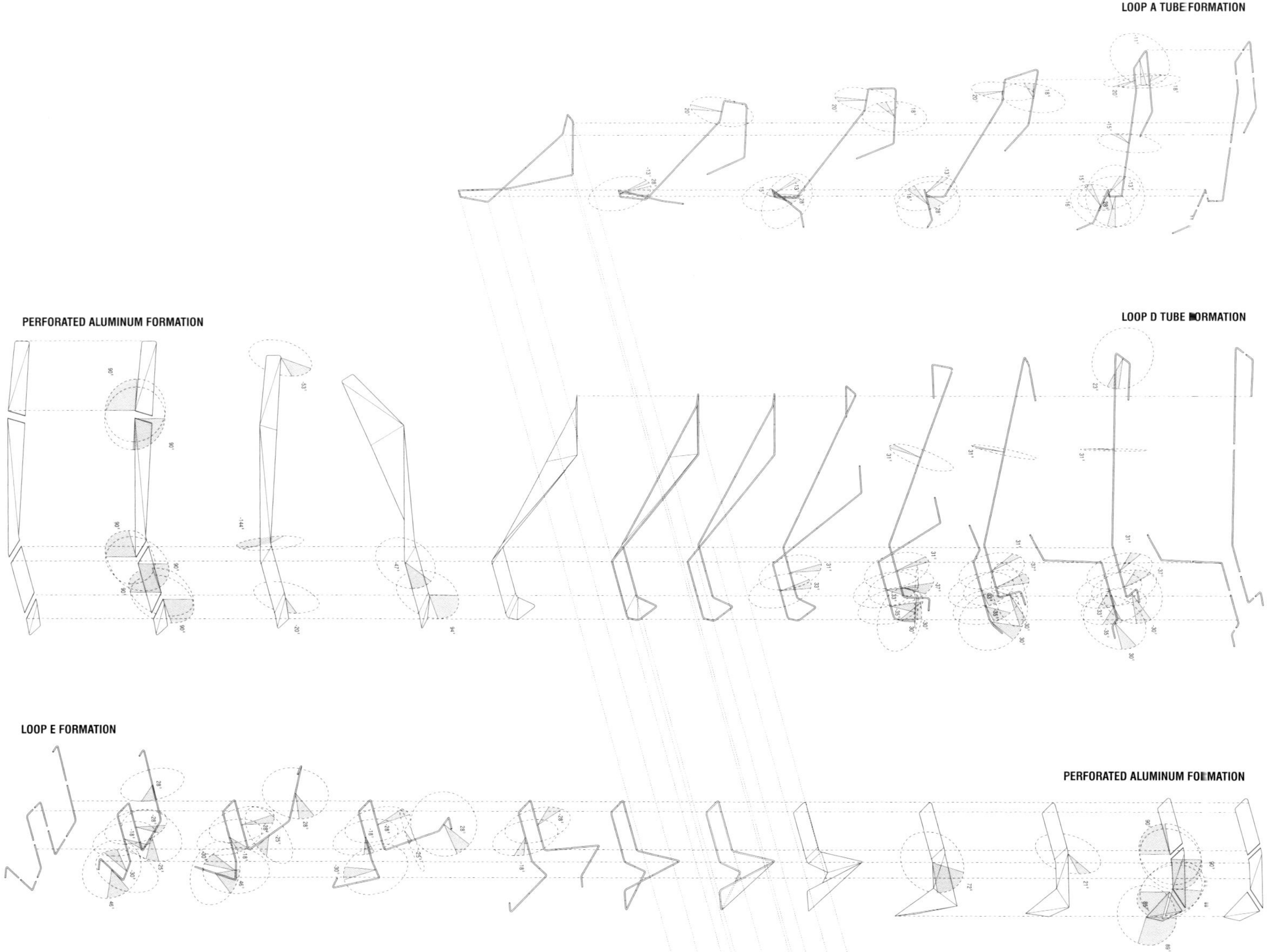

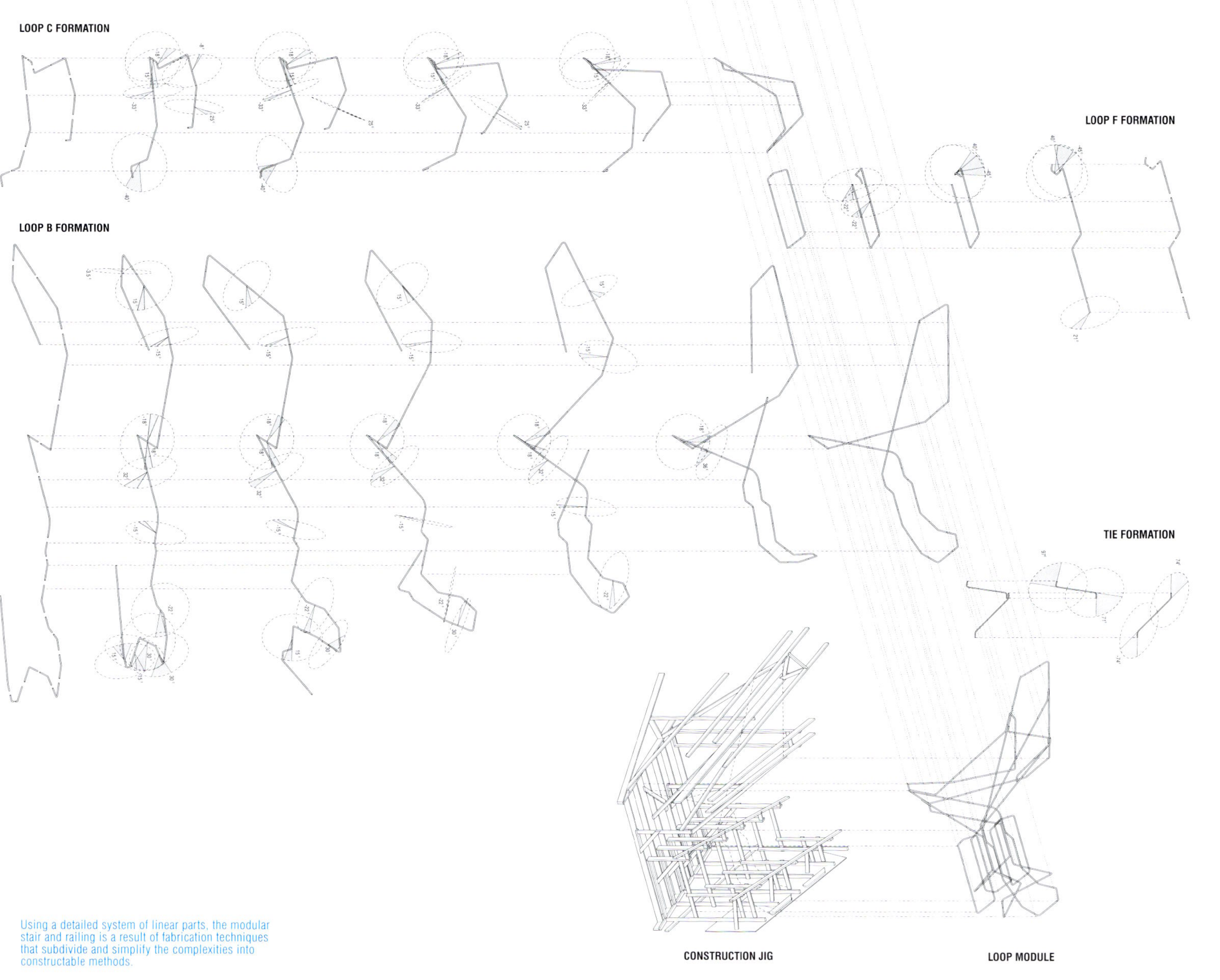

Using a detailed system of linear parts, the modular stair and railing is a result of fabrication techniques that subdivide and simplify the complexities into constructable methods.

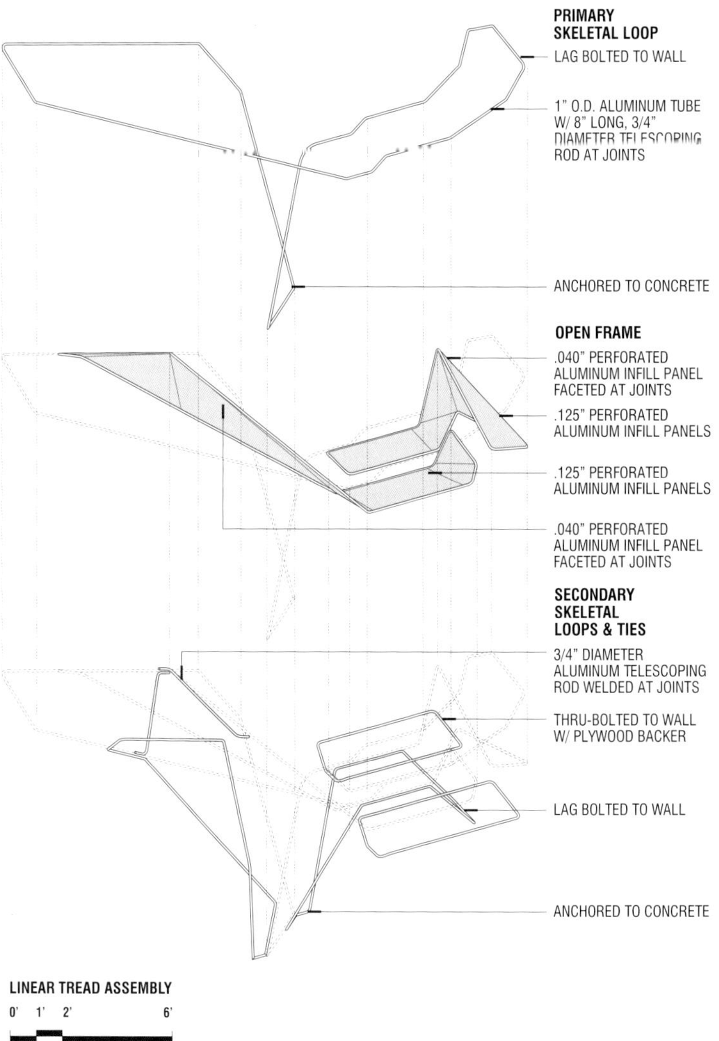

As a way of studying the continuous looping system, the design process used physical models to explore both spatial ideas as well as the ideas surrounding physical fabrication. Fabricated from approximately 2,400 linear feet of aluminum tubing and rods, the stair employs a combination of complex loops that merge together to form every part of its system. It also incorporates perforated aluminum panels of two different thicknesses, faceting the closed frame of its coplanar properties to create a continuous, semi-transparent tread surface.

Each part of the linear system is exposed and places progressively compounded forces onto each connected element. As the stair moves upward, the geometry subtly transforms to adapt to the limits of the material, relying on the tactical build-up of densely woven parts to carry the load. The stair assembly expands the definitions that underpin how architectural systems are assessed in design—as being evocative of something richly constructed for both function and experience.

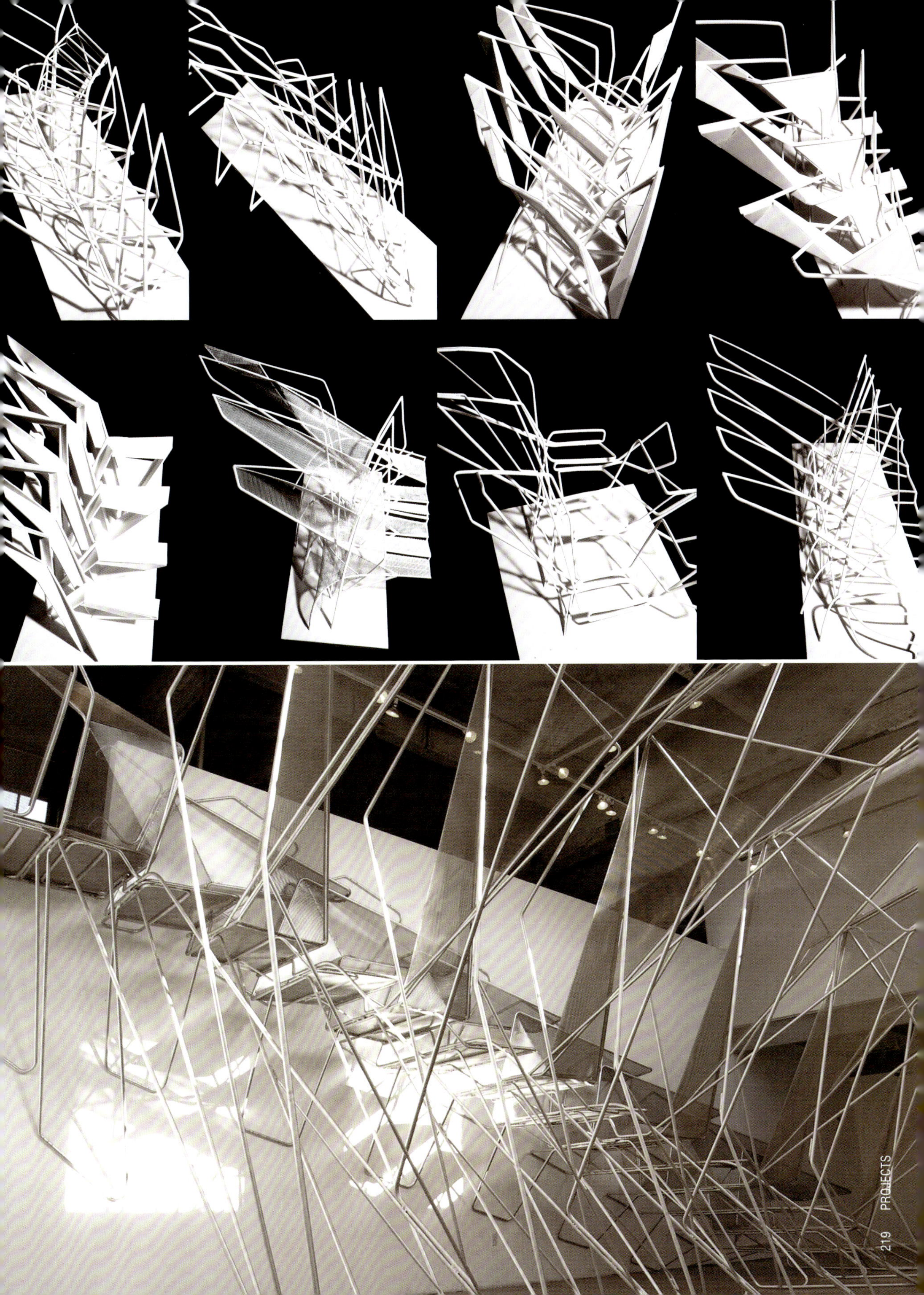

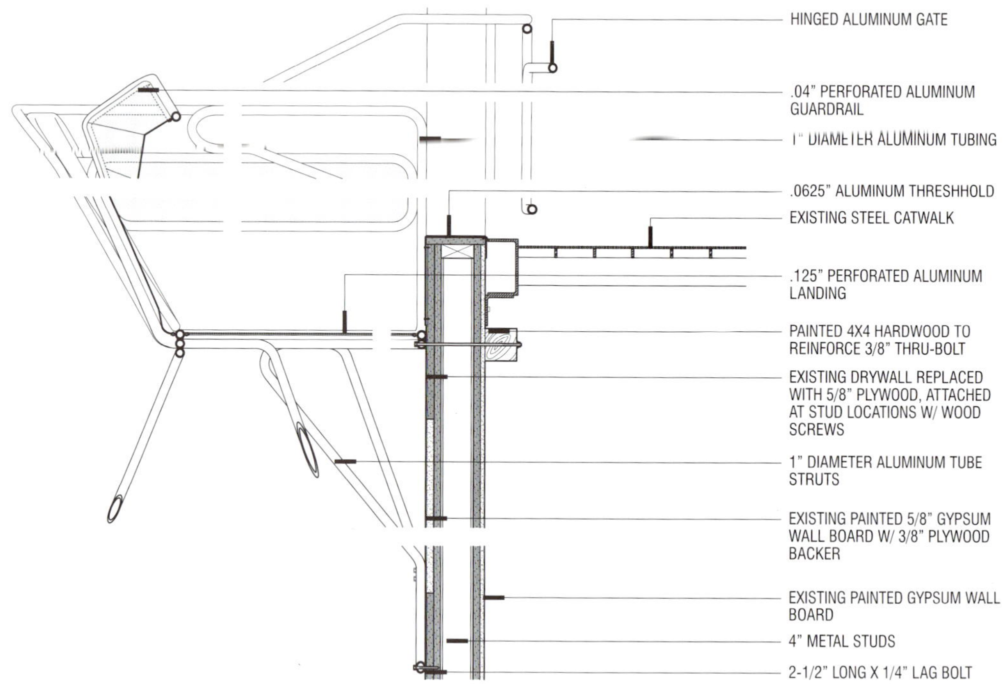

SECTION AT LANDING

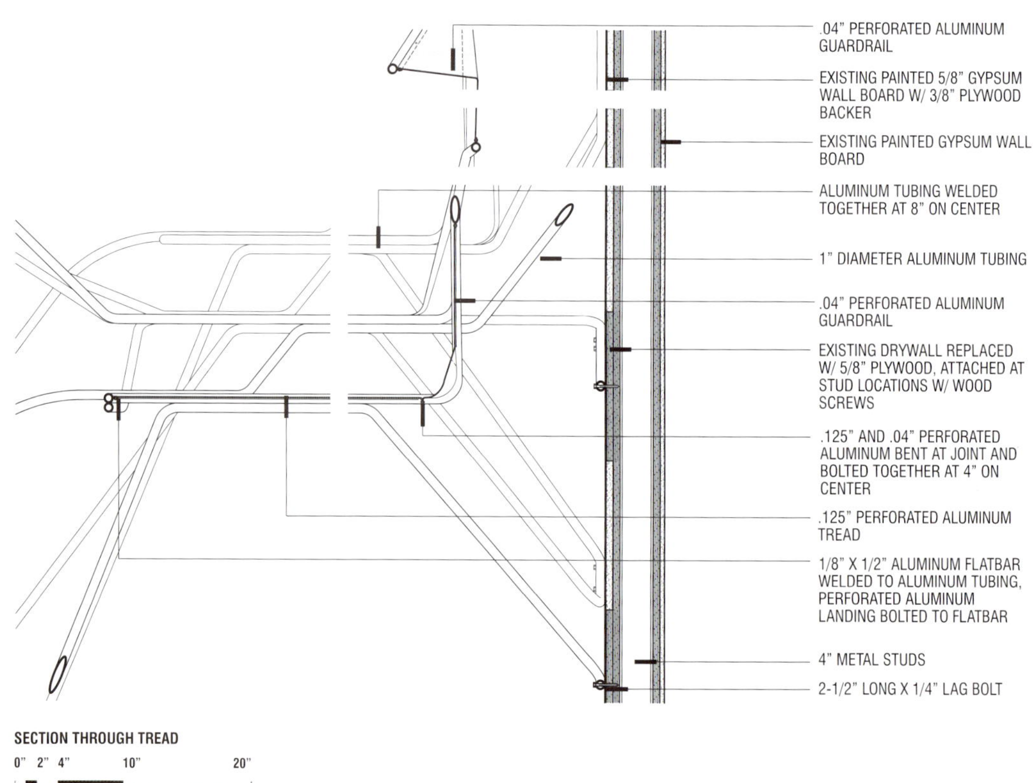

SECTION THROUGH TREAD

0" 2" 4"   10"   20"

QUICKSILVER

Designed as a site-specific installation for the JUT Art Museum in Taipei, Quicksilver continues the exploratory assemblies that foreground the qualities and vitality of the architectural stair. Unlike Live Wire, Quicksilver explores the elements of the stair as an object of assembly, without the restriction of functionality. Descending into the lobby atrium from the gallery above, the stair expressively echoes the existing museum stair that wraps the edges of the first floor, becoming the focal point that connects the spaces.

Visitors travel perceptually from the lobby to the second floor in a spiral, creating a dynamic sense of movement around an unoccupiable void. Filling this space, the installation becomes a mercurial centerpiece of the exhibition. Consisting almost entirely of one-inch polished steel tubes, its chandelier-like appearance explores loose-fit relationships with detailed construction techniques.

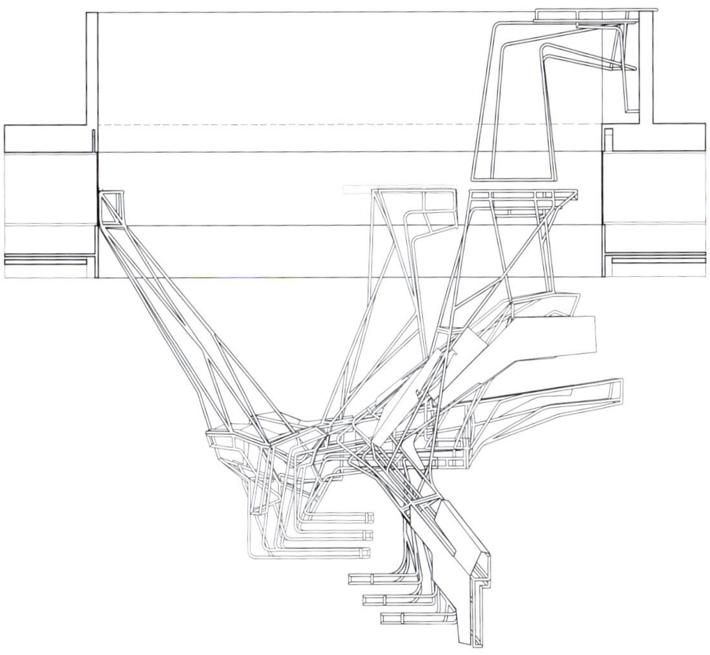

FRONT ELEVATION

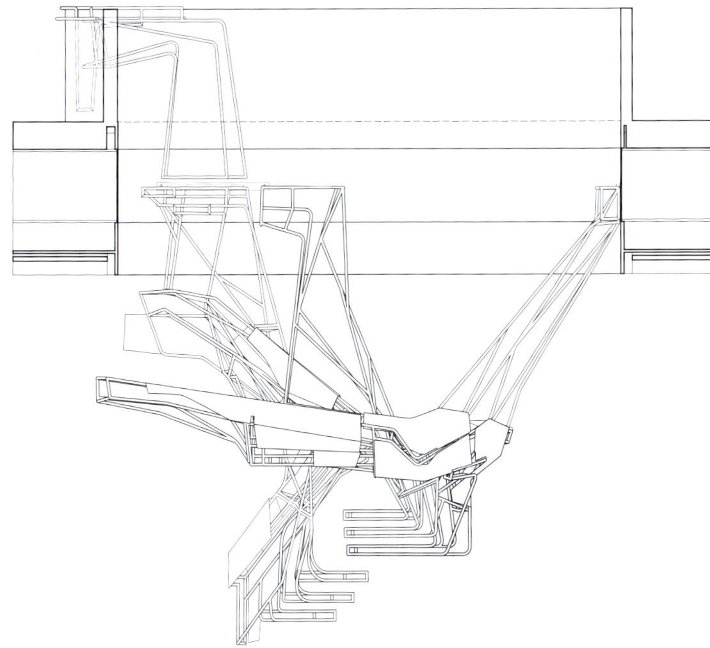

BACK ELEVATION

Both the linear tube system, as well as the accompanying planar surfaces, utilize multiple bending methods—resolving geometrically to create thickened railing elements and stepped treads as the components turn and warp. Developing these characteristics required customized tools for forming the creases of the metal panels to fit the linear volumes, using a custom-fabricated sheet-metal press that precisely folded each panel.

Reassembled on site in a sequence, the components connect along interfacing end profiles, completing the opening in the existing railing of the gallery above, while hovering over the entry space of the museum.

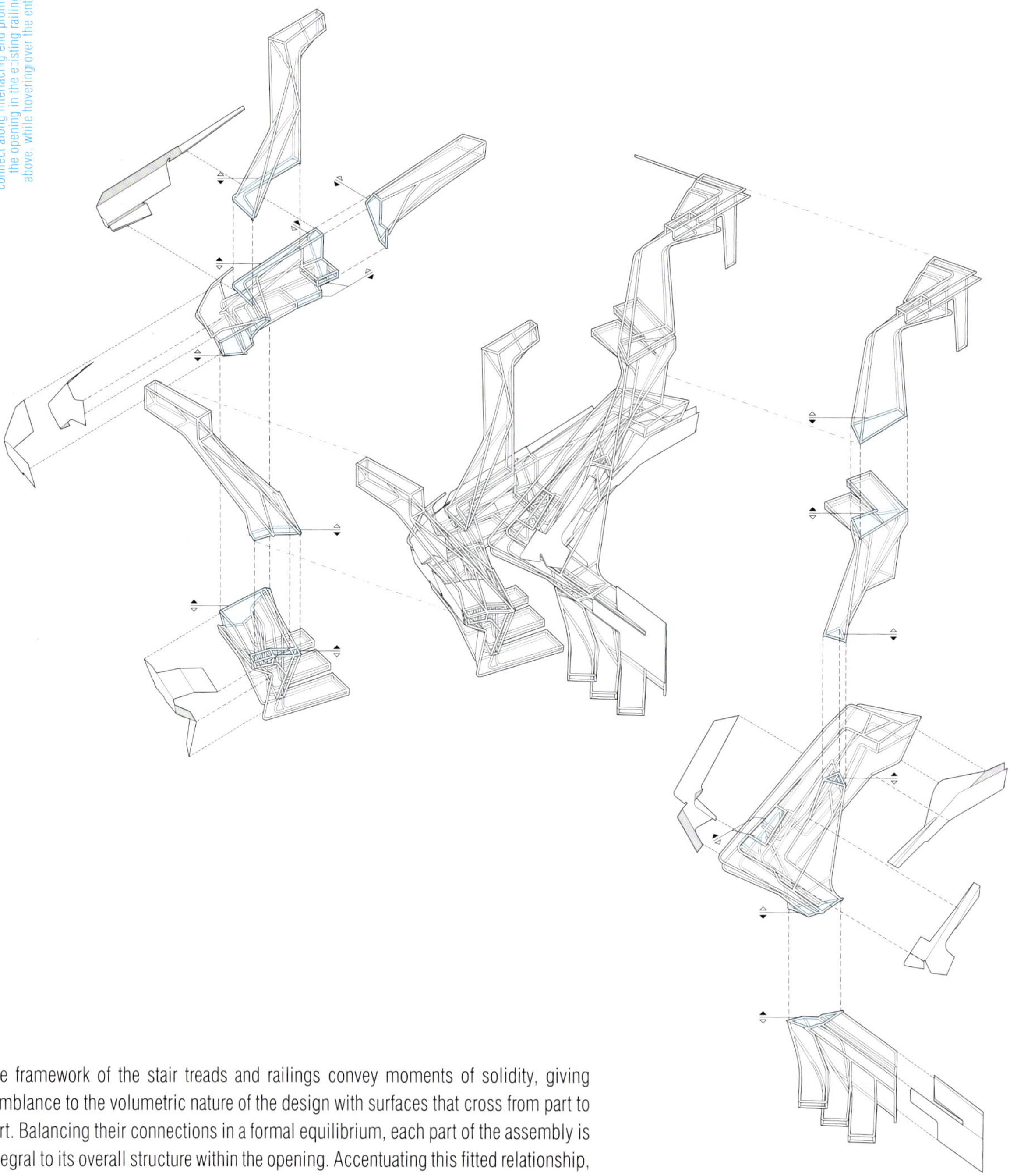

The framework of the stair treads and railings convey moments of solidity, giving semblance to the volumetric nature of the design with surfaces that cross from part to part. Balancing their connections in a formal equilibrium, each part of the assembly is integral to its overall structure within the opening. Accentuating this fitted relationship, the descending stair reaches into the upper gallery floor, locking the hinged access door of the guardrail into an open position.

SUSPENDED ASSEMBLY SEQUENCE

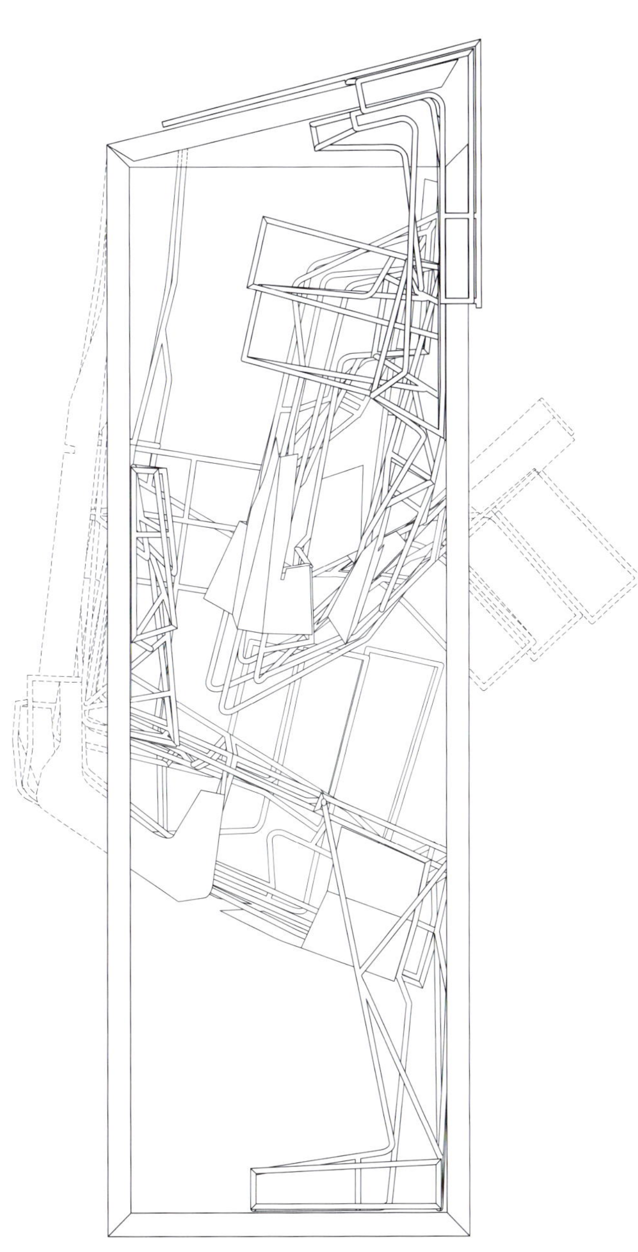

PLAN ABOVE GALLERY RAILING

KEELUNG CUBE

Designed as a sculptural centerpiece in Keelung, Taiwan's extensive port and harbor, the puzzled cube is an investigation of the logics of puzzling assemblies and their ability to produce dynamic perceptual effects through their part-to-part relationships, posture, and implied sense of movement. With the intention of subtly conveying a sense of its assembly sequence, the overall volume simultaneously conveys a clear holistic reading while highlighting the individuality of its parts. Creating a static object from individual parts, the completed cube conveys how these parts have sequentially found their place in the overall composition, activating the reading of subtle chamfers and notches with an implied sense of movement. Each of these parts has its own identity in shape, proportion, and material, but combine to complete the cubic assembly in an interlocking dialogue. Within this embedded relationship, the openings between connections compel the visitor to look deeper into the object to discover the subtle surfaces that enliven its formal and technical construction.

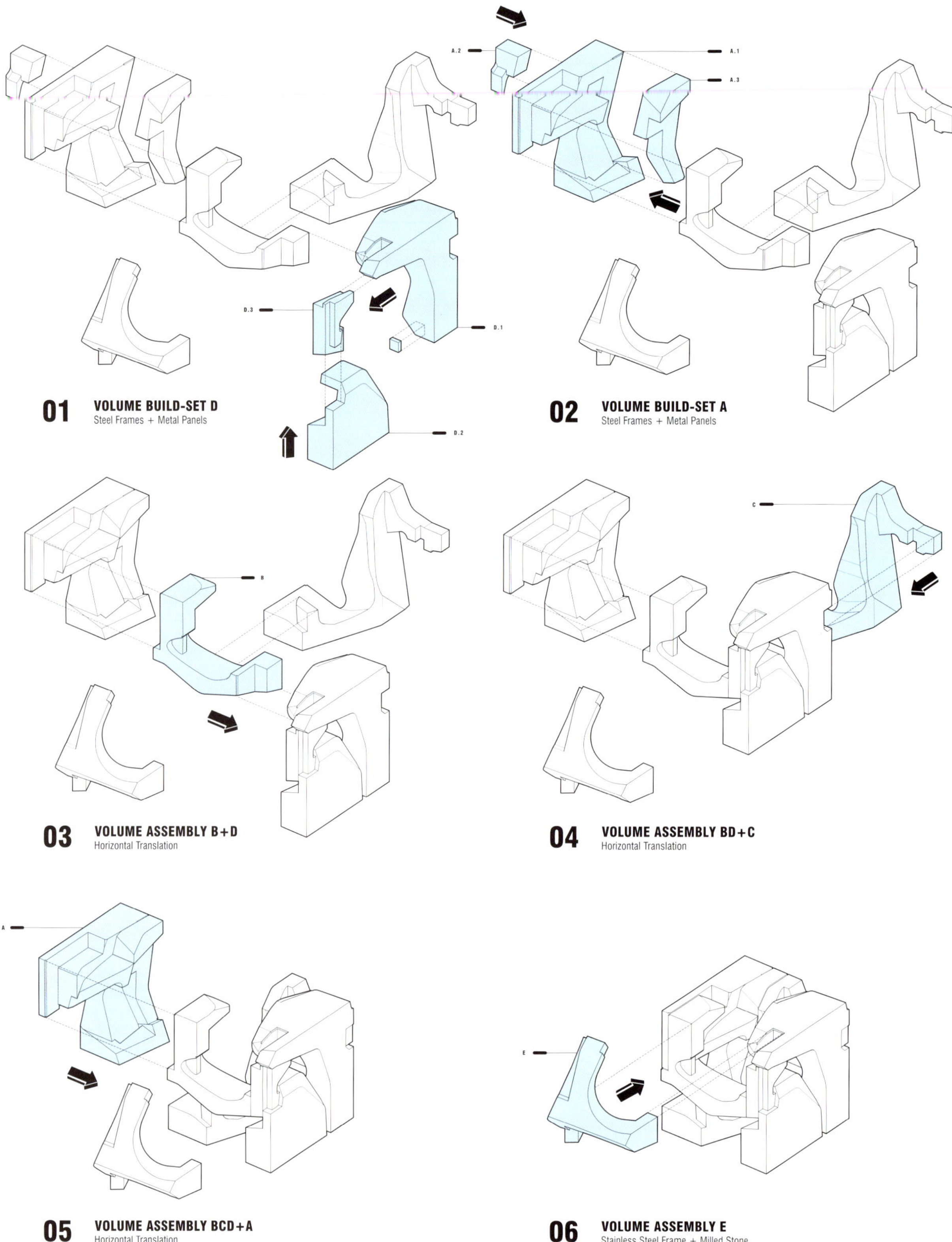

01 **VOLUME BUILD-SET D**
Steel Frames + Metal Panels

02 **VOLUME BUILD-SET A**
Steel Frames + Metal Panels

03 **VOLUME ASSEMBLY B+D**
Horizontal Translation

04 **VOLUME ASSEMBLY BD+C**
Horizontal Translation

05 **VOLUME ASSEMBLY BCD+A**
Horizontal Translation

06 **VOLUME ASSEMBLY E**
Stainless Steel Frame + Milled Stone

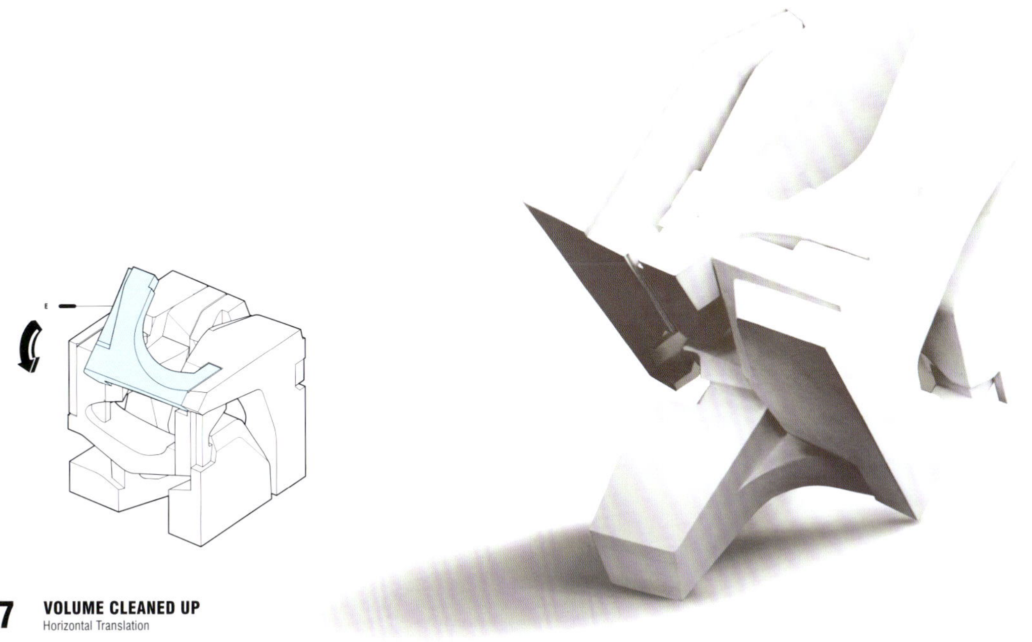

Though the assembly of the cube is a result of a buildup of parts, their relationship to one another is expressed as they are fixed in place within the cube. Creating gaps and edges that allow for shifts and slides in the fitting of parts, the openings on the exterior expose the volumetric relationships of internally sculpted surfaces, suggesting a more nuanced formal fit.

07 **VOLUME CLEANED UP**
Horizontal Translation

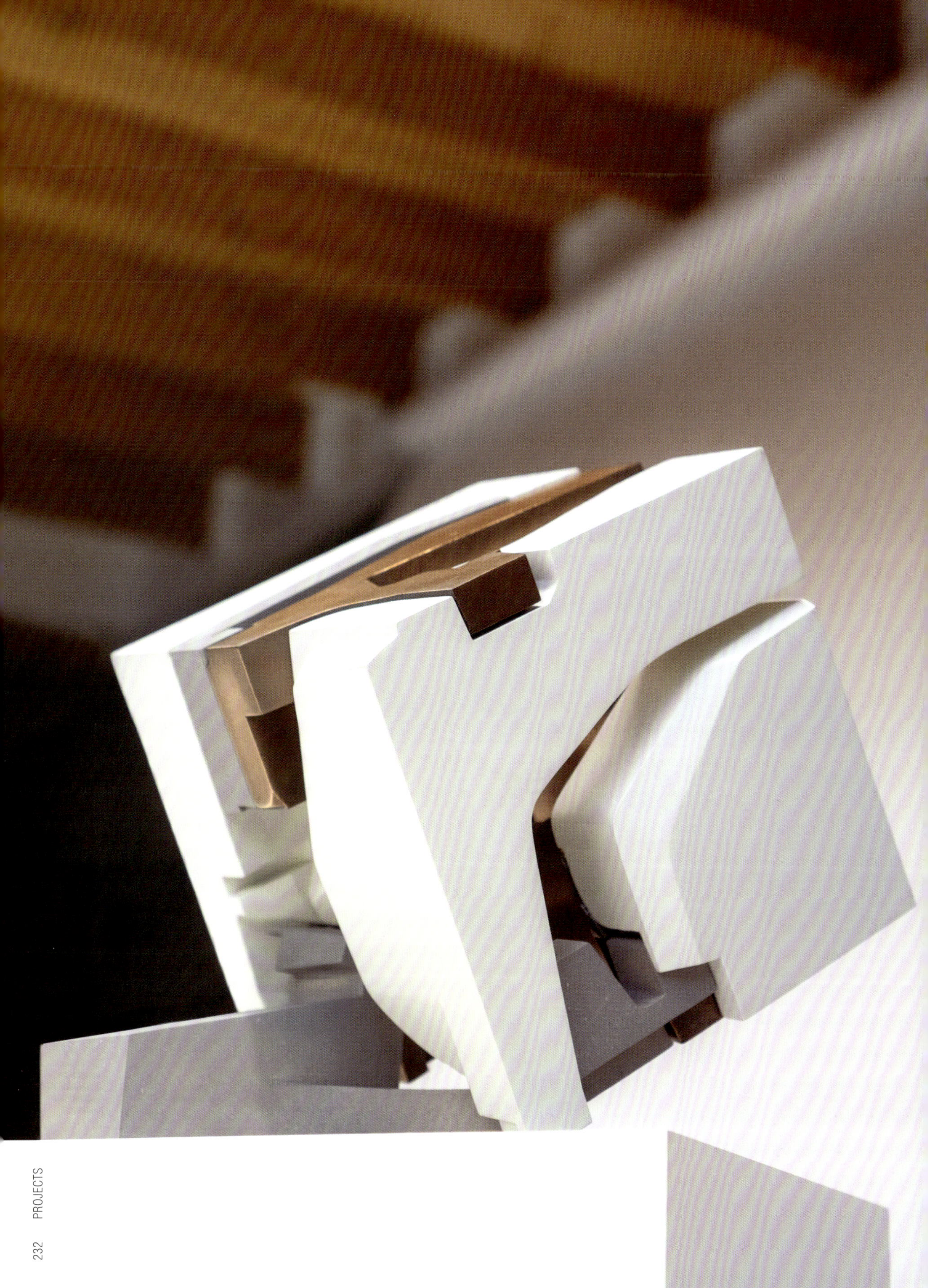

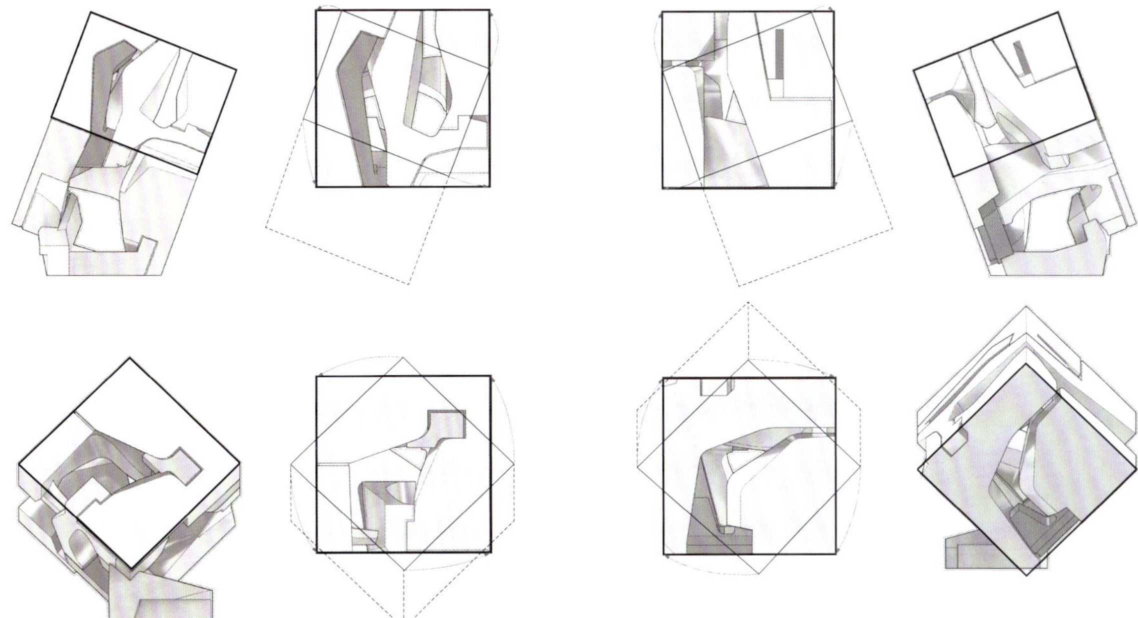

TILTED ELEVATIONS

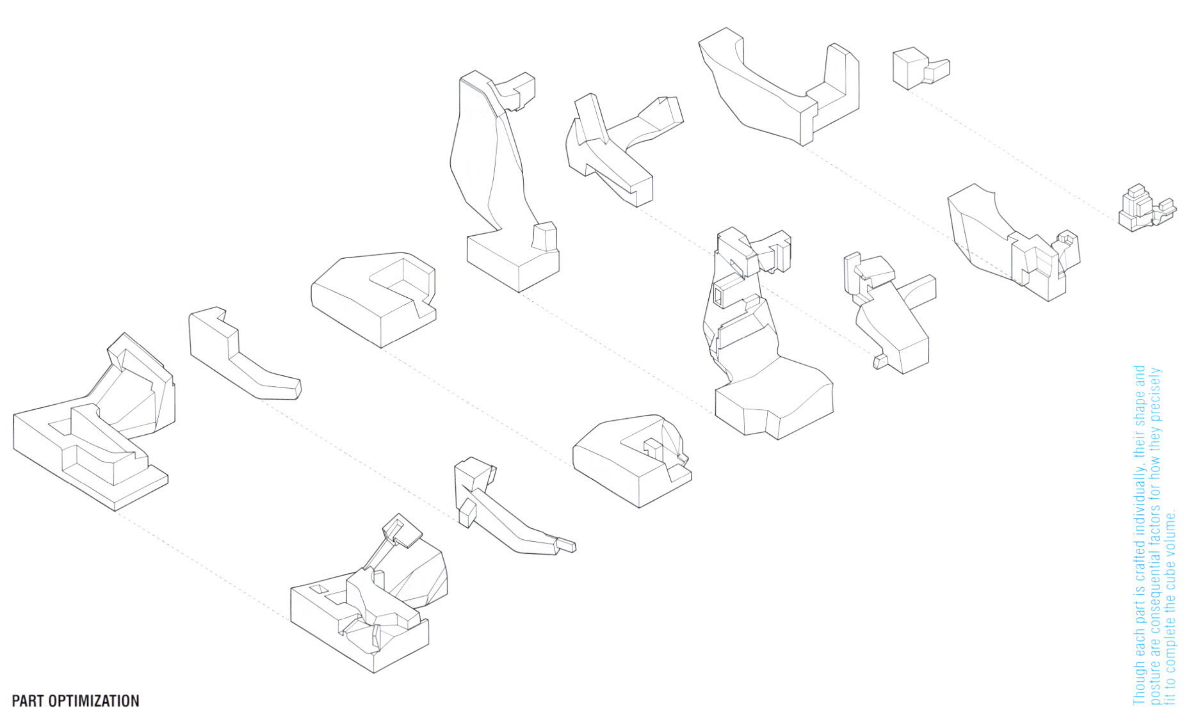

PART OPTIMIZATION

Though each part is crafted individually, their shape and posture are consequential factors for how they precisely fit to complete the cube volume.

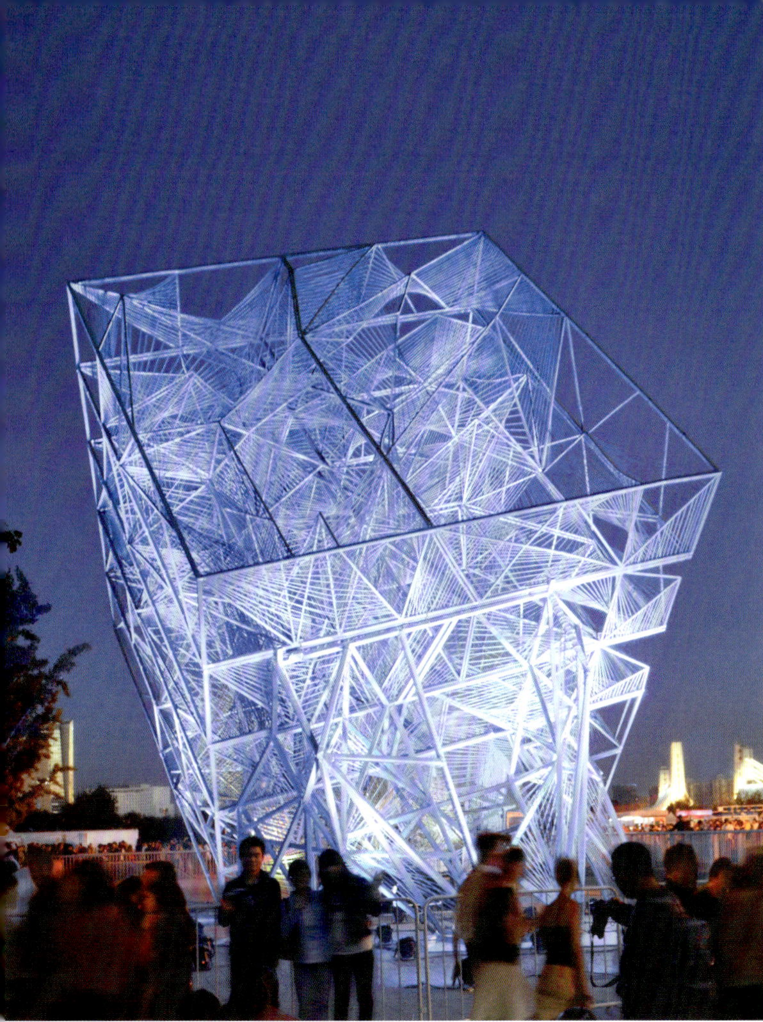

THE CUBE

Using a primitive cube volume as a spatially rich environment to study linear assemblies, this installation merges abstraction and tectonic construction. Conceptualized as a spatial field rather than a solid mass, the qualities of its perceived formal language challenge the reading of its overall form through woven surfaces and filigree. In a rhythmic field of lines, the twisting of implied surfaces is dense and complex—creating layered fields and coherent geometric patterns. The transformative effect engulfs the open space within the cube, and becomes a portal for viewing the intense interactions and deliberate relationships of its interior space: two-dimensional strategies transform into a dynamic experience in three dimensions.

This transformation is something that gives new readings to both the inside and outside of the cube, as its geometric boundary and sense of enclosure are redefined as a field of shifting trajectories. Stripping the cube of its typical readings as an object with mass, the design uses volume and space to reconstruct it with intricately assembled systems. Turning a linear system into a three-dimensional network, the fabrication is modular yet varies to position and arrange twisting geometries across the overall form. Systematizing the design into simpler components, this modularity is masked when fully assembled, but made the construction of these parts more logical.

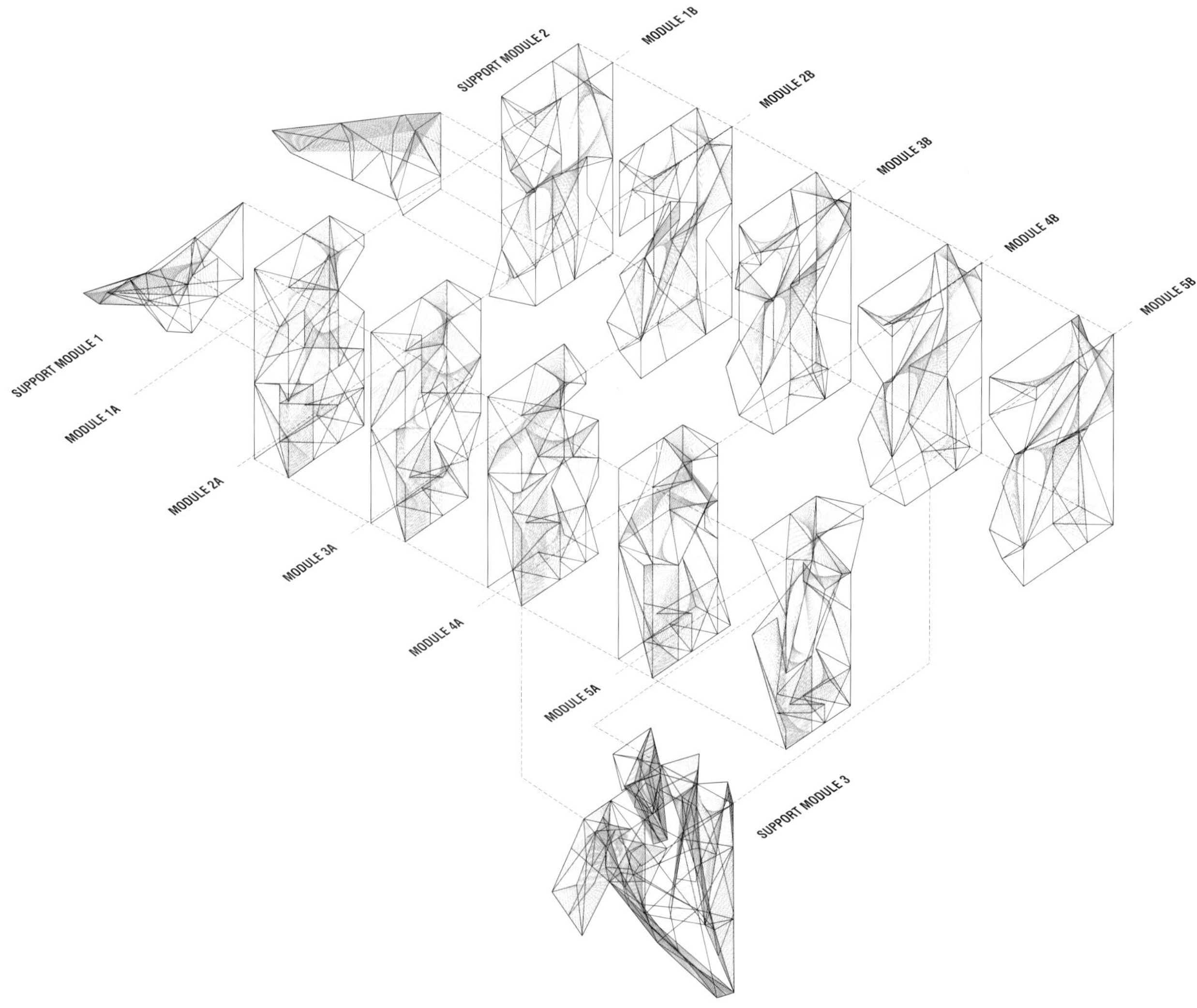

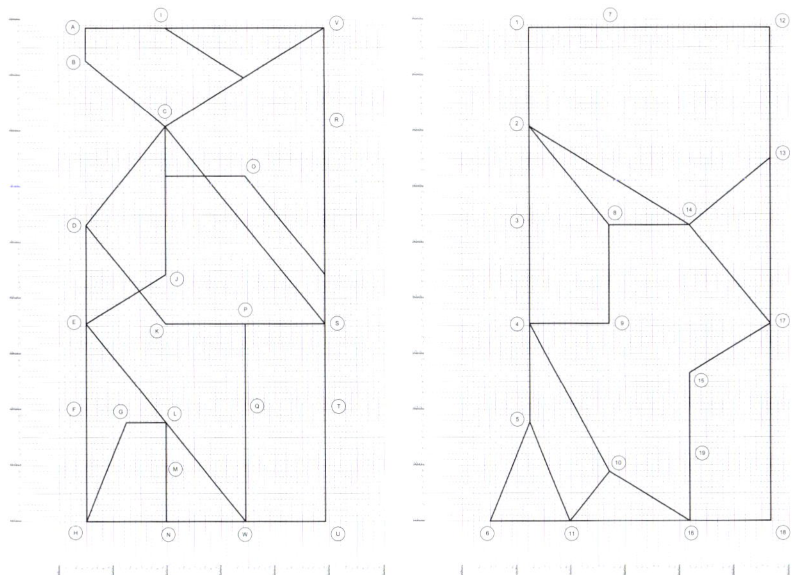

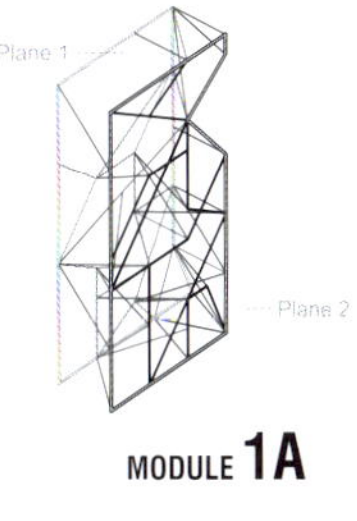

MODULE **1A**

Through a constellation of two-dimensional techniques and strategic connections, the entire system consisted of an armature of flat profiles on a metric grid. With point-to-point fabrication methods, both the structural steel armature and continuous rope system reach deep into the volume to become three-dimensional surfaces that stretch across the internal space.

MODULE PROFILES

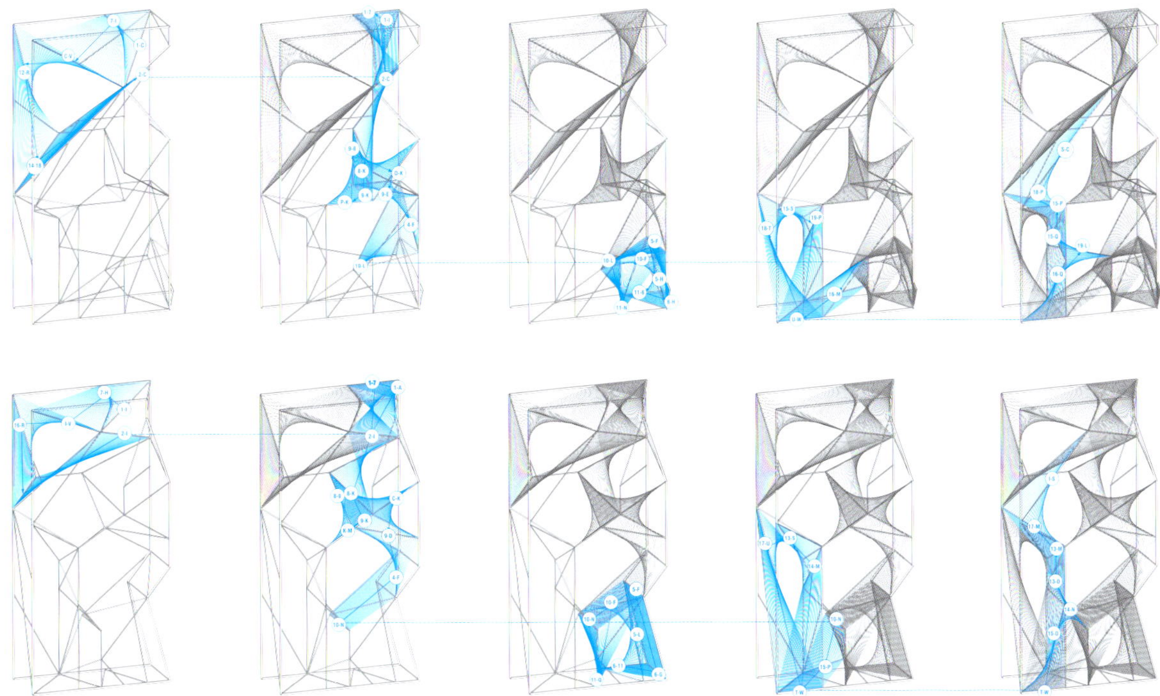

FILIGREE SEQUENCE

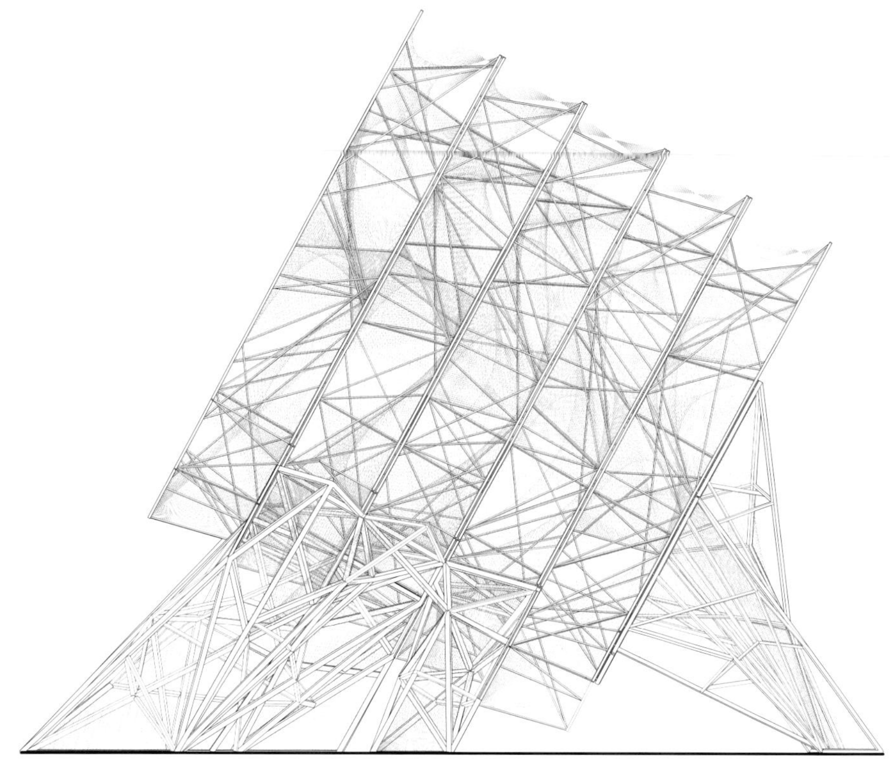

SIDE ELEVATION

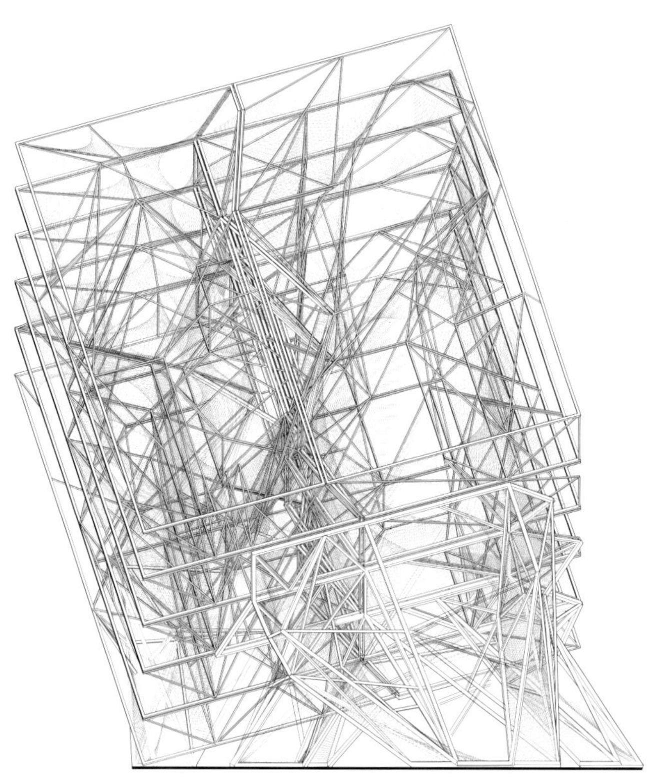

FRONT ELEVATION

0M   1M   2M   4M

Imagining continuous surfaces that flow from one to the other, each module contorts
the surfaces in variation from the others. These articulations transform the rope into a
linear texture, with fluctuations in coplanar alignment, implying a continuous, warped
space. Traveling through the volume continuously, these surfaces become active in
the system, spilling out to lift the cube into the air. Challenging the notion of a cube as
a solid object, the armature redefines the distinct boundary of a spatially rich volume,
optically transforming the linear geometries into a woven network.

3DS
CULINARY

Designed as a creative laboratory that celebrates the merging of technology and the culinary arts, 3DS Culinary reimagines its existing neoclassical building shell as an empty volume for embedding architectural objects. The interior of the shell consists of a concrete vault, masonry walls, and exposed steel roof trusses that once hung a coffered ceiling. In contrast, our intervention into the open space inside, like the technology itself, charts out new territory that brings together innovation and assembly.

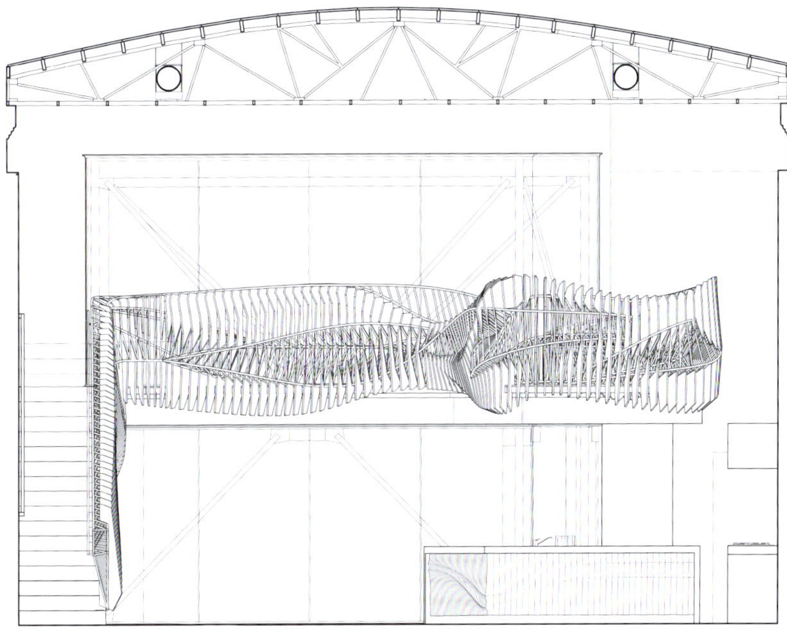

INTERIOR ELEVATION NORTH

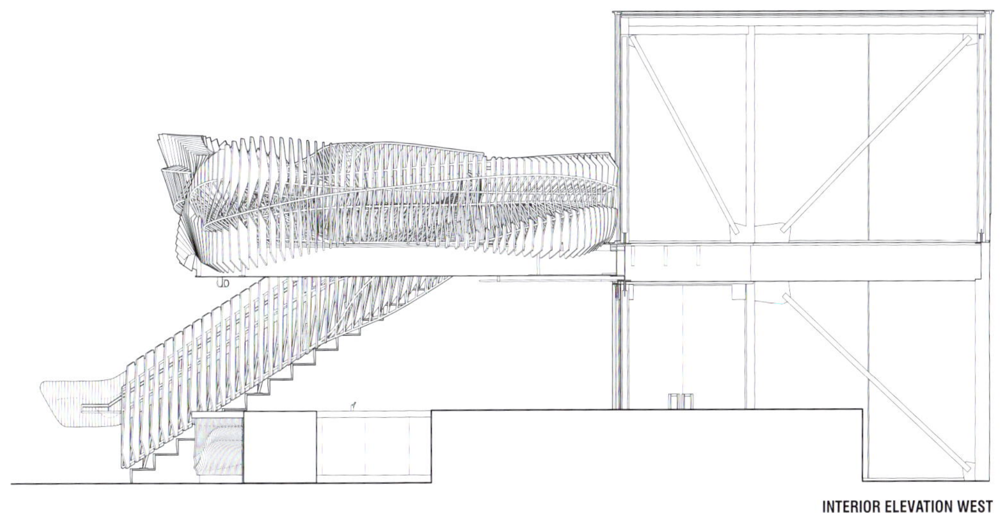

INTERIOR ELEVATION WEST

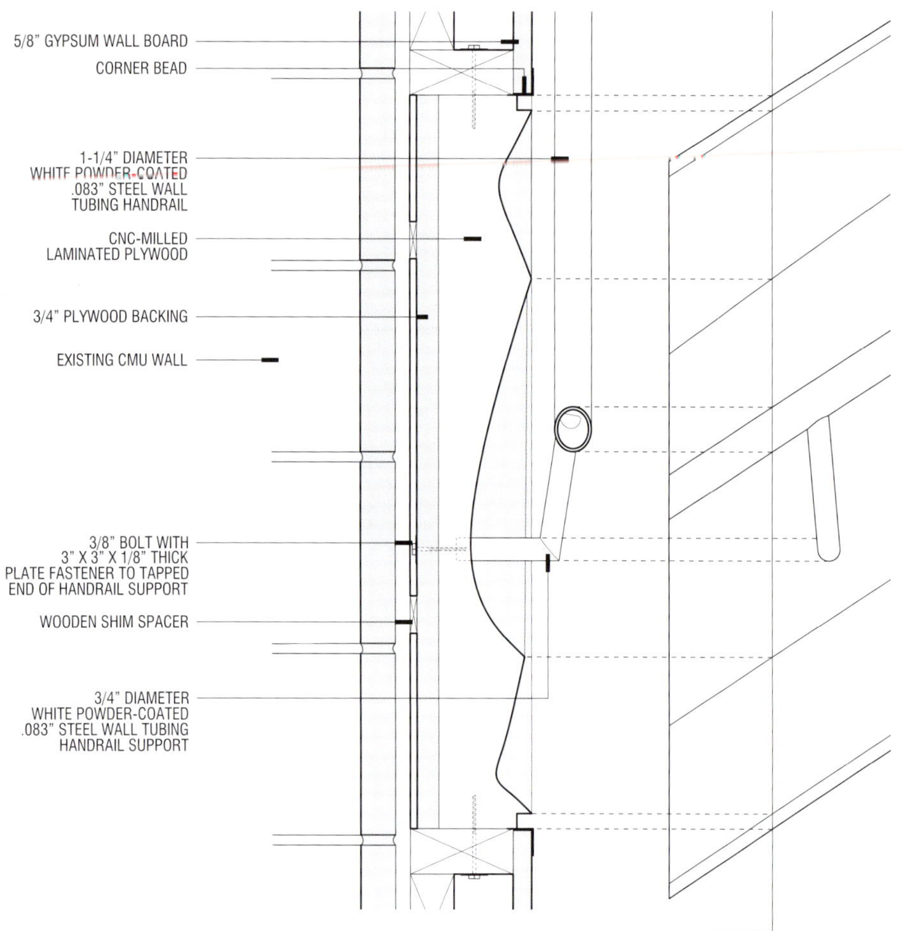

Volumetrically linking the key programs around an enclosed food-printing room, the stair and elevated mezzanine invite visitors to observe the processes of their innovative technology, as well as its potential in the culinary arts.

243 PROJECTS

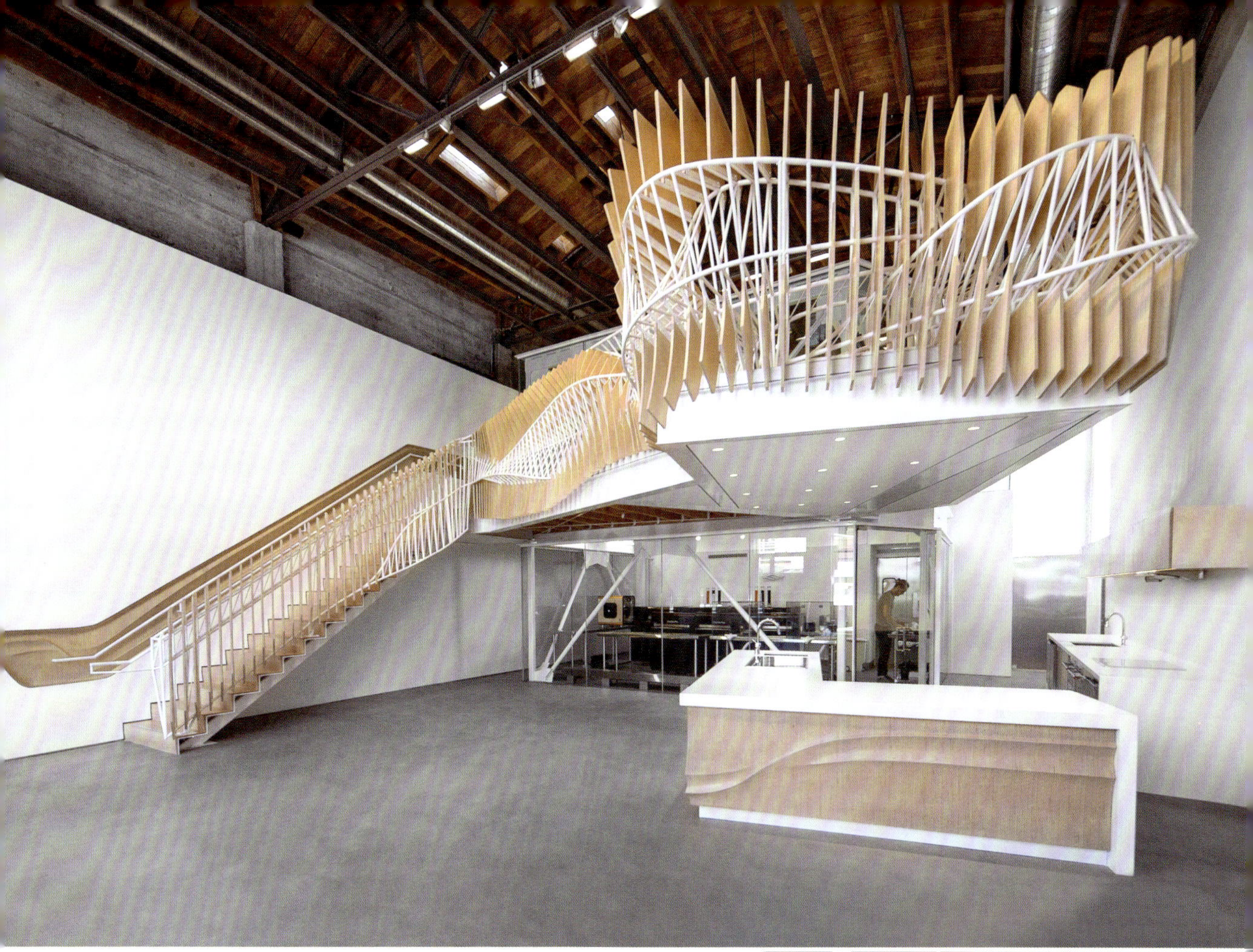

Balancing both the needs of the storefront entry with back-of-house program, the two-story, glass-enclosed production house and printing room is a central element, providing the necessary access to kitchen on the ground floor, and a visual line of sight to the private offices on the upper floor.

Unifying the divided spaces, and projecting from the glass volume, the mezzanine expands the interaction between the two areas. Exaggerating this relationship with a cantilevered lounge space, the mezzanine offers views into both the technical production space and the exhibition area on either side, physically connected through a stair. As the visual focal point for this transitional space, the stairs foreground this relationship with an intricately woven system, reflecting the conceptual ambiance of precious fabrication and artful configuration.

Apart from using CNC bending technologies for longer spans of steel tube, and fabricated directly by our office, the railing elaborately weaves linear filigree and plywood panels in segments for the contractor to assemble on site.

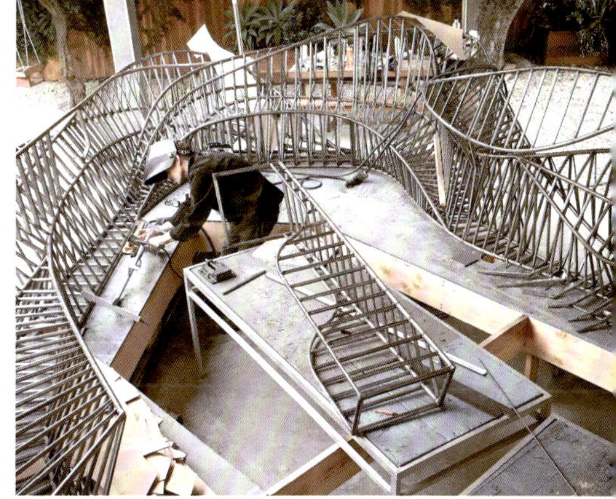

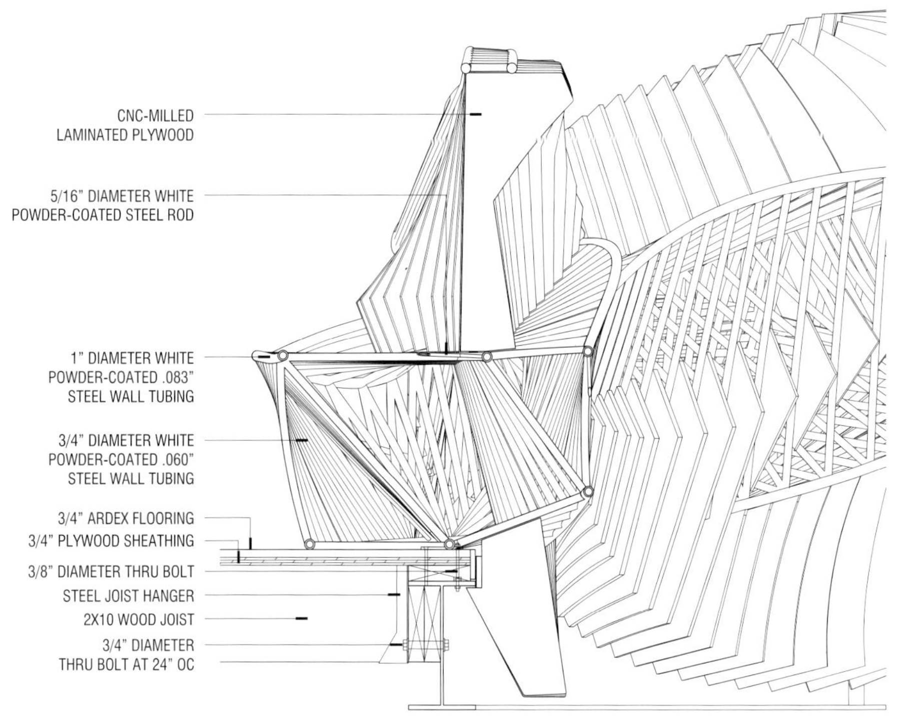

SECTION THROUGH GUARDRAIL SEAT

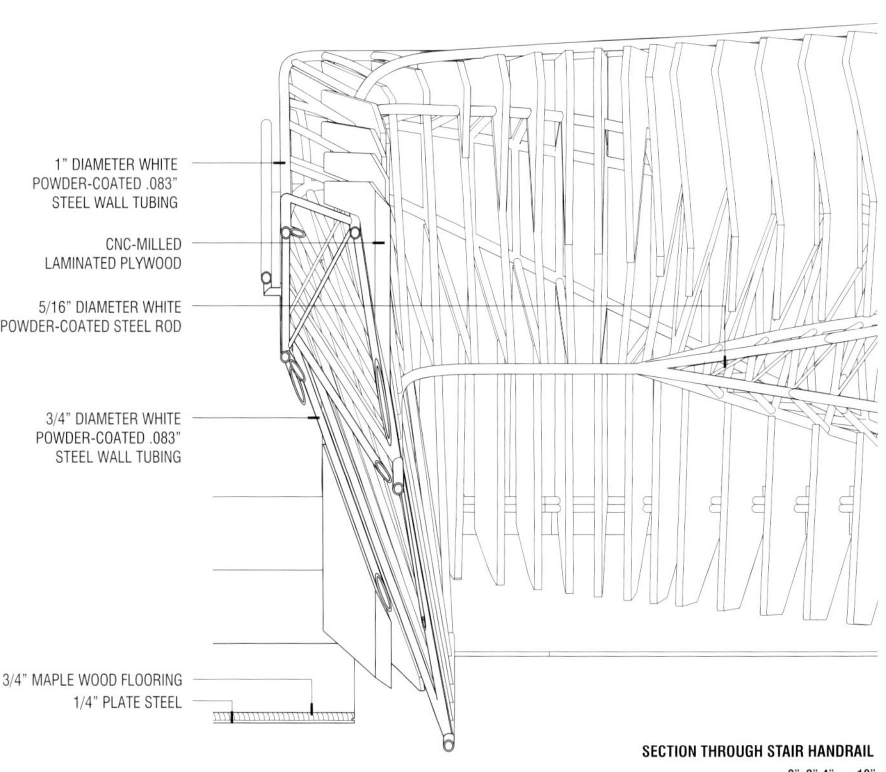

SECTION THROUGH STAIR HANDRAIL

Introducing a formally integrated guardrail of white frame elements and CNC-milled wood panels, the components of the assembly combine elegant massing with contrasting materials to emphasize their complex geometries. Built from hundreds of linear steel tubes and planar plywood surfaces, the railing is an interweaving of these systems, crossing in and out of one another to create seating elements and guardrails. Punctuating their tectonic interaction, these forms climb the stairs and railing, volumetrically twisting and swaying, leaving subtle impressions on the embedded railing in the wall and creating a dialogue with the exposed materials of the original building.

THE EXCHANGE

Designed as a part of Exhibit Columbus, the inaugural citywide design festival, the Exchange continues the heritage of design culture that dramatically shaped the city of Columbus, Indiana, since its famous modernist initiative. Incorporating the three existing canopies that formerly served as drive-through bank tellers in Eero Saarinen's original bank building, the design unifies the existing canopies to define a new public pavilion in the plaza.

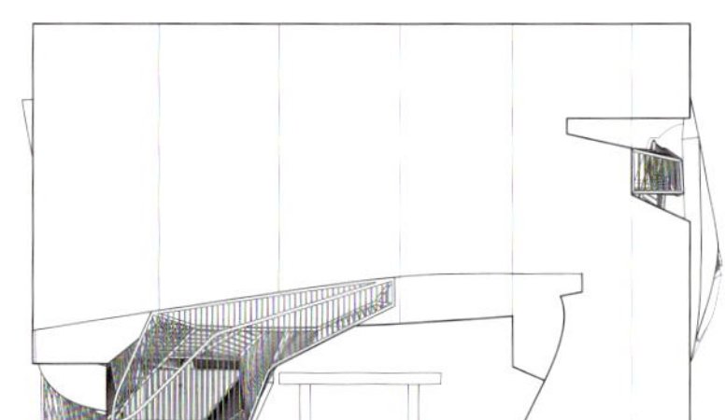

WEST ELEVATION

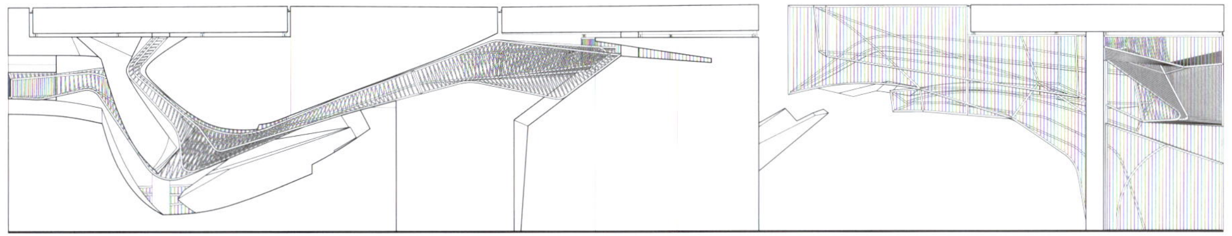

NORTH ELEVATION

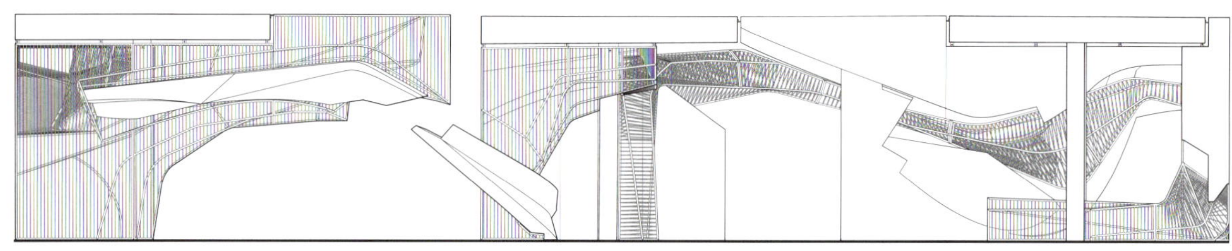

NORTH ELEVATION

EAST ELEVATION

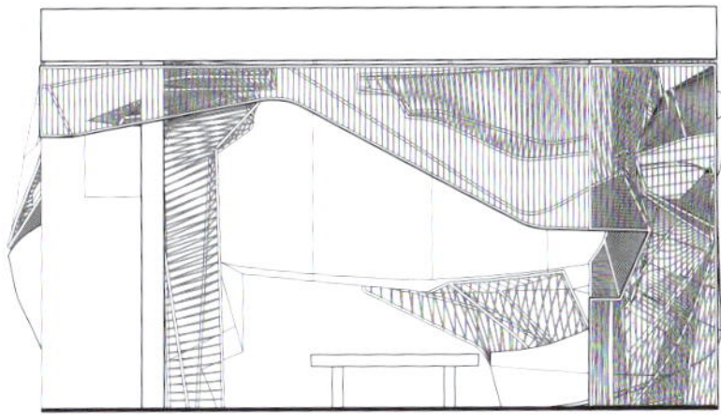

Creating a complete volume, the Exchange reflects Saarinen's influential design approach and lifelong architectural interests, reimagining the expressive curvatures and detailed filigree of architectural elements as a catalyst for exploring contrasting volumes of frame and solid. The pavilion highlights this interplay, utilizing solid curvilinear elements and a complex filigree of line work as the key components.

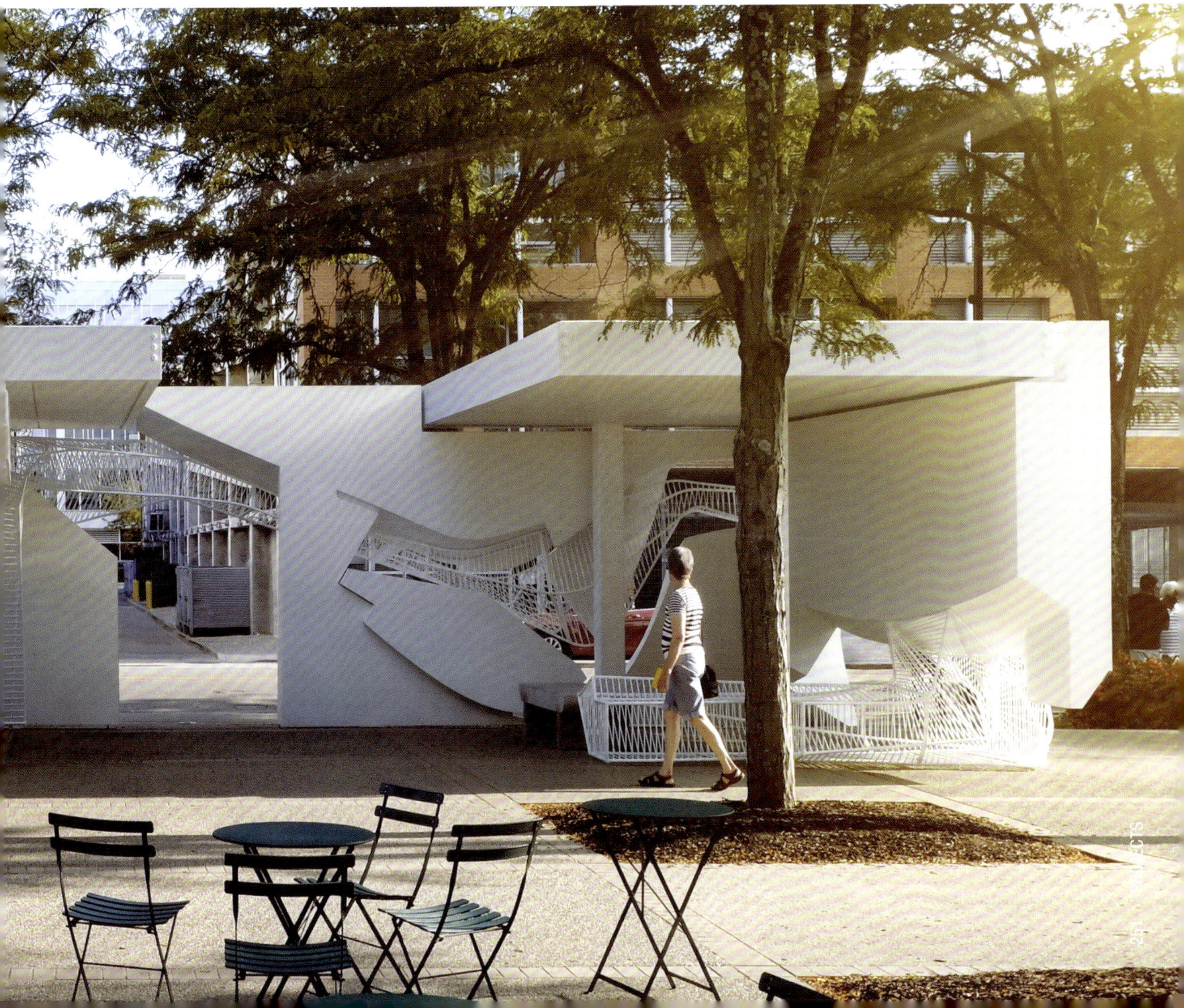

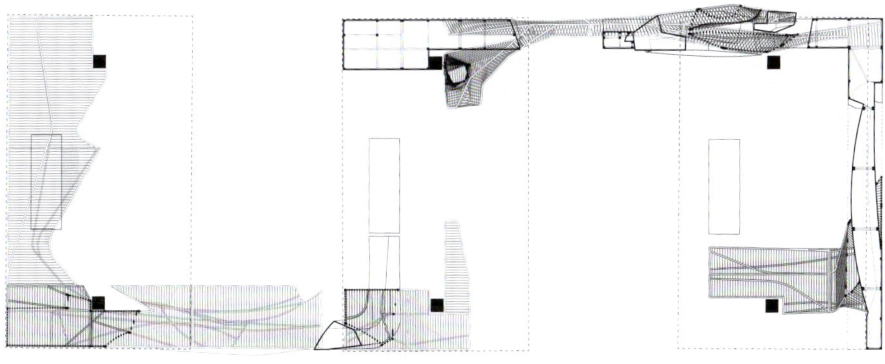

PLAN

0' 1' 2' 4'   10'

In plan, the shaped volumes create an open pavilion, where solid and framed elements create walls and benches that notch and slip to interlock with the existing canopy structure.

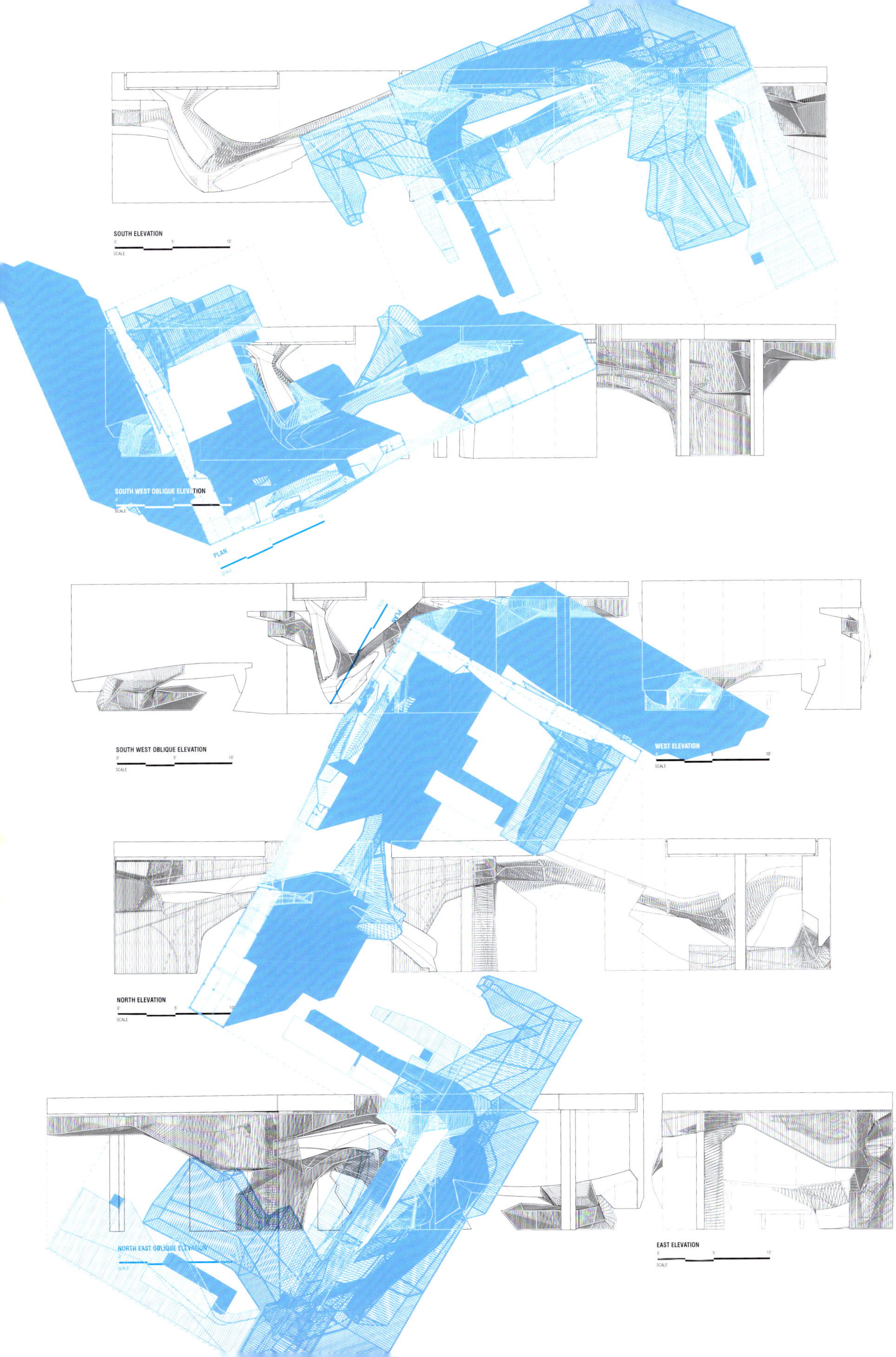

SOUTH ELEVATION
SCALE
SOUTH WEST OBLIQUE ELEVATION
SCALE
PLAN
SCALE
SOUTH WEST OBLIQUE ELEVATION
SCALE
WEST ELEVATION
SCALE
NORTH ELEVATION
SCALE
NORTH EAST OBLIQUE ELEVATION
SCALE
EAST ELEVATION
SCALE

Using a loose-fit placement of volumes within carved voids, the pavilion fills in the areas beneath the existing canopies with linear texture and white solids. Expressing this negative space through a connective series of embedded objects, the pavilion is fixed to its context, maintaining views of the bank and incorporating existing benches, alongside fitted interactions suspended within its sculpted walls.

Constructed to the exact dimensions of the existing canopies, each part of the design fits together in precise arrangements to be quickly assembled on site. In their combined forms the volumes of the frame and solid elements interact in loose-fit positions, articulating expressive scrapes and embedded fragments.

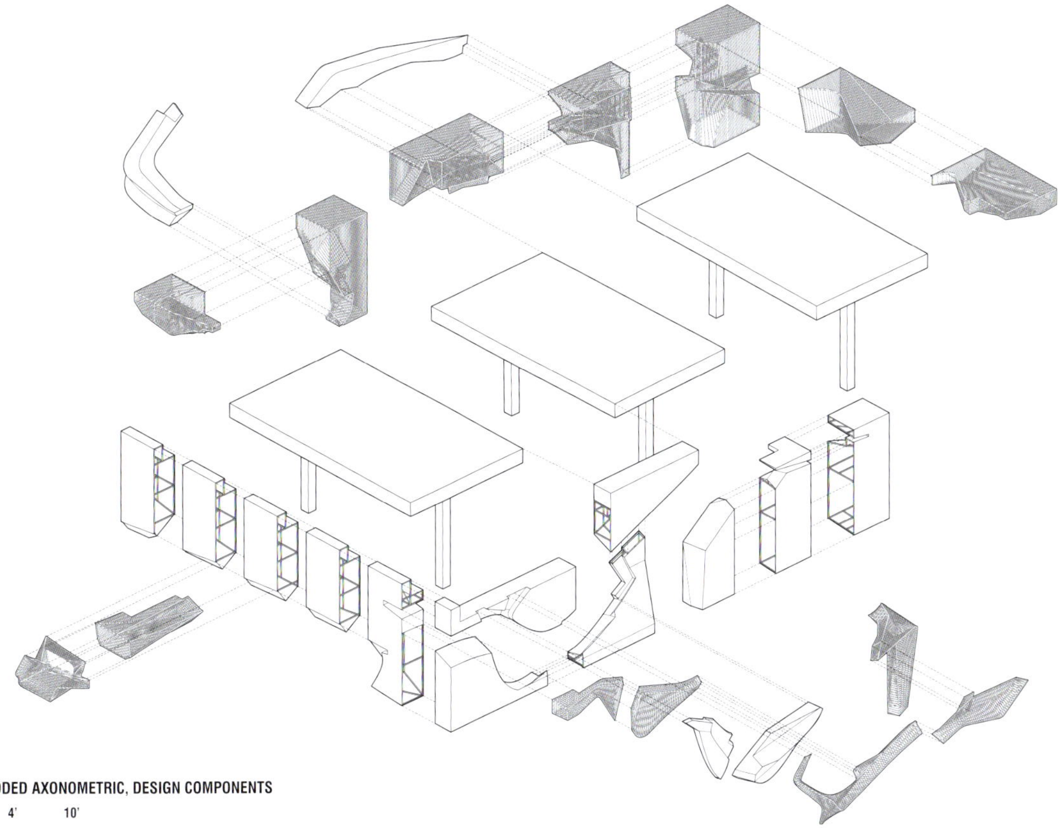

EXPLODED AXONOMETRIC, DESIGN COMPONENTS

0' 1' 2' 4'   10'

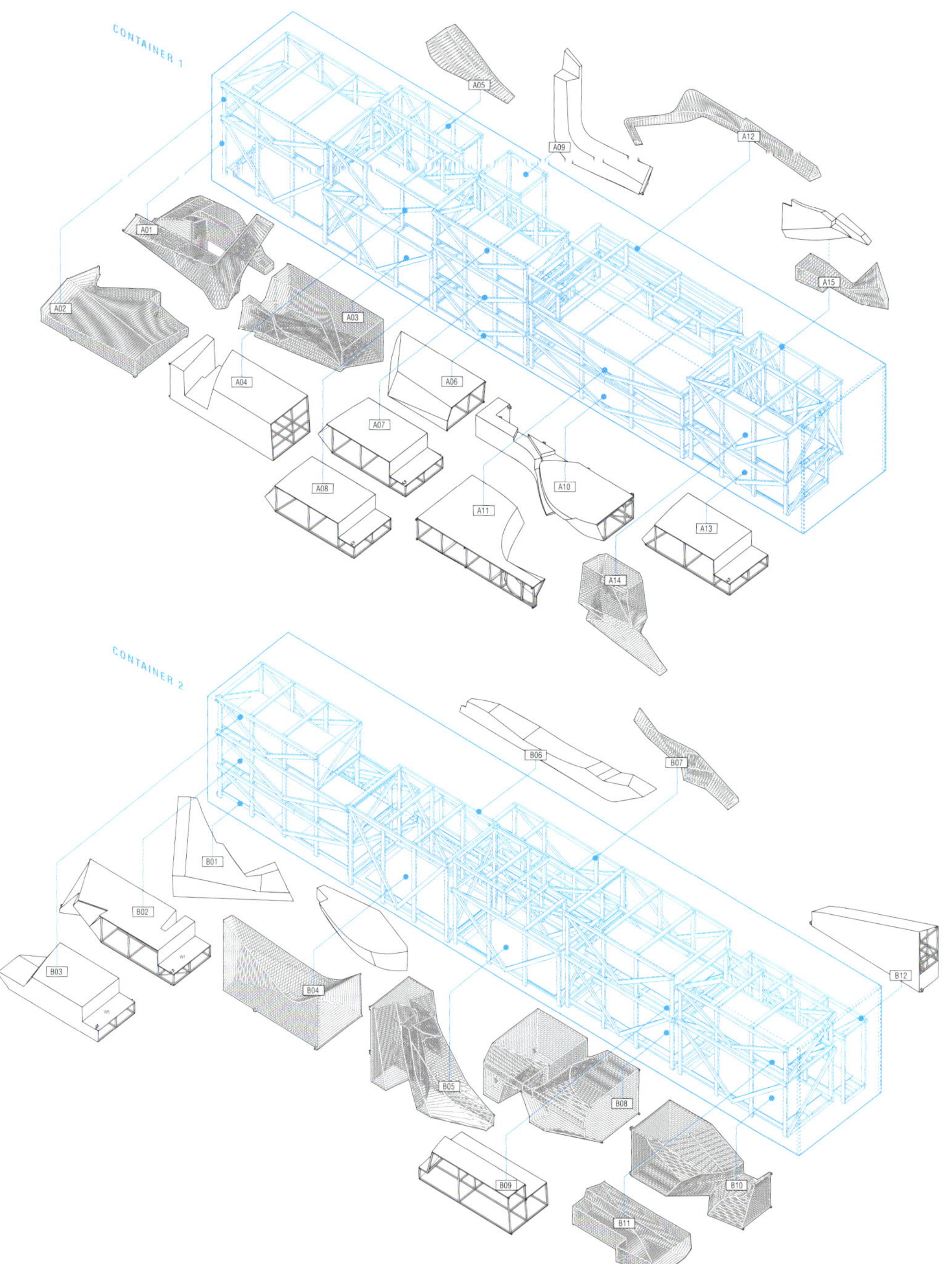

CRATING DIAGRAM

The pavilion provides a range of porosities, from semi-private spaces to open areas shaped by how the forms contain and unfold the internal space, activating the plaza with new areas of engagement and destination. The project reflects the character of Saarinen's formal shaping and is intended to reignite a curiosity of architectural experimentation, becoming a focal point that feels simultaneously brand new and as if it has always been there.

IVANHILL RESIDENCE

Located on a hillside lot at the northern edge of the Silver Lake neighborhood of Los Angeles, this project strategically positions three new single-family dwellings into two volumes: one in isolation and two combined together. Maximizing the square footage of all three houses, each volume skews to fit the setbacks of the site and the extents of its buildable space. The street-front residence shown here is tightly contained within this boundary, densely packing program volumes in ways that internally wrap and project into one another as objects that are organized into a cubic form.

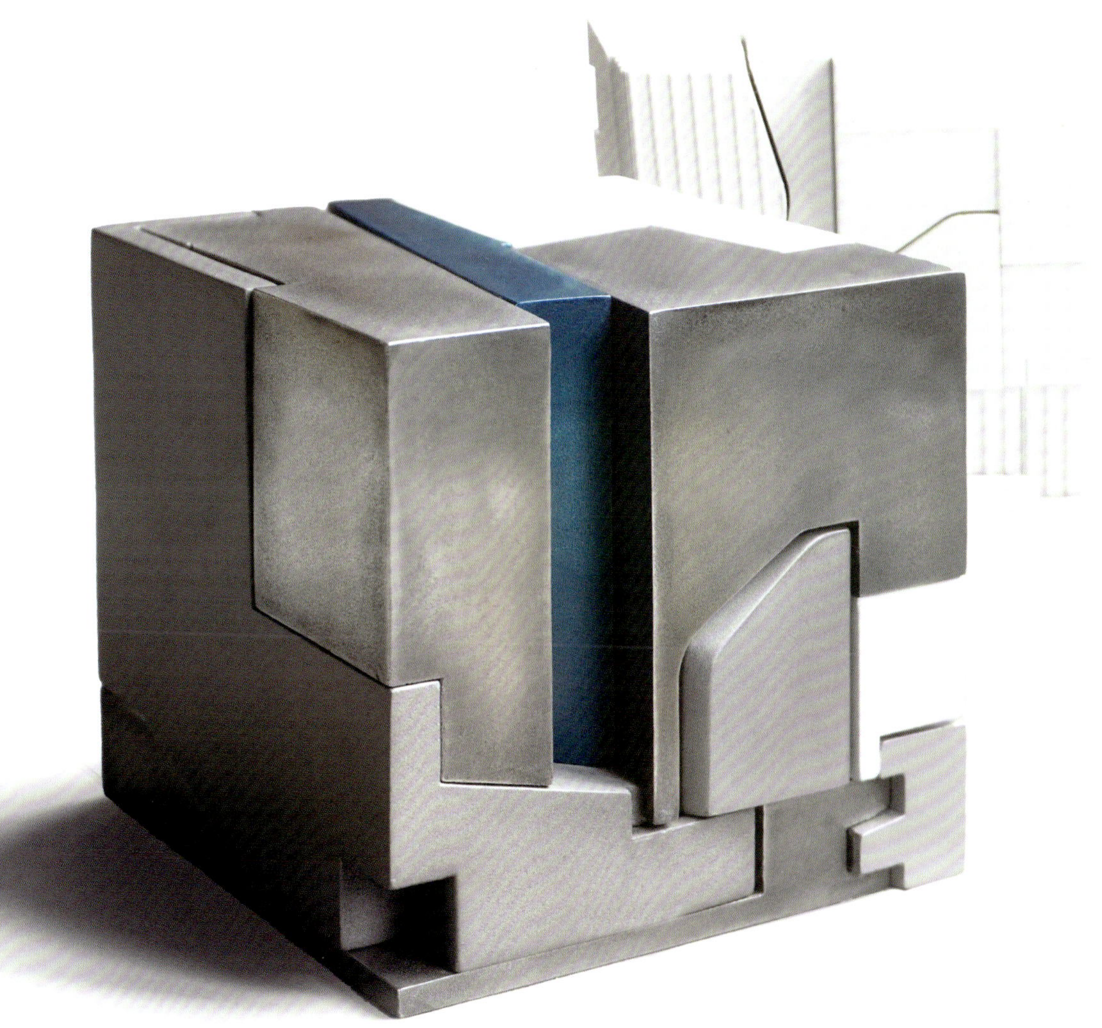

Rather than approaching voided spaces as the result of carved elements, the internal volumes are distinctly shaped to interlock—playing out to define the larger volumes of the house as well as punctuating gaps and reveals on the exterior. Accentuating these volumetric relationships, the facade uses both smooth and textured systems: differentiating between solids and louvered screens to express these inner alignments. Organizing these arrangements like programmed parts around a primary "voided object," the parts create small overlooking areas and courtyards within lightfalls that reach deep into the central living spaces. As physical objects, their interlocking shapes slide and pocket into place, intricately assembling the overall volume.

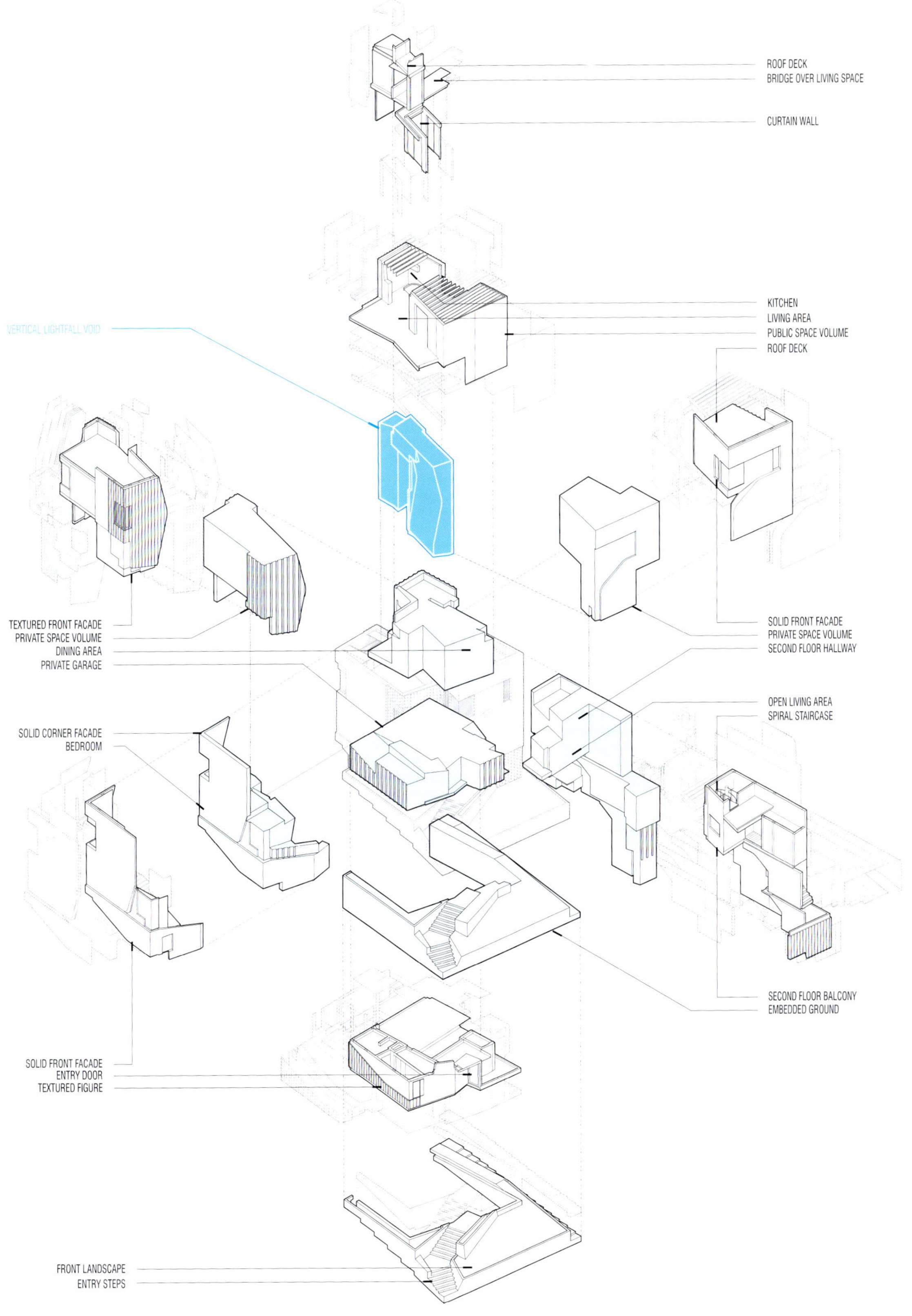

PROGRAM MASSING & BUILDING COMPONENTS

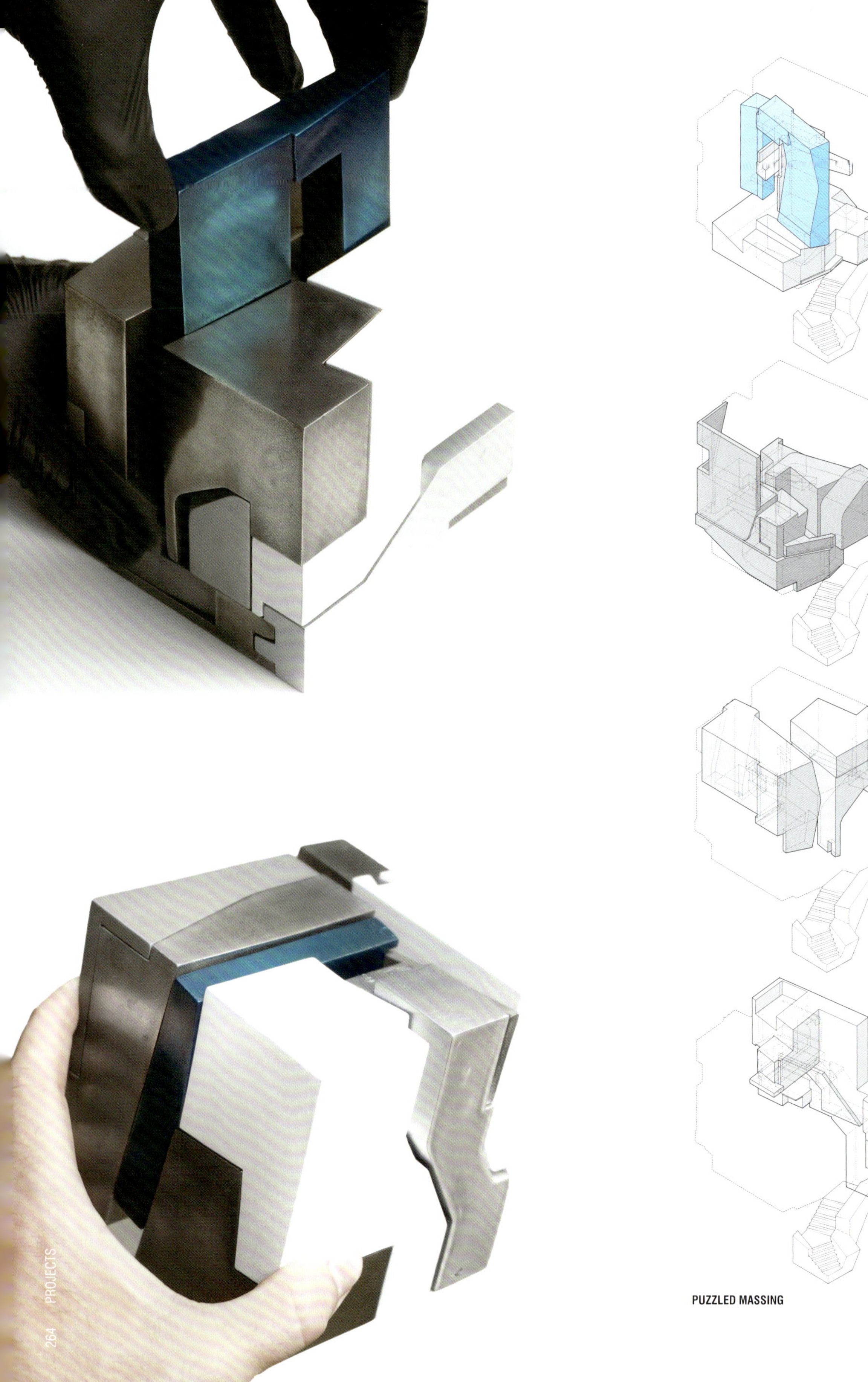

PUZZLED MASSING

2F PLAN

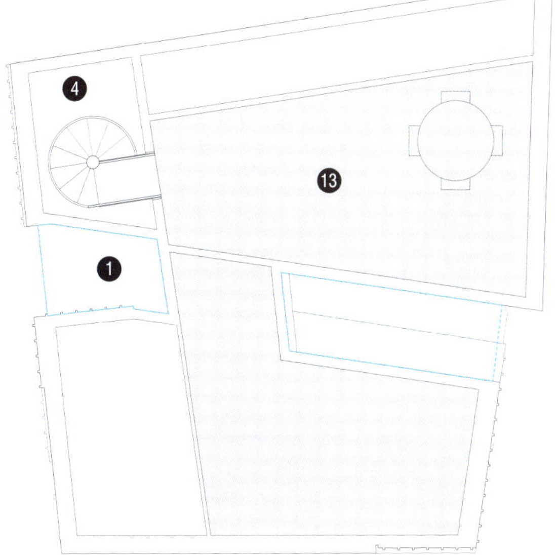

ROOF PLAN

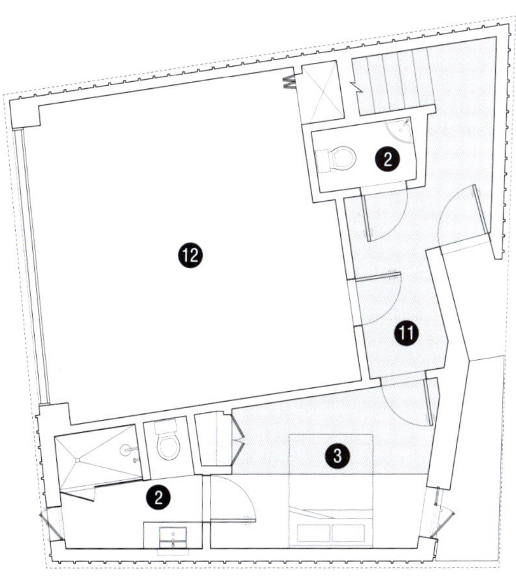

1F PLAN

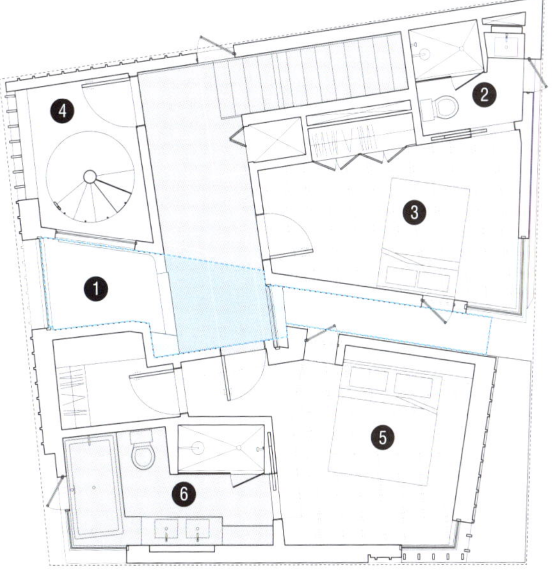

3F PLAN

1 VERTICAL VOID
2 BATHROOM
3 BEDROOM
4 BALCONY
5 MASTER BEDROOM
6 MASTER BATHROOM
7 KITCHEN
8 DINING
9 COURTYARD
10 LIVING
11 ENTRYWAY
12 GARAGE
13 ROOF DECK

LEGEND

COLD
WAR
VETERANS
MEMORIAL

In recognition of the profound complexity of the Cold War, the memorial, designed for the site of the Pritzker Archives in Somers, Wisconsin, draws on a range of artifacts and imagery to create a deeply moving and immersive experience. Organized as a set of circular "orbits" influenced by Diplomatic, Intelligence, Military, and Economic themes of the memorial, the design moves visitors along a journey through the park as an extension of the Memorial Archives, and as an iconic landmark destination in the region.

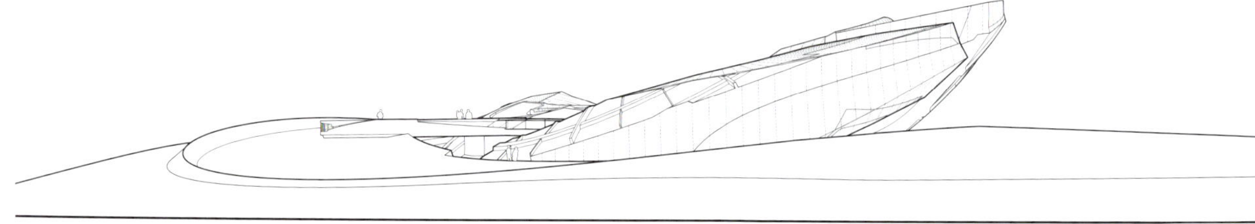

SOUTH ELEVATION

0' 5' 10'   25'   50'

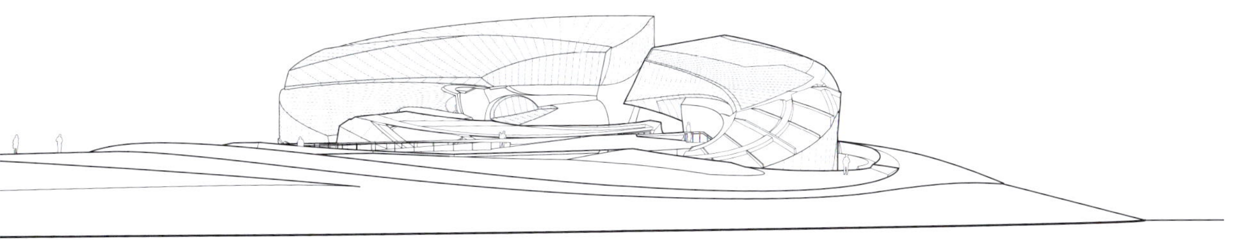

WEST ELEVATION

RING ASSEMBLY & ARTIFACTS

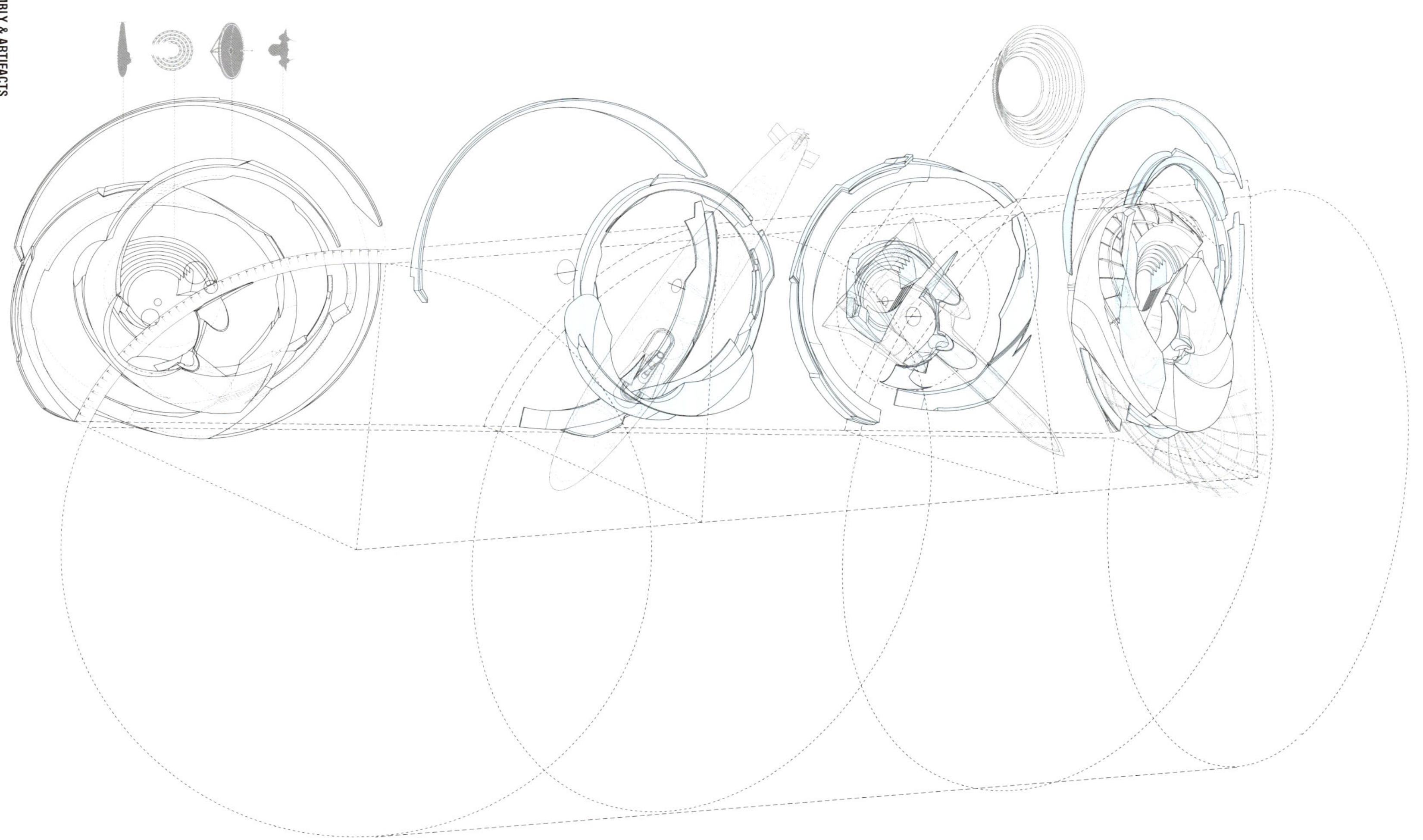

Embodying an intangible quality of the Cold War era, the crafting of these spaces creates architectural moments from the nuanced features of objects whose shape and appearance conjure the character and qualities of missile silos and communication satellites, war rooms, and underground bunkers.

Finding tectonic parallels to the layered history of the war, the sweeping forms and textural surfaces carve through the structure, leaving remnant objects on the architectural volumes and landscape, and embedding curious details and wondrous moments of light and spatial complexity. Studying an intertwined language of three-dimensional rings, these "artifacts" give form to parts that assemble on the site, reforming the landscape as they scrape and press into the ground.

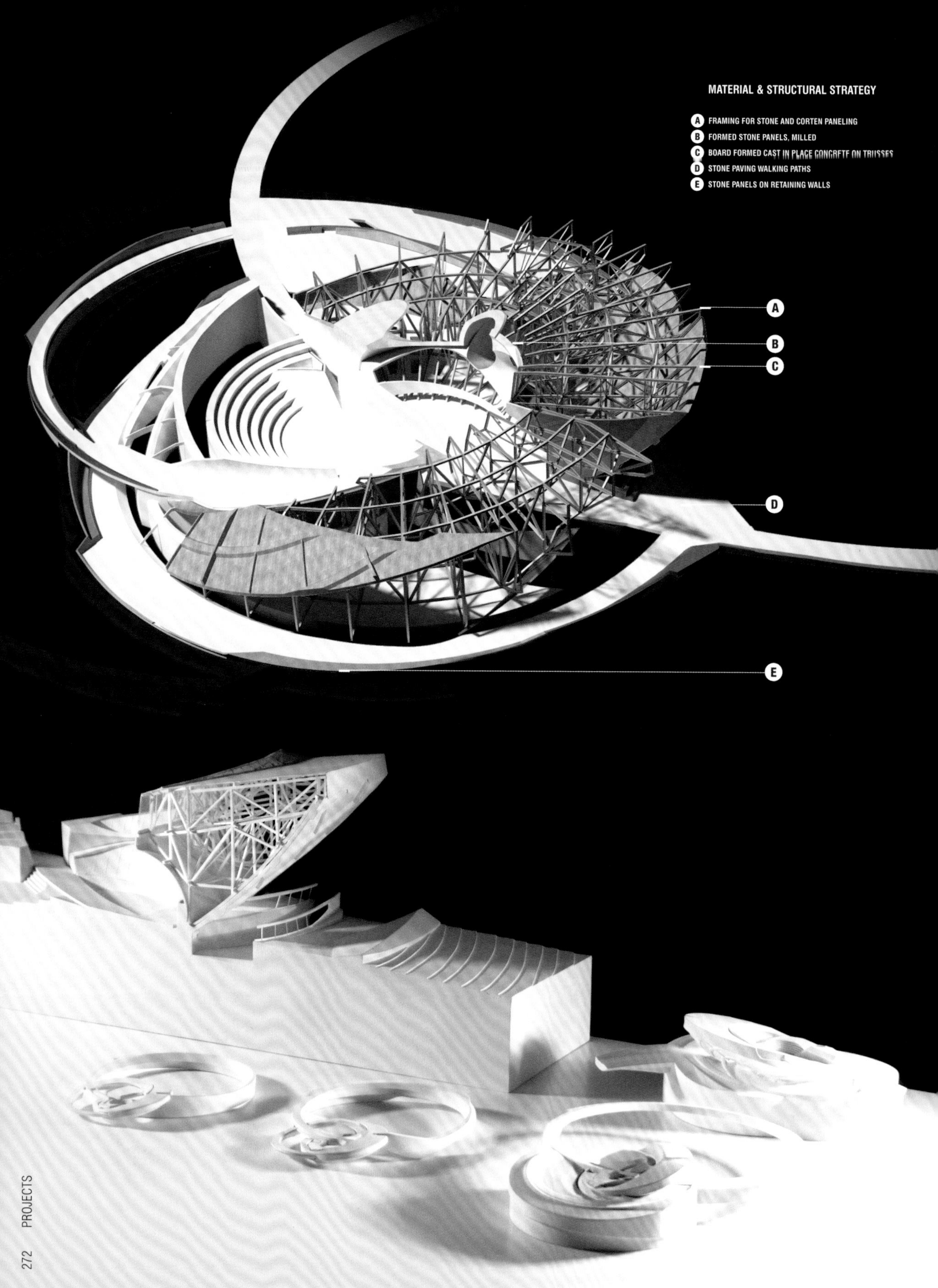

MATERIAL & STRUCTURAL STRATEGY
A FRAMING FOR STONE AND CORTEN PANELING
B FORMED STONE PANELS, MILLED
C BOARD FORMED CAST IN PLACE CONCRETE ON TRUSSES
D STONE PAVING WALKING PATHS
E STONE PANELS ON RETAINING WALLS
A
B
C
D
E

The large disc-shaped structure is partially embedded in the ground, as the memorial emerges from the earth with arcing pathways and gracefully curving walls to hover overhead and nestle in the bermed landscape. Each orbit around the structure takes shape differently, with the intention of evoking the broadest range of wartime associations: as surrounding elements evoke impressions that are both triumphant and ominous.

SECTION THROUGH STRUCTURE & LANDSCAPE

A BUTTRESS RETAINING WALL, STRUCTURE FOR CORTEN/STONE
B CONCRETE FOUNDATION LAID ON COMPACTED EARTH
C CONCRETE PILES CAPPED INTO FOUNDATION
D PILE CAPS ALIGN WITH RADIAL TRUSS TOUCHPOINTS
E STRUCTURAL FRAMING FOR STONE AND CORTEN PANELING
F FORMED STONE PANELS, MILLED
G BOARD FORMED CAST IN PLACE CONCRETE, SUSPENDED
H BOARD FORMED CAST IN PLACE CONCRETE
I STONE PAVING WALKING PATHS
J STONE PANELS ON RETAINING WALLS
K CORTEN MESH PANELS REVEAL STRUCTURE
L CORTEN PANELS
M CORTEN PANELS ON RETAINING WALLS

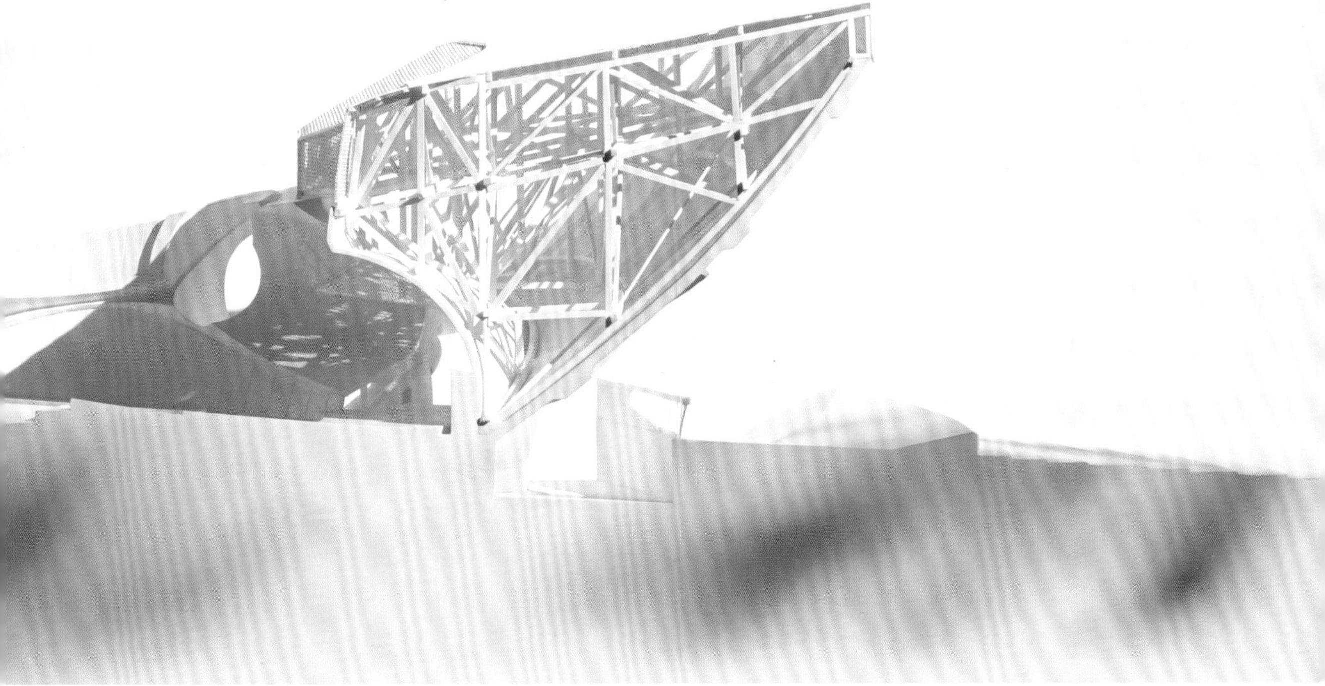

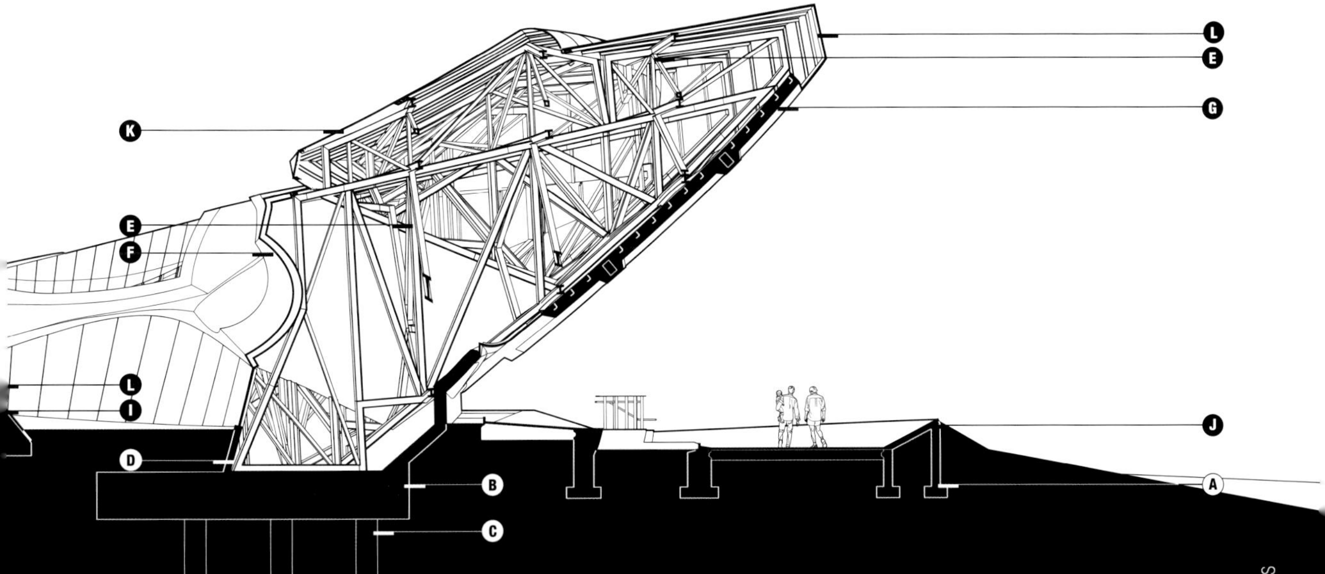

K

L
E
G

E
F

L
I

D

B

C

J

A

0'   5'   10'   25'   50'

INTERSPHERE

Like a city, museums are collections of diverse programs both large and small: an array of eccentric parts and dynamic movements that interact experientially. Encapsulating this idea within a simple container, Intersphere, designed for Helsinki's South Harbor, conceptually reimagines the museum as a programmatically dense solid.

With galleries and workshop spaces operating as embedded elements of this density, the spherical massing of the New Museum of Architecture and Design in Helsinki articulates formal and spatial maneuvers that make it characteristically volumetric. Each element is strategically assembled and disassembled, swiveled and rotated, interlocked and overlapped—forming the key public spaces in the residual areas in between.

These residual spaces are essential, creating openings that coalesce within the core of the building, and formally bridge the public space with the more malleable public and private functions of the museum. Spaces take shape through internally sculpted partitions, creating thickened shells and rectilinear masses that loosely fit to sleeve and socket within the public space.

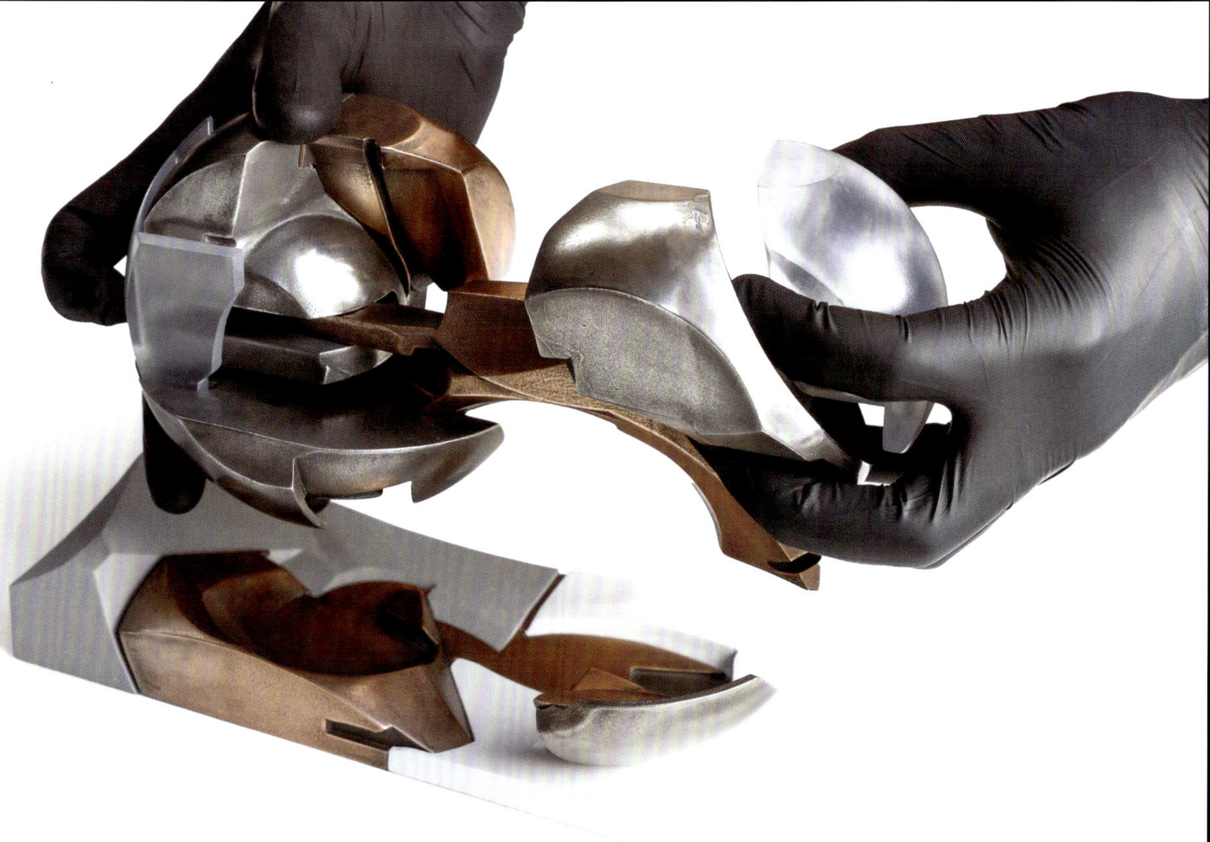

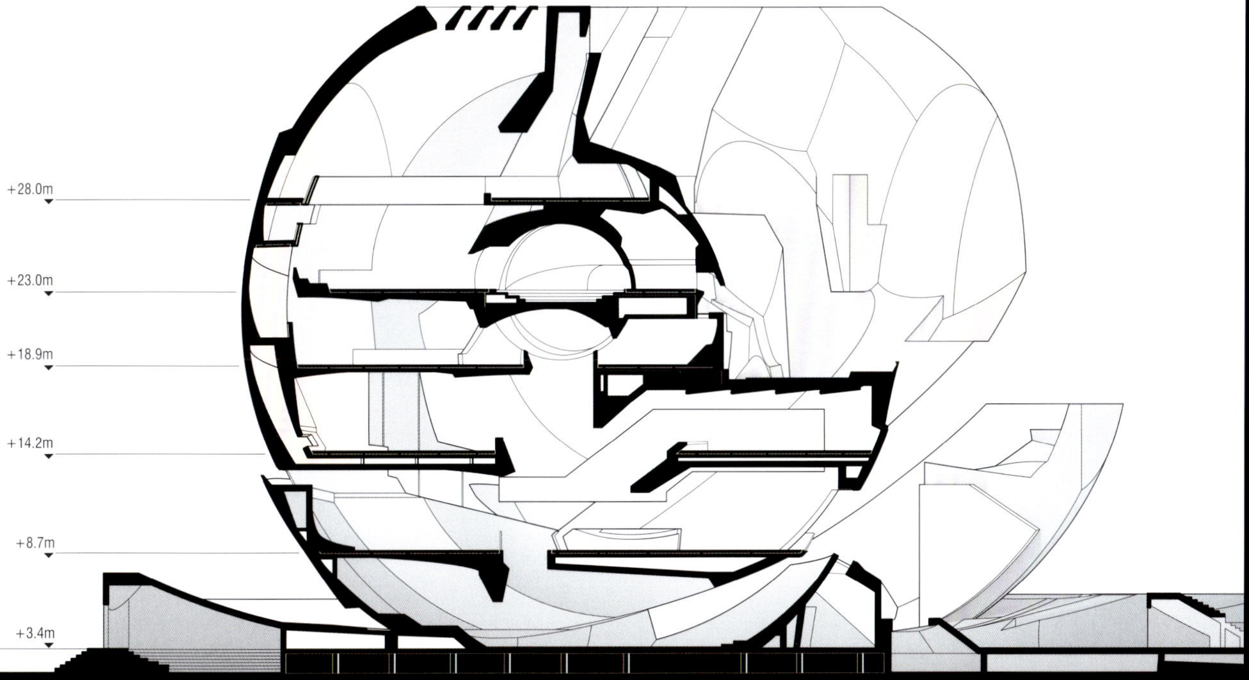

+28.0m
+23.0m
+18.9m
+14.2m
+8.7m
+3.4m

0m 1m   5m   10m   25m

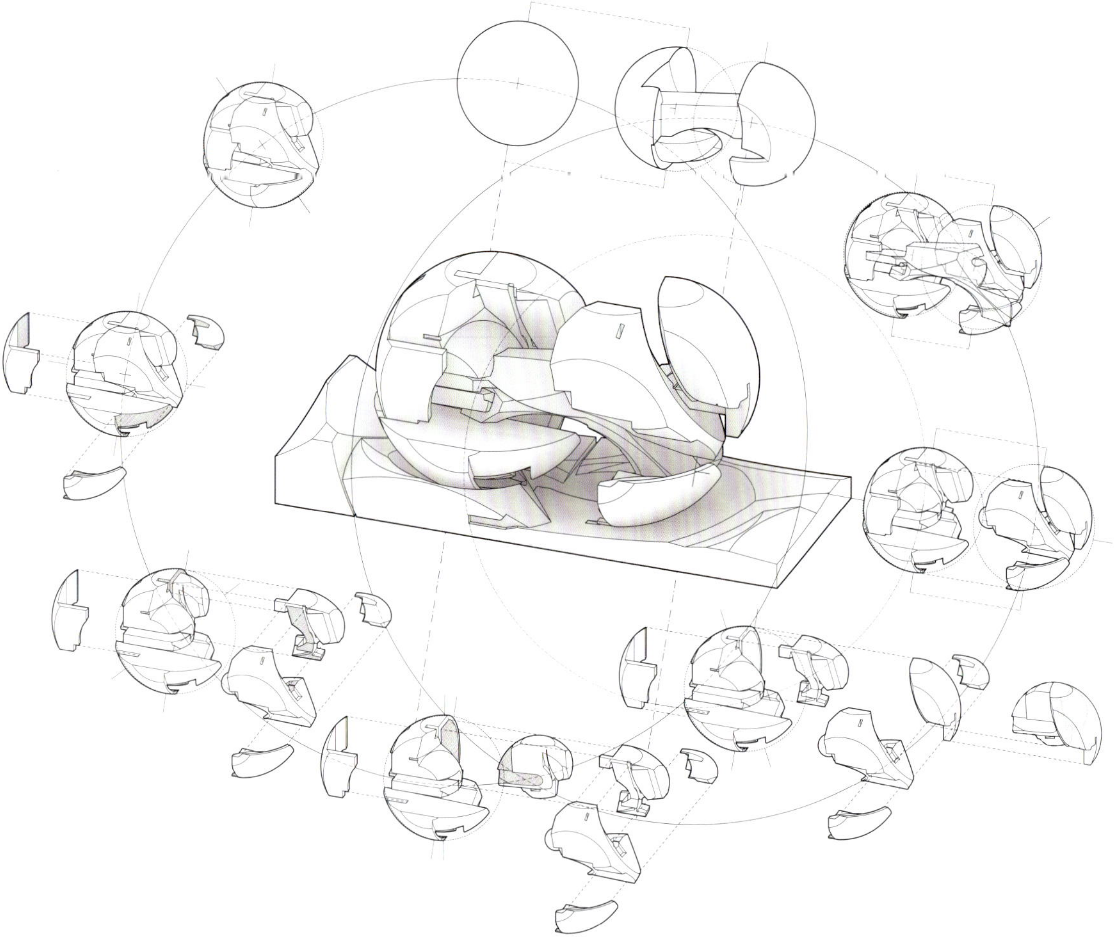

VOLUMETRIC ASSEMBLY

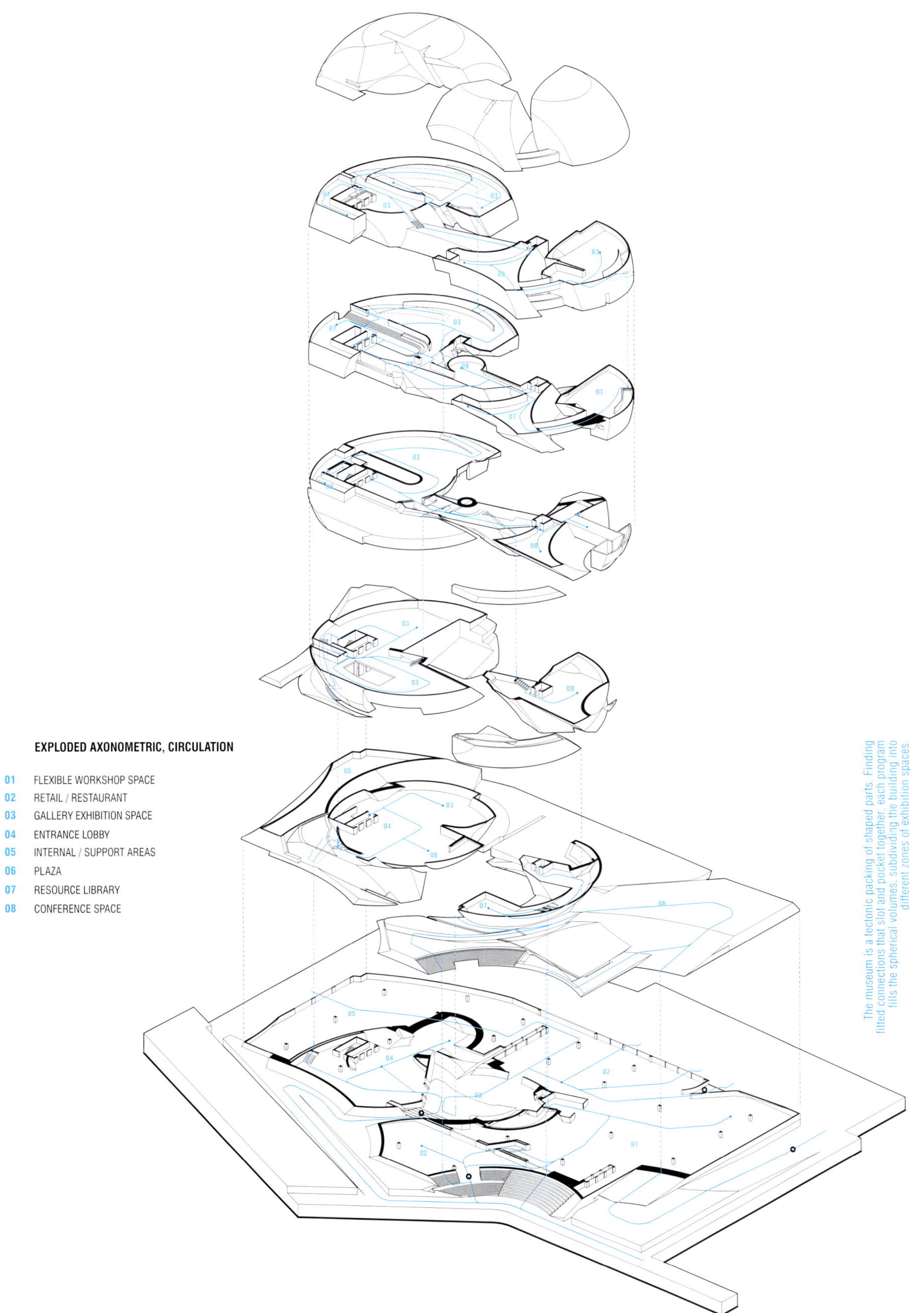

EXPLODED AXONOMETRIC, CIRCULATION

01 FLEXIBLE WORKSHOP SPACE
02 RETAIL / RESTAURANT
03 GALLERY EXHIBITION SPACE
04 ENTRANCE LOBBY
05 INTERNAL / SUPPORT AREAS
06 PLAZA
07 RESOURCE LIBRARY
08 CONFERENCE SPACE

The museum is a tectonic packing of shaped parts. Finding fitted connections that slot and pocket together, each program fills the spherical volumes. subdividing the building into different zones of exhibition spaces.

MONARCH TOWER

Consisting mostly of bulky concrete frame and curtain wall systems, the uniform appearance of typical tall buildings in Taipei reflect a design formula that maximizes their economic efficiencies. Challenging the conventions of typical high-rise developments, our design approach addresses these regulatory requirements in ways that strategically offer variation and modularity within a highly articulated facade.

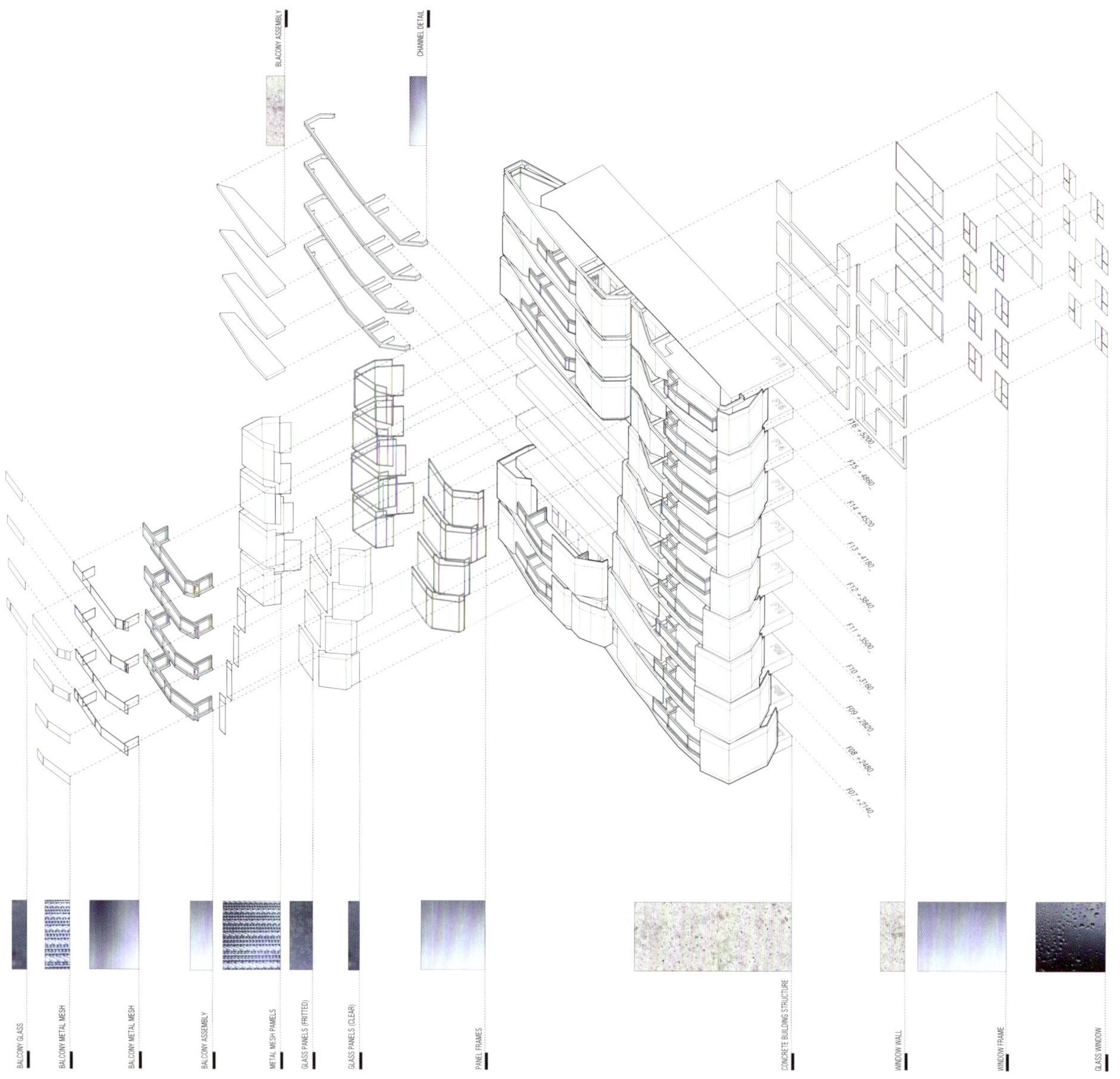

EXPLODED AXONOMETRIC, FACADE

As a series of interconnected elements, railing channels, framing tubes, window mullions, glazing, and mesh panels, the system shifts locally from floor to floor, weaving linear structure and transparent surfaces in modular order. In many buildings of this size, the spatial qualities of the exterior envelope tend to be visually flattened, and the physical enclosure is clear. Giving the illusion of varying depth, our design for the exterior envelope disrupts this repetitive vertical treatment, adding a spatial continuity to the meandering voids between panels.

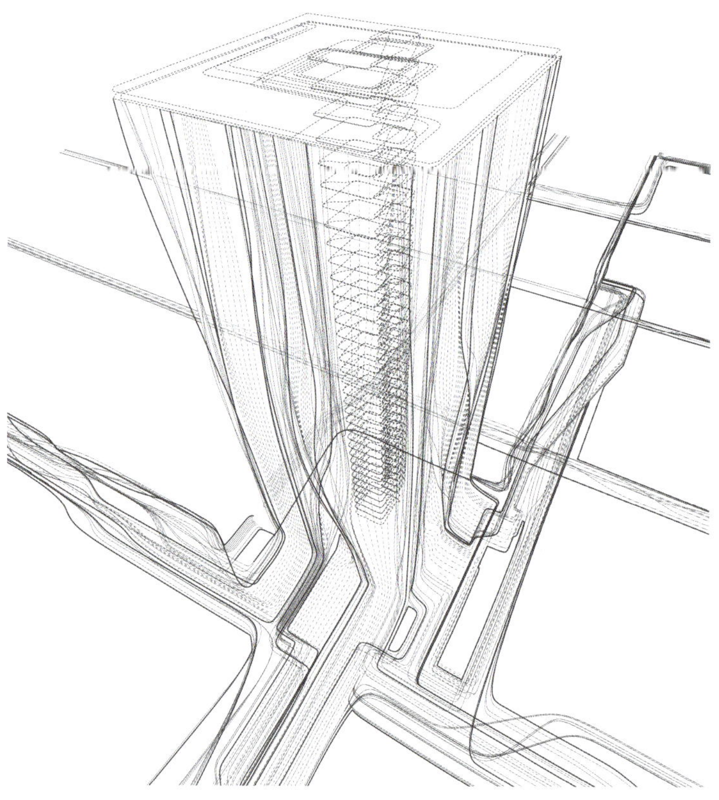

Deploying a strategy of linear splines to the faces of the building, the exterior paneling uses a system of incrementally shifting balconies and panels to pixelate movement from top to bottom. The facade systems are tactically positioned to shift and slide along steel channels to expand and compress in relation to one another, creating a sweeping effect as they move vertically up the facade.

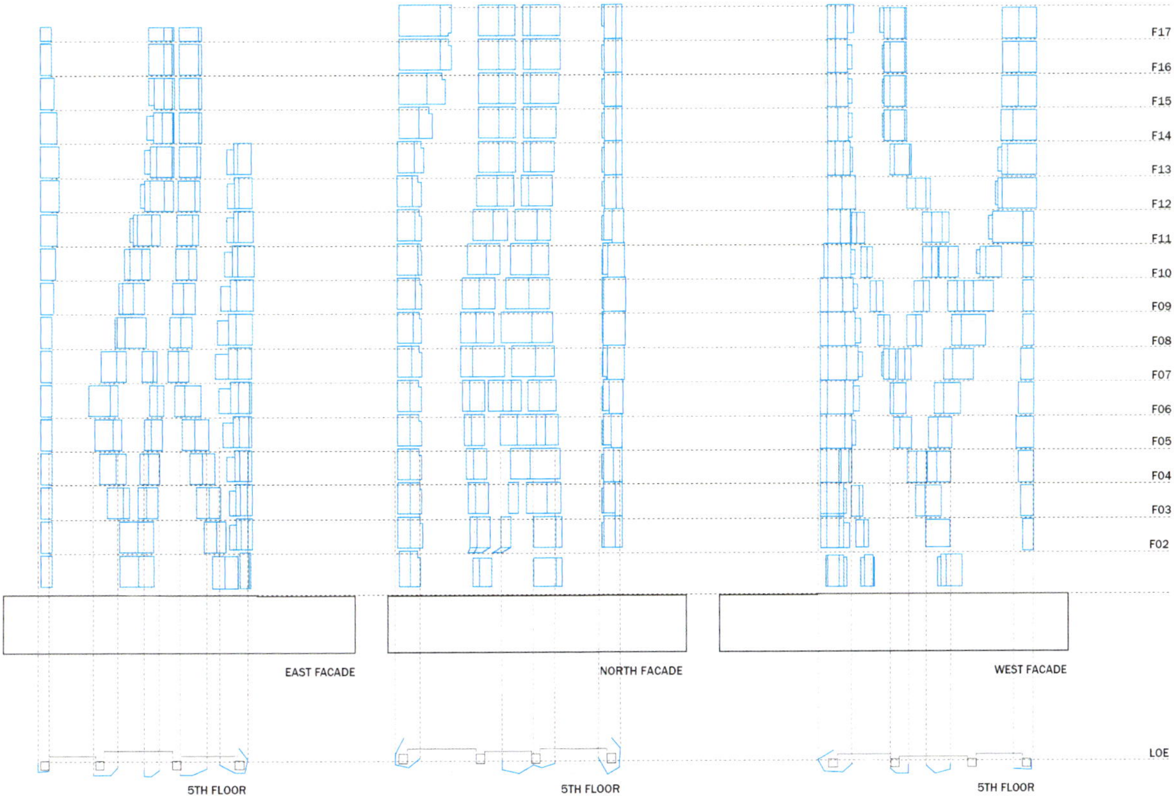

PANEL ELEVATIONS

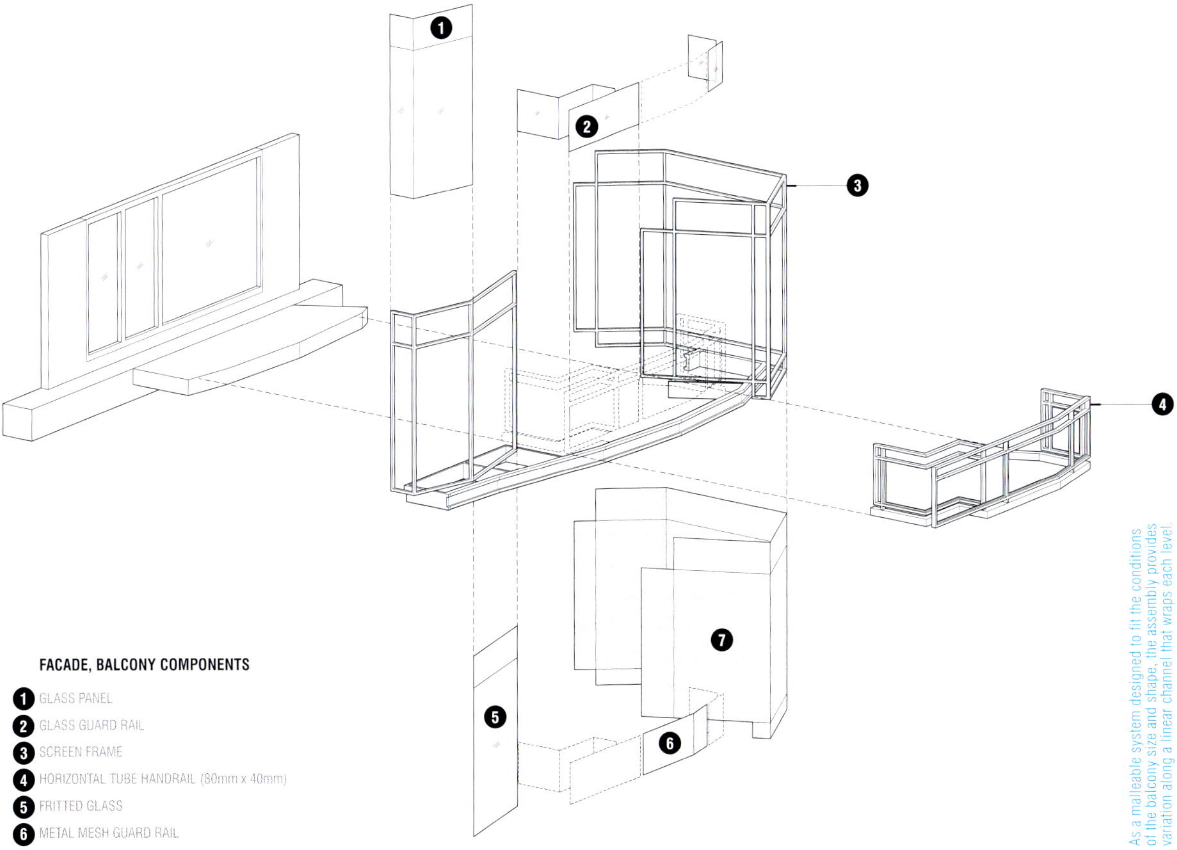

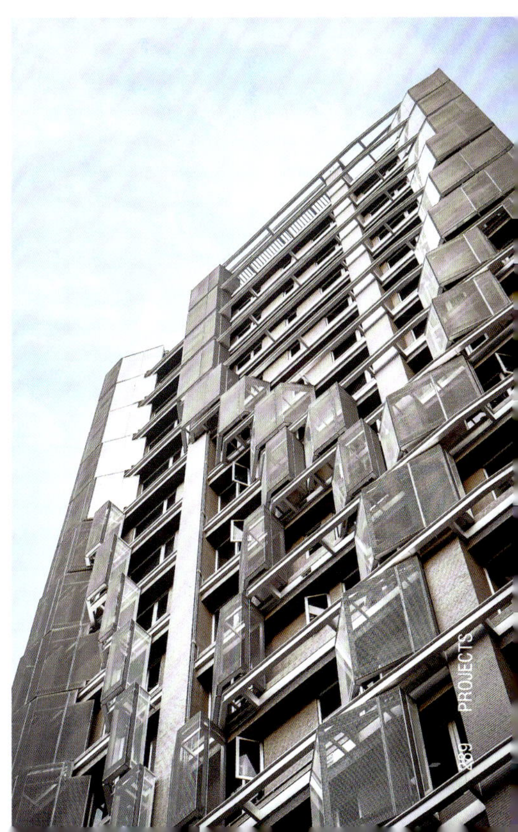

FACADE, BALCONY COMPONENTS

1. GLASS PANEL
2. GLASS GUARD RAIL
3. SCREEN FRAME
4. HORIZONTAL TUBE HANDRAIL (80mm x 40mm)
5. FRITTED GLASS
6. METAL MESH GUARD RAIL
7. METAL MESH SCREEN

As a malleable system designed to fit the conditions of the balcony size and shape, the assembly provides variation along a linear channel that wraps each level.

The interplay of screens disrupts the repetitive stacking of the tower form and absorbs the irregularities of the floor plans through a weaving of four materials—expanded aluminum mesh, fritted glass, solid panel, and steel structure. Finding a balance between performance and aesthetic, these screens are carefully proportioned to provide views of the city, shading and privacy for the residents, and to reduce heat gain. Adapting to the fixed positions of the balconies and window openings of the building, the modular components of the assembly offer spatial organization and variation to the facade.

DUNHUA TOWER

As a residential high-rise along a main promenade in the city, Dunhua Tower also counteracts Taipei's infrastructural tower typology with a modular approach. The facade uses shifting components of metal frame and fritted glass, but unlike Monarch, these layers accentuate a finely threaded lattice that spans the vertical openings between balconies in the stone exterior. Against this solid envelope, these gestural frameworks reinforce the faceted swaying of the facade, subtly pressing in and pushing out as they step in larger sections.

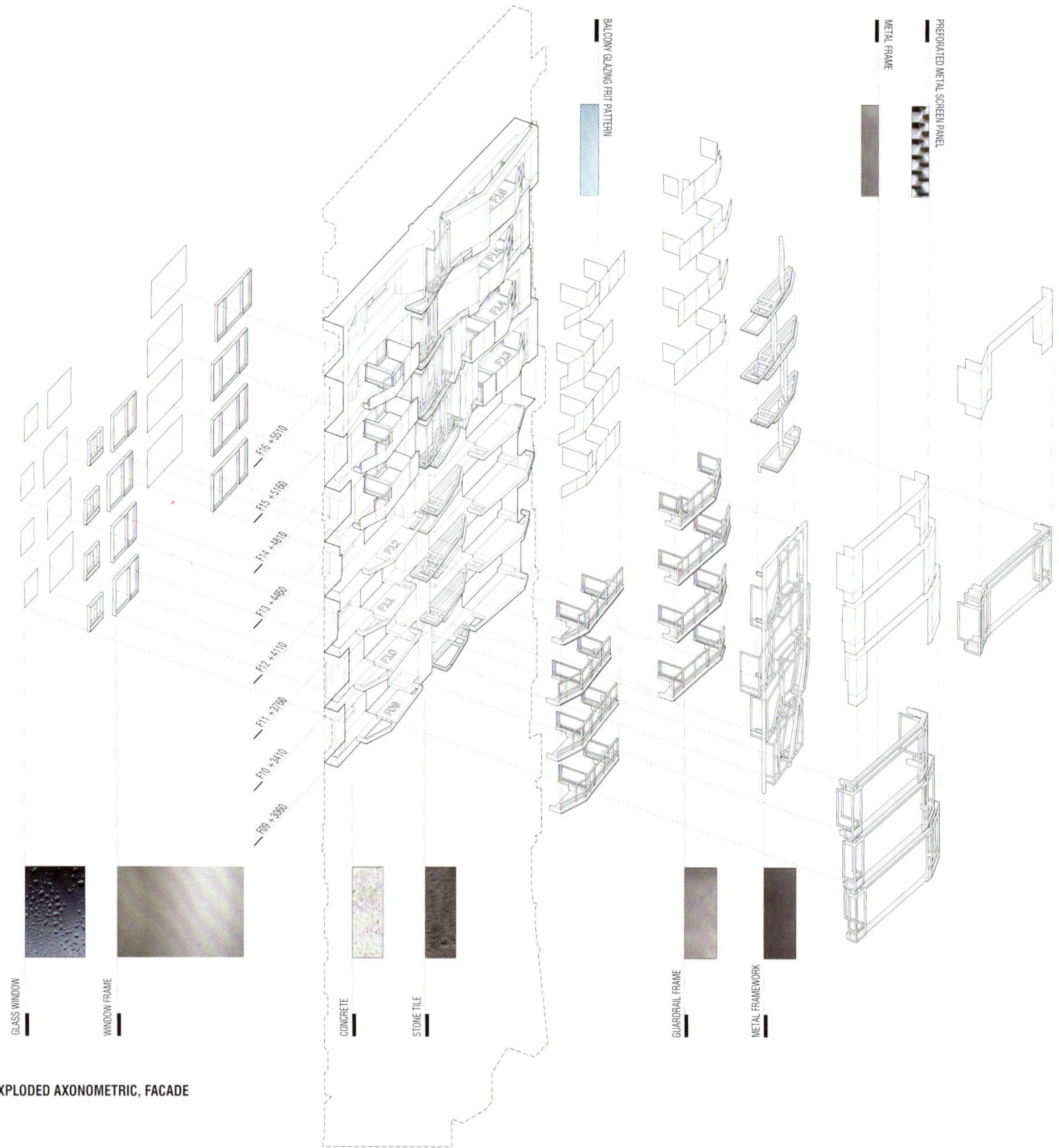

EXPLODED AXONOMETRIC, FACADE

Intricately weaving linear elements and metal panels to create an armature between balconies, the stone surfaces are embedded with figural frames. In addition to offering a performative quality for daylight screens and lighting, these frameworks accentuate the shifting movements of the solid modules, exaggerating their subtle rhythm with gestural lines. The linear metal armature intricately weaves through balconies to create a lattice of figural forms that facet and shift as they are embedded into the building's chiseled facade.

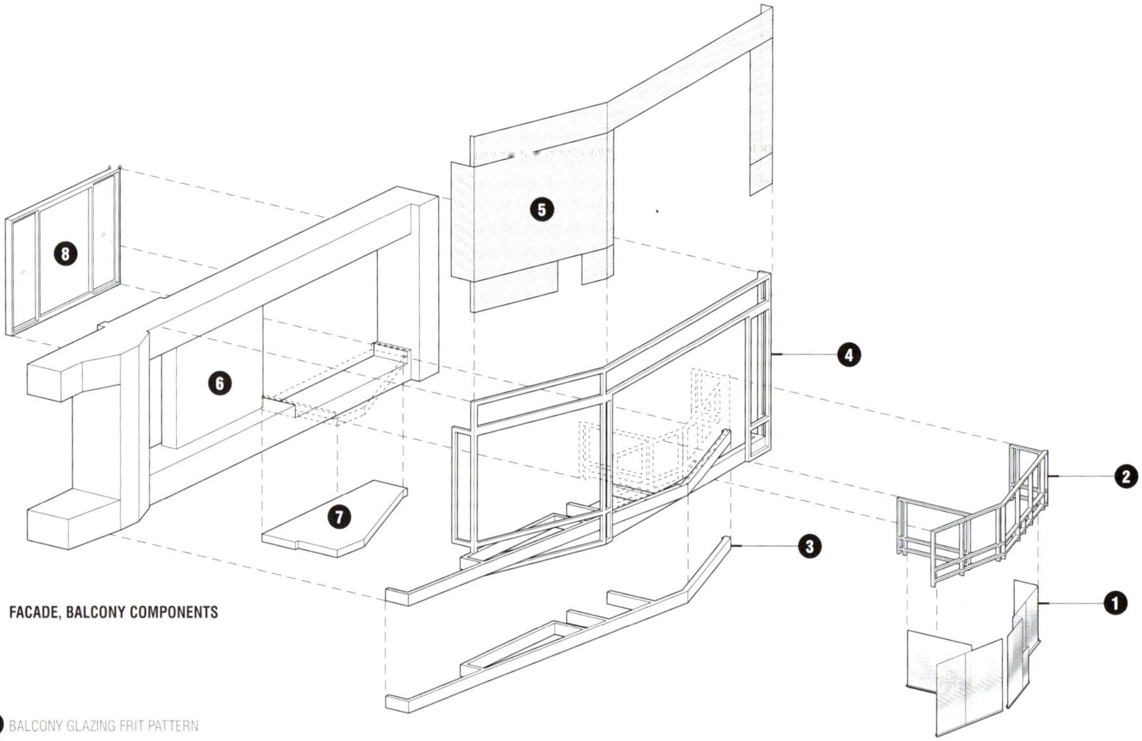

FACADE, BALCONY COMPONENTS

1. BALCONY GLAZING FRIT PATTERN
2. BALCONY RAILING
3. METAL FRAME
4. MESH FRAMEWORK
5. PERFORATED METAL SCREEN PANEL
6. FACADE THICKENED WALL
7. BALCONY FLOORING
8. WINDOW GLAZING

Finding alignments in the window openings, the facade uses this double-layered strategy of stone and frame to find a tectonic balance. Transforming vertically, the systems fluctuate in dynamic relationships to express the twisting contours of conceptual surfaces that swell and sway along the facade.

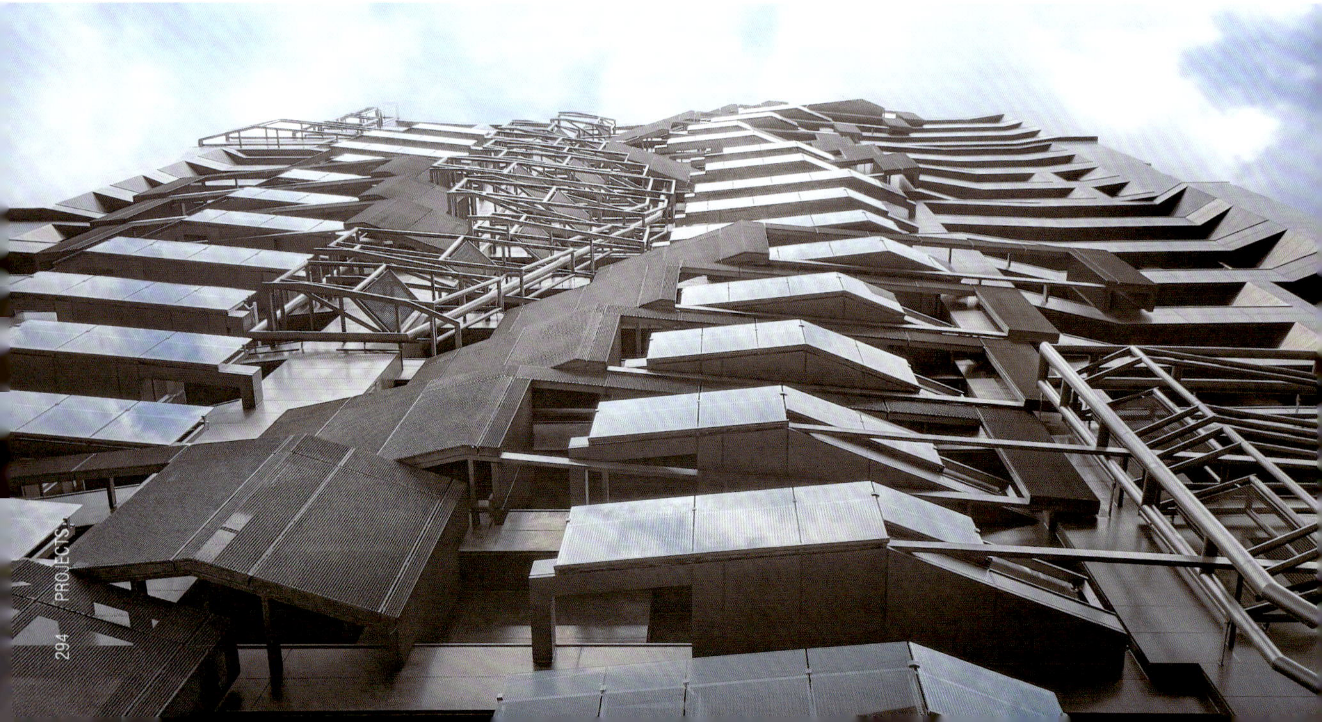

Comprised of steel channels, tubes, and perforated metal panels, the framework is designed to visually articulate the openings between balconies with a linear lattice of interlocking modules.

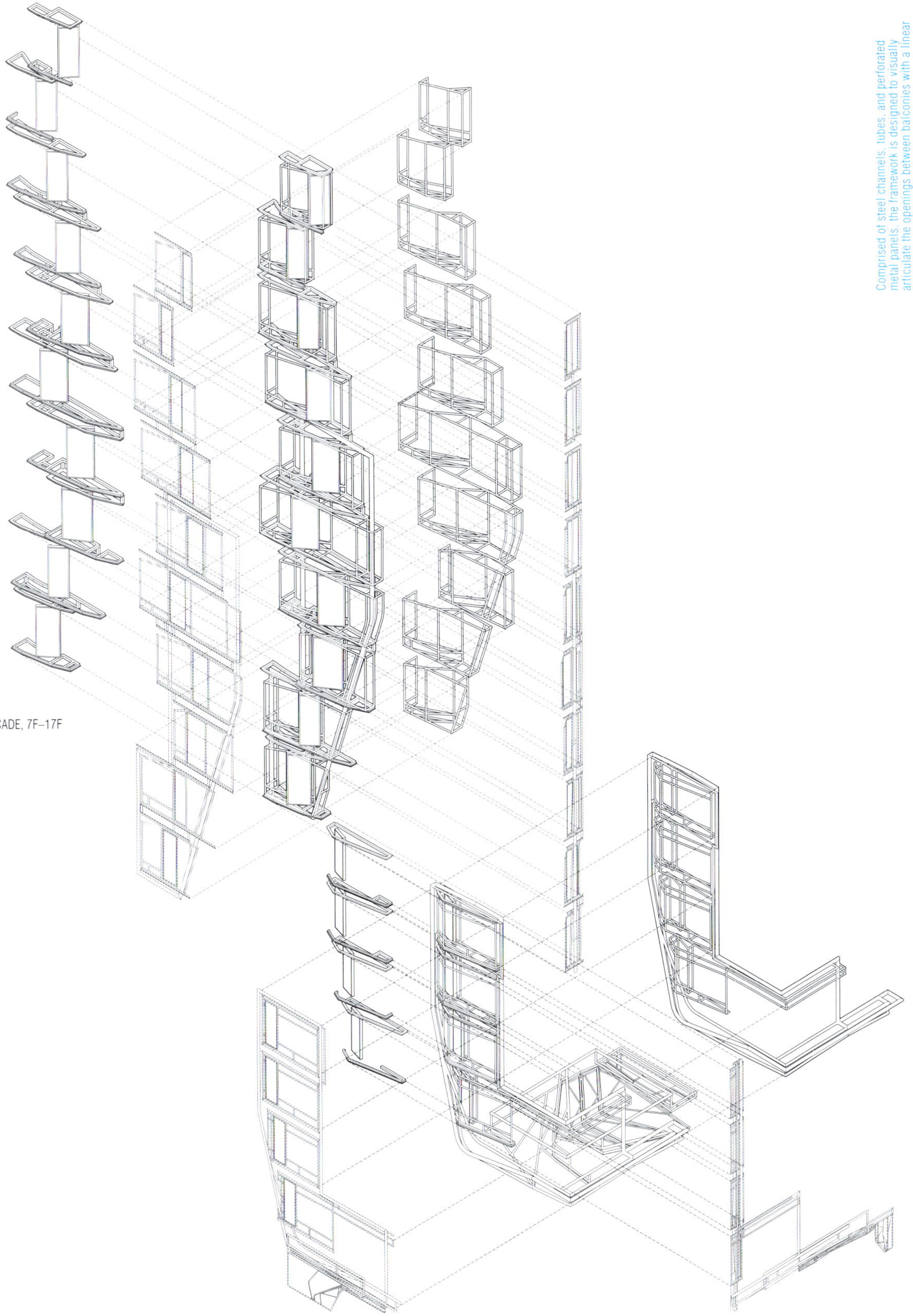

FACADE, 7F–17F

FACADE, 1F–6F

FRAMEWORK COMPONENTS

oyler wu collaborative

DWAYNE OYLER & JENNY WU

Dwayne Oyler and Jenny Wu established the architecture and design firm of Oyler Wu Collaborative in Los Angeles in 2004. The firm is recognized for its experimentation in design, material research, and fabrication. The office relies on the constant exchange between design and making, encompassing a variety of scales, with small, intense installations built alongside the design of large-scale projects. The work is driven by an insistence on striking a balance between design experimentation and technical feasibility, often finding creative solutions in the zones between the two.

In 2021, the firm was awarded the American Academy of Arts and Letters Award in Architecture, and they received the ACADIA Digital Practice Award of Excellence in 2018. In 2017, they were the J. Irwin and Xenia S. Miller Prize recipient and were awarded the Design Vanguard Award from Architectural Record in 2013. They were also awarded the 2013 Emerging Talent Award from AIA California Council, 2012 Presidential Honor Award for Emerging Practice from AIA Los Angeles, Taiwan's ADA Award for Emerging Architect, and the 2012 Emerging Voices Award from the Architectural League of New York.

Dwayne received a Bachelor of Architecture from Kansas State University and a Master of Architecture from Harvard Graduate School of Design. Jenny received a Bachelor of Arts in Architecture from Columbia University, and a Master of Architecture from the Harvard Graduate School of Design. Both Dwayne and Jenny have been full-time faculty members at the Southern California Institute of Architecture since 2004 and have taught visiting design studios at various other institutions such as Cooper Union, Columbia GSAPP, Syracuse University, the University of Tennessee, the University of Texas at Austin, and the Harvard Graduate School of Design.

In addition to the architectural practice, Jenny Wu also founded LACE by Jenny Wu, a line of 3D-printed fine jewelry in 2014. Since its launch in 2014, LACE has catapulted as a leader in the jewelry industry, producing statement pieces that are unique in their design, production, and material quality.

Like all aspects of our work, this book is made possible by the unwavering support of numerous colleagues, friends, and family. We would especially like to thank a number of key people that have been essential to helping us bring this work to light:

To all our colleagues at SCI-Arc, for creating an environment that has helped to fuel us creatively and intellectually for so many years.

To our students, who continue to inspire us with your energy, enthusiasm, and boundless talents.

To Dora Epstein for your wisdom, and for shepherding us through this process.

To Therese Kelly for the clarity of your voice and for the essential editorial help that made this possible.

To David, Anna, Ed, Paul, Nader, and Marcelyn for your incredible intellects and insights.

To Thom Mayne, for the inspiration that your profound love of all things architectural produces.

To Owen Duross, for your steady hand, insightful ideas, and unmatched design abilities.

To our parents, John and Sharon Oyler, and Grace and Allen Wu, for maintaining a profound sense of youthful excitement, pride, and thoughtfulness that continues to guide us every day.

To our boys, Emery and Ariel, who bring joy to every second of our day.

TO OUR STAFF

Since the inception of our office, we've been fortunate to be surrounded by some of the most talented young architects in the world, whose enthusiastic dedication, intellectual rigor, and boundless creativity have served as a constant source of inspiration for the evolution of the work—and without which it would not exist.

oyler wu collaborative

Abbey Chong   Abel Maqueira   Albert Chavez
Alex Urasaki   Alex Zhang   Andrea Sanchez
Andy Hammer   Andy Magner   Ange Long
Brad Goldpaint
     Burak Celik
Camille Thai   Carson Fischer   Chris Eskew
Clay Monarch   Clifford Ho   Clint Johnson
Cooper Liu   Cory Hill   Curt Budd   Cynthia Abi-Naked
Dan Hutchins
Danielle Kemble Dongwoo Suk   Dustin Columbatto
Ehab Ghali   Eli Ratansi
     Elliot Sauquet   Emilijia Landsbergis
     Emmet Holton   Eric Lalone   Erik Mathiesen   Esteban Ley
     Faris Ahmed   Fayez Ahbad
Hans Koesters   Hans Steffes   Harrison Steinbuch
     Hsiyuan Pan   Huy Le
Ibrahim Ibrahim   Irvin Shaifa   Isabelle Joannides
Jacques Lesec   James Choe   Jie Yang
Jordan Micham   Joshua Ehrlich   Jui Hong Weng
Junda Xiang   Justin Oh
     Kay Kofong Hsia   Kelly Dix Van   Kevin Foley   Kevin Murray
Laure Michelon   Lung-Chi Chang
Mariajose Meza   Marianna Girgenti   Matt Evans
Michael Chung   Michael Ho   Miguel Matos
Mike Piscitello   Ming Jian Huang   Mohamad Al Sharif
Nandini Parekh   Nathan Myers   Navid Simanian
Nick Aho   Nick Wu
     Oliver Hu   Onurcan Kusken   Owen Duross
     Paul Cambon   Paul Germaine McCoy   Peihao Jin
     Peter Rosa   Phillip Cameron
     Phoebe Ou-Yang   Piyush Panchal   Po Yao Shih
     Rakshith Raghu   Richard Lucero   Riya Venkatesh
     Sanjay Sukie   Shane Bugni   Shawn Rassekh   Shouquan Sun
          Sue Choi   Suhan Na
     Thompson Burry   Tice Hannemann   Tim Choi   Tony Morey
     Tucker Van Leuwen-Hall
     Vincent Yeh
          Wilson Chan
     Yaohua Wang   Yi Dazhong   Yu Shih   Yuan Wang
     Zack Matthews

CONTRIBUTORS

THOM MAYNE

Thom Mayne founded Morphosis in 1972 as a collective practice engaged in architecture, urban planning, and design. Working globally, his work represents a wide variety of scales and typologies. Mayne cofounded the Southern California Institute of Architecture in 1972 and has held teaching positions at UCLA, Columbia, Yale, Harvard GSD, Bartlett School of Architecture, and many other institutions. He co-heads the NOW Institute, a division of Morphosis that collaborates with communities, cities, and academic institutions to research and enhance urban environments. Mayne was awarded the Pritzker Prize (2005) and the AIA Gold Medal (2013). He served on the President's Committee on the Arts and Humanities under President Obama from 2009 to 2016. Morphosis's work has been featured in over thirty monographs and the firm has received over 120 AIA Awards. They have been the subject of various exhibitions, including a solo show at the Centre Pompidou in Paris in 2006.

DAVID ERDMAN

David Erdman is the Founding Director of Pratt Institute's Center for Climate Adaptation (CCA) where he is involved in the development of projects in NYC, Southeast Asia, and South America alongside partners in each region. Erdman was the Chairperson of Pratt's Graduate Architecture and Urban Design 2016–2023, where he is currently an Associate Professor and founded the Southeast Asia International Program. Erdman has also taught at HKU in Hong Kong and UCLA, as well as held visiting positions at Yale, SCI-Arc, UC Berkeley, University of Michigan, Syracuse, and Rice, and has received numerous awards including the prestigious Rome Prize. Erdman co-founded two practices, davidclovers (now plusClover) and servo, with works collected in museums, and published in leading journals in Hong Kong, China, and North America. He is on the editorial board of the Routledge Ocean and Island Studies Book Series, and is the author of *Introducing*, and co-author of *Future Real*.

ANNA NEIMARK

Anna Neimark co-founded First Office Architecture with collaborator Andrew Atwood to promote an exchange of ideas between the academy and the profession. Her research in techniques of representation, formal principles, and precedent analysis has been published widely, in journals such as *AD, Log, Khorein,* and *Future Anterior*, as well as the *Treatise* series *Nine Essays* in 2015, co-authored with Atwood. First Office has engaged in projects with the MAK Center for Art and Architecture, the Chicago Biennial, the A+D Museum in Los Angeles, and the Venice Biennale. They were awarded numerous honors for creative endeavors, including the Young Architects New York League Prize, the Architect's Newspaper Best of Young Architects Award, and were a finalist for the MoMA PS1 Young Architects Program. They recently completed several residential projects and developed a series of accessory dwelling units for the City of LA's ADU Pilot Program, using prefabricated Structural Insulated Panels (SIPs). Neimark previously worked at the Office for Metropolitan Architecture (OMA) in Rotterdam and New York, and at Johnston Marklee in Los Angeles, and is currently design faculty and Visual Studies Coordinator at SCI-Arc.

MARCELYN GOW

Marcelyn Gow is a partner at servo Los Angeles, a design collaborative focused on the intersection of architectural ecologies and material practices that engage multiple environmental histories and possible futures. Gow's doctoral dissertation, *Invisible Environment: Art, Architecture and a Systems Aesthetic,* explores the relationship between aesthetic research and technological innovation in the context of collaborative practices. Gow is an Undergraduate Programs Chair at SCI-Arc, and design and history-theory faculty, teaching in the postgraduate Design Theory & Pedagogy program.

PAUL LEWIS

Paul Lewis, FAIA, is a Principal at LTL Architects, based in New York City, and Professor at Princeton University School of Architecture. Paul received his BA from Wesleyan University and M.Arch from Princeton University. He served as President of The Architectural League of New York from 2018–2022. LTL Architects were the NY State AIA Firm of the Year in 2019, received a National Design Award, and was inducted into the ID Hall of Fame, and are the authors of several monographs: *Intensities* (2013), *Opportunistic Architecture* (2008), and *Situation Normal...Pamphlet Architecture #21* (1998), as well as *Manual of Section* in 2016 and *Manual of Biogenic House Sections* in 2022.

NADER TEHRANI

For his contributions to architecture as an art, Tehrani is the recipient of The American Academy of Arts and Letters' Arnold W. Brunner Memorial Prize, the highest form of recognition of artistic merit in the United States. He is also the recipient of the American Academy of Arts and Sciences, the National Academy of Design, and the Design Visionary by Cooper Hewitt and the Smithsonian Museum of Design National Design awards. Tehrani is Founding Principal of NADAAA, an interdisciplinary practice with a body of work in infrastructure, urbanism, architecture, and installations. Tehrani is also the former Dean of The Irwin S. Chanin School of Architecture at The Cooper Union, and his works have been widely exhibited at MoMA, LA MoCA, and ICA Boston.

EDWARD FORD

Edward Ford is the author of the two volumes of *The Details of Modern Architecture* and *The Architectural Detail,* as well as *Searching for Authenticity: Rustic Architecture in America 1877–1940*, with articles published in *Architectural Design*, *L'Architecture d'Aujourd'hui*, *Detail*, *Harvard Design Magazine*, and *Perspecta*. Ford was a consultant to the *1992 American Heritage Dictionary*, and is on the Editorial Board of *Architectural Graphic Standards*. He has taught at Washington University, the University of Texas, Austin, the University of Virginia, and the University of Arkansas, and his architectural works are the subject of *Five Houses, Ten Details*, which has been featured in *Arq* and *The New American House*.

ORO Editions
Publishers of Architecture, Art, and Design
Gordon Goff: Publisher

www.oroeditions.com
info@oroeditions.com

Published by ORO Editions

Copyright © 2025 Oyler Wu Collaborative and ORO Editions.

Contributors: Foreword:
                        Thom Mayne

                        Contributing Essays by:
                        David Erdman, Edward Ford, Marcelyn Gow, Paul Lewis, Anna Neimark, Nader Tehrani

                        Contributing Editors:
                        Dora Epstein-Jones
                        Therese Kelly

Edited by   Owen Duross

Author: Oyler Wu Collaborative
Book Design: Oyler Wu Collaborative, Owen Duross
Publishing Project Manager: Jake Anderson

10 9 8 7 6 5 4 3 2 1 First Edition

ISBN: 978-1-961856-90-5

**Prepress and Print work by ORO Editions Inc.
Printed in China**

ORO Editions makes a continuous effort to minimize the overall carbon footprint of its publications. As part of this goal, ORO, in association with Global ReLeaf, arranges to plant trees to replace those used in the manufacturing of the paper produced for its books. Global ReLeaf is an international campaign run by American Forests, one of the world's oldest nonprofit conservation organizations. Global ReLeaf is American Forests' education and action program that helps individuals, organizations, agencies, and corporations improve the local and global environment by planting and caring for trees.